Mormon Rivals

Copyright © 2015
The Salt Lake Tribune
90 S. 400 West, Suite 700
Salt Lake City, Utah 84101

ISBN: 978-0-9862245-2-2

Library of Congress Control Number: 2015934425

Also by The Salt Lake Tribune:
Mia Love: The Rise, Stumble and Resurgence of the Next GOP Star

Published in the United States of America

Mormon Rivals

The Romneys, the Huntsmans
and the Pursuit of Power

Matt Canham and Thomas Burr

Contents

Introduction

It was his first chance to sell himself as a presidential candidate, and Mitt Romney was determined to make it memorable. The Massachusetts governor stood in a Memphis convention hall before a gathering of Southern conservatives who knew little, if anything, about him.

And he began to sing.

"Born on a mountaintop in Tennessee, greenest state in the land of the free. ..."

Just about everyone attending the 2006 Southern Republican Leadership Conference knew the lyrics — the opening lines to the theme song from the Disney television series "Davy Crockett." It's something Romney may have watched as a child. (It premiered in 1954, when he was 7 years old.)

Romney, though, had changed the last line, turning his impromptu concert into a tepid joke about Tennessee Sen. Bill Frist, a physician who was obviously a popular local.

"Doc-torr, Doctor Bill Frist, king of the wild frontier."

The crowd chuckled politely. One columnist winced.

"This sucking up to the hometown favorite coupled with Clark Griswold goofiness made me want to dive under the desk out of embarrassment for

Romney and mankind," wrote Slate's John Dickerson. "The audience didn't care. They liked him and were still talking about him two days later."

Tall and lean, Romney wore a charcoal suit and a blue-and-white checkered tie. He stood behind a presidential-looking podium, and he fit the part, with ramrod-straight posture and rugged good looks. Each strand of his trademark hair knew its place.

The 1,800 Republicans, mainly from the South and Midwest, came to size up the candidates. They wanted to know if Romney shared their conservative values and beliefs. After his opening musical number, he dived into more traditional political fare.

He criticized President George W. Bush for the growth in federal spending, then he praised Bush for fighting terrorism.

He jumped to gay marriage: "Every child in America has the right to a mother and a father!"

The crowd leapt to its feet and cheered.

He moved to immigration: "I say, if you're going to be successful in America, you have to speak the language of America."

Enthusiastic applause.

When he finished his short speech, Romney made a beeline for the airport and left the wild frontier. He had no interest in being around when the conference concluded with its presidential straw poll, the first of the 2008 election cycle.

More than 2 ½ years before voters would pick the next president, nobody expected much of Romney, especially with Frist and eight others in the pack.

From the instant he entered the race, one question hung over the son of George Romney, a one-time presidential hopeful and governor of Michigan: Would voters elect a Mormon? Nowhere was that question more pertinent than in the South, where evangelicals — many of whom consider the LDS Church a cult — dominate Republican politics. And yet in the straw poll, Romney placed a surprising second.

Maybe the crowd liked his baritone.

In any case, the Romney acolytes went wild and, 1,500 miles away, Utah Gov. Jon Huntsman cheered along with them. He sent Romney a handwritten note on his gubernatorial stationery: "Mitt, well done in Memphis! You made us all very proud. It was just a hint of what is to come! Respectfully, Jon."

That note, previously undisclosed, sits in a thin manila folder labeled "Misc.," tucked in one of the dozens of archived boxes holding records of Huntsman's time in office.

A wiry man with thick salt-and-pepper hair and a boyish face, Huntsman first met Romney while running for governor in 2004, though their families have been intertwined for decades. Their fathers — Jon Huntsman Sr.

and George Romney — were friends and wildly successful business leaders. Huntsman's mother had shared a college dorm room with Romney's sister. And now, Mitt and Jon were governors, seen as rising Republican stars.

On top of all of that, they were on the same team — Huntsman helping Romney's campaign on foreign-policy issues.

Within four months, though, their relationship would be in tatters. In place of an admiring friendship rose a bitter rivalry that has festered in the years since.

Huntsman jumped ship to endorse Sen. John McCain — a betrayal Romney learned about from a story in The Washington Post. Feeling humiliated and abused, Romney picked up the phone, reached Huntsman and delivered the harshest criticism he could think of: "Your grandfather would be ashamed of you!"

In the pantheon of put-downs, this would rank pretty low, but unpacking the power of those seven loaded words says everything about the way Romney perceived Huntsman's disloyalty. The grandfather Romney referred to was David B. Haight, a beloved Mormon apostle and one of the most influential people in Huntsman's life. Haight, who had died in 2004, was also a close friend of George Romney.

For Mitt, this was politics fused with religion and family, and it was unfathomable that Huntsman wouldn't even afford him the decency of a heads up. Endorsements are often overrated, but losing this one was embarrassing. How could Romney fail to secure the backing of the Mormon governor from Utah, a state that loved him for leading the 2002 Winter Olympics?

Insiders say the problem was that Romney took Huntsman for granted. He was slow in returning Huntsman's calls, and so were his advisers. He made Huntsman feel like just another Utah groupie instead of part of his team.

Huntsman didn't believe he had promised Romney anything close to a full endorsement, and he didn't feel Romney had earned any advance notice of his plans, either. So when McCain, a politician Huntsman had long admired, asked for his support, the Utah governor didn't hesitate. He agreed despite knowing that he'd face a backlash for snubbing the great Mormon hope. What he didn't worry much about was what Romney would think.

"There were some angry calls," Jon's mother, Karen Huntsman, said in a nonchalant voice, dismissing Romney's outrage. "If I had a son running for president, and my best friend voted for his opposition, it wouldn't make me mad. That's your choice."

Karen Huntsman passed down that cool detachment to her eldest son, who repeatedly has torn down Romney in small digs and outright slams without so much as an emotional blip. He compared Romney to "a perfectly lubricated weather vane" in the same tone he might order a taco from one of his favorite street vendors.

The Romney clan hit back, accusing Huntsman of being a coldblooded opportunist who put himself before party.

Caught in the middle of the spat was Huntsman's father, a billionaire who had long backed Romney's political aspirations. He helped Romney run for Senate and governor in Massachusetts and, despite his son's surprise reversal, Huntsman Sr. remained a co-chairman of Romney's 2008 presidential push. But the frayed relationship unraveled in the years to come.

The big split in 2008 was just the beginning. Four years later, the 2012 election would fan smoldering resentment into flaming disgust in full view of the political world. Huntsman, then ambassador to China and an employee of President Barack Obama, left his dream job for his own White House run. He wouldn't have made the move if he didn't view Romney as a weak front-runner. Romney, for his part, saw Huntsman as another GOP gnat to swat aside on his path to the nomination — one he would relish crushing.

Members of both families deny a feud exists and instead offer polite, politically correct compliments about their counterparts. They often say they just don't know one another very well.

Behind the facade, though, lie two political tribes that deeply dislike and distrust one another. Family friends, confidants and former aides, given anonymity so they could speak without fear of reprisal or of damaging relationships with the families, say the raw feelings have persisted.

"It's almost like they are trying to be king of the Mormons," said one person who has professional and personal ties to Romney and Huntsman. "They are two royal clans who have had so much success financially and politically and in other ways. It is not easy for them to be second place. ... I know they all feel some real harm."

Since his painful defeat to Obama in 2012, Romney moved to Utah and reinvented himself as an elder statesman and a potential kingmaker in the Republican Party.

Each summer he hosts the E2 (Experts and Enthusiasts) Summit at a posh mountain resort a mile from his vacation home in Park City. It offers a mix of business and politics. In June 2014, Romney's biggest donors hobnobbed with Denver Broncos quarterback Peyton Manning, enjoyed early-morning yoga sessions and afternoon golf rounds, while spending hours hearing from potential 2016 candidates such as New Jersey Gov. Chris Christie and Kentucky Sen. Rand Paul.

Despite the convergence of all these GOP luminaries, Romney emerged as the event's brightest star, and he made the biggest headlines for criticizing

Hillary Clinton while humbly brushing aside chatter about a "Draft Mitt" campaign.

"There is a thing called a Romney Republican," said Spencer Zwick, a top Romney aide. "We are almost two years after the election — how many other people could bring all these people together?"

Romney's insistence that he wouldn't make a third run for the White House eroded slowly over the fall of 2014 and then collapsed in January, when he told Wall Street donors that he wasn't yet ready to step aside.

It took just minutes for the news to break, setting off a frenzied month when Romney courted GOP moneymen and sought to reinvent himself as an authentic politician more comfortable talking about his Mormon faith and concerned about stagnant wages and the poor. News outlets covered his speeches but also started reporting on his four mansions, including one in a suburb of Salt Lake City that the architectural plans said had a hidden room.

In the end, Romney knew he couldn't outrun his past. The 2008 and 2012 campaigns branded him as a rich politician, out of touch with the working class. He would have to combat that throughout a third bid, and he worried that doing so may cost his party a shot at victory.

At the end of January 2015, Romney announced that he wouldn't return to the campaign trail. Yet he left the door open just a crack, in case the party needed a savior in the months to come.

He still yearned to be president and while he didn't see a clear path to victory, Romney was heartened that Republicans didn't reject him outright after his loss.

Huntsman was met with a far different reaction since bowing out of that 2012 race. Republicans and the media have used him as a cautionary tale: The moderate Republican with a good résumé who is willing to challenge his party's orthodoxy and yet isn't that interested in mixing it up with his fellow primary contestants.

When former Florida Gov. Jeb Bush expressed interest in running in 2016, more than one commentator warned that he could be the Huntsman of this cycle.

Huntsman has acknowledged his campaign's many flaws, but he also hasn't backed away from his critiques of the modern GOP. He has continued to argue that the party of Abraham Lincoln, Teddy Roosevelt and Ronald Reagan needs to take a step to the center to regain relevance and credibility. If it does, he would consider another presidential pursuit. Huntsman Sr. has dropped hints about 2020.

In the meantime, Huntsman has turned himself into a secretary-of-state-in-waiting, leading a think tank known as a stopping-off point for potential Cabinet members.

It seems ludicrous to think that Romney and Huntsman will clash again, but it is possible the family rivalry may extend to the next generation. Each man has ambitious, talented offspring. In the increasingly dynastic realm of politics, it wouldn't be surprising to see a Huntsman daughter, such as MSN-BC's Abby Huntsman, or one of the Romney sons, likely Tagg or Josh Romney, enter the arena.

Within the insular circle of Mormon politicians, the rivalry between the Romneys and the Huntsmans is the clash of the century and, in a way, stands as a moment of LDS pride.

No legitimate political analyst continues to publicly question whether voters would reject a candidate because she or he is Mormon. Romney and, to a lesser extent, Huntsman erased that question, even if their political successes had their limits. Their acceptance among conservative voters helped their faith cross a threshold into the political mainstream.

Each man handled the issue of religion in his own way, which in itself became a point of friction between these proud families, estranged now despite being tied by blood and history.

To understand how Romney and Huntsman see the world and envision their place in history, you have to look back to the creation of the Mormon faith, when a farm boy from New York named Joseph Smith proclaimed he had discovered engraved golden plates and translated them into a restored gospel of Jesus Christ.

And you have to understand the story of Smith's contemporary: a 23-year-old Baptist named Parley Parker Pratt who, after picking up one of the first published copies of the Book of Mormon, was baptized in the icy, trout-filled waters of Seneca Lake in September 1830 and became one of the faith's original apostles.

Pratt was among the pioneers who fought their way through the Rocky Mountains and into the Salt Lake Valley. In this remote desert enclave, Mormons led by Brigham Young would multiply and flourish, in part through polygamy. Pratt did his part. He married and married and married, tying the knot a dozen times.

Eleanor, wife No. 12, was something of a polygamist in her own right, since she never divorced Hector McLean, her abusive, alcoholic first husband, whom she abandoned in San Francisco. Eleanor's parents in New Orleans disapproved of her conversion to this odd faith, and they tipped McLean to her new life.

Riled and relentless, he jumped on his horse and tracked Pratt across half the country, finally catching up with him in a small Arkansas town, where

McLean stabbed him twice in the chest and shot him in the neck. Before bleeding to death, Pratt told some farmers of his unwavering devotion to the LDS Church, proclaiming: "I am dying a martyr to the faith."

As many as 50,000 descendants have come from Pratt's storied family line, among them Romney and Huntsman. That makes them distant cousins, and in genealogy-rapt Mormonism, both families are well aware and deeply proud of their history.

They draw much of their identity from their pioneer roots, with ancestors ranging from temple builders to saloon owners, from rugged expatriates who fled Pancho Villa to a spirited frontier wife who boldly, so the story goes, threw coffee in a prophet's face.

chapter two

Rise of the Romneys

Five framed portraits dominated the foyer of Mitt Romney's mansion in Belmont, Mass. On the far left was Miles Archibald Romney, an Englishman who came to America to join his Mormon brethren. Next came Miles' son and his son's son and so on. On the far right was a picture of Mitt. There's an obvious resemblance among the men — square chins, tall foreheads, thin lips, deep-set eyes — even if Miles and Mitt were born 140 years apart. And the similarities cut far deeper. They share a fidelity to their faith, an industrious nature and a penchant for leadership.

Of all the portraits, one stands out for Mitt Romney — that of his father, George. His dad always has been his hero, the man he measures his life against. George Romney became a titan of the auto industry and a governor. He graced the cover of Time magazine and ran for president.

For a boy born in Mexico, who hailed from a long line of polygamists, his rise is remarkable.

George's great-grandfather Miles A. Romney converted to Mormonism at age 32. He packed up his belongings and, with family in tow, set sail from England. He landed in New Orleans and then chugged up the Mississippi River, arriving in Nauvoo, Ill., then the heart of Mormondom, in the summer of 1841.

As a skilled woodworker and cabinetmaker, Miles not only built a home for his family in this burgeoning city, but he also became the master mechanic for the grand LDS temple, which later was burned by a mob. The Mormons, persecuted by government leaders and Protestant masses, fled from city to city and eventually trekked west to Utah, entering the Salt Lake Valley through Emigration Canyon — though Parley P. Pratt soon found a shorter route, which now is named after him.

Miles also helped build the iconic Salt Lake LDS Temple. He had 12 wives and by all accounts was poor. Miles P. Romney, his son, became a polygamist as well, heeding the orders of LDS leader Brigham Young. The Romney clan dutifully followed all of the prophet's requests. That included an arduous move 300 miles south to St. George, where the family members were instructed to turn the red sandstone into another temple and a tabernacle. The elder Miles, then 71, fell to his death while working on a high window.

The Romney odyssey continued when Young ordered the family to help settle St. Johns, Ariz., a desolate place sparsely populated by migrant farmers, a few Mexican families and some Apache and Navajo indians. The Romneys, as Mitt Romney once proudly wrote, fought "against the arid terrain, the cactus, alkali, quicksand and rattlesnakes."

Mitt Romney has said he disdains polygamy but that he understood why his great-grandfather practiced the lifestyle. "They were trying to build a generation out there in the desert, and so he took additional wives as he was told to do," he said. "I must admit I can't imagine anything more awful than polygamy."

Authorities in St. Johns didn't like Mormons any more than had the people of Illinois, viewing these strange new neighbors as interlopers. Federal authorities prosecuted Mormon polygamists and on two occasions marshals tried to arrest Miles, but he essentially had stashed the evidence, having sent two wives into hiding.

The whole community started to turn on Miles Romney and his ilk. He claimed two Mexican men bullwhipped him unconscious, and the Apache Chief newspaper lashed him with the written word. Editor George A. McCarter wrote in 1884 that Romney was "a mass of putrid pus and rotten goose pimples; a skunk, with the face of a baboon, the character of a louse, the breath of a buzzard and the record of a perjurer and common drunkard."

While calling him a skunk or a baboon-faced louse was overly harsh, there was truth to the drunkard charge. He was known to have a weakness for wine, something he fought throughout his life.

LDS leaders told Romney and other Mormon polygamists to high-tail it to Mexico, where they could start a community safely beyond the reach of federal authorities. In 1885, the Romneys and a collection of other families settled on an elevated plot some 90 miles south of New Mexico along land that hugs the Piedras Verdes River. There, they grew peach and apple trees and helped launch the Colony of Juarez in the Mexican state of Chihuahua.

On Sept. 24, 1890, LDS Church President Wilford Woodruff, under heavy pressure from the U.S. government, issued his famous "manifesto," which in part read: "I now publicly declare that my advice to the Latter-day Saints is to refrain from contracting any marriages forbidden by the law of the land."

The manifesto marked the beginning of the end of Mormon polygamy, but the Romneys, like many families, didn't stop immediately. Miles took a fourth wife, Emily Henrietta Eyring, in 1897. He was the last in the family line to practice "the principle."

Son Gaskell, by then a community stalwart and a talented craftsman, had but one wife. He married Anna Amelia Pratt, granddaughter of Parley Pratt. While Gaskell started as a carpenter like his father and grandfather, he eventually owned a cattle farm and a door factory that made him the first wealthy Romney and a leader in the colony. He lived in nearby Colonia Dublán, where his wife gave birth to their fourth son, George Wilcken Romney, Mitt's dad, in 1907.

The fighting began when George was 4 years old. He said he could remember hearing gunfire in the distance, the sound of revolution. President Porfirio Diaz had lost control of the country and, in the chaos, Pancho Villa's raiders roamed freely over vast tracts of territory.

The Mormons, trying to stay neutral, hunkered down to maintain their farms. But the rebels, needing horses and guns, saw the LDS enclave as an easy target. More than once, little George's beloved pony, Monte, was stolen only to slip out of his rustlers' grasp and return in the night.

Gaskell Romney and other Mormon leaders negotiated with Villa's rebels, who agreed to offer safe passage to the women and children. They left Juarez by train. A few days later, Romney and his uncle Junius were among the 235 men who rounded up some 500 horses and rode north in a hurry.

All told, about 2,300 Mormons fled the colony. A few daredevils stayed behind, and eventually some families returned. To this day, Mitt Romney has relatives who carry the Romney name south of the border — kin he never has met.

Gaskell and the Mormon men rode for three hard days in the August heat to get out of Mexico. He reunited with his wife and children in El Paso, where they were living with other refugees from the war. After a few months of struggle, with no prospect of employment, Gaskell, Anna and their boys moved on, eventually buying a farm in southern Idaho. It turned out to be a mistake. The stubborn land produced few potatoes. Young George remembered it as a period of profound poverty.

"We fed potatoes to the hogs and this gave us a little pork for variety in our diet," he said, "but it wasn't much variety."

Maurice Romney, George's older brother, was more to the point: "It was the worst period and Father finally gave up. ... The only thing we had in abundance was potatoes."

Gaskell almost regained his fiscal and social standing when he launched Rexburg Home Builders in Idaho. He bought his first car and had visions of constructing a five-story building before World War I ended and the nation's economy tanked.

Ruined again, the nomadic Gaskell moved his family one last time, returning to Salt Lake City in 1921. He taught George, then 14, to work with lath and plaster, building interior walls in red-brick bungalows in the days before drywall became ubiquitous. When he wasn't at school or playing sports, George was often at one of his dad's construction sites, plying his new trade.

Gaskell finally earned a significant and stable living and became the family's first real politician, winning two terms on the Salt Lake County Commission. He also served as chaplain to the Utah Legislature.

His son was the last in the Romney line to work a craft. George would become a successful businessman and politician, but he didn't start with such ambitions. His break from the family business had everything to do with a pretty girl who carried an unusual confidence and a ukulele.

Occie Evans, a star on the Latter-day Saints University High School basketball team, persuaded George Romney to be his wingman on a canyon picnic during the summer of 1924. His girlfriend, Genevieve, brought some reinforcements of her own, among them Lenore LaFount. She had reddish-brown hair, hazel eyes and a slender 5-foot-6 frame. Put bluntly: Lenore was a knockout. George was instantly smitten, and that was before her impromptu ukulele concert on the slow drive home. Lenore noticed that her new admirer wasn't bad-looking himself. At 5-foot-11 and about 175 pounds, George had jet-black hair, steel-gray eyes and a warm grin.

"From that time on," Occie said, " it was Lenore and George."

That was true, even if Lenore wasn't as quickly committed as her devoted suitor. She attracted plenty of boys and had rebuffed them all. George was harder to shake — enrolling in drama club because she was a member and then almost getting into a fight with a guy who kissed her as that day's script had required. He followed her everywhere, including to a junior college in Salt Lake City.

But after his mother died of a brain hemorrhage, George found solace in his LDS faith and decided he should shelve his courtship to serve a mission abroad. The church doesn't pay to send its young men and women to find converts. Their families generally do. Gaskell Romney didn't have the resources to fund his son's mission, so George threw himself into building homes. He scraped together $700, sending $70 to the church as tithing and using the remainder to support himself during his two-year mission to Liverpool, England, close to his ancestors' birthplace.

While he was away, President Calvin Coolidge named Lenore's father one of the first members of the new Federal Radio Commission, so the entire LaFount family moved to Washington, D.C. When George's mission ended in 1928, he went straight to the nation's capital instead of going home, spending two weeks with Lenore before returning to his family.

George then enrolled in George Washington University, where Lenore was continuing her studies. To pay his way, he landed a job as a stenographer with Sen. David Walsh, D-Mass. He turned out to be terrible at it. Instead of firing him, the senator shifted George to the Senate Finance Committee, where he worked as a clerk on tariffs. It gave Romney his first insights into the world of business, and he made connections that would serve him the rest of his life.

He was a natural at politics and probably would have stuck with it at the time had Lenore not moved to New York to try her luck at acting. She soon caught the eye of a talent scout with Metro-Goldwyn-Mayer and went to Hollywood, where she appeared in supporting roles with some of the era's biggest female leads, Greta Garbo and Jean Harlow among them. She also started dating other guys, something George couldn't abide.

He took a job with the Aluminum Company of America and soon asked to be transferred to Los Angeles. There, he followed Lenore in his car while she was out on a date, and she angrily vowed to never, ever marry him. While his over-the-top pursuit almost backfired, it ultimately achieved the desired result. Lenore turned down an MGM contract worth $50,000 to marry an apprentice aluminum executive and college dropout making $125 a month. Years later, George would call it "the best selling job I ever did."

Lenore seemed to suggest it was her plan all along.

"I had no intention of staying in Hollywood and taking their $50,000," she said. "I really was anxious to get married — to George Romney."

They wed July 2, 1931, in the Salt Lake LDS Temple and soon returned to Washington, D.C., where George lobbied Congress for the aluminum company. There, he caught the eye of the Automobile Manufacturers Association, and before their first wedding anniversary, George and Lenore moved again, this time to Detroit, where George became the association's top man.

The couple were quite the team. George made a great first impression but could be impatient and hard charging. The industry boys liked his spunk, but they also wanted someone who could schmooze. George Romney's mentor, Pyke Johnson, credited Lenore with smoothing out her husband's "rough edges," saying she "could hold him down a little and possessed the social graces that George would have regarded of little importance in his intense desire to get on with whatever he was doing."

As an example of that drive, George thought it would be professionally advantageous if he learned to golf, so he joined a country club. He often could be spotted chasing three balls at the same time and for six quick holes. He called it "a compact 18."

His father, Gaskell, described his son's hard-charging nature this way: "He set his eyes on a goal early in life, and he never took them from it."

Within a few years, George became the lead spokesman for the national automakers lobby and his pay rose accordingly, allowing him to live in a fancy Detroit suburb as his family grew. The Romneys had two daughters, then a son, but his birth was complicated. Doctors said Lenore was not physically able to have more children.

They were wrong.

Not only did she get pregnant again, but she also was able to carry her "miracle baby" to term. George wrote friends marveling at his wife's endurance and faith. In that letter, he also announced the birth of Willard Mitt Romney, who was born March 12, 1947, with — yes, he noted this — "strong features" and "dark hair."

"We consider it a blessing for which we must thank the Creator of all," he added.

George and Lenore named the baby for their close friend J. Willard Marriott, founder of the hotel empire, and they selected the middle name Mitt in honor of Milton Romney, a cousin and former quarterback of the Chicago Bears.

While Mitt was an infant, George jumped from the auto association to the front office of an automaker, taking a job with Nash-Kelvinator, a maker of cars and refrigerators. He spent two years with front-line workers learning the business before he assumed the role of vice president. The company merged four years later with Hudson Motor Car Co., becoming American

Motors, and when the president died after developing pneumonia during a hunting trip, the board turned to George Romney to lead the company.

American Motors was a scrappy newcomer surrounded by entrenched giants. It had to do battle on two fronts. On the car side, American had to elbow for room among Detroit's big three of Ford, General Motors and Chrysler; on the appliance side, it wrestled with General Electric, Frigidaire and Westinghouse.

Romney's plan was to follow the path staked out by his predecessor: Sell the Rambler, a small fuel-efficient car. The problem was that the industry was promoting bigger, flashier vehicles as road-hogging status symbols. Little cars made people feel small.

To shake things up, Romney, in a stroke of prescience, waged a public-relations campaign in which he disparaged full-size automobiles, calling them "dinosaurs" and "gas guzzlers."

"Cars 19 feet long and weighing 2 tons are used to run a 118-pound housewife three blocks to the drugstore for a 2-ounce package of bobby pins and lipstick," he said with obvious derision.

Rambler sales rose, but his company remained mired in debt for another three years. Then it took off.

American Motors was making $60 million in annual profits by 1960 — ranking it the nation's 32nd most-profitable corporation. (Rival GM was the most profitable, making $873 million.) Romney's annual salary swelled to $250,000. The success allowed him to venture into more civic projects that piqued his interest. He already was leading the Detroit Citizens Advisory Committee on School Needs, a program in which business leaders helped develop a financial plan for troubled schools. Romney was also the lay president of Detroit's Mormon stake, the rough equivalent of a Catholic diocese.

In 1959, Michigan had such financial problems that 26,000 state employees went without a paycheck. The crisis was exacerbated by political warfare between Republicans, backed by the carmakers, and Democrats, aligned with the unions.

Romney stepped in, fashioning a private-sector solution. He created the nonpartisan Citizens for Michigan and invited Detroit's business titans to help address the state's fiscal and political woes. Among those he recruited was Robert S. McNamara, then a vice president of Ford who would go on to become the secretary of defense and a major political adversary.

After a lengthy series of committee meetings, the group joined with more progressive organizations, such as the League of Women Voters, to call for a state constitutional convention and a complete rewrite of Michigan's charter. Romney became one of three vice presidents of the 144-member group, which received heavy media scrutiny.

He thought briefly about a Senate run in 1960 but dismissed it, vowing to stay out of electoral politics while working on the constitutional convention. In a halting, highly political process, the convention slowly churned out a plan. It proposed doubling the governor's term from two years to four, reducing the number of elected statewide officials and creating a civil-rights commission in hopes of developing better relations with the state's large African-American population.

Democrats loved it, but Republicans were skeptical and succeeded in pushing a vote past the 1962 election. That was fine by Romney. It made it easier for him to run for governor.

Everyone in Michigan political circles assumed Romney would run as a Republican, though up to this point he had eschewed any sort of partisan allegiance. He even went so far as to ask his own family: "Should I run as a Republican or a Democrat?" While he was clearly a moderate, he never seriously considered siding with the Democratic Party, which would have been a shocking move by an auto executive.

Before he even declared for office, his political stock skyrocketed. Former President Dwight Eisenhower and former Vice President Richard Nixon already were floating Romney's name as a potential 1964 presidential candidate.

Romney stoked the hype by saying he would make up his mind by Feb. 10, 1962. Two days before his self-imposed deadline, he told reporters he had begun a religious fast.

"My final step in making such an important decision is to seek divine guidance," he said, displaying how comfortable he was discussing his Mormon faith, which he brought up regularly.

Romney appeared before the microphones that Saturday wearing a blue suit, a blue shirt and a blue tie with a dinosaur on it, a clear nod to his campaign to sell the Rambler. Wife Lenore and son Mitt, who was then 14, stood by his side.

George Romney said he would take a leave from American Motors to challenge Gov. John Swainson, a Democrat, though he said he wouldn't campaign until the constitutional convention finished its work. He beat back talk of higher office, saying: "As a gubernatorial candidate, I will have no interest in any other position in the state or nation — elective, appointive or otherwise."

This was George's big moment in the spotlight. It was also Mitt's first turn on the political stage, and he ended up creating a minor stir by telling reporters his father made the decision to run on Friday, during the constitutional convention, where George said he would do no politicking. George quickly corrected his son and said he didn't make the "final decision" until he was driving away from the convention to his home in posh Bloomfield Hills.

Young Mitt made headlines again a few months later when, at an Independence Day event, he said: "It's really fun to be here in the United States for the Fourth of July for the first time."

The eyebrow-raising comment, which drew groans from the campaign staff, was true. The Romneys had a vacation home in Canada, where they celebrated the most American holiday each year. Years later, Mitt Romney would laugh about it.

"That wasn't a great line," he said. "Yeah, I was not particularly adept at my communications with the media."

But Mitt was enthusiastic and far more into the campaign than his siblings. His father loved having him around. Mitt would man the campaign headquarters' switchboard and helped set up booths at county fairs.

"I would introduce myself and shout out to people walking past, 'You should vote for my father for governor. He's a truly great person. You've got to support him. He's going to help make things better.' "

Mitt believed it. The GOP believed it. The unions didn't. Gus Scholle of the AFL-CIO called George Romney a "big clown" and thought he was pompous and self-righteous. Scholle insisted the constitutional convention was nothing more than an elaborate attempt to build Romney's brand.

"This business of trying to put on an act of having a pipeline to God in order to become governor of Michigan is about the greatest anticlimax to a phony stunt that I've ever seen," Scholle said shortly after Romney's announcement.

Conservative Republicans weren't big Romney fans, either. They didn't understand why he would call on the Legislature to pass the state's first income tax and bristled at his criticism of "extremists" in the party, filled with members of the John Birch Society.

Romney heard the complaints.

What he didn't hear much about was his faith, largely because Swainson was a former member of the Reorganized Church of Jesus Christ of Latter Day Saints, a splinter group from mainstream Mormonism that never recognized polygamy. Swainson downplayed any questions about religion, though reporters still occasionally asked Romney about the LDS Church's prohibition on black men holding the faith's priesthood, a ban that remained until 1978.

Romney responded by pointing to his record on civil rights, including his support for integrating schools, for fair-employment practices and a statewide civil-rights commission. As the campaign continued, he actively sought support from the black community, calling for new apprenticeship programs for African-American members of labor unions.

At one event, he told an overwhelmingly black audience to "get away from the practice of permitting anyone to take you for granted."

Romney ran as a centrist who understood the economy and could attract jobs, a person who put himself outside the standard partisan divisions. He didn't identify himself as a Republican on any of his campaign materials and was known to say: "I'm a citizen who is a Republican, not a Republican who is incidentally a citizen."

It was part personality, part political strategy. There was a reason Democrats held all of the statewide seats at the time, and they desperately wanted to keep it that way.

President John F. Kennedy came out to campaign on Swainson's behalf in early October. In the days to follow, so did Vice President Lyndon Johnson and former President Harry Truman. The Kennedy administration even handed Swainson a $102 million missile contract to announce three days before voting started.

It didn't matter.

Romney was too popular. He captured 51.4 percent of the vote, making him the state's first GOP governor in 14 years. He brought on Mitt as an intern, and his aides later would remark how often the young Romney would get involved in policy discussions, even challenging his dad at times. The dynamic felt an awful lot like a protégé being groomed by a mentor.

The new governor received an early victory when voters approved the state's new constitution, although by a tiny majority. He also suffered an early defeat when Republicans in the Legislature killed his income-tax plan. No matter, an economic turnaround helped the state's sagging finances.

Romney was a popular national figure, and Michigan voters liked his no-nonsense, post-partisan image. But state lawmakers from both parties bristled at his leadership style. Some argued it led to the early demise of his tax plan, which he would resurrect and see enacted.

A profile in The New Republic included this unflattering description: "Associates complain that the governor is a self-righteous, fiercely ambitious man with a bad temper and a messianic sense of destiny. Taken separately, none of these traits is especially uncommon in political figures; it is the combination that appears to cause difficulty.

Also, he has an oversimplified horse-opera sense of morality, which neatly divides the world into good guys and bad guys; and an unshakable conviction of the rightness of anything he undertakes, which permits him to rationalize personal inconsistency and contradictions. When something goes wrong, Romney tends to look around irritably for a scapegoat. This has led one critic to remark that he is like a little boy who has dropped an egg; it isn't his fault, it's the egg's."

George had spent years leading American Motors, where he had employees to execute his every plan, but he had yet to develop a rapport with lawmakers, who refused to be treated as subordinates. He also learned rather quickly that while he may have wanted to focus on the economy, events outside his control often altered his plans.

When Medgar Evers was assassinated in 1963 in Mississippi, civil-rights protests took on a new urgency throughout the nation. Romney didn't attend the first two movement rallies in Michigan, but he made an unexpected appearance at the third. It was held in the fancy all-white suburb of Grosse Pointe, where the NAACP gathered to criticize the use of race as a determining factor in reviewing applications of would-be homebuyers. Romney received a standing ovation for saying the "elimination of injustice and discrimination is the most critical and urgent problem."

The issue played heavily into his re-election drive in 1964 and his early flirtations with a run for president. He never campaigned outright for the job that year, but he made it clear that, if drafted, he would take the Republican nomination. There was no effort to draft him despite his positioning himself as "a favorite-son candidate" from Michigan. That allowed him to control the state's delegates throughout the nomination process at a time when convention battles were far more dramatic than today's scripted coronations.

Sen. Barry Goldwater, the conservative firebrand from Arizona, and Gov. Nelson Rockefeller, the moderate insider from New York, were locked in a primary battle. It wasn't long before Goldwater, the more aggressive candidate, gained the upper hand. That bothered Romney, who saw Goldwater as far too conservative, in part for voting against the Civil Rights Act that year. When Goldwater won California and was poised to claim his party's nomination, Romney made an unusual request. He wanted a panel of Republican governors to meet and grill Goldwater about his positions.

"If his views deviate as indicated from the heritage of our party," Romney warned, "I will do everything within my power to keep him from becoming the party's presidential candidate."

The other GOP governors considered the idea absurd and the scheme fizzled, but the episode marked the start of a public rift between Romney and his party's standard-bearer. Romney wouldn't endorse Goldwater at the convention in San Francisco's Cow Palace, and he pushed an amendment to the platform to denounce extremism, a move the Goldwater people rebuffed and one that prompted the nominee's most quoted remark: "I would remind you that extremism in the defense of liberty is no vice."

Romney never relinquished control of his 41 delegates from Michigan, but Goldwater didn't need them. He had 883 delegates — four times more than his nearest competitor.

Distancing himself from Goldwater played well for Romney in urban and moderate Michigan, but it also became a bit personal. He accused Goldwater, a one-time supporter of the NAACP, of trying to "finesse" the issue of race relations, securing the vote of white people who still held bigoted views while also saying he would enact the Civil Rights Act. Unlike the vast majority of Republicans and Democrats, Goldwater had voted against that landmark legislation.

The two men met privately to try to work out their differences, but they forged an unsteady truce. Romney never would publicly support Goldwater. He went so far as to have his campaign distribute instructions to voters on how to split their ticket in favor of Lyndon Johnson for president and Romney for governor.

Johnson won in a landslide, carrying Michigan and 43 other states. Still, enough voters split their tickets that Romney won a second two-year term by 380,000 votes over one-term Democratic Rep. Neil Staebler, a much stronger victory than Romney had achieved in his first go-round.

In the ensuing months, Romney wasted no opportunity to say Goldwater's campaign failed miserably to appeal to moderates. One of those occasions was during an appearance on CBS' "Face The Nation," which Goldwater watched. The senator wrote Romney a letter going point by point through his criticisms.

"You further state, 'We need to win elections and serve America as a broad-based political party.' How does that statement possibly square with the actions of leaders like you and Nelson Rockefeller? Where was this broad-based feeling on your part when you repeatedly refused to back the national ticket?

"You stated during your television interview that you would never compromise your principles, but you made it rather clear that you expected me and others to compromise theirs. Now, George, I happen to be just as proud of my principles as you are of yours, and I don't intend to compromise any basic feelings of mine any more than you do. Frankly, I don't understand what principles of mine you disagree with."

Goldwater demanded a response.

He got one.

"I cannot accept the blame for the divisiveness in the party when you, your representatives, and your campaign strategy refused to encompass those of us who had reservations based on basic American and Republican principles," Romney wrote.

"For these philosophical, moral, and strategic reasons, I was never able to endorse you during the campaign. Of course, millions did because they believed your leadership would inspire a rebirth of Americanism and a strengthening of constitutional government. I, too, am one dedicated to these objectives, but I know they cannot be realized if foundation principles of American freedom are compromised. The chief cornerstone of our freedom is divinely endowed citizenship for all equally, regardless of pigmentation, creed, or race."

The conversation didn't continue beyond that correspondence, but Romney knew mending his relationships with the conservative wing of his party would be essential if he were to have a shot at the nomination in the next presidential election. Before he could turn his full attention to that race, though, he had to win a third term as governor. It turned out to be a cakewalk. The state had a hefty surplus, and voters were happy with a recently passed minimum-wage law. He won by 580,000 votes.

As the 1968 presidential chase began coming into view, Romney was a leading contender, but the decks were far from cleared. His biggest rival was the rejuvenated Richard Nixon, the former vice president and California senator.

Mitt would play no role in his father's presidential campaign. He was in France serving a Mormon mission. The best he could do was exchange letters with his dad and read news clippings his family would mail him. He tracked his father's rise and his trouble coming to grips with the political morass that was Vietnam.

George Romney had started as a skeptic of the war, saying he didn't see the justification for being involved in the conflict. To bolster his credentials, he took a quick trip in 1965 to the front lines, where he met with generals and visited the troops. When he returned, he said he could voice his general support for the war waged under President Johnson's leadership. Then, about eight months later, he appeared on CBS' "Face the Nation" and called for an escalation in force.

"I don't think that you can bring the North Vietnamese to the bargaining table by simply saying that you are going to demonstrate to them that they can't win," he said. "Now, I think they have to be confronted with the fact that they are going to lose."

Questions about the war dogged him wherever he went, though he tried to change the topic. He embarked on a six-state trek in early 1967 to highlight his Western roots and get a feel for what a major campaign trip would be like. He started in Washington, then hit Alaska before stopping in Utah, where he had dinner at the house of Amy Pratt Romney, who, in a quirk not uncommon among former polygamist families, was his aunt and his stepmother. He also met with the president of the LDS Church between giving three speeches and holding one news conference, touching on the economy, Vietnam and blacks in the Mormon priesthood.

"I have fought for 25 years in Michigan to eliminate discrimination," he said. "I believe I'm entitled to be judged on the basis of my actions, not someone's ideas of what may be the precepts of my church."

The next day he went to Rexburg, Idaho, where he visited his boyhood home and brought reporters to the Rexall Drugstore, where as a child he used to get a banana split and take the occasional five-finger discount.

"While you were there, you probably swiped 50 cents' worth of candy and other stuff," he said impishly.

The trip did nothing to divert calls for him to make a clear statement on Vietnam, given his seemingly wandering stance, from skeptic to supporter to troop-escalation hawk. At that point, he was being accused of playing politics on the most pressing issue of the day. Romney tried to clarify his views in April 1967, delivering a lengthy address in which he said withdrawal was unthinkable and that the nation must use its military might to shield the South Vietnamese from Communists. His speech placated many of his critics, and his poll numbers rebounded, but the bounce was short-lived.

Police in Detroit busted an illegal after-hours club early in the morning on July 23, 1967, and attempted to detain about 80 people. Members of the crowd, believing cops were targeting them because they were black, started throwing rocks and bricks. A riot ensued that lasted five days and left 43 dead and more than 1,000 injured.

Seeing that the police were outmanned, Romney called in the National Guard. It still wasn't enough, and he demanded 5,000 Army troops. But the Johnson administration wouldn't send them unless Romney agreed to say he had an insurrection on his hands that was out of control. Romney wasn't ready to do that. After a daylong delay because of the political tussle between the potential presidential rivals, the troops quickly restored order.

In a televised address, Johnson said: "I am sure the American people will realize that I take this action with the greatest regret — and only because of the clear, unmistakable, and undisputed evidence that Governor Romney of Michigan and the local officials in Detroit have been unable to bring the situation under control."

Romney eventually shot back: "I think the president of the United States played politics in a period of tragedy and riot."

The governor vowed to improve living conditions for inner-city blacks and went on a national tour of ghettos to show he was serious. Already an advocate for equality, Romney pressed others to take up the cause.

"The Negro people are quite justified to say they are entitled to the same rights as everyone else," he said. "Cities must declare themselves and provide leadership in this area."

The fervor died down and Romney returned to a regular campaign schedule, during the course of which he appeared on a new Michigan interview program called "Hot Seat."

It was mostly standard fare until anchor Lou Gordon homed in on the war.

Gordon: "Isn't your position a bit inconsistent with what it was? And what do you propose we do now?"

Romney: "Well, you know when I came back from Vietnam, I had just had the greatest brainwashing that anybody can get. When you ..."

Gordon: "By the generals?"

Romney: "Not only by the generals, but also by the diplomatic corps over there. They do a very thorough job. Since returning from Vietnam, I've gone into the history of Vietnam all the way back into World War II and before. And, as a result, I have changed my mind in that particular. I no longer believe that it was necessary for us to get involved in South Vietnam to stop Communist aggression in Southeast Asia."

Gordon was fine with Romney's answer. Romney saw nothing wrong with what he said, and neither did his press secretary, Travis Cross, who was in the WKBD-TV studios for the interview. Romney was trying to impart that the Johnson administration had been misleading Americans on the war and that he had he bought into their dog-and-pony show while in Vietnam.

The show aired on Labor Day. The next morning, articles in newspapers nationwide led with Romney's brainwashing comment. His political adversaries, including Nixon and Johnson, pounced, and his fellow GOP governors didn't come to his defense.

Democratic National Chairman John Bailey said: "Governor Romney's statements this week have proved that anybody who tries to brainwash the governor has very little to work with."

Romney tried to remedy the mess with a news conference the next day followed by a tour of American ghettos to refocus on civil rights and poverty. It didn't work. His campaign went into a tailspin.

The conservative editorial board at the Detroit News had backed Romney in every race, but now published a damning editorial: "We do not demand that every presidential candidate agree with us on our Vietnam stand. But there is a requirement that every candidate have a firm policy on so critical an issue and a capacity to state it. Governor Romney fails that requirement."

His poll numbers plunged from a healthy 31 percent of the GOP vote in February to 14 percent in November. Romney still staggered forward, launching his formal campaign that lasted only a few brief months. He called it off Feb. 28, 1968, when Nixon piled up a 5-to-1 victory in New Hampshire.

"It is clear to me," he said, "that my candidacy has not won the wide acceptance with rank-and-file Republicans that I had hoped to achieve."

Nixon won the White House and that December named George Romney, then 61, as his secretary of Housing and Urban Development, a job he would hold for only a short time. It was as close as he'd get to the Oval Office. While upset at the loss, it didn't take him long to be able to poke fun at it.

"It was a mini-campaign — much like a miniskirt — very short and revealing," he said. "I didn't really expect to come out victorious in the battle. I contemplated each move before it was made. I knew the consequences of many of my statements, but I felt they needed to be said regardless of the outcome."

Michigan Republicans later tried to resurrect Romney's career, urging him to run for Senate in 1970. He declined and remained in Washington as HUD secretary, but Lenore jumped in, with the support of House Minority Leader and future President Gerald Ford.

She had movie-star charisma and keen political instincts, but many in the state were uncomfortable supporting a woman. Lenore secured the party nod by a thin margin, beating back accusations that she was simply her husband's puppet. The press even fed into the line of attack, with one headline reading: "George won't run, he'll let Lenore do it."

Lenore didn't duck the gender issue. Her campaign slogan was: "Never before has the voice and understanding of a concerned woman been so needed."

Following George's example, Lenore chartered a Cessna and flew all over the state, addressing any group that would have her, and her children made their own appearances on her behalf. Mitt, then 23, took a break from college to speak at schools and county fairs.

Lenore called for new laws to crack down on crime and drug abuse and new aid for the poor, but voters never warmed to her. George Romney, busy in Washington, joined the campaign only for its final days, but by then it was long over. Incumbent Democratic Sen. Philip Hart cruised to a 67 percent to 33 percent landslide.

Four years later, when Utah Sen. Wallace Bennett announced his retirement, George offered himself as a potential candidate.

"If I had sufficient reason to believe that the people of Utah wanted me to serve them for the next term and the Republican Party, independents and concerned Democrats wanted me to be their candidate, I would probably respond favorably, as I have to previous requests from Utah, and resume residency here."

But two months later, back in Bloomfield Hills, Romney realized he didn't have the fire in the belly. In a letter, he wrote: "I have searched diligently and prayerfully in arriving at a decision. As a result, I have concluded not to run for the U.S. Senate seat from Utah."

It would be another 20 years before George Romney would return to the stump, but the campaign wouldn't be in Michigan or even Utah. It would take place in Massachusetts, where his youngest son was trying to take down a liberal lion.

chapter three

Building the Huntsman empire

From his prime spot in the balcony of an ornate concert hall, a proud Jon Huntsman Sr. watched his son, Utah's new governor, deliver his inaugural address, fulfilling his father's aborted political ambition. Huntsman Sr.'s elevated seat mirrored his role in society. He saw himself as a benevolent caretaker of the state.

Huntsman Jr. saw his dad as a great man, his best friend and closest confidant. His father had regaled him with family lore about the gregarious ancestors who helped turn the Huntsmans into one of Utah's most storied families. They were proud of their lineage, the Mormons and the not-so-Mormons.

"In my own family, I have war veterans and teachers; public servants and private business owners; proselytizers and saloon keepers," Huntsman Jr. said as he laid out his agenda as governor. "Regardless of our origin or family background, we as Utahns share an undeniable bond — a link to our past."

The Huntsman past includes a proud farmer who became so enamored of the LDS faith in 1833 that he was willing to give up his land and a prominent place in an Ohio township to follow Joseph Smith.

James Huntsman IV and his wife, Mary, along with their nine children, moved to Independence, Mo., then Nauvoo, Ill. Each move brought the Latter-day Saints strife and trouble from angry mobs. In Independence, James Huntsman was arrested with Smith and Parley Pratt, only to be released after a vicious beating, according to James' son Peter. Pratt and Smith were locked up for weeks, and the Missouri governor eventually issued a notorious executive order saying Mormons should be "exterminated or driven from the state." A mob in Illinois murdered Smith. About a dozen years later, Pratt met his own bloody end. James Huntsman was more fortunate: At Brigham Young's request, his family settled Fillmore, Utah, named for the U.S. president at the time.

Fillmore was picked as the territorial capital to give some perceived separation between the Mormon church, headquartered in Salt Lake City, and the government, though no gap really existed. Fillmore was in the geographic center of the territory, an area dominated by Paiute Indians.

The Paiutes and these pioneers fought frequently. In reaction, the Mormons began building a fort out of large stones, mud and straw. After two years, they had constructed an 8- to 10-foot-high wall that spanned four football fields in length and was a quarter-mile wide. The settlers used the fort as the back wall of their small homes. One was occupied by James and Mary, another by their adult son, Gabriel Huntsman.

Family lore relays that one day Young stopped by the Huntsman homes while James was chopping wood and, after a brief chat, abruptly said: "What I really came to ask you is, why don't you take another wife?"

James asked his prophet to talk to Mary and get her permission. When he obliged, Mary thought about it for a second and then threw a cup of coffee in Young's face, saying, "This is my answer."

Brigham went out of the house, dried himself off and said: "James, you have all the wives you can handle."

Whether the story is true or not, James Huntsman took no more wives and neither did his sons — though the Huntsmans had other relatives who lived the "principle." (For the record, Mormons today are taught not to drink coffee, but that prohibition was not in force in the 1850s.)

When the hostilities with the Paiutes died down, the family built a 24-room hotel in the area. It became an iconic building in the state, a rest point for anyone traveling between Salt Lake City to the north and St. George to the south.

Gabriel Huntsman added a general store and tapped the profits to become a real-estate baron, selling off parcels for homes as Fillmore grew. Townsfolk saw Gabriel as a rock-solid pillar of the community, a man of great means. He also had a cheap labor source at the hotel and nearby ranch: his 11 children.

As the eldest, Gabriel Riley took care of the horses and, early each morning, milked the cows. He became a dependable rancher and a filthy-mouthed rebel who loved a good party. Women loved him. He had a fancy carriage led by well-kept horses that he used for entertaining. He was a graceful dancer, a decent singer and, like his dad, he could play a mean accordion.

He waited until he was 29 to get married, an uncommonly late age for Mormon men. When he wanted to get hitched, it wasn't easy. His eventual wife, Hannah Hanson, rejected his advances for a considerable time before relenting in 1885.

The couple became regulars at Fillmore's dance hall, where Gabriel Riley and buddy Can Melville would attend the occasional costume party dressed as twin girls, complete with corsets and women's shoes.

Around town, Gabriel was known as "Doc Huntsman," even though he wasn't a physician. He took over the Huntsman Hotel when his father died in 1907 and updated it throughout the years. The biggest change was adding a saloon, which he did while his wife was out of town. That turned out to be the last straw. Hannah and Doc, who had been fighting for some time, divorced upon her return, said Gabriel's grandson Knox Huntsman, who still lives in Fillmore.

Jon Huntsman Jr. grew up hearing stories of the famed hotel and its colorful operator. His father even paid for a replica to be built in a Salt Lake City park, where the "saloon" now is an ice-cream parlor. Huntsman not only mentioned the hotel and bar when he became governor, but also as he campaigned for president, using it as a signal that he wasn't as devoutly Mormon as Mitt Romney.

"It was the greatest saloon in the entire state," Huntsman said in 2005. "It was a very famous watering hole."

The family demolished the hotel shortly after Doc Huntsman died of a heart attack in 1936. The story goes that his grieving family members knew the eccentric patriarch had a cache of gold coins, but they couldn't find them. Believing he had hidden them in the hotel, they decided to raze it. They found no gold.

The family, now out of the hotel business, turned to the classroom. Doc's firstborn, Gabriel Alonzo Huntsman, became a schoolteacher, working his way up to superintendent of the Millard School District. And son Alonzo Blaine Huntsman — Jon Jr.'s grandfather — became an educator, forcing him to move out of the area due to anti-nepotism rules.

A former bar owner and a gifted violinist, Blaine went to LDS Church-owned Brigham Young University, where he earned an education degree. He ended up teaching music in Thatcher, Idaho, a tiny town south of Pocatello, in 1935 and later moved north to Blackfoot. There, Blaine and his wife, Kathleen

Robison Huntsman, would have three sons, including Jon Meade Huntsman, who would become a billionaire industrialist, noted philanthropist and the father of a governor.

Jon was born eight weeks premature on June 21, 1937. The doctor declared him stillborn, an outcome an assisting midwife refused to accept. She instructed Blaine to plunge the limp newborn into cold water, then into hot water. Cold then hot, over and over until the baby gasped for air.

In retelling the story, Jon Huntsman Sr. likes to say: "I've been in and out of hot water since."

Jon and his family lived in Blackfoot only a few years. His dad made $99 a month, and the family lived in a two-room house without indoor plumbing. The outhouse was 40 feet away, but seemed like a half-mile on frigid winter mornings. The Great Depression cost his father his teaching job, and the family moved to Pocatello, a metropolis compared with tiny Blackfoot.

Jon remembers a rough upbringing. Blaine was a surly disciplinarian who fell away from the Mormon faith and in love with booze.

"I wouldn't tolerate the son-of-a-bitch," recalls Fillmore's Knox Huntsman, who saw Blaine only at family gatherings. "He was a problem. He was a big problem, as a matter of fact. He was a mean drunk."

Jon Huntsman said his father badgered his mother.

"My dad never let her drive, never let her go to church, never let her write out a check, didn't trust her," he said. "There was all this tension in the family."

And when Blaine Huntsman drank, he was more inclined to use the belt on Jon and Blaine Jr., whom he called Sonny.

"It would have been child abuse today, no question about it," Jon Huntsman said. "But in those days, people brought kids in line pretty fast.

"Sometimes when he would get really upset he would say, 'This is for all the things I didn't know about that happened today.' "

To blunt the impact from his kicks in the rear, the boys would shove plywood down their pants.

Huntsman Sr. believes part of his father's rage stemmed from an inability to take care of his family on a teacher's meager wages, forcing his boys to work. Jon said he took his first job at age 8 and his first full-time work at 10. Like young George Romney, Huntsman later worked on a potato farm, where he said he got 6 cents for every 50 pounds picked. He earned about $3 a day, but he remembers the labor fondly.

"I loved working out in the potato field," he said. "I mean, they let school out for two weeks every year during harvest time and we worked hard, but my brother and I always got in potato fights with everybody."

At a young age, Huntsman vowed to be a different man than his dad.

"Most of my life growing up was in less-than-ideal conditions," he said, "but it also drove within me a great desire to not raise my own children that way."

Jon Huntsman Sr.'s young life revolved around two places: rural southern Idaho, where his father, Blaine, taught music in public schools, and Fillmore, Utah, where he would spend summers in the town of his ancestors, fishing and playing with his many, many cousins.

That all changed in 1950, when he was 13. His dad decided he wasn't satisfied. He wanted more money, more authority, and to get it, he needed more education. In his late 30s, the World War II Navy veteran turned to his GI Bill benefits to get a master's degree and then a doctorate from Stanford University in Northern California.

The family moved into Stanford's married-student housing in an old Quonset hut — think of a silo knocked on its side and cut in half. The long metal structure was sliced into 16 apartments divided only by heavy industrial cardboard. Each family had about 600 square feet to call home and remarkably little privacy.

"With my parents and two brothers, the quarters were cramped and embarrassing for a teenager," Jon said. "But it was home."

To him, this was worse than the two-room shack they called home in Blackfoot, the one with no indoor plumbing.

His father did two stints as a full-time student at Stanford, with a season of work in Idaho in the middle. Money was scarcer than ever. Jon and Blaine Jr., who was one year younger, mowed lawns, set pins at a bowling alley, sold shoes at a department store, worked as janitors and took jobs in a cannery to help support the family. They essentially paid for the family's medical bills and made sure the car kept running, while their father went to college.

When Blaine Sr. graduated at age 42, a nearby school district hired him as an assistant superintendent, and the family's financial stress slowly eased.

Despite the distractions growing up, or maybe because of them, Jon became adept at juggling responsibilities. He worked his odd jobs and did well in class, academically and socially. He was elected class president in three separate schools. And even though his parents had drifted from their religious roots, he insisted on spending his Sundays at a Mormon meetinghouse.

Jon, then in the eighth grade, would hitchhike to the nearest church. On his first visit, he was asked to pass communion — the sacrament, in LDS lingo, small pieces of bread and cups of water consumed by members in remembrance of the body and blood of Jesus Christ. It is a scripted rite, but

Huntsman paused for two reasons: First, he had yet to meet his Mormon bishop, and the bishop always received the sacrament first; second, he was smitten by a pretty girl at the piano.

Huntsman decided to offer the sacrament to the piano player before approaching the men on the stand, leading to a scolding from the bishop. Huntsman listened, apologized and then returned to the comely keyboardist and asked for her phone number.

"I had never done that. I was very shy and I never really had a date before," Huntsman said. "But we struck up a conversation, and nine years later we were married."

That's how Huntsman met Karen Haight, the straight-talking, popular daughter of a man who owned a chain of hardware stores. David B. Haight would rise to mayor of Palo Alto and, later, one of the highest-ranking apostles in the LDS Church. He became a role model for his eventual son-in-law.

Jon's courtship of Karen wasn't quick.

"I was 15 before I got up the nerve to hold her hand at an LDS ward dance, and even then a chaperone told us to knock it off," he said. "It was another year before I again reached for her hand and two more years before I kissed her."

Those high-school years were glory days for Jon. Naturally quick of mind and engaging, he was elected student-body president at Palo Alto High and captain of the basketball team. He had decent grades and an attractive girlfriend who was a student leader in her own right. He had everything, except for the money to go to college or a plan for his future. Turns out, he didn't need them.

Harold Zellerbach, the head of a paper company headquartered in San Francisco, had set up a scholarship at the University of Pennsylvania's prestigious Wharton School of Business. He contacted Ray Ruppel, principal of Palo Alto High, asking who would be worthy of the award. Ruppel, after a chat with his friend David Haight, summoned Jon to his office. Huntsman said he would love to accept the scholarship but he didn't know if he could cut it at an Ivy League school or how he would pay for room and board. Zellerbach worked out a separate deal to cover those expenses, too.

"I had been in the right place at the right time and was thrust into a situation by those who, at the time, had more confidence in me than I had in myself," Huntsman said later. "It was a life-altering break."

The transition wasn't easy. His early grades were not great, and he felt like an outcast among the Eastern elite, but he gained his footing with the help of his brothers at the Sigma Chi fraternity.

"Jon came from zip," said wife Karen. "He didn't know how to even tie a tie, and here he was going to school with people whose fathers were cornering the cocoa market."

He eventually became the fraternity president and in his senior year won the International Balfour Award, given to the most outstanding Sigma Chi in North America.

Huntsman was more than just a fraternity man. He also earned a spot on the varsity basketball team, though he scored only one point and saw little action. He became the senior class president. And throughout high school, he was a member of the Navy ROTC, following his family's legacy of military service. That NROTC uniform became his ticket to Utah.

It wasn't uncommon for men in military uniform to hitchhike in the postwar years, and that's how Huntsman got from Philadelphia to Salt Lake City to see his girl.

Karen, a year younger than her boyfriend, was attending the University of Utah, sharing a dorm room with Jane Romney, Mitt's older sister. This wasn't by chance. David B. Haight and George Romney were childhood friends and remained close throughout their lives. On occasion, George Romney would go to Utah and throw dinner parties, inviting Jane's close friends, who invariably included Jon Huntsman and Karen Haight. Through these visits, Huntsman said, he developed a "great respect and admiration" for George Romney.

His cross-country escapes from Penn also gave him a chance to fall in love. He became determined to ask for Karen's hand in marriage during the Christmas break of his senior year. He just didn't know how he would be able to afford an engagement ring.

Huntsman went to Philadelphia's jewelry district and haggled with a diamond dealer. If he got two of his friends to buy diamonds at full price, the dealer would give him one at half. But even with this discount, he needed $300 to get an emerald-cut diamond, which he knew Karen preferred.

He took the little money he had and put it on the poker table, playing some well-heeled classmates. He cashed out with $120. Next, he persuaded a friend to drive him to the Garden State Park Racetrack in New Jersey, where he bet on the horses. He got lucky twice, winning the money needed to buy Karen's diamond.

Before he proposed, Huntsman asked David B. Haight's permission and confessed how he scraped together the money for the ring (gambling is frowned upon in the LDS Church). Haight, then a stake president over a group of Mormon congregations, gave him a pass.

Karen left college a year early to be with Jon and the couple married in June 1959, weeks after he graduated from Wharton. Nine months later, on March 26, 1960, in Palo Alto, they had their first of nine children. They named the boy Jon M. Huntsman Jr.

Like his father, Jon Sr. became a Navy man, a post that at times separated him from his young family. He served two years as a gunnery officer, including a stint on the USS Calvert in the South China Sea, while Karen and little Jon Jr. resided in a basement apartment just outside the naval base in San Diego.

Huntsman's ship helped transport military advisers to Vietnam through Laos in the early days of the Southeast Asia conflict, though his military service ended before the United States became mired in war.

When Huntsman left the Navy, the Haights helped him land a stable job. David Haight's brother-in-law ran one of California's major egg-producing companies, Olson Farms. Dean Olson gave Huntsman his first taste of the corporate world and nudged him along as he learned the poultry business. Olson previously had paid for Jon and Karen's honeymoon to Hawaii.

The Huntsmans moved from the base to North Hollywood, where, Jon Jr. said, they lived in a classic 1960s suburb dotted with rambler homes, one step removed from the hippies and musicians who congregated down the street.

While in elementary school, the young Huntsman remembers going with his dad on sales calls, where he would pitch Olson Farms products to grocery stores throughout Southern California.

Within a few years, Huntsman Sr.'s entrepreneurial flair emerged. He started night classes at the University of Southern California, where he eventually got his master's degree in business administration, and he started his first stand-alone enterprise. He called it Continental Dynamics, a lofty, albeit confusing, name for a company that bought the rights to old music and Christmas songs and then sold them to people looking for a little nostalgia.

Huntsman notched his first sale by persuading a Safeway grocery store — also a big Olson Farms customer — to let him set up a display for a Christmas record. From there, he earned enough money to push his $1 records and cassette tapes through major television ads featuring has-been stars, such as Chubby Checker. Through the years, Continental Dynamics racked up 13 albums that sold more than 1 million copies each.

The music business may have brought in big bucks, but it remained a sideline, especially when Olson Farms and Dow Chemical launched a joint venture to create the first Styrofoam egg container. They named their new company Dolco Packaging and asked Huntsman, then 30, to be its president.

"I was in over my head," Huntsman later acknowledged. Still, the job allowed him to learn the corporate ropes and interact with investment bankers. He saw insider secrets that turned various chemicals into a goop that, when cooled, became a hugely profitable foam.

He observed everything closely for three years and suddenly left Dolco in 1970, taking 14 of its employees to launch a direct competitor, Huntsman

Container Corp. To say hard feelings arose with Dow and Olson Farms doesn't begin to describe the feud that ensued. There were lawsuits and countersuits, furious uncles and animosity that lasted decades. It was messy, but Huntsman maintains he acted honorably throughout.

"To leave a company you're with for some time, people don't like that," he said. "They want to be captive over able young men and keep you as a slave there forever, and I don't believe in that."

Those early disputes would come back to haunt Huntsman's political aspirations nearly two decades later, but they did nothing to hamper his soaring business success. The fledgling Huntsman Container Corp. built its first chemical plant in Fullerton, Calif., with $1.3 million that he and brother Blaine rounded up with the help of a few investors. In the following years, Huntsman Container outpaced Dolco, mainly by landing the first contract to make clamshell containers for McDonald's legendary Big Mac.

Strangely, for a man known for being hands-on, he hardly hovered over the day-to-day operation of his signature company. Instead he moved across the country, diving headlong into government service and the "Mormon Mafia."

Not only had President Richard Nixon tapped George Romney to be his secretary of Housing and Urban Development, but he also asked Romney's buddy J. Willard Marriott to organize his inauguration. Shortly afterward, Sen. Wallace Bennett, R-Utah, sent Marriott a note that said: "You will be interested to know that there is a comment up here among some of my colleagues that the Mormon Mafia has taken over Washington, and of course you are the number one man."

Huntsman joined that group, becoming an associate administrator in the Department of Health, Education and Welfare. Fred Malek, a Wharton man, lined up the coveted presidential appointment just months after Huntsman incorporated his packaging business, so while Blaine handled the chemical plant, Jon packed up Karen and their six children at the time — including 10-year-old Jon Jr. — and moved to Washington.

Huntsman worked for HEW for all of six months, because Malek had taken a job on Nixon's personal staff and recommended him for a higher-profile post that would place him a few feet from the Oval Office.

Malek was able to give Huntsman a warning exactly 10 minutes before H.R. "Bob" Haldeman, Nixon's chief of staff, called. He wanted Huntsman at the White House immediately. When Huntsman got there, Haldeman had him cool his heels in the West Wing waiting room for 90 minutes. The interviews lasted two grueling days and included questions from Vice President Spiro Agnew. Finally, Haldeman ended his inquisition with: "Are you a full tithe payer for your church?"

The question stunned Huntsman. He'd never had anyone outside the LDS Church ask him that question. He said, yes, he did give the church 10 percent of his income.

"Good," Haldeman said, "we don't have to worry about your integrity then, do we?"

Huntsman became the president's staff secretary in February 1971, a job that paid $6,000 a year less than his HEW post, but came with some heady responsibilities. He started three days later, the same day his seventh child, James, was born. He held the job for one year.

He later would say he left because his company needed him and so did his large family, which may have been true, but he also was exhausted and frustrated. The man was burned out, unwilling to deal with the intense pressures of the West Wing any longer. And the feeling was mutual. Haldeman had had his fill of Huntsman and wanted him gone.

Reflecting decades later on his year on Nixon's staff, Huntsman was full of warring emotions. He told interviewers it was "a great experience" and professed his eternal love for Nixon. At the same time, he displayed his loathing for Haldeman. He called his secretary position "by far the most difficult job in the White House," where he was nothing but "a robot" working more than 15 hours a day.

That may be a tad dramatic, but it says something that subsequent administrations have divvied the responsibilities Huntsman handled among a handful of employees.

Nixon's staff secretary managed office-space allocation in the White House and each employee's pay. Huntsman decided who was important enough to merit a limousine and driver. He drafted one-page summaries for Nixon on every meeting he was about to have, complete with background information on his guests and suggested topics of conversation. He was the keeper of every slip of paper that went to and came from the president. Only the highest-priority items ever made it in an all-important red folder.

He regularly fielded calls from upset Cabinet members complaining they didn't get more time with the president, most of which he ignored. But he didn't ignore calls from HUD Secretary George Romney, for whom he'd launched a presidential campaign office in 1968.

"He was one of the men in my life that I not only admired immensely but felt a great closeness and respect toward," Huntsman said. "I always had a wonderful relationship with George."

He used his position to help Romney, slipping in memos or requests to the president that normally wouldn't get through. One time, he sent in a nomination note making one of Romney's friends an ambassador to a Scandinavian country. Nixon signed it. Haldeman blew up.

" 'How did we ever get that guy in as an ambassador? How did we ever let that happen?' Haldeman demanded to know," Huntsman said. "I just sat there shaking, you know? But anyway, it got in there."

Romney wasn't the only fellow Mormon Huntsman took care of, according to Nixon insiders. He was said to often arrange tours and perks for Latter-day Saints.

"He sort of set himself up as the Mormons' man in the White House," said a senior Nixon aide. "It was nothing unusual to see Jon walking eight to 10 people through on a private White House tour."

Possibly the hardest part of Huntsman's job was deciphering and responding to Nixon's scribblings on his ever-present yellow legal pad. The president took it to the residence with him each night. In the morning, Huntsman would have a new list of questions to answer, some vitally important, others passing interests that Nixon would promptly forget. But Huntsman was required to respond to all of them within 48 hours.

"His handwriting, honestly, was terrible, and he had this initial system down, where he only used the initial letter of the person's last name," Huntsman said. "After a month or so, I could decipher any code on any little thing."

He even tried to emulate the president's system, signing a memo simply, "H." It wasn't long before the chief of staff noticed.

"The door flew open and Haldeman was there screaming at the top of his voice, 'If you think H stands for Huntsman and not Haldeman, you're one dumb son-of-a-bitch.' "

Huntsman became J.

Every error or perceived goof would result in a clash with Haldeman, who not only screamed, but also bullied. Huntsman called it "a terrorizing time in my life."

Huntsman participated in the 10 a.m. meeting, when Nixon heavyweights would plan the president's day. At one of these meetings, Haldeman complained about a California senator who was giving the White House grief about a woman nominated to be the U.S. treasurer who had employed illegal immigrants. Haldeman asked Huntsman to use some Latino workers at his Fullerton plant to go on an undercover reconnaissance mission at a nearby business once owned by the troublemaking senator.

"If there had been employment of undocumented immigrants," Huntsman said, "the information would be used, of course, to embarrass the political adversary."

Jon called his plant manager and put the plan into motion. But 15 minutes later, with a gnawing feeling in his gut, he phoned back. "Let's not do this. I don't want to play this game."

He informed Haldeman at the next day's 10 a.m. meeting and the chief wasn't pleased, but he didn't press the issue. It was the only time, Huntsman said, he heard or saw anything unethical in the West Wing, though he had his suspicions. He ended up leaving the White House four months before the June 1972 Watergate break-in, which eventually would take down Nixon and send Haldeman to prison. Huntsman escaped the scandal untouched.

Months later, he would realize how close he came to being a co-conspirator. In December 1971, Haldeman asked Huntsman to approach one of his first employers with an offer. The president would nominate Dudley Swim, a California recluse and a brilliant investor, to become the ambassador to Australia for $100,000 in cash. Swim, for whom Huntsman worked briefly, initially resisted, but eventually consented. The plan was for Huntsman to fly to California to pick up the money. Huntsman says he didn't understand why Swim couldn't just write a check, until Watergate press coverage disclosed that the Committee to Re-elect the President was collecting illegal contributions and using them for nefarious purposes.

Swim died of a heart attack the day before Huntsman was expected to make the trip.

"His passing saved me from becoming a bagman in an illegal contribution scheme," Huntsman said. "And for that, I remain forever grateful."

Huntsman had a hard time reconciling the Nixon he knew with the one who resigned in disgrace.

"There was obviously a dark side to Nixon. History has proven that. I didn't see it. His behavior didn't suggest it. I was treated extremely well by the president. I loved him," he said. Later he added: "Nixon was my hero and my kids' hero."

He blames Watergate on Haldeman, a charge that would raise the eyebrows of many historians or anyone who listened to the secret White House tapes. But to Huntsman, Nixon was everything Haldeman wasn't. He was kind and appreciative of the long hours Huntsman logged. Nixon would visit with his children. Haldeman was the bully, the instigator, the man who drove him to leave.

When asked what he took from his White House experience, Huntsman immediately says: "I didn't take anything but fear out. It took me years to get over the fear of Haldeman, the fear of my work not being perfect, and the need to please the president with every little letter in place, every word in place, everything done with a ruler and every briefing paper exactly right. What did I learn? I didn't learn anything that's helped me productively. I learned a lot of things that I would not implement in a business.

"You asked what I learned: I learned I didn't want to serve in government anymore."

Haldeman tried to get rid of Huntsman by appointing him to lead the

Peace Corps, but Huntsman declined. Malek tried to get him a job leading the Bureau of Land Management, and Huntsman turned him down, too.

Huntsman and Haldeman hashed out his exit over a heated two-hour conversation. Huntsman left the White House as a part-time, unpaid consultant who would help find nominees for sub-Cabinet-level appointments from time to time.

He presented Nixon with a parting gift, a leather-bound Book of Mormon. Nixon read a few verses aloud to the family before thanking Huntsman for his service.

He left the White House on Feb. 5, 1972, and moved his family to Utah for the first time, taking with him a wealth of connections and a determination to turn his company into an empire.

By 1973, Huntsman's assets topped $3 million from Huntsman Container and his record business. That was a year before his company started making the McDonald's clamshell and profits exploded. Huntsman and brother Blaine felt financially secure enough to buy a tract of land along the foothills of the mountains that circle Salt Lake City. They built identical houses on their own cul-de-sac.

Huntsman had moved on from the White House, but The Washington Post had not. In a front-page article that year, the paper suggested Huntsman used his White House ties to better himself. It was the first news article focused exclusively on Huntsman, and it was devastating to him.

The story said Huntsman offered Malek, the man who helped him get the staff-assistant job, 2,500 shares of his music company for $1 each, even though they were worth far more. Huntsman later denied such a stock sale.

The Post also reported that Huntsman set up a private White House tour for Julius Goldman, a leading egg producer in California, and later helped arrange a meeting between Goldman and Agriculture Department officials to discuss a government program that paid farmers whose chickens were struck with the deadly Newcastle disease.

Goldman ended up getting $2 for every bird he had to euthanize, which added up to $8.8 million. No poultry producer received a higher amount or a higher per-bird rate.

After Huntsman left Washington, his company secured a big contract with the supermarket giant Kroger, which was a majority stockholder in Goldman's Egg City. Huntsman said Goldman promised him no business, and he denied any connection between the contract and the help he provided while at the White House.

Huntsman considered the article wrong and unfair. He said it cost him business. Despite the piece, he was able to merge the container company with Keyes Fibre in 1976. The deal netted Huntsman and his brother $8 million, their first substantial taste of wealth. It also resulted in him losing some control of that company and vowing to forgo future joint ventures.

Huntsman also had started dabbling in Utah politics, getting elected as the state's Republican National Committeeman and becoming Ronald Reagan's Western states finance chairman. By 1980, Utah politicos regularly mentioned him as a gubernatorial candidate, though he declined to challenge Gov. Scott M. Matheson, the last Democrat to serve in that position. He wrote a letter to the state's GOP bigwigs saying he wouldn't run because he was focused on his international business interests. He could turn down the Republican Party, but he couldn't turn down the LDS Church when apostles came calling.

The faith sends tens of thousands of young men and women out into the world to hunt for converts. At the same time, it selects some established couples to serve as leaders in the mission field. The LDS Church sent Huntsman to his old stomping ground of Washington, D.C., to serve as a mission president, a three-year assignment. While spending most of his time counseling young missionaries, he also looked after some business. It was there he launched Huntsman Chemical, the company he would have sole control over and that would turn him from a millionaire into a billionaire. It also would make him a household name in Utah.

To get Huntsman Chemical up and running, he mortgaged his house, put up $500,000 and then persuaded ARCO Chemical, Shell Oil and Union Bank to finance an additional $42 million. The entire sum went to buy a polystyrene plant in Belpre, Ohio, earning him the nickname "the riverboat gambler" by Modern Plastics magazine.

He borrowed even more to buy a second polystyrene plant and then another. The world was awash in cheap polystyrene, and chemical companies were eager to sell their plants. Huntsman bet heavily on a plastics industry that would expand exponentially — making cheap silverware, car dashboards, toothbrushes and just about everything else.

What he didn't expect was how fast the surplus would evaporate and the price for his product would rise. The turnaround in plastics began in 1986, and by 1990 his net worth exploded to $450 million. He was one of the richest men in America. Six years later, his net worth reached $2.5 billion.

Along the way, he began establishing another reputation — as a philanthropist. He made his first headline-grabbing donation in 1987, giving $5 million to the University of Utah. In appreciation, administrators named the basketball arena in his honor. But wealth and fame have their price, as he soon discovered.

Huntsman's son James was about to drive away from the family house on the evening of Dec. 8, 1987, when two masked men rushed at him with a knife.

The men handcuffed and blindfolded him before forcing him into their car. They drove the 16-year-old across town to Budget Bob's Motel, where they chained him to a bathroom sink and one of the men pressed a blade to his throat, telling him to be quiet or die.

The kidnappers turned out to be two of James' classmates from Highland High School. When they nabbed him, one panicked and took off. The other one went forward with the plan. In a phone call answered by James' brother Paul, the kidnapper demanded $1 million and warned that if the family called police, he'd cut his victim into little pieces.

Paul called his father, who was away in Ohio with his mom and some of his siblings for a company Christmas party. Huntsman Sr. immediately sought help from a pair of neighbors, M. Russell Ballard, a member of the LDS Church's Quorum of the Twelve Apostles, and Cal Clegg, an FBI special agent who was active in the local Mormon ward.

Clegg was also attending a Christmas party when he received Huntsman's frantic call. Huntsman wanted the FBI on the case, but worried about bringing in Salt Lake City police for fear that broad knowledge of the kidnapping could endanger his son. Clegg agreed, and in a matter of minutes, the phones of FBI agents throughout Utah were ringing.

Agent Al Jacobsen was getting ready to turn in for the night when he got the call. He threw on a sweatshirt and corduroy pants and rushed to Ballard's house, where Huntsman family members were gathered. Jacobsen was stunned to see that such a wealthy man was listed in the phone book, which told him everything he needed to know about Huntsman's lax home security.

The kidnapper said he'd call again, so the FBI set up a "trap and trace" on the family phone. Agents coached Huntsman, who by now had arrived back in Salt Lake City, to stay calm and keep the kidnapper on the line as long as possible.

"I have never been as nervous in my life as when I was awaiting that call," Huntsman said, "rehearsing over and over what I would say."

The kidnapper phoned at 7:42 a.m., and Huntsman performed his role perfectly, stretching the conversation by negotiating the amount and denominations of the cash ransom: $1 million, with $100,000 of it in $100 bills. The FBI traced the call to a pay phone at a Farmer Jack supermarket on Salt Lake City's west side. At the FBI's suggestion, Huntsman told the kidnapper he'd gather the money, but only after the kidnapper called back and put James on the line, so he could confirm that his son was alive.

Agents rushed to the grocery store and tracked two suspects hurrying to a truck with a gun rack. They tailed the truck as it sped north on the interstate. It turns out they were following two innocent shoppers.

Clegg and Jacobsen replaced these agents, staking out the pay phone in an unmarked car parked across the street. Within 40 minutes, Huntsman's phone rang again. The kidnapper put James on the line to let Huntsman hear his son's scared voice.

"I'm OK, Dad," he said. "Do whatever he says."

The FBI radioed to Clegg and Jacobsen, and they spotted two men next to the pay phones. They were wearing sunglasses, and one of them had his arms around the other's neck. Clegg thought he recognized James, whom he knew from church, but Jacobsen wanted to make sure. He got out of the car and walked through the parking lot, making a point not to look directly at the suspect and his victim.

Finally, about 75 feet away, he turned his head and saw they hadn't noticed him. Jacobsen, a burly 6-foot-4, decided to go for it. He made straight for the kidnapper and just as he was about to grab him, the boy turned and plunged his 4-inch butterfly knife into his chest.

"I thought he had hit me with his fist," said Jacobsen, who felt no pain. "I think what surprised him was if you did that in the movies, the guy falls down, but I kept standing and I had a gun in my hand."

When the kidnapper saw the Smith & Wesson .357 Magnum revolver Jacobsen had drawn, he dropped the blade and ran. It wasn't until the knife hit the concrete that Jacobsen realized he had been stabbed. Clegg ran after the assailant, and Jacobsen grabbed the dangling pay-phone receiver, giving a rapid update to Huntsman and agents listening in as James stood frozen next to him.

"This is Al Jacobsen of the FBI. James is all right. I've got to go."

Clegg tackled the kidnapper and held him down until backup arrived. Jacobsen got on the ground to slow his heartbeat, while Clegg returned to James, who had thrown off his sunglasses and was frantically trying to remove the cotton balls taped over his eyes.

"James was just beside himself," said Clegg, who approached just as James was able to see again. "He said, 'Oh, Brother Clegg, Brother Clegg,' and he was crying. It was very emotional."

While Clegg took care of James, other agents and an off-duty paramedic tended to Jacobsen, who had turned a ghastly gray and was bleeding internally.

They rushed him to Salt Lake City's LDS Hospital, where doctors determined the knife sliced an artery and his chest was filling with blood, so much so that his left lung collapsed. Doctors siphoned the blood out of his chest and put it back into his leg. He was awake through it all and he remembers thinking that bleeding to death was relatively painless.

While Jacobsen was in surgery, Clegg reunited James with his family. James told him he recognized the voice of his kidnapper. It was Nicholas Byrd, a fellow Highland student, who had visited the Huntsmans' home and swam in their pool with a group of boys. Byrd was 17 years old.

Salt Lake City police weren't informed about the kidnapping until shortly before Byrd was in handcuffs.

Later that day, Jon and Karen Huntsman, visibly shaken, appeared before TV cameras. With his voice breaking and tears clouding his vision, Jon Huntsman said: "Our family is deeply grateful to the FBI and the Salt Lake City Police Department who acted in a swift and professional manner to save the life of one of our children. Our family extends its deepest sympathy and heartfelt gratitude to Special Agent Jacobsen and his family. He truly placed others' lives before his own."

The kidnapping and the FBI's dramatic rescue of James dominated Utah's news.

Huntsman Jr. was out of town when his brother was taken and was devastated by his inability to get good information. Years later, upon reflection, he says that event, more than the $5 million gift to the University of Utah or his father's business success, catapulted his family into the public eye.

Jacobsen had never been wounded in his 27 years in the FBI, where he investigated hundreds of cases from white-collar crime to kidnappings to murders. Byrd stabbed him just three weeks before his planned retirement.

When Jon and Karen Huntsman visited Jacobsen in the hospital, they didn't come empty-handed. They told him they would be honored if he would become the first director of security for Huntsman Corp. He accepted. When he started, his first act was removing the Huntsmans from the White Pages and installing a home-security system. Huntsman then hired bodyguards, erected a big fence around his house and got some dogs.

"It changes your lifestyle," Huntsman said, "and, unfortunately, is a negative side of wealth and philanthropy."

Jacobsen also helped beef up security protocols at company plants in Ohio, Texas and countries around the globe. And he kept Huntsman up to speed on the criminal case against Byrd, who was tried as an adult.

Nearly three years later, Byrd, then 19, pleaded guilty to first-degree felony aggravated kidnapping and third-degree felony aggravated assault. In accepting his 5-years-to-life prison sentence, Byrd apologized to the Huntsmans.

"I'm willing to deal with the consequences," he said, as his relatives sobbed in the courtroom. "I wish there was a better and more constructive way to deal with this. But I know by law I will go to prison."

The Utah Board of Pardons and Parole released Byrd from prison in January 1995. He hasn't had any run-ins with Utah authorities since.

When Jacobsen left his job at Huntsman Corp. to go on a Mormon mission, Huntsman immediately called Cal Clegg, who retired from the FBI to become his second director of security. Clegg offered Huntsman a recording of the FBI tapes of Byrd's calls during the kidnapping, but Huntsman declined. He said his loved ones just wanted to put the episode behind them.

Through the years Clegg has heard rumors in police circles that James was somehow implicated in the kidnapping, and he denies them adamantly.

"I know that James wasn't involved in this," he said. "I'm absolutely sure he wasn't involved in this."

In the days after his son's dramatic rescue, Jon Huntsman Sr. promised to keep a lower public profile. It was a promise he didn't keep long.

Just three months later, in March 1988, he floored Utah's political establishment when he announced that he would run for governor.

On the face of it, his announcement shouldn't have been surprising. Huntsman had considered a run for governor previously, and Republican Gov. Norm Bangerter was far from the most popular man in the state.

In the midst of a wrenching economic downturn, made worse when two of the state's largest employers — Geneva Steel and Kennecott Copper — temporarily shut down, Bangerter pushed through a $166 million tax increase to help fund public schools. He also was dogged by criticism over his controversial move to spend $60 million on massive pumps to divert Great Salt Lake floodwaters into the desert.

Early polls had Bangerter a whopping 26 percentage points behind Democrat Ted Wilson, the former mayor of Salt Lake City.

A Bangerter aide sarcastically noted Huntsman's vow to keep his family out of the headlines, saying: "I guess running for governor is taking a low profile."

The governor's campaign staffers long had suspected a possible Huntsman challenge and made several attempts at neutralizing it. In November, they had asked him to join the campaign as finance chairman. When Huntsman, who wasn't particularly close to Bangerter, declined, they asked him to help raise money, gave him a copy of their campaign strategy, stayed in regular contact and even offered to create a job for Huntsman Jr.

Campaign director David Buhler set up a lunch at Salt Lake City's swanky Alta Club with the younger Huntsman in mid-March. The meeting didn't go as planned. When Huntsman dropped the news that his dad was planning to run against Bangerter, Buhler dropped his fork.

Huntsman Jr. thought his father's campaign was a great idea. He knew his dad had long had political aspirations, and he thought Bangerter was weak.

"For a riverboat gambler," Huntsman Jr. said, "it seemed like an interesting opening."

The next day, his father went to the Governor's Mansion to deliver the news in person.

Huntsman Sr. recalls his message this way: "I'm here as a gentleman following up on our November 8th meeting; I indicated to you that I would be back. I'm back. I am recommending another candidate; it happens to be me in this case."

Huntsman, then 50, announced his campaign on the 6 o'clock news that evening.

"I have made this decision after hearing from hundreds of people who have urged me to run," he said. "I've heard from people in the halls, people in the streets. I've heard from plumbers, from repairmen. People want a change. They want a new direction."

He argued the state needed "an industrialist who is used to creating new jobs."

Bangerter responded to Huntsman's desertion — at least publicly — by saying: "It is a free country. He can do what he wants and I will do what I want.

"There are no friendships in politics. There are just coalitions, and I guess our coalition is over."

The governor argued Huntsman's entry into the race would "hurt my chances for re-election and it will hurt the Republican Party's chances." Early polling showed Bangerter was right. The Utah Poll, sponsored by The Salt Lake Tribune, had Huntsman up 3 percentage points just days after his announcement; after three weeks, his advantage over Bangerter grew to 8 points. A poll by Dan Jones & Associates gave Huntsman a 12-point lead. Both distantly trailed Wilson.

The next week, Huntsman paid the $300 filing fee to make it official. He then dumped about $600,000 into the race, half from his own pocket, while some he siphoned from his company and family. He named two campaign directors: Jon Jr. and John Romney, a cousin of Mitt's who was a Huntsman-family loyalist.

Huntsman's main strategy was to peel away Bangerter's supporters. He got former Rep. Dan Marriott to endorse him. Richard Eyre, who ran for governor four years later and became a best-selling author, publicly urged Bangerter to get out of the race. Joe Cannon, the head of Geneva Steel, commissioned his own poll and held a news conference to say there was no way for Bangerter to win.

Huntsman summoned Nolan Karras, then the Utah House majority leader, to his office, where Karen and Jon Jr. were waiting. After they peppered him with questions, a secretary ushered in Karras to see Jon Sr. for a second interview. The Huntsmans viewed Karras as a serious lawmaker who could help Jon Sr. deal with the Legislature and provide valuable political advice. Huntsman planned to serve only one term if elected, and he was already thinking about who would come after him.

The conversation was startlingly frank.

"We've checked you out," Huntsman told him. "I'm running for governor and I want you to be my lieutenant governor. You can be governor in four years."

Karras, who had not yet picked sides, was intrigued, but left without giving a definitive yes.

Bangerter's aides were alarmed by Huntsman's lightning-fast rise, but publicly said they didn't think his poll numbers would hold. Bangerter had held the support of Sen. Orrin Hatch and much of the Legislature. And Sen. Jake Garn, Huntsman's close confidant, remained in Bangerter's corner as well.

Wilson started taking a few light jabs at Huntsman in his public appearances. When people asked why he was running, the former mayor would say he wanted the job so he could live in a house slightly smaller than Huntsman's.

Still, even with all the Huntsman hoopla, Wilson said he saw Bangerter as his main rival.

"Jon Huntsman has an almost coronation atmosphere about him now. That's understandable. But the governor is still the man to beat," Wilson said. "No one is perfect, and the people know our warts; we've been in public life for so long. They don't know Jon's. Everyone has warts, and when the public sees Jon's, the Bangerter-Huntsman race will tighten up."

Wilson called it.

When Huntsman announced his candidacy, Rick Shenkman sat in the KUTV newsroom and thought: "Who the hell is Huntsman?" As an investigative reporter for the Utah TV station, Shenkman didn't spend much time on politics, but he was stunned that he didn't know anything about this wealthy businessman who came barreling into the race. His curiosity was piqued even before the station received an intriguing anonymous package.

A select group of news outlets in Utah received the same unmarked envelope with a Salt Lake City postmark that included a 15-year-old story from The Washington Post alleging Huntsman had used his position in the Nixon administration to better himself, and some legal documents pertaining to his business spat with his uncle-in-law Dean Olson.

Ogden's Standard-Examiner wrote a front-page story on the accusations.

Huntsman Sr. denied the thrust of The Post story and accused the Bangerter campaign of trying to smear him. Buhler said the governor's campaign received the same anonymous package, insisting it wasn't from Bangerter's team.

Huntsman Jr. remembers driving 40 miles to Ogden on that Sunday to pick up copies of the paper to bring back to his father.

"We both read it. It wasn't kind," Huntsman Jr. recalls. "And then the TV interviews followed that."

Shenkman wanted to explore the accusations in The Post story, but he saw something bigger — a family drama involving the very creation of Huntsman's vaunted business empire.

He flew to California to interview Dean Olson, the egg executive and Huntsman's uncle by marriage. Olson, in his 80s by then, had never gotten over the sense of betrayal he felt when Huntsman left Dolco to start his own polystyrene-packaging company and the rift it had caused. All these years later, he remained so angry that he was willing to torpedo his nephew's fledgling political career.

"I love my sister Ruby. I hate to see the family split, which in my opinion, Jon is the cause of it. And I feel very bad about that," Olson said in measured tones as he sat behind his desk. "I feel Jon's loyalty and integrity and his moral business ethics are not compatible with what I believe in. But I wish him well. I think he has probably done a lot for Utah, but I can only wish him very well as far as I'm concerned. ... In a business sense, I have lost confidence in him."

Shenkman asked Olson, a prominent Republican who previously served as the mayor of Beverly Hills, if he would vote for Huntsman for public office.

"No, I wouldn't."

What if the choice was Huntsman or a Democrat? Olson looked at his hands for a second and then back at Shenkman. "I would either not vote or I would vote for the Democrat."

Olson accused Huntsman of setting up his company on the sly while working for Dolco. When ordering new equipment, Huntsman would have a duplicate sent elsewhere for Huntsman Container, he charged. Huntsman had secret conversations with some of Dolco's top minds, and Olson said he "borrowed" a specialized dye from Dow Chemical that is critical in the creation of polystyrene.

When Huntsman announced he was exiting Dolco, Olson said, he left with the people, the tools and the know-how to compete head to head with his former employer.

"It was a matter of integrity and loyalty," Olson said.

Dow Chemical sued Huntsman Container, and Huntsman Container countersued, claiming Dow was paying potentially illegal kickbacks to Dolco. Both companies eventually backed down.

But Olson wasn't ready to drop it. At a poultry convention in February 1972, he publicly and repeatedly claimed that Huntsman had just been fired from the White House. Huntsman sued him for slander, seeking $11 million in damages. In the legal proceedings, Olson surprised Huntsman's team by producing a letter he mailed to himself back in December after claiming to get information from someone inside the White House.

He opened the sealed letter postmarked Dec. 9, 1971:

"About 10 days ago, I was informed that Jon Huntsman will be discharged from his position in Washington. The principal reason given was that he was peddling influence, spending a lot of time on his personal business, and, in general, that they were afraid of him.

"In order not to cause any 'stink' about the discharge, they will retain him as an adviser, but this will be without compensation and they are not planning to use him in any advisory capacity.

"It would be my guess that Jon, in his desire to look good, will blow this out of proportion, etc., etc. The confidential information that has come to me, however, is that he is fired. The termination date will be February first, allowing for vacations, etc."

He signed it simply: "Dean."

Huntsman left the White House on Feb. 5, exactly one year from his starting date, and he was kept on in an advisory capacity.

Olson's insurance company settled the slander suit by cutting Huntsman a $1,000 check. Huntsman claimed victory, saying any settlement implied that Olson's comment was wrong, while Olson said he settled to avoid paying legal fees and that he remained convinced Huntsman was fired.

The lawsuit played heavily into The Post's decision to probe Huntsman's White House service and how he may have helped Julius Goldman get millions from the Agriculture Department.

The paper highlighted a quote from Huntsman's deposition in his case against his uncle-in-law: "I think anyone who has served as special assistant to the president and has a fairly good knowledge of the workings of government could capitalize his earnings in that experience many times over."

Olson saw it as proof that Huntsman used his government ties to gain an unfair business advantage, helping brother Blaine set up their company from inside the West Wing.

"I don't think anybody should be working on the president's staff and building their business at the same time," Olson told Shenkman and his KUTV camera crew. "Using government influence, I would classify that as immoral or a lack of integrity and honesty, using his office to promote his personal wealth."

Unlike Dow, Olson didn't file a lawsuit and, at the time, he didn't take his disputes to the news media. Instead, he says he took Huntsman to "church court," a colloquialism referring to an LDS Church disciplinary council. Such councils often involve a serious breach of church principles, anything from murder to sex crimes to "apostasy" — standing in direct opposition to the Mormon prophet. But they can delve into other activities that go against the faith's standards. Olson claimed Huntsman's underhanded business dealings qualified.

"He hasn't followed the line as a good Christian, as far as I'm concerned," Olson said. "We have a process in the church where these things have to be adjudicated before a church court or a committee. We thought Jon's actions were not honest."

Huntsman doesn't think Olson's retelling of the episode is honest. He says it's horribly misleading to call what happened after their blowup in 1972 a "church court," where the potential penalty could be excommunication.

"I have never been involved in a church court," said Huntsman, who argues if Olson's claims were true, he never would have become a mission president or attained other high-level LDS leadership roles.

Instead, Huntsman says David B. Haight, then an assistant to the Quorum of the Twelve Apostles, arranged a "conflict-resolution committee," which included himself and two high-ranking Mormon leaders. Huntsman saw Haight, his father-in-law and Olson's brother-in-law, as a neutral arbiter of their dispute.

While Olson alleged Huntsman pilfered trade secrets from his company, Huntsman argued Olson tried to destroy Huntsman Container with lies and innuendo and defamed Huntsman personally.

Olson told Shenkman that, in the end, he had to pay $52,000 in restitution to Huntsman and Huntsman had to pay Olson $62,000.

The resolution was supposed to remain private, but Olson had no qualms talking about it on camera.

His broadsides even extended to his nephew's gift of $5 million to the University of Utah, when he remarked sneeringly that a friend was surprised Huntsman didn't demand his name on the basketball arena be in neon.

"I think his greatest weakness," Olson said, "is in seeking honor and publicity."

Shenkman left California with explosive footage, backed by legal documents and the tantalizing promise that Olson would expose even more personal details about Huntsman as the political contest unfolded. The reporter's next step was to sit down with Huntsman in his corporate headquarters in the Eagle Gate Tower, half a block from the Salt Lake LDS Temple.

George Hatch, a well-known Democrat, owned KUTV, which put the Huntsmans on alert, though Shenkman said his corporate bosses took no part in his reporting on the new gubernatorial candidate. At any rate, KUTV didn't send its investigative reporter out to do puff pieces, so Huntsman knew it was going to be a rough interview. He just didn't know how rough.

Shenkman started by asking Huntsman why he wanted to be governor. Huntsman answered that he could use his business knowledge to help Utah's sluggish economy. They then discussed Bangerter for a few minutes and moved on to Huntsman's upbringing in rural Idaho, but it wasn't long before Shenkman plunged into Olson's accusations. Huntsman became stiff, frustrated and increasingly hostile.

"This is the type of questions and trickery really — and I want you to put this on camera — it's why good men and women don't get into politics because people have tried to feed you information to discourage my running for office."

Huntsman made the accusation after the first tough question. He remained in the chair for another 40 minutes, defending the founding of his business and his White House service, while slamming The Washington Post for "a fallacious article with 51 errors" that made his children come home from school crying. He resisted going after Dean Olson personally.

"Mr. Olson is in his 80s, he's probably ... he is a fine man and I'm not going to say anything other than that," Huntsman said, biting his lip.

He tried to steer Shenkman back to Utah's economic problems and away from the nasty dispute.

"What Mr. Olson wants to say happened 20 years ago doesn't faze me in the slightest. I've been a man of integrity. I have put funds back into this community. I have raised a great family. I have built a business that has taken hard work, and it is the American Dream come true from the son of a schoolteacher. If people want to make these statements about me 18 or 15 or 20 years ago, it really doesn't bother me. All I want to do is help this state move forward economically."

Huntsman produced his own letter from H. Glenn Olson, Dean Olson's brother, that he received Oct. 15, 1979: "Dear Jon, during 1972 and 1973, in an attempt to embarrass you and your company as competitors, some of our former overzealous employees and associates presented inaccurate and exaggerated information to The Washington Post and other media. We regret that these incidents ever occurred. The people involved in this activity have since left our company. We all wish you the very best of luck in the future and stand ready to assist you where appropriate."

Huntsman told Shenkman that he didn't steal any equipment from Dow, denied using his White House job to benefit himself and disputed that he was fired. Huntsman pointed to the $1,000 check from Olson's insurance company in the slander suit as proof that Olson lied.

He fumed that Shenkman would spend so much time focusing on the start of his business while asking no questions about its incredible growth or his charitable works. He remained defiant and defensive, but Huntsman acknowledged that the early 1970s were tough on him and he had made some missteps.

"I have made mistakes in my life," he said. "As I have made mistakes, I have tried to benefit from those and grow from adversity."

As the interview went on, Huntsman kept directing his anger at Shenkman personally.

"You came over here under false pretenses. You said you were going to do a profile of my life."

Shenkman: "We are going to do a profile."

Huntsman: "Then get into this other 48 years then."

Huntsman's campaign manager, Lillian Garrett, tried to cut the interview short, saying Shenkman would get just two more questions, but Huntsman wouldn't have it.

"No, Lillian, I'm very disturbed about this, and this is something I'm going to go on television on," Huntsman said, pointing at Shenkman. "He came over here to tell me he was going to do a profile on my life. He's come over here, after he dug up all this dirt, to focus on two years of my life, and I don't believe there is a fairness doctrine in the media."

Shenkman more than once told Huntsman he could say whatever he wanted, but the candidate saw that as a cop-out. Shenkman then brought up a final letter, this one from an LDS apostle to Dean Olson that said, in effect, the church ought to put Huntsman in his place because he was "a young ambitious man who tried to destroy a good Mormon company."

"That is out there. We've got the letter. It is part of the questions that are out there," Shenkman told Huntsman. "I understand when you are a businessman you are going to make enemies, but this was a church apostle saying this. It wasn't like he was one of your competitors."

Huntsman seethed.

"If there is any church apostle who has said anything about Jon Huntsman over the last 50 years of my life — I served as a mission president and a stake president in the church. I have given my time and effort and I love the church. If somebody has said something about me in a letter, go ask them what they said."

A couple of questions later, Huntsman had had all he could handle.

"Why don't we end it, Rick. You've got your pound of flesh now. You can go back and do your thing with me."

Shenkman: "I'm not looking for a pound of flesh."

Huntsman: "I think you are, Rick. I'm going to have my day in court because … I'm not saying that legally. I'm just saying you came over here to do a profile on my life and you have not done it. You have not done it, Rick!"

Huntsman eventually ripped the microphone from his lapel and stood up, taking a step toward the still-seated Shenkman. The cameras kept rolling and the lights illuminated Huntsman's finger wagging in the reporter's face, while Huntsman's head disappeared into the shadows.

"I'll be around this community a long time. I don't care if I win this job or not. You misled me, buddy. I wanted a profile. You told me profile. Why didn't you say, 'I want to come over and talk to you about the Olson mess'? Why didn't you have the guts to tell me that?"

Shenkman told Huntsman that he had known what they were going to talk about beforehand. KUTV produced five separate pieces around 4 minutes each from Shenkman's work that would run on consecutive nights in mid-April. Each day Shenkman called a Huntsman adviser and read word for word what would appear in that night's installment, giving him a chance to challenge any factual inaccuracies.

Separate stories focused on accusations of Huntsman's White House improprieties, why he ran for governor, his philanthropy and the legal disputes over the start of Huntsman Container.

On the day after the third story aired, Shenkman called and not only read the script for that day's story but also gave a hint at the closing piece, two evenings hence, which would focus on the "church court" and the apostle letter.

A few hours later, Shenkman says Huntsman's campaign told KUTV the candidate was dropping out. The reporter and his station chief decided his withdrawal made Huntsman a private citizen again, and they backed off. Olson's church-court accusation never made the newscast. Shenkman also decided against reporting the allegation that Huntsman was axed from the White House after he had called H.R. Haldeman, who denied that he fired Huntsman. Given the animosity between Haldeman and Huntsman, that denial carried weight with the reporter.

The last thing viewers saw of the series was Huntsman ending the interview, shaking his finger in Shenkman's face and walking out. It was a searing image at odds with the public persona Huntsman had cultivated. Shenkman described the moment as unsettling yet revealing.

"My personal reaction was, 'Hey, if he can't handle Rick Shenkman, I'm just a reporter at a TV station, how is he going to handle the whole Legislature? How is he going to run the whole state?' Running a business is entirely different than running a whole state. You have to run a state through cooperation. You can't run a state through edicts."

Huntsman was half a world away when Shenkman's series aired, traveling with Garn in Taiwan, Singapore and Thailand. But that doesn't mean he wasn't paying close attention.

"He called every day for almost a week, saying he was going to sue," said Pat Shea, KUTV's lawyer at the time, who vetted the stories and stood up to Huntsman Sr.'s pushback. Huntsman didn't follow through on his threats of litigation. Later, he put Shea on retainer and the two became close.

While this drama unfolded, Garrett, Huntsman's campaign manager, was busy finding downtown office space for the effort and keeping tabs on Karras, who by then was leaning against accepting Huntsman's invitation to join the ticket. She insisted Karras wait to talk to Huntsman in person.

Unknown to Garrett — and to most everyone else — Huntsman funneled a back-channel note to Bangerter, who slipped past his security detail to meet his just-returned rival in a park near the Capitol. During a private stroll, Huntsman said he was bowing out.

The governor waited until after the 10 p.m. news was nearly over to tell his staff to meet him at Huntsman's office on the 20th floor of the Eagle Gate Tower the next day.

With Bangerter by his side, Huntsman faced the press, saying he was exiting the race 12 days before the Republican caucuses, two days before he was to hold a big campaign event in Fillmore and one month after declaring his candidacy.

Garn insisted he didn't pressure Huntsman during their swing abroad, and Huntsman said it wasn't bad press that drove his decision. Rather, he said during his economic-development foray he "discovered that, as a private citizen, I can be an effective and forceful advocate for doing business in Utah." He has since said his major suppliers threatened to pull away from Huntsman Chemical if he ran for office.

Garrett backs her former boss, saying the KUTV stories stung, but didn't force out Huntsman.

"I don't think so; I think Jon was pretty tough," she said. "You have to have pretty tough skin to be a politician or to be in business."

Political insiders didn't buy it, saying Huntsman couldn't handle the aggressive reporting on his past, which tarnished his carefully crafted image as Utah's patron saint. It was also believed that Huntsman had calculated — wrongly — that Bangerter would step aside rather than dig in for a fight. When it came down to it, Huntsman didn't really want to wage a bare-knuckled campaign with the prospects of exposing the "warts" of all the candidates and splitting the GOP.

"There were some pretty outlandish and difficult allegations against him," Karras said. "And I think he just thought, 'My Lord, I'm mega-wealthy, why would I put up with this?' "

Looking back on his father's short gubernatorial bid, Jon Huntsman Jr.

says there is some truth to Karras' analysis. Huntsman's son not only had helped set up the KUTV interviews but had sat through them as well.

"They weren't pleasant," he recalled. "It was a really tumultuous week or two. It should have shaded my view of politics forever, but it didn't. I'm too much of an optimist."

For his part, Huntsman Sr. says the Shenkman pieces had nothing to do with his withdrawal.

"I'd been in the Nixon White House; I pretty well knew how the game of politics was played," he said. "It became very apparent to me that if I was to seek a political career, that it would terminate any hope I would have of someday giving large amounts of money to public interests."

And yet, more than a quarter-century later, Huntsman still seethes at Shenkman: "I never met anyone who is as mean-spirited or as dishonest as he was."

Huntsman says he eventually reconciled with his uncle-in-law. Olson, he says, called in 1993 to ask if Huntsman would assume control of his egg-producing business.

"I said, 'Thank you, Dean, for asking me after all of these years, but no, I wouldn't be interested at all,'" Huntsman said. "He died a few months thereafter."

When Huntsman ended his short-lived political push, he pulled the plug on five TV ads he had produced to introduce himself to voters, losing the $115,000 he paid the stations to run them and whatever it cost to make the spots. One of the never-aired 2-minute ads opened with Huntsman walking in the Fillmore cemetery, where his ancestors are buried, and concluded with him saying: "I'm Jon Huntsman. I'm running for governor because I can lead Utah to the future it deserves."

Out of the race, Huntsman held a news conference where he raised Bangerter's hands in a show of unity before the TV cameras as their wives politely hugged.

"From this day forward, I will work to unite our party and do all that I can to re-elect Governor Bangerter," Huntsman said. "I give to him my unwavering support."

Despite residual skepticism in the Bangerter camp, Huntsman proved true to his word. He contributed money and cut at least one ad for the governor. In return, Bangerter named Huntsman an economic "ambassador," an unpaid position in which the industrialist would tout the state as a good place to do business.

In the ensuing months, Wilson refused to hit Bangerter on his tax increase or much else and the Republican governor's numbers started inching up. By November, what had looked like a surefire win for the Democrat turned into a narrow victory for Bangerter, who snagged 40 percent of the vote. Wilson netted 38 percent and independent candidate Merrill Cook claimed 21.

Jon Huntsman Jr. told reporters at the time that his father was on newly elected President George H.W. Bush's short list to be commerce secretary, but said he wasn't interested in going back to Washington. Huntsman Sr. never ran for another public office, redirecting his political hopes and dreams to his eldest son and namesake.

Huntsman Sr. returned his focus to his business, which was still expanding into international markets. He was buying smaller companies and making a financial killing. It was his kingdom, and he could run it the way he wanted, without having to answer to stockholders, partners or the press. He didn't like what he couldn't control, and that's part of the reason a routine medical checkup gone wrong was such a devastating blow. At the same time, it also gave him a new life's mission.

In 1992, four years after his ill-fated political run, Huntsman learned he had prostate cancer — a disease that had killed his father two years earlier. His mother perished in his arms of breast cancer in 1968. He was scared, describing it as getting a guilty verdict for a crime he didn't commit, but he put on a brave face in revealing his illness publicly.

"We have gone through many interesting things in this life," he said, "but my family has developed a strong determination to never give up, to be positive no matter what hand we are dealt."

Huntsman faced the prospect of surgery. Only then would he know if the cancer had spread. The day before he went under the knife, he and his family went to the homeless shelter in downtown Salt Lake City and gave the director a handwritten note and a check for $1 million. They then walked across the street to the soup kitchen and food bank operated by the Roman Catholic Church and delivered an identical envelope and donation.

"Our prayers are with Mr. Huntsman and his family," said the Rev. William K. Weigand, then the bishop of Salt Lake City's Catholic Diocese. "His thoughts and actions today reached out to the lives of others in need. We are deeply grateful for his remarkable act of selflessness. We ask our Lord that Mr. Huntsman be granted a full and hurried recovery."

But Huntsman wasn't done yet. He also stopped at LDS Hospital and gave $500,000 for the program that detected his prostate cancer.

"Dad thought it would be nice to focus on people truly in need of help," said Jon Huntsman Jr., acting as the family spokesman. "It had a cathartic effect on the family — it helped us reflect on others during our own time of need."

Huntsman's prostate removal lasted four hours. Karen, Jon Jr. and seven of his eight siblings were on hand. The only Huntsman missing was Jennifer, who was on a Mormon mission. The surgery succeeded, though it resulted in impotence and temporary incontinence that left Huntsman frustrated. But he had his life, and doctors were confident that they removed all the cancer. The family patriarch spent 11 days in the hospital, often surrounded by family, but the nights were long.

"I was terrified the whole time," he said. "And I was incredibly lonely."

He slowly recovered as his pre-surgery generosity caught more and more attention. "Good Morning America" planned to run a piece on it. That segment was seen in the western United States, but it was pre-empted elsewhere for extended coverage of President George H.W. Bush getting sick and throwing up at a state dinner in Japan.

Two months after his surgery, Huntsman invited every health professional who had helped him — from the doctors to the orderlies — to his Deer Valley home for a dinner. He gave each of those 40 people a 20-inch color TV.

A year after that, the Catholic Church wanted to say thank you, inviting Huntsman to Rome for a 10-minute private audience with Pope John Paul II in recognition for his generosity toward the homeless and his help in restoring Salt Lake City's Cathedral of the Madeleine.

The pope kissed Huntsman on the cheek and thanked him for his contributions. They talked about charity and faith, but they also touched on a shared experience.

"We both have had prostate cancer and similar surgery, so I was paying particular attention to his vigor," Huntsman said. "He appeared very strong and in good spirits. I was impressed by the vibrancy and vitality of his presence."

Huntsman called that papal visit one of the "greatest honors of my life," and he counts John Paul II and LDS Church President Gordon B. Hinckley as the two men he has most admired.

Huntsman long had given tens of millions to universities and arts programs. In more recent years, he had turned his generosity to building hospitals and schools in Armenia after a horrendous earthquake in 1988. But his experience with prostate and, later, skin cancer sparked an intense desire to fight the disease that had ravaged his family and countless others.

He toured cancer centers throughout the country and decided to help build one in Salt Lake City. He started small, giving $1.25 million to the University of Utah's School of Medicine to endow a chair in urologic oncology a month after his visit with the pope. Three months later, he announced his initial $10 million gift to create the Huntsman Cancer Institute. He promised much more, and he delivered.

In 1995, he pledged $100 million to the institute, at the time the world's largest donation to medical research from an individual. And he had raised $51 million from business associates. Hinckley, the LDS president at the time, and then-Gov. Mike Leavitt were on hand to celebrate Huntsman's commitment.

His donation led to the construction of a six-story glass-and-stone-veneer complex in Salt Lake City's eastern foothills, where researchers delve into the genetics of cancer and patients have hotel-like accommodations while they wrestle with the disease.

Huntsman and his wife designed the rooms to offer everything he didn't have when he fought prostate cancer. They are bright and comfortable, with stunning views and restaurant-quality food unlike the usual hospital fare.

Jon Huntsman Jr. was the president of the Huntsman Cancer Foundation's board in 2015 and his brother David served as CEO.

The cancer hospital remains visible from anywhere in Salt Lake City and rests just north of the headquarters of Huntsman Corp., a similarly gleaming glass behemoth nestled in the foothills.

The lobby of the corporate office features an image of the globe with "Huntsman" splashed across it in big bold letters. Nearby are glass cases that explain what the company's plants look like and display some of the products they have helped produce. Others tell the story of Huntsman Sr.'s life, pictures of his kids with him and Nixon and Reagan. Then there is the plaque near the the door that tells of Orson Pratt, Parley P. Pratt's brother, who was the first Mormon to enter the Salt Lake Valley, not far from the Huntsman headquarters.

Jon Huntsman Jr. was the heir apparent at Huntsman Corp., but he had other ideas about where his life would take him. So his father began to hand over the reins to the second-oldest son, Peter, who has moved the company away from polystyrene and its huge volatility to the more stable market of designer chemicals.

Huntsman Sr. remained the heart of his company even as he devoted more time to other endeavors, such as philanthropy and a new prominent role in the LDS Church. In 1996, he was named as an Area Seventy, a high-ranking quorum in the faith. His release from the prestigious, though short-term, position preceded his son's 2012 presidential run.

As Huntsman Sr. rose in prominence and wealth, in his faith and in the esteem of the community, one thing that never wavered was his fierce instinct to protect his family and reputation at any cost.

Take the story of the student journalist who almost cost the University of Utah its cancer hospital.

Dave Hancock was an exceedingly smart but cocky editor of The Daily

Utah Chronicle, the school's independent student newspaper. In the fall of 1999, Hancock wrote an editorial questioning why Karen Huntsman, who had never graduated from college, deserved to be on the state Board of Regents. The editorial also included a pejorative line saying her life's biggest accomplishment was marrying Jon Huntsman.

This infuriated the billionaire. He wanted Hancock fired and the student newspaper reined in. If he didn't get what he wanted, he threatened to pull all future donations. University administrators panicked. Past presidents and the football and basketball coaches leaned on Hancock to publicly apologize. He refused.

University trustee Randy Dryer tried to talk down the school's very important, very irate donor.

"I had to explain to Mr. Huntsman that The Chronicle was part of the free press," Dryer recalls. "We made it clear the university president didn't have the ability to shut The Chrony down or fire [the editor]."

Hancock heard Huntsman was threatening to yank planned contributions to the cancer center and eventually relented, writing a front-page retraction. Huntsman then befriended Hancock, a survivor of testicular cancer, and eventually invited The Chrony staff up to Huntsman Corp. for a free lunch to make peace.

Huntsman acknowledges that he often reacts strongly when angry, a trait of which he's not proud.

"I am an emotional person," he said, "but my outbursts are rare and end quickly, and I spend the next three weeks apologizing for them."

Huntsman's contributions to the cancer center never stopped nor slowed as a result of The Chrony dust-up. They actually increased.

The philanthropist led three successive expansions. All told, he has given $450 million to the cancer center. Construction began in June 2014 on the latest wing, which will focus on cancers affecting children. At the groundbreaking, Huntsman recalled that when he was serving as White House staff secretary, he received one of the pens that Nixon used to sign the National Cancer Act of 1971, proclaiming war on the disease. Karen Huntsman recalled that when her husband was diagnosed with prostate cancer, he vowed to tap all of his resources to fight cancer. While his health has waned — he has a condition that swells his feet, making walking and standing difficult at times — Huntsman has vowed that he isn't done with his namesake cancer center yet.

"I'm not supposed to say anything. ... But I've already got the next phase ready to go," he told reporters. "This is the time, the season and the place to cure cancer."

During his lifetime, he has given more than $1.5 billion to charity, making him one of only 19 people on the planet who have donated more than $1 billion. He was one of the first people to sign the Giving Pledge, a promise proffered by Warren Buffett and Bill and Melinda Gates to give half their wealth to charity. Almost instantly Huntsman called on his fellow philanthropists to do even more.

"My suggestion was to give 80 percent away. Why do they need half of $10 billion to live on?" he said. "The people I particularly dislike are those who say, 'I'm going to leave it in my will.' What they're really saying is, 'If I could live forever, I wouldn't give any of it away.' "

His plan is to end his life without any fortune at all, giving most of it to the cancer center. In 2014, he was trying to sell his palatial Deer Valley home, with its 22-car garage, and has said the proceeds will go to his charitable works. He also published his autobiography, "Barefoot to Billionaire," and he's spent years building Huntsman Springs, a major housing development in Driggs, Idaho, complete with its own business district and golf course. He's promised to plow all of the proceeds from his book sales and housing development into the battle against cancer.

"I am certain the genesis of my philosophy of giving springs from my humble beginnings and the memory of having been on the outside looking in," Huntsman wrote. "Throughout my life, I have hustled to outrun the shadow of poverty."

Outrun it, he did.

In looking back on his life, Huntsman, who turned 77 in June 2014, said he has accomplished three things: He and his wife have created a large and accomplished family; he built Huntsman Corp.; and he gave his money to fight cancer. That's how he wants to be remembered, though he would be just fine if folks eventually knew him as the father of the president.

chapter four

The rebel and the honor student

George Romney and Jon Huntsman Sr. were men whose long shadows gloomed over their children. In his formative years, Jon Jr. struggled to come to terms with his family's surging wealth and status, and he ended up faltering in high school. When he found his footing, he relied on his father's considerable connections to launch a career in public service.

Through it all, he maintained a close, if unorthodox, relationship with his dad even as he tried to establish his own identity.

Mitt Romney never really rebelled. He instead wanted desperately to be like his famous father. He grew up expecting to run a car company because his dad did. He ran for office largely because his dad did. Even Romney's love affair with young Ann Davies resembled his father's instant infatuation with Lenore LaFount. The difference was Lenore made George work for it, moving from one coast to the other, while Ann didn't require such a long trial-by-courtship. But she did make Mitt sweat a little.

The Romneys and the Davies family lived about a mile apart in Bloomfield Hills, a swanky suburb about 20 miles northwest of Detroit. Mitt, who went by the nickname Billy as a young boy, met Ann briefly in elementary school, where he saw her riding a horse. They wouldn't connect again until they were teens.

That's because Mitt went to Cranbrook, an elite all-boys boarding school, from the time he turned 12, while Ann, who is three years younger, went to Kingswood, the nearby all-girls school.

Cranbrook and Kingswood were modeled on British boarding schools where grades were called "forms" and teachers "masters." The campuses had sweeping grounds, fountains, columns and buildings bedecked in frescoes and fancy chandeliers. Students were treated like future business executives, and they acted the part.

Mitt already displayed his trademark perfect hair and stiff bearing, but he was far from the leader he later would become. He wasn't Cranbrook's most popular kid nor the best student. He wasn't much of an athlete, either.

"He was your typical gawky, tall, skinny adolescent boy," recalled Jim Bailey, a classmate.

But he wasn't shy. He packed all kinds of activities on top of his structured life, which revolved around church and chores on the weekends and Latin and advanced math on weekdays. Mitt picked up after the school's hockey players as team manager and led cheers at Cranbrook Cranes football games. He joined 14 student groups from the glee club to the pre-med club.

George Romney was the president of American Motors at the time, and many of Mitt's 75 classmates were sons of auto executives. He even got teased because American Motors and its little Rambler were small potatoes compared with GM or Ford.

"That's not a car," some scoffed. "That's a bicycle with a dishwasher for an engine."

Mitt didn't stand out until his dad moved into the governor's mansion in 1963. The taunts then shifted, belittling the son as "no George Romney."

"I had the impression that Mitt was struggling for respect when he was at Cranbrook," said Eric Muirhead, a classmate who is now a writing teacher in Texas. "Mitt suffered because of his father's importance."

That didn't make the younger Romney resentful. He interned for his father when he was 16, viewing the state's top political leader in action. This proximity to power also let Mitt become chummy with the state troopers assigned to protect the governor. And those ties gave him the opening to pull off an elaborate prank.

Mitt borrowed a trooper uniform, badge and siren, which he placed atop a car. He then pulled over two friends who were in on the gag. Their girlfriends, though, got nervous. When "Officer" Romney searched the trunk and found empty bourbon bottles, the girls got scared. When the two boys peeled off and Romney chased after them with the police siren blaring, they freaked out.

Candy Porter, a Kingswood student, feared she would not only get arrested, but also expelled.

"I just remember being like a deer in headlights," she said. "I just remember being terrified."

"It wasn't a very funny joke for them," added Graham McDonald, one of the pranksters. "But it was a funny joke for us."

Not every trick went over so well; one in particular drew cringes.

Mitt apparently couldn't stand the bleached blond hair that hung over one of John Lauber's eyes. Lauber had transferred into Cranbrook and never really fit in. Classmates teased him because they presumed, correctly, that he was gay.

Romney rallied a group to make Lauber conform. The boys tackled him and held him down while Mitt approached with scissors. Lauber screamed for help as Romney started snipping the boy's prized blond hair. Five students, including Mitt's friend Matthew Friedemann, recounted the bullying to The Washington Post.

"He was just easy pickin's," said Friedemann, who expressed regret for not stepping in to stop the ambush.

Cranbrook never disciplined Romney for his actions, though school officials did expel Lauber later for smoking. Mitt says he didn't recall cutting Lauber's hair, but he later apologized generically for pranks that crossed the line.

That may have included a time where he led a vision-impaired teacher into a closed door and giggled at the collision.

Classmates don't remember Romney as mean-spirited, even if he did go too far a few times. He and Friedemann were known for late-night antics that drew appreciative crowds.

"If you should ever by chance be walking down the corridor at 2:00 a.m. and hear rising tones of boisterous, exuberant laughter, you are almost sure to find its source is Mitt Romney," said a blurb in the Cranbrook yearbook during Romney's senior year. "A quiet joke, a panicky laughter and another of the Friedemann-Romney all-night marathon contests has begun."

As Mitt matured, his penchant for pranks gave way to a growing devotion to self-discipline. He made the cross-country team, not because of his stamina or his speed, but based on resolve. Muirhead, the team captain, got sick early in the season and lobbied for Romney to take his spot at one meet. It was largely a symbolic move because the Cranbrook team regularly dominated the competition. As long as Mitt crossed the finish line, his team would likely win.

As expected, Romney fell behind as the race got under way. Near the end, he gasped for breath and fell. When teammates rushed to help him up, he waved them off. He got up, took a few more steps and fell again. He staggered a few more steps and then collapsed, the race long over. The quiet crowd stared at the governor's son as he continued to stumble toward the finish line. When Romney finally made it across, the audience erupted.

"He got an ovation like I never heard. He won a lot of people's respect that day," said Muirhead. "In all my years, I never saw a guttier performance."

By this point, Romney was getting used to the spotlight. He was the spunky kid often at the governor's side, and he didn't shy away from reporters. He became a mini-celebrity in Michigan. When Mitt had his appendix out, it made the papers. Reporters wrote about the $2,000 he raised from his neighbors for his dad's campaign. One Detroit News story declared "Romney Son Helps Fight School Fire," when actually he just pointed firefighters in the direction of a small blaze in the Cranbrook art building.

Romney became a big man on campus, outgoing and confident, even with the opposite sex. He wrote letters to Kingswood girls, a number of them addressed to Lyn Moon Shields, his girlfriend in the fall of 1964.

"Things were so innocent," she said. "We kissed each other; I think Mitt would admit to that."

The letters then stopped.

At one of the Cranbrook-Kingswood parties, he ran into and instantly fell for Ann Davies. She was a 15-year-old sophomore, tall, blond and beautiful with bright brown eyes. He was so smitten that he persuaded her to let him drive her home. Ann was interested in him but cautious.

"He dated a lot of my friends," she said. He would see them for a month or more and then break up. "I kept him at bay, and I think that drove him crazy."

It was weeks before their first date in 1965. He took her to "The Sound of Music." After a few months, they had fallen deeply in love. He brought her to the governor's mansion. She took him to her family's cottage on Lake Michigan, where her father caught them smooching one night.

"Chaperone rules were tightened," she said.

At his senior prom, Mitt told Ann that he wanted to marry her one day.

George Romney gave Cranbrook's commencement address, telling the young men about the impact one person can make on the world and the need to be persistent in good times and bad. He then offered those 76 graduates some advice that may have been directed at his son more than anyone else.

"Friends will also shape your future, particularly your girlfriends," the governor said. "Your girlfriends, especially that special one, probably have more influence on your life than anything else."

Those words turned out to be prophetic, but, at age 18, Mitt still had some personal exploring to do. He loved Ann, and yet religion was an issue. She was a mainline Protestant; he was a Mormon, though he later would acknowledge that at that young age his faith was shaky. For the most part, he followed the strict LDS rules, though after his graduation, Romney drank enough beer that he got sick, according to his pal Phillip Maxwell.

In the fall of 1965, Romney enrolled at Stanford University, leaving Michigan for sunny Palo Alto, Calif., where Jon Huntsman Sr. was living, working on behalf of Olson Farms, and Jon Huntsman Jr. was starting kindergarten.

That first year away from home was hard. Romney used his ample allowance to secretly fly back to Michigan to spend time with Ann on weekends. Once he even drove across country just to see her for a day. He tried to time these clandestine trips for weekends, when his dad was away on gubernatorial duties in Lansing.

"He didn't want his parents to know," Ann said. "They had no idea he was coming home weekends."

Eventually, the couple got busted.

George Romney implored his son's friends at Stanford to stop him from coming home at the same time he restricted his allowance. The governor worried the jaunts would hurt his son's grades. But love was calling and young Romney wouldn't be stopped. He went so far as to sell his clothes and belongings to buy another airline ticket home.

When he wasn't pining for Ann, Romney got involved on campus. He bunked with the quarterback of the football team and the two became fast friends, regularly going to parties together. He joined the Axe Committee, a group of students who would build a massive bonfire before the rivalry game against the Cal Bears and protected the ceremonial ax given to the winner of the previous year's game. Cal students would try to destroy the bonfire and steal the ax. Romney guarded the site day and night until the big game.

He also became active in the Republican Club on a campus where most students abhorred the Vietnam War. Some anti-war protesters even stormed the president's office and staged a sit-in. In reaction, Romney helped gather 350 counterprotesters. He held a sign that said "Speak out, don't sit in," and shouted, "Come out of the office and let school continue!" His picture appeared in the Palo Alto Times, which declared, "Governor's son pickets the pickets."

Romney had no real fear of going to Vietnam. He had a deferment as a college student, and when that tumultuous freshman year ended, he got another one as he prepared to depart on his Mormon mission.

For a short time, Romney considered staying home and forgoing what many LDS families see as a rite of passage. He couldn't stomach the idea of leaving his girlfriend for 2½ years, but she urged him to go, saying he would always regret it if he didn't. He knew she was right.

So a few months after he left Stanford, never to return, Romney made his way to France.

About that same time, Ann Davies, then 16, expressed a desire to explore Mormonism, but her father, Edward Davies, the mayor of Bloomfield Hills, resisted. He disliked organized religion and relented only after George Romney came to his house. The two politicians struck a deal. The mayor's daughter could listen to the LDS missionaries as long as her mother was in the room.

Within weeks, Ann had decided she wanted to get baptized into The Church of Jesus Christ of Latter-day Saints, and she asked George Romney to do the honors. Through this religious conversion, Ann Davies stayed close to the Romney clan as her boyfriend struggled to persuade French families to set aside their red wine and Catholicism and give a uniquely American faith a chance.

Romney had about two weeks of language and cultural training in the summer of 1966 before he found himself in the windy coastal city of Le Havre, a major port in northern France rebuilt after the horrors of World War II.

It became an instant struggle. He missed his family and his girlfriend, and he could barely communicate with residents, though he had no problems picking up on their hostility toward Americans.

He lived in a one-bedroom apartment with three other missionaries, not all of whom he liked. He woke up at 6 a.m. daily, studied scriptures and then biked to neighborhoods, where he would knock on doors all day. Those that opened often were slammed in his face. He would return to the apartment and get six hours of sleep on an air mattress, then do it all again. By Sunday, he had a hard time keeping his eyes open at church services.

Tired of the relentless rejection, Romney dreamed up alternative ways to spread his message, everything from public singing to basketball games to archaeology lectures. In a letter home, he wrote: "Why even last Sat. night, my [companions] and I went into bars explaining that we had a message of great happiness and joy, and that we would like to talk to anyone who had a few minutes. Amazing how that builds one's courage."

Courage, maybe, but the tactic didn't win any converts. In reflecting on his mission, Romney has called it a "watershed" moment, where his faith grew iron strong and he learned to handle adversity. In those 30 months, he would say he helped convert 10 to 20 people.

"As you can imagine, it's quite an experience to go to Bordeaux and say, 'Give up your wine! I've got a great religion for you!' " he said. "It was good training for how life works. I mean, rejection of one kind or another is going to be an important part of everyone's life. Here I'd grown up as the son of a governor, from a wealthy home. No one had asked me about my religion, or cared, and now I was on the street, lower than a Fuller Brush salesman, in a place where Americans were not particularly liked, where I couldn't speak the language very well, and where selling religion, particularly Mormonism, was going to be very painful."

In letters, Romney complained. His father sympathized. George Romney wasn't sure he converted anyone during his mission to Britain. He tried to buck up his son by pointing out that Ann Davies and, later, her little brother, Jim, now were Mormons because of him.

"This makes two converts here that are certainly yours so don't worry about your difficulty in converting those Frenchmen!" his father wrote in a birthday message to his son in March 1967. "I am sure you can appreciate that Ann and Jim each are worth a dozen of them, at least to us."

George also tried to ensure Mitt felt connected to Ann, seeing the distance as only a small break in a relationship he hoped would thrive.

"Your gal looked lovely as always. I sat next to her in church and asked if that ring of yours on her engagement finger meant what it usually means and she said it did. So now I guess it is a pre-engagement ring."

Beyond the stream of letters from his parents and his siblings, the family regularly sent Romney a collection of newspaper clippings about his father's presidential run. He tracked it all: his father's rise in prominence and his struggle dealing with the Vietnam issue, on which Mitt Romney faced daily chiding from anti-war French families, some of whom counted relatives among the thousands who died during the eight-year Indochina War.

Romney agreed to give a lecture on the American political system, and he sent his father a letter asking for brochures explaining presidential primaries.

"The rest of our system I know pretty well — only one thing I can't understand: How can the American public like such muttonheads?"

The missionary read about the riots in Detroit and his father's tour of U.S. slums. He followed along as his father was pilloried for his "brainwashed" comment. The only time Romney was able to participate in the campaign was when his parents came to France in December 1967. His son helped translate for George as he spoke with French leaders before embarking on another trip to Vietnam, where he vowed he wouldn't be misled by military leaders again. At that point, nothing could stop George Romney's slide in the polls, and he dropped out in February 1968. Mitt, who had no access to a TV, radio or phone, heard about it in a letter from his dad.

"Your mother and I are not personally distressed. As a matter of fact, we are relieved," George Romney wrote. "We went into this not because we aspired to the office, but simply because we felt that under the circumstances we would not feel right if we did not offer our services. As I have said on many occasions, I aspired, and though I achieved not, I am satisfied."

Mitt would take that saying to heart, even as he remained frustrated at his lack of tangible achievements in the mission field. Few worked harder or were more inventive, and his mission president, H. Duane Anderson, noticed it. As a reward, Romney became his assistant. In this new role, he moved to Paris to help oversee the LDS Church's efforts throughout the country at a time of great upheaval. Union workers were holding mass strikes and talking about revolution. Back in the United States, Martin Luther King Jr. and then Robert F. Kennedy were assassinated. But Anderson kept his young aide busy, leaving little time for him to worry about the outside world.

In the middle of June 1968, a dispute among women in the outlying area of Pau had threatened to split an LDS congregation in two. Anderson asked Romney to accompany him and his wife on the seven-hour trip to settle the matter. It took them only one evening to soothe the hurt feelings and the troubleshooting group, now with a couple from Bordeaux and a young man from Salt Lake City, began the return drive with Romney behind the wheel of their Citroen DS.

The roads, particularly in the south of France, were windy and treacherous. They drove past a car that had earlier slammed into a tree. About 90 minutes into their trip, a tipsy Catholic priest named Albert Marie took a curve at about 70 mph, veering his Mercedes into Romney's lane.

"It happened so quickly that, as I recall, there was no braking and no honking," Romney said. "I remember sort of being hood to hood. And then pretty much the next thing I recall was waking up in the hospital."

The horrific collision had knocked him unconscious, trapping him between the steering column and the driver's side door. Duane Anderson in the front passenger seat was able to turn off the car. He had liver damage, a broken wrist and five cracked ribs. The passengers in the back were all injured as well. But no one was hurt as severely as Duane's wife, Leona, who sat between her husband and Romney. The crash thrust the engine into the cab, crushing her. She died 2½ hours later.

When the police arrived at the bloody scene, one officer thought there was more than one fatality. He picked up Romney's passport and wrote in it "Il est mort" — he is dead. Romney eventually would wake up in a little hospital in Bazas. Police blamed Marie for the accident, though Duane Anderson never pressed charges because he didn't want a dispute between a Catholic priest and a Mormon mission president.

Romney's family heard of the accident amid sketchy reports that he had died. George Romney called Sargent Shriver, the U.S. ambassador in Paris and Sen. Ted Kennedy's brother-in-law, who calmed him down, assuring him that his son was alive. He had hit his head pretty hard and had a broken arm. Concerned about the medical care, George Romney dispatched his son-in-law

Bruce Robinson, a medical resident married to his daughter Jane.

"He probably came within a hair of not surviving," Robinson would report back.

While Romney's injuries were serious, they were far from life-threatening. Wire services reported that he was "not seriously hurt" and "suffered a slight head injury." At no point did Romney seriously consider ending his mission early.

Duane Anderson went back to the United State to bury his wife, while Romney and a companion led the mission in his absence, gaining occasional help from the president of the LDS mission in Geneva, Switzerland. Romney threw himself into the work, as much to hide his grief as to help his fellow missionaries be successful. He refused to share his feelings with anyone but family.

"It was a very difficult and heart-wrenching experience to lose someone that I respected and admired, and to see someone who I loved — the mission president — lose the love of his life," Romney said. "I didn't want to, if you will, carry to all of the people in France a posture that would suggest that I didn't have the emotional strength and the spiritual confidence to carry on."

Missionary companions did see a break in the Romney façade when he received a troubling letter from Ann Davies. She had moved to Provo, Utah, to attend LDS Church-owned Brigham Young University and on occasion would go on a date, but said she felt nothing for her suitors. That changed when she met Kim Cameron, a member of the basketball squad. She said he reminded her of Romney. The note left him horribly jealous and worried. He had heard story after story of missionaries who received "Dear John" letters.

"He became really, really distraught that she had indicated she had gone out with this guy," said Dane McBride, one of Romney's missionary companions.

Romney wrote a series of heartfelt letters home and asked those around him for help in making sure he used just the right words. Duane Anderson returned to the mission, bringing with him his son Andy Anderson, who got to know Romney in Paris.

"He had served well, but like most missionaries he looked forward to his release date and getting on with the rest of his life. Ann in particular," Andy said. "He didn't talk about it much, but the few times he opened up, you could tell he was fiercely determined to get what he wanted. And Ann was what he wanted, no question about that."

Mitt's mission ended just before Christmas 1968. His family, along with Ann Davies, greeted him at the Detroit airport, and he slid in next to his girlfriend in the back seat of his sister's Oldsmobile Vista Cruiser for the ride home. Mitt wasted no time asking Ann to marry him before they even reached the family's driveway. It turned out that Cameron wasn't as big a threat as Romney had dreaded.

"I said yes without a second thought," she said later. "That night we told our parents that we wanted to get married right away. They pleaded with us to wait three months so that all the formal wedding preparations could be made. … We allowed that concession to our parents' sense of propriety, but I knew that Mitt and I were meant to be together and that's all that mattered."

Their nuptials became big news in Detroit, where society columnists cataloged in vivid detail who appeared at what event and which gifts were most appreciated. Ford Motor Co. President Semon "Bunkie" Knudsen threw a party in honor of the couple at the Pontchartrain Hotel three days before their wedding, where they received gifts of silver and fine china and had their astrology charted by the exotic Cleo Abuin.

Miss Cleo said the couple "will be very happy because their personalities go well together." She predicted they would have a musical and artistic child, which Davies thought was funny because neither she nor Romney had much artistic flair.

About 60 friends and family watched the two exchange plain wedding bands at a makeshift altar in her parents' living room March 21, 1969. The Bloomfield Hills house was covered in orchids at Davies' request, and a reporter described her as "the picture of a very happy but tearful Victorian bride."

Her maid of honor was her BYU roommate, Cindy Burton, while Romney's brother, Scott, served as his best man, though his missionary companion Dane McBride was also part of the wedding party. The couple gave their attendants and ushers gifts of gold, jewelry boxes for the women and travel clocks for the men.

Mitt Romney, 21, told Detroit reporters: "We met exactly four years ago tonight, so we've been waiting for this day to come for a long time."

The entire wedding party boarded two chartered planes to Salt Lake City the next morning, where the Mormons in the group observed the couple's temple wedding. Then the newlyweds went to Hawaii for their honeymoon, returning in early April to continue their college educations.

Romney transferred to BYU, and they moved into a cramped one-bedroom basement apartment that cost them $62.50 a month.

There, they lived a life of contradictions, a tiny home where they seemed the average struggling college couple and yet they had luxuries that would have stunned their classmates: a light blue Rambler sports car and new TV that George Romney gave them as wedding gifts, along with Clarendon pattern china by Royal Doulton and the Lalique crystal that Romney bought his bride-to-be in Paris. They decorated their living room and bedroom with early American antiques that the new Mrs. Romney had collected. Years later, she would cause her husband some embarrassment on the campaign trail by saying their financial situation got so dire they were forced at one point to cash in some stocks to pay the bills.

At the same time, they used a fold-down ironing board as the kitchen table and when their first son, Taggart, was born on their first wedding anniversary, Romney built a contraption over the foot of their bed to hold the crib because there was no other room. The couple even stitched their own rug from carpet remnants.

Romney wasn't known around campus for his money, but for being the son of the new Housing and Urban Development secretary for President Richard Nixon.

"Even though they came from pretty successful and affluent backgrounds, they just didn't throw it around at all," said Alan Layton, a college friend. The Laytons also had a small child, and the couples would spend time together. Romney and Layton were members of the Cougar Club, a booster club that raised money for the athletic department.

"He was the smartest guy I knew in college," said Layton, who now owns a construction company among the top 100 largest contractors in the country. "I absolutely knew he would be successful."

Romney took his studies at BYU far more seriously than he had at Cranbrook or Stanford. He graduated with a degree in English literature and was the school's valedictorian. In addressing his fellow classmates, he said that for people blessed as they were, much would be expected.

"I pray that this graduating class will choose a different kind of life, that we may develop an attitude of restlessness and discomfort, not self-satisfaction. Our education should spark us to challenge ignorance and prepare to receive new truths from God."

At his father's prodding, Romney continued his education, enrolling in a grueling new program at Harvard that combined a master's in business administration with a law degree. After four years, he graduated cum laude from the law school and was in the top 5 percent of his business-school class.

The family, which at this point included two sons, settled in the affluent neighborhood of Belmont, Mass., while Romney attended school. He passed the Michigan bar exam after he graduated in 1975, but that was only a backup plan. He had accepted a job with Boston Consulting Group, where he would help companies scour their financials to find efficiencies. It engaged his analytical mind, and he shined.

Three years later, Bain & Co. recruited him. Bill Bain became Romney's mentor and Mitt became Bain's star consultant. It was a lucrative relationship for all, but Bain thought Romney could take on more. In 1983, he persuaded Romney to lead a new venture, Bain Capital. Instead of consulting for companies, Romney now would invest directly in them, taking troubled ventures and making them profitable with the potential of reaping huge rewards.

Leading a private-equity spinoff seemed like a big risk, and Romney initially tiptoed into this new venture. But in the years to follow he would manage billion-dollar funds and earn loads of cash for himself and his partners. He had little involvement with some deals, while in others he sat on a company's board of directors. He often would buy companies with borrowed cash, heaping debt on their books as he sought to make them quickly profitable. At times that meant layoffs — sometimes lots of them. Romney either would make money as the businesses gained solid footing or he would sell them off, almost always at hefty profits. Occasionally a deal would be a stinker.

Flush with cash, he started buying vacation homes, one in Lake Winnipesaukee in New Hampshire and another in Park City, Utah. He eventually added a home in California.

Romney led Bain Capital for 15 years, closing nearly 100 deals that made him fabulously wealthy, and yet he often was seen as risk averse by his employees, some of whom were itching to chase more aggressive, though chancier, deals.

"I always wondered about Mitt," one partner said, "whether he was concerned about the blemishes from a business perspective or from a personal and political perspective."

In a speech at BYU, Romney cast it in terms of faith, saying business for Mormons is "a test for us to see whether we fall in love with money or whether we can instead be true to our covenants and worship our Father in Heaven."

During this period of professional success, Romney also rose in stature in his church. He became the lay bishop of his ward and later the regional president of a stake.

With these demands on his time, Ann Romney reared the five boys largely on her own, without the help of a nanny or a housekeeper.

"Mitt was often away. His work generally took him out on the road two or three nights a week. I remember some of his calls. He could hear the boys fighting in the background and he could hear the weariness in my voice," Ann recalled. "More than once, he said: 'Ann, what you are doing is more important than what I am doing. You're raising the kids who will be part of our lives forever; I'm just trying to earn the money to pay the bills.' "

Romney was good at paying those bills, but that didn't satisfy him. Through the years he had toyed with the idea of political office, but often considered it far-fetched. How would a Republican, even a Romney Republican, win in Massachusetts, one of the most liberal states in the land? Then, in the middle of 1993, on a morning when they had a few quiet minutes to themselves, Ann suggested that Mitt take on Sen. Ted Kennedy, the state's most dominant politician who was seeking a sixth term the following year. Romney pulled the covers over his head, but she wasn't about to let him off that easy.

"You can gripe and gripe and gripe all you want about how upset you are about the direction the country's going," she said. "But if you don't stand up and do something about it, then, you know, shut up and stop bothering me."

He thought it over in the coming days, balancing his restlessness at work against the long odds of unseating a political icon.

"I kept asking myself, 'Do I really want to stay at Bain Capital for the rest of my life? Do I want to make it even more successful, make even more money? Why?' " Romney said. "I thought of my dad."

His father's 1968 presidential campaign was far from a success, but as George Romney stated in that letter to his missionary son: "I aspired, and though I achieved not, I am satisfied." George was proud of his campaign and believed he accomplished some good by speaking out on poverty and race. Mitt Romney thought maybe he could push the debate in a productive direction and at least make Kennedy work for it. It wasn't as if there was a line of Republicans ready to take on the challenge.

George Romney wasn't the only politician in the family. Lenore Romney had run a U.S. Senate campaign in Michigan, though she fell short. Her style was a contrast from her husband's — a peacekeeper and behind-the-scenes strategist — a style that her son noticed.

"Mitt's more like my mother," his sister Jane once said. "Mitt's the diplomat. Mitt knows how to smooth things."

But it was George Romney whom Mitt revered. And he viewed politics as a possibility, largely because his dad had been a candidate.

"I really believe the reason we are involved in politics is because of George Romney," Ann Romney said. "I don't think it would have even occurred to us to get involved in politics."

One person who wasn't particularly keen on the idea of Mitt Romney taking on Kennedy in 1994? George Romney. He wanted his son to wait another six years. "I thought he ought to get better known," said George, who then was 86.

The elder Romney always had told his kids that if they were going to run for office, they should hold off until they were financially stable and their children old enough to handle the public scrutiny. Clearly money wasn't a problem and, at this time, Mitt Romney was 47 and his youngest boy was 14. When George first ran for governor, Mitt was 15.

His dad's skepticism didn't stop Romney from talking to GOP insiders and figuring out how he could take a leave of absence from Bain if he became a candidate. He followed the pattern his father set in 1962. He sequestered himself and his family. They fasted and prayed. A short while later, he announced his run for the Senate, vowing to give it everything he had, even though he privately thought he would lose.

"We recognized that there was no way I was going to beat him. A Republican, white, male Mormon millionaire in Massachusetts has no credible chance," Romney said. "Even when the campaign was riding high, I never put our odds at better than 1 out of 10."

His first task was to become a Republican, at least officially. Romney always had registered as an independent and even had voted for Massachusetts Sen. Paul Tsongas in the 1992 Democratic presidential primary. He changed his voting registration shortly before announcing his campaign, fashioning himself a Republican in his father's mold: conservative but not an ideologue, a man with a solid business background, but socially moderate. Romney preferred the term "socially innovative."

George Romney wasn't his only model. William F. Weld, a Republican moderate, narrowly defeated Boston University President John Silber to become Massachusetts' governor in 1990. Republicans held the seat for the first time since 1975 and were riding high, while Kennedy was at a personal low.

Over Easter weekend in 1991, Kennedy, his son Patrick and his nephew William Kennedy Smith went to a bar near the family's Palm Beach estate. The two young men brought women home. One accused William of raping her on the beach. The police were slow to investigate, and the Kennedy political machine tried to derail any probe, but it soon became national news. Kennedy got skewered on late-night shows for his infamous boozing and womanizing, and he was lambasted in Newsweek as "the living symbol of the family flaws." The senator eventually felt forced to apologize publicly for his behavior.

"I recognize my own shortcomings — the faults in the conduct of my personal life," he said. "I realize that I alone am responsible for them and I am the one who must confront them."

That didn't end the matter. Smith was acquitted, but his trial in December 1991 was nationally televised, and the senator had to testify. The episode tarnished the Kennedy brand and dredged up old stories about Chappaquiddick. In that 1969 scandal, Kennedy accidentally drove off a bridge on the small island of Chappaquiddick, and while he was able to swim to safety, his female passenger, Mary Jo Kopechne, died. He didn't report the accident for nine hours, eventually pleaded guilty to leaving the scene of an accident and was slapped with a two-month suspended jail sentence.

The 1994 campaign coincided with the 25th anniversary of Chappaquiddick. That, together with the new family dirt on display in the rape trial, stoked a public weariness of Kennedy's antics. A Boston Herald/WCVB-TV poll found that 62 percent of voters thought he shouldn't run for re-election and a vast majority believed he had misled Palm Beach authorities.

Kennedy's troubles clearly played a role in Romney's calculations and, while he wouldn't hit the senator hard on Chappaquiddick, he did contrast his squeaky-clean Mormon image with that of the hard-partying senator.

"I will not embarrass you," Romney told Republican delegates, while Ann let reporters know that she never had heard her husband swear during their 25 years of marriage.

Once Romney formally entered the race, his father lent his full support, making public appearances around the state on his behalf and eventually moving into the apartment above his son's Belmont garage so he could campaign full time. Voters often asked George Romney about the similarities between himself and Mitt.

"He's better than a chip off the old block," the father would say. "No. 1, he's got a better education. No. 2, he's turned around dozens of companies while I turned around only one. And No. 3, he's made a lot more money than I have."

Romney asked his son Tagg, who had just graduated from BYU, to act as a surrogate as well, burnishing his image as a father figure.

He had the campaign apparatus, the looks, the cash, the family and a political opening, thanks to Kennedy's woes. What he didn't have was a set of issues on which to run. He took on the problem like he took on a troubled company at Bain. Mitt wanted all of the data. He weighed the pros and cons, and he tried to make smart business decisions. It wasn't natural for him to just say what he personally believed.

"Everything could always be tweaked, reshaped, fixed, addressed," said a former Romney aide. "It was foreign to him on policy issues that core principles mattered — that somebody would go back and say, 'Well, three years ago you said this.' "

Another aide said he had difficulty "connecting to folks who haven't swum in the same rarefied waters that he has." On top of that, he was a bit gun-shy with the public, worried he would have his own "brainwashing" moment. His sister Jane said his father's public stumbling affected how he campaigned.

"Mitt is naturally a diplomat, but I think that made him more so," she said. "He's not going to put himself out on a limb. He's more cautious, more scripted."

He took positions that were popular with Massachusetts voters, even though they were hardly loved by the Republican Party. He backed an increase in the minimum wage and a plan to tie it to inflation. He supported an assault-weapons ban and made it clear that he wasn't on board with Newt

Gingrich's Contract with America. He said he favored gay rights short of marriage, and while he and his faith opposed abortion, he wouldn't seek to overturn Roe v. Wade. At one debate, he even distanced himself from President Ronald Reagan.

"Look, I was an independent during the time of Reagan-Bush," he said. "I'm not trying to return to Reagan-Bush."

Romney also hit Kennedy on his lifestyle and for being soft on crime. It was all working. Right before the Republican primary, which he would easily win, polls showed him even with Kennedy. Romney heard from backers that Kennedy was getting old and didn't have the fight he once had.

"I was getting ready for this guy that was going to be kind of a doddering old fool," Romney said. "I'd be able to crush him like a grape."

Then the Kennedy apparatus belatedly sprang to action, beginning by contrasting Romney's personal beliefs with his public positions. On abortion, Kennedy said: "He's not pro-choice, he's not anti-choice, he's multiple choice." The senator's campaign team jumped on a report that Romney called homosexuality "perverse" when he was a Mormon bishop.

These were but appetizers. Kennedy's main course was a relentless barrage of attacks on Romney's business record, painting him as a ruthless corporate raider who profited by slashing jobs from ailing companies. The Democrat's team developed six television ads starring laid-off workers from an Indiana paper plant that Bain Capital bought. It didn't matter to the campaign that that purchase happened after Romney took a leave of absence. It was Bain, and Bain was Romney's brand.

Romney's campaign did little to respond, having never prepared a counteroffensive to what now seems like an obvious strategy for Kennedy. The challenger instead tried to hit Kennedy on the senator's opposition to the death penalty. Kennedy ignored that dig and launched into dessert: Romney's faith, particularly questioning why he would support a church that previously had discriminated against black people.

"Where is Mr. Romney on those issues in terms of equality of race prior to 1978 and other kinds of issues in question?" Kennedy asked.

The displaced-worker ads irritated Romney, but this race line of attack infuriated him. Romney's father had been an outspoken supporter of civil rights and was dogged by this same question. Mitt, who was a counselor to an LDS stake president in 1978, said he first heard that his faith would let blacks hold the priesthood on his car radio. He pulled over and wept with joy.

Romney responded to Kennedy's assault by calling a news conference in late September 1992. Reporters crammed into his Cambridge campaign headquarters to hear Romney echo the words Ted's brother John F. Kennedy used 32 years earlier when questioned about his Catholic faith. "I do not speak for my church on public matters, and the church does not speak for me." He scolded Kennedy for trying to "take away his brother's victory."

Romney then took questions from reporters, while his father stood near the TV cameras. At one point, George Romney got so worked up that he blurted out: "It is absolutely wrong to keep hammering on the religious issues, and what Ted is trying to do is bring it into the picture."

The Romney team went so far as to create its own TV ad, with Mitt Romney standing in his driveway in short sleeves saying: "All my life I've been guided by a set of strongly held beliefs. One is my religion. Another is tolerance of others. Unfortunately, some in this campaign have chosen to use religion against me."

The ad never aired, because Kennedy started to walk back his questions on Mormonism. That didn't stop others, including members in Romney's own LDS ward, from keeping his faith in the news. Throughout the campaign, liberal Mormons, such as Judy Dushku, a professor at Suffolk University, hounded Romney.

"We have a long tradition in our culture to never criticize the brethren," Dushku told The Boston Globe. "I'm afraid Mitt's grown up with this sense of entitlement not to be criticized, and to interpret criticism as never constructive and as always coming from the enemy. I think this is very dangerous for a political leader."

She approached Romney early in the race, saying that while she wasn't going to vote for him, she would help him on some issues, particularly women's rights, homosexuality and abortion.

"He said that was part of the church. I said, 'That's part of your life. People will be interested in that.' He said, 'Oh, no. I've talked it over with my campaign manager. We're going to keep the religious stuff separate.' I said, 'You're living in a dream world. The press is going to look at the way you've conducted yourself in all spheres of your life, including as a religious leader.' "

Romney disputes Dushku's characterization of their chat, but either way, the news media did poke into all facets of the candidate's life. They found that Romney, under heavy pressure, held a meeting with frustrated women in the Belmont area. He allowed Mormon girls to confide in women on topics they didn't want to discuss with the all-male church officials. Mormons in his community jumped to his defense, saying he was a generous person, willing to extend considerable amounts of time and effort, and sometimes even money, to assist those in need.

"The truth is, he's an incredibly sensitive guy. He often reflects on experiences that have nothing to do with wealth and privilege, but are just human to human," said Kent Bowen, a Harvard Business School professor who knew Romney from church.

But skepticism of his faith became more pronounced when he faced an accusation that, as a bishop, he threatened Peggie Hayes with excommunication if she didn't give up her baby for adoption. Hayes had a blood clot in her pelvis that doctors said could threaten her life, and she wanted to get an abortion. She was dismayed and hurt that Romney wouldn't support her. Hayes wrote about the incident in an essay for Exponent II, a publication for liberal Mormon women, though she didn't identify herself as the author or Romney as the bishop until confronted by reporters during that Senate campaign.

Romney said he couldn't recall the incident but added: "I certainly can't say it could not have been me."

All of the bad publicity in a state with such a Democratic tilt made the race a foregone conclusion. In the end, Romney spent $3 million of his own money and lost to Kennedy 58 percent to 41 percent. He gave an upbeat concession speech with his wife by his side, but when it was all over, and Ann was just out of public view, she burst into tears. Mitt wasn't able to move the public debate or pump up the state's Republican Party. Unlike his father, he left the campaign far from satisfied.

"The loss felt worse than we had imagined," Romney said. "For several months, we would say to ourselves, 'Why did we do that?' "

He returned to Bain Capital almost immediately, ready to put the 1994 defeat behind him. The next summer, George Romney had a heart attack and died at age 88 while on a treadmill in his home in Bloomfield Hills. Lenore knew something was wrong when she woke up and didn't see the single rose that George placed daily on her dresser. Three years later, Lenore died of a stroke, and just a few months after that, Mitt Romney was hit with news that would rock him to his core.

For a while, Ann had noticed that she wasn't as stable on her feet as she used to be. She thought it had to be a virus or maybe some kind of persistent nerve injury. When she finally went to her doctor, she said swallowing was difficult, and she couldn't feel pinpricks in her feet. The doctor referred her to a neurologist, and Romney took her to see John Stakes at Massachusetts General. She failed test after test. When Stakes left the room, Mitt and Ann broke down.

"We hugged each other," Mitt said, "and I reminded her that as long as this was not fatal, we could deal with it."

Stakes diagnosed her with multiple sclerosis, a chronic debilitating disease of the central-nervous system that afflicts people in different ways. Ann tried to put on a brave face in the days to come, but she became so weak that she could barely take care of life's necessities and the drugs were making her sick.

Romney told their children about her illness. Their oldest, Tagg Romney, refused to believe it at first.

"It just didn't make sense to me. That's my mom. She doesn't have multiple sclerosis. They've misdiagnosed her somehow and didn't realize it," he said. "A couple of weeks later, this is for real. She's really sick. It was right around Thanksgiving time and it was really hard. I mean, this is your mom. This happens to other people. It doesn't happen to you, and then all of a sudden it's happening to you."

Ann would rally for a few days, showing vast improvements in her energy level, and then relapse. She fought the pain and the exhaustion along with the depression that came with it.

"I frankly would have rather died than be the way I was," she said. "At the time, I wished I had cancer instead of this, something more tangible. We didn't know what was in store for me. This would take bits and pieces of you."

But through a slow process of trial and error, she found a way to build back her strength. She mixed yoga and reflexology, acupuncture and a strict diet. And she rekindled her love of horses.

"Riding exhilarated me," she said. "it gave me a joy and a purpose. It jump-started my healing."

She was still healing when she received a call from an old family friend, Kem Gardner. Once a Mormon mission president in Boston who had since moved to Salt Lake City, Gardner ran a successful development company. He also was intimately involved in Utah's planning for the 2002 Winter Olympics, which were foundering amid an embarrassing bribery scandal.

The Salt Lake Organizing Committee was seeking a new leader to save the Games from financial ruin, and Gardner knew just the man for the job. He also knew the best way to recruit Romney was to get Ann on his side. She instantly liked the idea, seeing it as a fresh opportunity for her husband, who was unfulfilled by his work at Bain. But just as with his Senate run, Mitt took convincing.

"She called me at the office. Before I could get beyond hello, she put me on notice. 'Now, whatever you do, don't just say no out of hand. Hear me out on this before you dismiss it,' " Romney recalled. "She proceeded tentatively, 'I talked to Kem. He thinks that you ought to consider running the Olympics. …' But before she could say another word, I immediately blurted out: 'Why in the world would I ever consider going to Utah to run the Olympics?' I couldn't help myself."

§ § §

The West Wing is not as big as you think. Outside of the Oval Office, the most coveted spaces in the White House are small, relatively unadorned and connected by narrow hallways. And, in 1971, they served as the weekend playground of Jon Huntsman Jr. and his brother Peter.

Their father, then President Nixon's staff secretary, didn't get days off, so Huntsman Sr. often brought his older boys to the office on weekends. And when Dad was working, the young Huntsmans goofed around with the son of Jeb Magruder, a Nixon aide who later went to federal prison for his role in the Watergate scandal. They would play in the offices of Henry Kissinger, then national security adviser, and Alexander Haig, a senior adviser. Both men later became secretaries of state.

A few times, the Huntsman boys bumped into Nixon, who seemed to enjoy their youthful exuberance. The president gave them golf balls embossed with the presidential seal and took them into the Oval Office for mini-history lessons.

Jon Huntsman Jr. knew these men were important, but, like any 11-year old, he didn't grasp how unusual his weekends were.

"You could walk around freely and run into major political players," he said. "I didn't know who they were. I didn't have much appreciation for that at 10, 11 years old. But you certainly developed a respect and appreciation for people who are serving their country at that level."

More than anything, Huntsman remembers "a stiffness and a formality" — and George Romney's backhand.

Huntsman recalls playing tennis with Mitt Romney's father, then a Cabinet secretary, at summer retreats at the Marriott family's New Hampshire vacation home.

"I thought George Romney was about the most impressive human being I'd ever met," Huntsman said. He remembers Romney as relentless and always in motion. Those tennis sessions and his days at the White House reinforced what his father had been drilling into him and his siblings: the importance of a strong work ethic.

Huntsman Sr. expected his children to work, and work hard. He had as a kid, and even though he acted out of economic necessity at the time, he thought it built character.

"We were always kicked in the fanny. Work, work, work. Jobs, jobs, jobs," Huntsman Jr. said. "That was probably the most prominent part of my upbringing."

Huntsman mowed his neighbors' lawns and delivered The Washington Star when he wasn't darting around the White House. Three years later, he was working as a stonemason in Salt Lake City. And as a 15-year-old, Huntsman earned his Eagle Scout by building trails in canyons near Salt Lake City while spending his weekends as a dishwasher and a busboy at Mikado, a Japanese restaurant.

That transition, from D.C. to Salt Lake City, was a big one for Jon Jr. He had spent plenty of time in Utah, but almost all of it had been in Fillmore, where he went on deer hunts with his cousins and heard wild tales of his eccentric relatives from the frontier days. He relished those visits, going so far as to call Fillmore the "center of my universe," but all in all, they were just visits. The bulk of his life was spent in the Bay Area or around Los Angeles or in the suburbs of Washington, D.C., larger and far more diverse places than Salt Lake City in the early 1970s.

The family drove down the canyon named after Mormon pioneer apostle Parley P. Pratt, and Huntsman remembers seeing the skyline from the backseat window.

"One thing that came to mind was, this is a very, very small town compared to what I was used to," he recalled.

He loved the easy access to the mountains, where he would go shooting with his friends and build trails with the Boy Scouts. He loved riding his motorcycle on dirt trails. But other parts of the transition proved challenging.

While his family was active in the LDS Church, Jon Jr. was unprepared for how dominant the faith is in the everyday lives of Mormons in Utah, where church-related events are scheduled throughout the week.

"It was a shift. In Los Angeles you go to church, you do your Scouting stuff. And in the Washington area, it was the same, but my best friends were other religions," Huntsman said. "And then you find it's a much different demographic when you get out to Utah in that there are continuous religious activities and it's much more focused on people's lives."

In addition, his father was unfairly tied to the Watergate scandal because he had worked for Nixon. For a time, the Huntsman family stayed in the small cabin grandfather David Haight built in Oakley, about 40 miles east of Salt Lake City.

"I'm not going to say in isolation, but my dad was kind of coming down from the government work and the Nixon fallout, and it was a very tense time for our family," said Huntsman Jr., recalling that a junior-high teacher pointed him out in class as a child of someone tied to Watergate. "That's not the way you want to start out your journey in a new community."

Jon Jr. also had to get used to his family's increasing wealth, which really came on as he transitioned from junior high to high school.

The year before his 15th birthday, his father struck a deal with McDonald's to make the clamshell for the Big Mac. The year after, his dad cleared $8 million in a stock deal. The Huntsmans built a big house in the foothills of the Wasatch Mountains, and while they were not yet one of the state's most famous families, they were fast gaining notice.

"Everybody knew who the Huntsmans were," said Eric Malmquist, a friend. "They lived in the castles on the hill.

"If you didn't know Jon was Jon, he was like one of the guys. That was one of the things that was neat about him. He obviously knew he had wealth. At 16, his dad bought him this incredible silver Bronco with a red interior. It was the dream car of any 16-year-old boy," Malmquist said. "But he didn't flaunt it. He'd go out and get dirty with anybody. He was a really grounded kid."

Music and motorcycles dominated Huntsman's teen years. He followed his mother and grandfather and became a classically trained pianist, though his musical interests evolved to jazz and later progressive rock. He started dabbling in high-school bands. His second love was motocross. He relished fast runs on the dirt courses where the boys hit a jump at full throttle and didn't mind an occasional crash.

Putting it all into perspective: He was the son of a wealthy man who drove a cool Ford Bronco, loved music and rode motorcycles. He was also slim as a reed, had penetrating eyes that somehow displayed confidence and compassion instantaneously and sported some stellar 1970s hair.

"In my late teens, you wouldn't have recognized me. My hair was Rod Stewart shaggy," he said. "I wouldn't wear anything but super skinny jeans."

Yes, girls found him attractive. And it would take a single glance across the high school's open-air courtyard for a girl from Florida to feel a spark. That ember wouldn't transform into the full flame of romance for years, but she felt it and he felt it, too.

Charles Floyd Cooper worked at a savings and loan in Orlando, but at a financial conference, he received an unexpected job offer. If he moved to Salt Lake City, he could be the highly compensated executive vice president of Prudential.

The offer was just too good to pass up and, by this time, two of his three children already had moved out. Mary Kaye Cooper, his third daughter, found out she was leaving sunny Orlando for the winter wonderland of Salt Lake City in the middle of ninth grade. She wasn't pleased.

"We might as well be moving to China," she complained to her parents, without knowing that years later she actually would move to the Far East.

The Coopers arrived in Utah in January 1976, moving into a home one block from the Huntsmans. That meant Mary Kaye attended Highland High School, where she was one grade younger than Jon Huntsman Jr. She didn't make the grand entrance she would have liked.

"I'd never been to Utah, never lived in the snow and knew nothing about the state or about Mormons," she said. "The first day I came to school, my mother dropped me off. I got out of the car and slipped and fell on some ice. The day kind of went downhill from there."

The kids couldn't get over her Southern accent and would tease her or ask her to read things aloud. Slowly "you all" replaced her natural "y'all" and the ribbing subsided. While she may have been mortified early on, Cooper was a charmer, with her blond bouffant hair and gymnast's physique. She had a boyfriend almost instantly and dated him through most of high school. It wasn't Huntsman.

"I was dating somebody else, too," he said. "She went through some steadies, and I was never really able to break into that orbit."

But he wanted to. Cooper was not only beautiful but also exotic.

"She had reminded me of the kind of folks I had grown up with," Huntsman said. "She had a Southern accent. She was different and she had lived elsewhere. And here she was, dropped in the middle of this school where people were pretty much marked by their similarities, not their differences."

Cooper and Huntsman may never have been high-school sweethearts, but they were close.

"We were best friends with a spark," she said.

She called him Jonny, and he called her Kaye Kaye. He still does.

By chance, they both landed jobs at a Marie Callender's restaurant, where he once again washed dishes and she served up salads. He says he once playfully doused her with the sink sprayer. She says it never happened. Then they both got jobs at Al's Garage, a store selling Levi's, again by chance, they say.

Spurred by Spencer Kirk, a mutual friend, they eventually went on a few dates between relationships. On their first outing, Huntsman picked up Cooper in a borrowed rust-colored 1977 Thunderbird, and they joined another couple at the Arnold Palmer miniature golf course, where they giggled far more than kept score. They finished the night at a nearby Hawaiian restaurant.

Huntsman was a popular student at Highland, a mainstay in the jazz band and junior class president, responsible for organizing prom. His junior yearbook described him: "Jon's easygoing personality and handsome appearance made him a person of which every junior could be proud."

He ran for senior class president in the fall of 1977. Candidates made posters to hang around the lockers and performed a skit in a school assembly. Cooper went with Huntsman to the hardware store, where he picked up plywood to make an outhouse after deciding to go lowbrow, shooting for chuckles by peppering his act with jokes about the john.

After emerging from the outhouse, Huntsman performed a skit based on Johnny Carson's character Carnac the Magnificent in which the "Tonight Show" star donned an elaborate turban, held an envelope up to his forehead and divined an answer to the secret question. Huntsman's secret question revolved around who would become senior class president. Naturally the answer was him.

His chief rival, Kenneth Hadlock, didn't tell any jokes. His posters were all about "senior spirit," and his skit was a speech. He took aim at the false perception of high-school seniors as apathetic. As he spoke about seniors as captains of sports teams and leaders of clubs and art programs, images of Hadlock with groups of Highland students flashed on the screen behind him.

The seniors responded to Hadlock's straightforward sincerity. He won.

Huntsman also tried out to be a cheerleader, which he called "probably the most prestigious position of all," but he didn't get that, either. The defeats shook him. He was a Huntsman, and Huntsmans didn't lose. Humiliated and confused, he stopped going to school in 1978, only a few months short of graduation.

"He was sort of depressed by the fact that he didn't have the kind of charisma with his peers that he thought he might have," said Don Barlow, an administrator who later became Highland's principal. "He dropped out, and I don't know what happened to him. I didn't even see him or hear from him again. When he re-emerged 15 or 20 years later, I couldn't believe it was the same guy."

Hadlock, now a junior-high principal in Utah, didn't know Huntsman dropped out, and he suspected many at Highland were unaware of it, though they all remembered their classmate when he became an ambassador, then governor and, next, a candidate for president.

Huntsman acknowledges the high-school setbacks were devastating. He felt that his friends abandoned him and that he was "the world's biggest loser."

"It's kind of like, 'Well, screw this,' " he said.

He stopped going to class and devoted his energies to a place where he felt accepted, an area of his life that excited him greatly and where he thought he could turn a passion into a profession — rock 'n' roll.

He played drums and keyboards in pickup bands named Holiday and Rockwater, which performed at weddings, school dances and corporate events on the weekends. That was before he caught the attention of four guys from nearby East High, who had designs on hitting it big. He joined Wizard. The group got gigs in bars and Mormon dances throughout Utah, spilling over into Nevada now and again. They performed covers of REO Speedwagon, Led Zeppelin and Eric Clapton and threw in their own original tunes on occasion. They had fun, but the guys yearned to do more than rock out with their friends. They wanted to go pro.

"When Jon came on board, we were trying to make a serious run at making money at this and making it a career," said Eric Malmquist, who played bass guitar. "This wasn't just a whim. We thought we could do it."

The band would gather at the now-defunct KCPX radio station and practice around the guys' school schedules. Huntsman didn't let on that he was essentially a full-time musician.

"I always thought he was going to school," said Howard Sharp, Wizard's drummer. "We'd practice like eight hours a day. I don't know if that was part of his issue. We took it more seriously than we should have."

Huntsman's father didn't like that his son dropped out, but the hard-charging industrialist surprisingly took it in stride.

"In many young people, there is a certain restless period of their life and often it comes about in your junior or senior year of high school," Huntsman Sr. said. "I think it was very important for him to call a timeout in his life and to do something that he personally wanted to achieve."

The younger Huntsman jammed on a Hammond C3 organ, with accompanying synthesizer, and Senior bought other gear for the band.

"It was the nicest equipment you could get," Malmquist said. "It made us look a lot bigger."

At the same time, Jon Jr. wanted to be smaller in some ways.

"He liked to fly underneath the radar screen or wished he could fly underneath the radar screen," Sharp said. "He never really flashed money around, in fact. ... He would never want to go to expensive restaurants. He liked seedy dives."

The band members were regulars at Bill and Nada's Cafe, an all-night diner where the group's mix of Mormons and non-Mormons felt at home. The diner scene in Salt Lake City is one of the rare places where partiers who closed down a bar grab a table next to high-school Mormons hanging out for hours sipping hot chocolate or Diet Coke and eating cheese fries. Now demolished, Bill and Nada's was known for its orange pancakes and its brains-and-egg special. No Wizard member ever ordered the brains and eggs, though they liked to joke about it. When Huntsman became Utah's governor, a painting of Bill and Nada's earned a prominent spot in his office.

Huntsman moved with relative ease across the unseen wall dividing the devout from everyone else in the Salt Lake Valley, a skill developed in those early years in Los Angeles and Washington, D.C.

"Very few straddled in between, but Jon was very good at being in between," Malmquist said. "He was faithful to his faith from everything I can see — but he also would go out and hang with guys and may not partake in things."

Some of his bandmates would smoke a joint in their cars before band practice. That wasn't Huntsman's thing, but he also wasn't completely strait-laced.

"I think Jon probably — like most teenagers — probably experimented with a few things," said Sharp, Wizard's other Mormon member. "I honestly don't ever recall him smoking marijuana. He was not a pothead."

Sharp did say that once, for a practical joke, Huntsman smoked a cigar in the office of a guy who couldn't stand the smell of stogies and he dumped a bucket of water on an unsuspecting bandmate. Huntsman fondly recalls his rocker days — the music, the camaraderie, the hijinks.

"We rolled in the ugliest green Ford Econoline van you could ever imagine with fold-up chairs in the back. It was pretty awesome until those inconvenient intersections, curves and stoplights caused those chairs to move around just a little bit," Huntsman said. "Seat belts weren't exactly enforced in those days."

The guys drove that van to the Utah Technical College (now Salt Lake Community College), playing for an older crowd, and as far south as St. George, a Utah city far closer to Las Vegas than Salt Lake City. They slipped into Sin City for a few hours of fun before heading back. Their mainstays were Mormon "stomps," where they'd have to censor the lyrics of some of their favorite tunes.

"We'd play Eric Clapton's 'Cocaine,' but instead of singing 'cocaine,' which you probably wouldn't say in church, we'd change the word to 'propane,' " Malmquist said.

Mary Kaye saw a show or two. Even Huntsman Sr. showed up and watched his son rock out.

"Oh, he thought he was going to make it big with a rock band. I knew he wouldn't, but I knew it was temporary," his father said. "I'd stand and listen to his rock band and think, 'Oh, I'll be happy when this is over.' "

The band hooked up with Jimmy Pitman, a former guitar player for Strawberry Alarm Clock, remembered for its hit song "Incense and Peppermints." Pitman had started Way to Gold productions and became the group's manager. He helped rent a recording studio, and Wizard started working on an album. It never came together, the recordings now lost to history.

Slowly the band broke apart, with Jon, at age 18, as one of the first to split off.

"He learned his first lesson in fiscal management when the band went bankrupt," Huntsman Sr. said. "Many people loved to hear them play, but none of the people wanted to pay for it."

"That's why I went into medicine and Jon went into politics," said Sharp, who is a gynecologist and sees Mary Kaye and her daughters as patients.

Huntsman Jr., though, said he'll "never regret following my passion."

"It was a momentary teenage desire to want to be a musician. You dream big and try to achieve your dream. Sometimes they work out, sometimes they don't. And then I ended up choosing a traditional pathway in life."

Traditional?

There's nothing traditional about Jon Huntsman Jr.'s life, not his childhood, not his high-school days and certainly not his journey through adulthood. Not many people bounce between posts in government and a family chemical empire, become ambassadors and, finally, try their hand at presidential politics.

His untraditional life was just beginning, but at this young age, Huntsman already felt restricted by the expectations others placed upon him because of his father's wealth and fame. At the same time, he remained loyal to and respectful of his family. He didn't rebel against his father. Yet he did rebel against the idea of being his father's firstborn son.

"It's clear he really wanted to do his own thing," Sharp said. "And I think he always loved and respected his family. They're great. But Jon kind of went his own way. And he really kind of was his own man."

His father and his grandfather had served in the Navy, but Huntsman wanted no part of that. Mitt Romney may have been a man of the 1950s living in the raucous 1960s, but Huntsman was all '70s, and a career in the military wasn't exactly groovy.

"I grew up right toward the end of the Vietnam War, where people were coming back from a very unpopular war," Huntsman said. "It seemed to be a much different mindset in those days than it is today."

And yet, Sharp said, Huntsman had his father's voice bouncing around the back of his brain, encouraging him to do more, be more.

"We talked about if the band didn't work out, what would we do?" Sharp said. "Jon talked about going to Germany to work in his dad's factories."

With Wizard not growing the way Huntsman expected, he jumped on that backup plan, moving to Germany for four months and working as a shipping manager at a firm with ties to his father's company. It gave him an escape from Utah and a chance to reconsider his future.

"That, for me, was an eye-opening experience of sorts and I thought, 'You know, there are other things I want to do in life,' " Huntsman said. "You know there is more to life than being in a band and really kind of spinning your wheels. That led me to getting serious about going out as a [Mormon] missionary."

As his German improved and he absorbed the culture, Huntsman hoped LDS leaders would keep him right where he was. Instead, they sent him to Taiwan. If Germany was a step away from isolated Salt Lake City, Taiwan was a thousand-mile journey.

He spent a few weeks in language and culture training before flying to Taipei. He realized almost from the start that the few phrases he learned essentially were useless. Huntsman and his missionary companions lived in what he described as "cockroach-infested dives" throughout a sprawling mega-city in a developing nation. They had to adapt to a different culture, learn a complicated language and then sell their American-grown Christian faith. In that scary, challenging environment, Huntsman found a new passion.

"There were no organized classes that helped us to understand what we were living with, the context of the Chinese experience," Huntsman said. "I became so taken by the history of Taiwan, particularly as it went back to the mainland and the revolution that took place in 1949."

He arrived in the country right after the United States cut diplomatic ties with Taiwan. The Carter administration recognized communist China and its dominance over this island off its eastern coast.

"I got to Taiwan and wondered why people hated Americans," Huntsman said. "Why we were yelled at and spat upon. Nobody stopped to mention that America had just withdrawn diplomatic relations with Taiwan. It left an indelible impression. For the first time, you could see the power of the U.S. at work overseas. It left me hungry to learn all I could."

He scavenged bookstores for history volumes that government censors hadn't already cleansed. He read all he could when he wasn't "knocking on a lot of inhospitable doors."

"It was so colorful. It was so complex. It was an extension of my country, an aspect of American power I have never grown up to study or understand," he said. "You are thrown into this milieu and it shocks your senses."

Among his missionary companions was Jeffrey Mollerup, who is now a postal worker in Salt Lake City. He recalls interacting with an angry populace, but unlike Huntsman, he tried to ignore international politics.

"We were there on God's errand," Mollerup said, "so we didn't get into the politics too much."

Mollerup did, however, take note of Huntsman, who was serving as the assistant to the mission president at the time.

"He was very sharp back then," Mollerup said, "and I think we all had the idea he was destined for greatness."

That didn't mean he was great at converting people to Mormonism. Huntsman has said his mission likely had a bigger impact on him than it did on the few people he helped to baptize.

The experience was "an opportunity to discover your strengths," he said. "A hardworking environment, a very regimented environment. You live in conditions that are darn close to poverty, killing cockroaches every night before you go to bed. Dingy apartments. So you learn a lot about yourself. You learn how to organize yourself. You learn how to work hard."

And, Huntsman said, it helped crystallize his life goals, giving him direction after his rock-star dreams faded.

"You get to see your own country, your own world, a little differently," he said. "I wanted to better understand America's role in the world, particularly in Asia. I was absolutely fascinated by what I learned there."

He returned to Utah with a deep desire to reinvest himself in school, but his mission did more than help focus his career goals. It also made him take stock of his personal life.

When he returned to Utah in 1981, he felt compelled to walk a block from his parents' home and knock on a door. The girl he wanted to see wasn't there.

Mary Kaye Cooper worked as a dental assistant throughout her senior year at Highland High and was on the job when her old friend stopped by the house. Her mother answered the door, and after Huntsman left, she couldn't wait to tell Mary Kaye the news, so she called the dental office.

"I said, 'I hope you told him to come back.' I actually didn't think he would," Mary Kaye said. "But he did, and I reached out to give him a hug. Instead, he reached out to shake my hand and he said, 'I don't know why, but you are the first person I came to see.' "

Huntsman's appendix became infected in Taiwan, and he spent the last week of his mission in a hospital. He jokes now that he looked like a "prisoner of war" when he returned home. He felt something for Mary Kaye, a crush, maybe more, and wanted to explore it, but she was dating someone and it was serious.

"It was a pretty quick conversation and a pretty cold hug," Huntsman said, "and we went on our separate ways."

While Huntsman was off in Taiwan, Mary Kaye had slowly grown more familiar and comfortable with the LDS Church. She went to young women's meetings on Tuesdays during which Mormon teens held short gospel sessions and enjoyed the busy social calendar of the faith.

"It's a way of life," she said.

Mary Kaye converted in her senior year, a decision in which Huntsman played no part. Her parents remain Episcopalian, and Mary Kaye says the move wasn't a rejection of her previous faith.

"I didn't feel I needed to abandon one to accept another," she said.

She enjoyed reconnecting with Huntsman, but their relationship stayed in the hazy realm between friendship and courtship.

Huntsman took classes at the University of Utah as a nonmatriculated student, never having earned a high-school diploma or a GED. He tried to join his father's fraternity, Sigma Chi, but didn't make it through the pledge process before Sen. Orrin Hatch, R-Utah, offered him an internship in his

Washington, D.C., office.

Hatch was the first of a trio of Utahns who gave Huntsman a chance to gain political experience. Huntsman jumped from his internship with the senator to one with Republican National Committee Chairman Richard Richards, who was from Ogden. After nine months in these political jobs, he received an offer to join Ronald Reagan's White House, working for Stephen M. Studdert, a former police chief in Brigham City, Utah, who was in charge of planning all presidential trips.

It probably didn't hurt that Huntsman Sr. was Reagan's Western states finance chairman in 1980 or that one of his closest personal friends happened to be Republican Sen. Jake Garn of Utah. Garn would land a spot as a Huntsman Chemical vice president when he left office in 1993.

Garn lobbied on behalf of Huntsman Jr.

"He asked if I was willing to support him," Garn said. "I didn't have any conversations with his dad about it. ... I just always thought he was wise for his age — everything is relative in life — but at that time I thought, 'What a sharp, outstanding young man.' "

Huntsman Jr. was 22 years old when he joined the president's advance team, a job that took him to almost every state in the union and a number of countries abroad. He even had a 45-minute conversation with Reagan on one of those Air Force One flights.

As an advance staffer, his job was to visit a location ahead of the president to scope the planned route, check out the restaurants and ensure every detail was considered before Air Force One touched down.

"There's nothing more exciting than when things go smoothly, as planned, and when the work pays off with cheering spectators and a happy president," Huntsman said. But, he noted, "you only really hear about your work when something goes wrong."

In January 1983, the White House sent Huntsman to Scottsdale, Ariz., where Nancy Reagan's parents lived, to prepare for a visit. He was just a 20-minute drive from Arizona State University, where Mary Kaye Cooper was continuing her education. He called ahead, they met and finally that spark caught fire. She visited him in Washington during spring break and then received a fortuitous call from an old family friend in Orlando offering her a job at the Florida House, a hospitality center in Washington, D.C., catering to tourists from the Sunshine State. Their romance blossomed in the nation's capital along with the cherry trees.

They returned to Utah together that fall and celebrated her 22nd birthday on Sept. 10. He gave her a card with a growling monkey on the cover. Inside, he had written: "Thanks for being such a good friend, love Jon."

That was it. The card with its mixed message and no gift.

"I was so baffled," she said.

Her boyfriend did at least ask her to go on a nice fall drive through Emigration Canyon near Salt Lake City, pulling off on a dirt road with a stunning mountain view. They walked around for a bit, while Huntsman summoned his courage. Suddenly, he hugged her and whispered in her ear that he wanted to get married. She felt the same. When he asked when they should announce their engagement, she stopped him.

"I said, 'You didn't ask me,' and I made him ask me. Then I said yes," she recounted.

Huntsman didn't have a ring and felt deeply uncomfortable in what he called "the awkward romantic encounter."

At that moment, a group of high-school kids drove by in a Chevy Vega and did a doughnut in the dirt, covering the lovebirds in dust.

When they left, Huntsman said: "I didn't know what to get you, so I thought I would just give you myself."

They married in the Salt Lake LDS Temple in November 1983, during Thanksgiving break. On the day of their wedding, Huntsman handled the romance better than he did the proposal. He presented his bride with a dozen roses and said: "I hope you're ready for an exciting life."

Throughout his time in Washington, Huntsman had plugged away on correspondence courses through the University of Utah, trudging his way toward a bachelor's degree, even though he didn't have a high-school diploma or a GED. He took advantage of the university's open-enrollment policy. He started going to actual classes again in Salt Lake City in the months before his wedding and took a second run at joining Sigma Chi, a pledging process that involves paying dues and committing to spending time each week doing the drudgery that the upperclassmen didn't want to handle.

Pledges scrub the frat-house bathrooms and pick up after parties. It's not fun, but everyone has to do it to join the brotherhood. Except Huntsman.

He stopped showing up with his pledge class, and the guys thought he was done with Sigma Chi. Those who stuck it out and were deemed worthy gathered on the morning of Dec. 10, cramming into the small ornate initiation room on the third floor. The wood-lined walls are covered with photos of the fraternity from the early 1900s and symbolic items known only to members. This room holds the secrets of the chapter, and only the worthy are allowed to enter.

During initiation, the young men often are accompanied by a father or a family friend who was a Sigma Chi. About 25 men were assembled on that morning in 1983. Right before the secret ceremony began, the door opened and three men walked in — Sen. Jake Garn, Jon Huntsman Sr. and Jon Huntsman Jr.

The fraternity brothers were stunned.

After the ceremony, Huntsman Jr. shook some hands, took a few family pictures and left. He didn't return to the house.

"The way it happened so abruptly left a sour taste in the mouth of more active members," said one of Huntsman's fraternity brothers. "He may be a Sigma Chi, but he never spent any time at the house. He didn't go to a single formal or attend any of the fundraising events that I recall."

Another said: "He's probably a Sigma Chi more in name than he is in practice."

Huntsman's initiation was a hot topic when senior members of the fraternity met the next night. The decision to let him join came from the Sigma Chi national office, and his fraternity brothers assumed it was facilitated by Garn and Huntsman Sr., both members of the fraternity.

Huntsman Jr. recollects the episode differently. He stopped the pledge process because "there were things going on in there that I thought were wrong."

"I just didn't want to hang around, and I told them basically to shove it and they came around later and said, 'You invested in the pledgeship for a better part of the semester or term,' so I ended up going through initiation."

Asked if his father pulled strings, Huntsman said: "I'm not sure it is anything for which one needs to pull strings. It really isn't too important in life. It wasn't a big part of my life at all."

Huntsman Sr. said: "I don't recall that I had anything to do with it."

Instead of participating in Sigma Chi, Huntsman took his first high-profile job with Huntsman Corp., serving as a project manager and secretary of the corporation while in college. Then, in February, he got a call from his friends at the White House that would change the course of his life.

Reagan was going to China, and the White House advance team knew how much Huntsman would want to be a part of this trip. The president was seen as a hard-liner when it came to relations with Beijing. During his campaign, Reagan vowed to fight against China's economic and political rise, a position he softened slightly when in office. Nonetheless, those tough public statements made the trip not only a dicey proposition, but also an opportunity to forge new ties.

"This was a real chance to build a relationship from scratch between two countries," Huntsman recalled.

When he arrived in Beijing, Huntsman and a contingent of officials from the military, the State Department and the Secret Service immediately met with U.S. Ambassador Arthur Hummel. The group discussed where Reagan should go and where he shouldn't, whom he could meet with and whom he had to avoid, and how to get a whole bunch of phone lines to the Great Wall so reporters could file their stores after the president made a stop there. During the discussion, Huntsman, then 23, was asked for his take on the political calculus.

"I remember sitting in Art Hummel's living room thinking, 'That is what I want to do someday,' " Huntsman said. "From that point on, my goal was to someday be able to serve in a capacity like that where you could make a real contribution to a relationship, an important relationship.

"You have to set goals for yourself, and I thought it was something completely out of reach, would never happen. But, nonetheless, I thought that that would be something to which I should aspire," Huntsman said a full 15 years before he became ambassador to China.

On his return to the states, Huntsman finished every class the University of Utah taught in Asian politics and Mandarin and then transferred to his father's alma mater, the University of Pennsylvania, which had a more robust Asian studies program. The high-school dropout had made it to the Ivy League. His now very wealthy father wrote a recommendation letter, but Huntsman had also recommitted to his schoolwork, posting what Huntsman Sr. described as "excellent grades." The younger Huntsman also won accolades for his work at the White House, giving him multiple people who supported his request to transfer schools.

Huntsman Jr. and Mary Kaye had just had their first daughter, Mary Anne, whom they named after Mary Kaye's mother. During these years, the young family took a trip to Virginia and spent a few days with Garn, whom Huntsman called his "political guru" and "almost like a second father growing up."

Garn already had helped Huntsman get the job as an advance man for Reagan, and the senator would be a Huntsman cheerleader for future jobs. But on this visit, they ruminated about the young man's future, his father's expectation that he go into the family business and Huntsman's desire to get involved in foreign affairs.

The way Garn remembers it, Huntsman said: "You know I'm very proud of my dad and my family and what they've accomplished. But in addition to what he's done, I would really like to make my own mark."

That mark, quite possibly, could have been as an American spy. His mentor at Penn, the late Alvin Rubinstein, set up an interview for Huntsman with the CIA.

"I thought that was maybe a career worth pursuing, as I did with the foreign service," Huntsman recalls, "and Mary Kaye put her foot down after we got a little way into the interviewing process."

She wanted no part of that lifestyle, but Mary Kaye wasn't an impediment to Huntsman's dreams of a life abroad. The Huntsmans moved to Taiwan for a year, giving Huntsman Jr. a chance to work as the vice president of Huntsman Pacific Chemical Corp., living this time in a nice place free of cockroaches. It allowed him to explore the city of his religious mission through the eyes of a resident businessman. During the year, he locked down deals to further the company in Thailand, Indonesia and India. His main job, though, was to launch a joint venture creating polystyrene to sell to the burgeoning consumer electronics plants in Japan, China and elsewhere.

Little Mary Anne was the only American in her Chinese preschool and Abby was just an infant. Mary Kaye was pregnant with their third daughter, Liddy. While her husband traveled for the company, she took care of the girls and soaked in the culture that had so captivated Huntsman. Nearly every day she walked past the door of St. Anne's Home, a Catholic orphanage. One day, she stopped and knocked. A nun opened the door, and the two fumbled over their language barrier. Mary Kaye eventually was invited into a large, dimly lit room, where children with physical and mental disabilities were lying on mats. None of these children was likely to be adopted.

Mary Kaye returned later the same day with an armful of children's clothes.

"I was so taken by the feeling I had in there of these innocent little children who needed a home," she said. "That never left my mind."

She wanted to adopt. Her husband didn't say no; he just stated the time wasn't right.

It was during that December they learned in a frantic call from family that Huntsman's little brother James had been kidnapped. At first, they thought the news was far worse than it turned out to be.

A relative called Huntsman's secretary in Taipei to pass on the dire development, and it got bungled in translation. She told Huntsman that his brother had been killed, not kidnapped. It took hours before Huntsman could secure a phone line and get an update. Jon Jr. and his family waited out that tense 12 hours in their home in Taipei, helpless and distraught. It was one of those episodes that expose how fragile life can be and how powerful the pull of family is.

About three months later, the Huntsmans moved back to Salt Lake City, allowing Mary Kaye to deliver Liddy in the states and, and while the kidnapping wasn't a motivation, the relocation gave Huntsman Jr. a chance to reconnect with his family. He helped lead his father's over-before-it-really-started gubernatorial campaign in 1988 while continuing work on international ventures for the now-sprawling chemical empire.

Huntsman never relinquished his dream of a career in international relations, and he was well-placed to ride out the changes in politics, bouncing between jobs with the government and stints with his father's company.

Shortly after President George H.W. Bush took the baton from Reagan, Huntsman landed back in Washington. This time he took an appointed position in the Commerce Department, first working on deals with the International Trade Administration and later taking a post as deputy assistant secretary for East Asian and Pacific affairs. His father used his connections to lobby for his son for this and future posts.

"He doesn't take no for an answer," said a former official during the Reagan and Bush I administrations who didn't want to use his name because he feared angering the Huntsmans.

Bush appointed Huntsman in March 1989, and he came on board that May, helping to get U.S. products and firms involved in the Soviet Union. The move came shortly after Huntsman Corp. teamed up with Marriott and Aeroflot to create Aeromar, one of the first joint U.S.-Soviet companies after the Cold War. It made plastic utensils for the Russian airline. Huntsman Jr. earned $75,000 a year at the Commerce Department, managed a staff of 60 and received accolades for his work.

"Competent, capable and hardworking, flashes of real brilliance and just a very nice guy," said Wayne Berman, a former assistant secretary at Commerce who hired Huntsman.

Huntsman left the job in August 1991. He says it was because he had promised his dad he would return to Huntsman Corp. within two to three years.

"I was of the opinion that if you spent more time than that, you lose your effectiveness because you have to bring something to the job," Huntsman said. "You can't just take a job without anything to give."

There was more to it than that.

Utah Republicans were urging Huntsman to consider a run for the Senate, since his "political guru," Jake Garn, was retiring, or a run for the House, taking on a seat held by a Democrat. Huntsman pledged he'd seriously consider each opportunity.

"I'm keeping all the options open," he said. "I have a strong commitment to return something to society. I'm not sure whether I can be most useful with public or private involvement."

Huntsman said serving in Congress never really appealed to him. He didn't see himself as an elected official. He saw himself as a diplomat. In January 1992, Huntsman announced he wouldn't be a congressional candidate, partly because his father was battling prostate cancer and he didn't want to leave the company. Around that same time, top Bush aides came calling again. They were willing to make Huntsman an ambassador — the youngest in more than 100 years — and that was something he couldn't turn down.

There were jokes that Huntsman, then 32, could be ambassador to Armenia because his father had donated millions there after a horrendous earthquake. The problem was the United States had not formally recognized Armenia. But over time, there grew to be some mutual interest. The president wasn't against sending a young ambassador overseas, and Huntsman had the strong backing of Sens. Orrin Hatch and Jake Garn, along with Commerce Secretary Bob Mosbacher.

"I thought that this was silly, I should be older, but if an opportunity presented itself, I would really think about it," Huntsman recalls. "It would have to be the right country. I would not leave to serve in any country just to serve."

What about Singapore?

Huntsman Corp. had a joint venture there, and Huntsman Jr. had made a lengthy visit, learning much about its culture. He also saw the place as an emerging trading partner. He wanted it.

Huntsman had a decent work history, and friends within the Bush administration from his Commerce days lobbied on his behalf. Still, it would have been inconceivable to be named ambassador at age 32 had it not been for his family's connections.

"I don't think there's much question that he would not have been ambassador to Singapore without his father's strong support, and his father had a very good Rolodex in those days," said then-Sen. Bob Bennett, who had won the race to replace Garn that year. Garn spoke directly to Bush about Huntsman's potential appointment and Huntsman Sr. launched a full-fledged campaign, even enlisting Fred Malek, the man who got him a job back in the Nixon White House.

"Our families have been very close," Malek said, adding he saw Huntsman Jr. as "a bright, kind of earnest young man, cut out of the father's cloth."

Huntsman Jr. was one of 15 applicants who interviewed for the diplomatic post, and while he wasn't the White House's first pick, he was a tantalizing option. He got a call back from Sam Skinner, Bush's chief of staff.

"He called me into his office. I remember it very well. He looked at my résumé and then at me and I was very intimidated, thinking, 'This is the president's chief of staff, what am I doing here? I should be out doing what I have been doing the last six months, building the family business.' I didn't think the job would ever come to fruition. He said, 'Well, I have a son about your age,' " Huntsman recalls. "He said, 'What do you think you can contribute to a position like this?' We got to talking and we became friends, and he took me to the White House mess and we had lunch together after the meeting."

"That interview with the president's chief of staff did it, I am convinced, because I got a call a week or two after that from the person who runs personnel in the White House saying, 'The president is prepared to nominate you to become the ambassador to Singapore.' I couldn't believe what I was hearing."

Bush nominated Huntsman in June, but that didn't guarantee him the job. The Senate still had to confirm him. And before that vote, Huntsman had to win over the Senate Foreign Relations Committee and Sen. Paul Sarbanes. The Maryland Democrat was on a crusade against nominees who had been big campaign donors to the president. Huntsman fit that label, and he got the Sarbanes treatment.

Huntsman spent weeks studying Singapore, learning about past diplomatic interactions and the backgrounds of key players. Then he set about arranging meetings with each member of the Foreign Relations Committee. Sarbanes turned him down, saying he didn't like to meet with nominees before a confirmation hearing. Among those who did meet with him was Sen. Joe Biden, D-Del., who went on to become chairman and, later, vice president.

Huntsman said he told Biden: " 'Please don't hold age against me. Look at experience. You were elected to the Senate when you were 30 years old. You couldn't possibly use age as an argument against me.' And he said, 'Absolutely not, I wouldn't think of doing that. I am going to base my vote on merit.' "

Senate aides warned Huntsman to expect a lively exchange before the committee members, since his age and his family's campaign contributions were big targets.

"I was fearful that they were going to do their best to torpedo me," Huntsman said. "I was concerned. I was scared. But I was in a very feisty mood. I thought, 'I am not going to just go down in flames, I am going to put up a fight if that is what they are going to do.' "

Huntsman didn't just study Singapore, he also studied Sarbanes. He read the testimony of nominees who never made it through the Senate and he focused on the ones Sarbanes liked and the ones he didn't. He read Sarbanes' favorite books, such as "The American Ambassador." And he consulted with some of Sarbanes' close associates, including Pat Shea.

Before Shea was the attorney for KUTV, battling Huntsman Sr. after that disastrous interview with Rick Shenkman in 1988, he worked for the Senate Foreign Relations Committee and became chummy with Sarbanes. Later, he worked for Huntsman Corp. and became a friend and supporter of Huntsman Jr.

Shea called Sarbanes on Huntsman's behalf, saying that while the nominee was young and came from a wealthy, politically active family, he also was well-versed in Asian affairs and had a long work history, starting with a job as a dishwasher in a Japanese restaurant.

"He is very street smart as well as intellectually smart," Shea told Sarbanes.

Shea also counseled Huntsman that Sarbanes would soften up if he could prove he wasn't a token political appointment, but a serious person prepared to represent the country abroad.

Huntsman appeared before the committee in late July 1992. Sarbanes started out complimentary.

"He is young, but he's had a pretty impressive career," said the senior senator. "His proficiency in the language is a real credit. He lived in Taiwan as a missionary. He has worked in business in the area. And he has experience with the Commerce Department in the area."

Huntsman could sense the next word out of his mouth would be "but."

"I have some concerns about the number of contributions your family made to the Bush-Quayle campaign about the same time as your nomination. Were you aware of them?" Sarbanes asked.

Huntsman said he wasn't, though he was the chairman of the Utah fundraising committee for the president. He noted Barbara Bush visited Utah around that same time and he volunteered that he and his wife each gave $2,000 to the campaign. What was left unsaid at the time was that the rest of his immediate family gave another $10,000.

Sarbanes seemed persuaded, saying afterward: "That's not a large amount really. It's a large amount for ordinary people."

The types of nominees who really got his attention were those who had given $100,000. "I would not put Mr. Huntsman in that category," Sarbanes said.

The senator moved on to the nominee's age, asking if he thought his inexperience would be a detriment. The man he was replacing was nearly 80. Huntsman noted the population of Singapore was young and that men his age were being groomed to take senior roles there. He also threw in a well-rehearsed joke.

"Even though I do not have the requisite number of gray hairs, I have tried to sprout them. But all I got was an ulcer."

Huntsman easily handled policy questions, wowing the senators by dropping the names of obscure officials and going into detail on international disputes. He also made a point to mention Sarbanes' favorite book on diplomacy.

"I was staggered," Garn said. "He even knew the name of the naval attaché."

Garn sat through the hearing, which led to a humorous aside from Sen. Alan Cranston, D-Calif.: "Jake personally called me at least 876 times on the Huntsman nomination."

Garn didn't win over Sarbanes, but Huntsman did, turning what Huntsman thought would be "a disastrous moment" into a triumph. The committee supported him unanimously a few weeks later and, a short time after that, so did the entire Senate. He received his credentials as an ambassador Sept. 22.

Within a month, Jon Huntsman Sr. and his chemical company donated $75,000 to the Republican National Committee, far more than he had given in previous years. He threw another $5,000 to the GOP a month later.

By that time, Bush was locked in a three-way race with Arkansas Gov. Bill Clinton and independent candidate Ross Perot. Clinton's eventual victory resulted in a quick end to Huntsman's ambassadorship. He held the post for nine months before leaving in June 1993. He would have held it for an even shorter time, had not Sarbanes talked Clinton's people into letting Huntsman remain in the country for the first six months of the new president's term.

Huntsman relished the opportunity to serve as a diplomat and went to great lengths to make a good impression on career foreign-service officers.

"My dad was just so happy in his job there. He loved it," Abby Huntsman said. "It was such a family job."

Entertaining guests is a big part of any diplomat's responsibilities, and Huntsman didn't shy away from using his daughters as part of the show. Mary Anne, 9, would play the piano and Abby, 7, would sing. Their favorite was "Castle on a Cloud" from "Les Misérables." The notables who watched their performance weren't limited to dignitaries from Singapore, but also others who stopped by the embassy, including Elton John and MC Hammer. The 1990s pop star even gave the girls a Mattel doll of himself with his trademark parachute pants.

The way Abby recalls the experience is reminiscent of how her father remembers his boyhood days in the West Wing.

"When I reflect back on that, it was a time in life where I think you mature and are taught at a very young age how to handle yourself — how to have this confidence," she said. "It wasn't a normal life for a 7-year-old."

It wasn't a normal life for a 32-year-old Jon Huntsman, either. He helped relocate military units from the Philippines to Singapore, worked on trade deals and assisted U.S. companies in gaining a foothold there.

With the change in administration, Huntsman returned to the family business, this time serving as vice chairman. All the while, he dabbled in outside foreign-affairs groups such as the Asia Society, the Singapore Economic Development Board and Johns Hopkins University's American Institute for Contemporary German Studies.

Huntsman was his own man overseas, but back at home he was often known as his father's son. Their relationship has always been a warm one, even if it is a bit unorthodox.

"I've always kind of used his life as a yardstick by which I measure my own life. But I'm not the kind of second-generation person who considers throwing himself out of a third-story window because you can't measure up," he said. "We have what probably would be considered by some to be a peculiar relationship. He has been a business partner of sorts, a father, a best friend."

That business partner/friend/father started to step back from the day-to-day management of Huntsman Corp. in 1996. He was ready to give up the title of president and CEO, though he still planned to head the company's board. Huntsman Jr. didn't want to take the reins, instead urging his father to pick his younger brother Peter. That same year, Republicans tried to persuade Huntsman Jr. to run for Congress. He again declined. They made a third try in 2000, but he still wasn't interested.

He instead led the Huntsman Cancer Foundation, raising money for the family's philanthropic masterpiece, the Huntsman Cancer Institute, and he kept his eye out for that next great adventure.

One appeared — not in China or Singapore or some other exotic locale, but right there in Salt Lake City. The organizers of the 2002 Winter Olympics were mired in scandal and needed a fresh face to take over. Who better than a former ambassador to work with the International Olympic Committee? Why not a man with international business experience?

Huntsman said he would be willing to take on the challenge and, with that, his father began making calls to Utah power brokers.

chapter five

The Games begin

Utah, it's the Toilet of the West!

As Olympic slogans go, this one is horrible, and yet it appeared on brochures supporting Salt Lake City's first bid for the Winter Games in 1966. Not in English — the promoters weren't that dumb — but in French, the product of poor translation. A University of Utah professor caught the appalling error before the state became an international laughingstock.

"It shows you how unsophisticated we were," said Walker Wallace, a retired businessman and former ski racer who was on the organizing committee.

The goal wasn't to win the 1972 Games, but to get free publicity for Utah's fledgling ski industry. Bid leaders, backed by the governor, sold faux Olympic pins to raise $24,000 and created a rough slide show that persuaded the U.S. Olympic Committee to back Salt Lake City's effort.

When the International Olympic Committee cast the deciding vote for Sapporo, Japan, it crushed Salt Lake City's chintzy bid, but that was fine with the Utah ski industry boosters, who had used the competition to launch their "Greatest Snow on Earth" campaign.

"We'd have been horrified if we won," said John W. Gallivan Sr., a booster and past publisher of The Salt Lake Tribune.

That didn't stop Salt Lake City from pursuing the 1976 Olympics, though that effort didn't get far. That seemed to end Utah's Olympic aspirations, until nearly a decade later when a bad economy had political leaders on the hunt for ways to give the state a lift.

In 1985, three years before they became gubernatorial rivals, Gov. Norm Bangerter and Salt Lake City Mayor Ted Wilson convened a lunch at the stately Alta Club, where they schmoozed a corporate attorney and posed this intriguing question: "What are you going to do with the next 10 years of your life?"

They were trying to persuade Tom Welch to give up a cushy job with Smith's grocery stores to chase their Olympic dream. In Welch, they saw the perfect point person — a strategic, affable, obsessive salesman. He was all that and more. It's not hard to argue that without Welch's skills and unrelenting drive, a Utah Winter Games would have remained nothing but a tantalizing pipe dream.

During that lunch, Welch, a stocky man with a round face, arching eyebrows and light brown hair, was intrigued by the Bangerter-Wilson offer and soon accepted. He began immersing himself in the peculiarities of the "Olympic family," the quirky and highly political fiefdoms of sports federations and national committees that operate side by side with the IOC. Welch had 30 days to hatch a plan for the 1992 Games, and the result wasn't much of an improvement on the first two attempts.

More realistically, he set his sights on 1998 with the understanding that it would take more than salesmanship for Utah to land the Games. The state needed a product to peddle.

In 1988, the same year Jon Huntsman Sr. jumped in and out of the race for governor, Welch led a ballot initiative to divert $59 million in sales taxes to build ski jumps, a bobsled/luge track and a speedskating oval. The proposal was structured in such a way that, if Utah won the Games, that investment would be returned to the state. Voters signed off on it.

The next year, Welch took a team to an IOC meeting in Puerto Rico to tout the project, but he had a hard time getting the attention of the men and women in charge of picking the Olympic cities.

"When we arrived there, the Greeks were entertaining on their yacht, with gorgeous hostesses," he said. "Atlanta had rented a mansion, shipped in furniture from Atlanta and called it the Atlanta House. Toronto had set up a whole wing out by the pool and were serving breakfasts, lunches and dinners to the IOC.

"Everyone was giving wonderful gifts — I think there were crystal vases and jewelry," Welch said. "Bid cities each had limousines. We showed up with nothing — on a bus. We called home, and they went and got some letter openers for us and brought them to us so we'd have something."

He went from feeling slightly embarrassed to being utterly demoralized when Atlanta won the 1996 Summer Games. He was convinced the IOC wouldn't give the Winter Olympics to the United States so soon after it was awarded the bigger Summer Games. But Welch trudged on, buoyed by words of encouragement from some IOC voters.

A delegation of 220 Utahns went to Birmingham, England, in the summer of 1991 for the vote on the '98 Games. Bangerter, Sens. Jake Garn and Orrin Hatch and the rest of the contingent handed out Stetson hats in a hospitality room lined with pine trees. Back in Salt Lake City, bid organizers set up an elaborate celebration in the public square surrounding the Richardsonian Romanesque-style City-County Building. Bands played, revelers attempted a mini-ski jump and big-screen TVs carried a live feed of the IOC announcement. At the nearby international airport, Delta Air Lines, a bid supporter, had prepared its own victory party with a live band, flag-waving crowd and two fire trucks that would spray streams of water in an arc over the plane bringing home the state's triumphant delegation.

The night before the vote, Jean-Jacques Ganga, the son of an IOC member from the Republic of Congo, sidled up to Welch and made him an offer. For $35,000 in cash, he'd secure some votes from the African delegation. Welch declined, partly because he didn't have the money.

Salt Lake City lost the bid to Nagano, Japan, on the fourth ballot by a mere four votes. The crowd of 6,000 in Salt Lake City let out a collective groan at the news and fell silent. On big screens, they watched the people of Nagano celebrate. Bid-committee lawyer Jim Jardine asked that the TVs be muted, then he picked up a microphone and quoted Winston Churchill: "Some may say that this is a blessing in disguise, but I must admit it is well disguised."

He delivered an impromptu inspirational speech to the disheartened crowd, and by the time he wrapped up, the people were chanting "Two thousand and two, two thousand and two!"

After such a painful loss, Welch faced two choices: Quit or up his game. Welch wasn't a quitter. He directed Dave Johnson, the vice president of Salt Lake City's bid committee, to find out everything he could about IOC members. Johnson, a baby-faced ex-car salesman whom Welch met through the LDS Church, had charisma. He was suave and tenacious. He memorized the names and ages of all the IOC members and their relatives. He learned what they liked to eat, what music they listened to and, most important, what it would take to lock up each vote.

"He could tell us their favorite toothpaste," said Fred Ball, a bid-committee member. "If they liked Godiva chocolate or a certain kind of wine, Dave would have it available in their rooms."

Salt Lake City had the venues and now the experience to put together a top-quality bid, but Welch and Johnson didn't want to leave anything to chance. Their strategy: Focus on the African IOC members because they didn't have a vested interest in the Winter Games, often voted in a bloc and were willing to deliver that bloc if provided the proper incentives. While some might see that as bribery, Welch looked at it as goodwill gift-giving and playing the game established by the IOC.

He reached out to Congo IOC member Jean-Claude Ganga, whose son earlier had sought a cash payment in England. The elder Ganga was the president of the Association of National Olympic Committees of Africa. Next, Welch cozied up to Rene Essomba from Cameroon, the secretary general of the continental organization. Whatever they wanted, they got. Period.

Ganga received medical treatment for hepatitis, his mother-in-law had her knee replaced and his wife received plastic surgery, all on the bid committee's dime. Welch and his team also set up a land deal that scored Ganga $60,000, and Welch handed him another $70,000 in cash. Ganga's wife even maxed out the credit card of a bid staffer during a Walmart shopping spree.

Salt Lake City's bid team gave Essomba $60,000 and paid for his daughter to attend American University, personally helping her move into an apartment in Washington, D.C. The tuition bill topped $100,000. SLOC also sent Essomba on all-expenses-paid vacations to Paris.

The largesse to these two men and their families totaled $500,000, and that was only half of what Welch and Johnson directed toward IOC members. More than 20 of the top Olympic officials took gifts in excess of their own rules, which allowed one visit to a bid city and permitted acceptance of a gift valued at $150 or less.

One son of an IOC member would show up unannounced at the bid committee's nondescript downtown Salt Lake City office every few weeks to ask: "Where's my check?"

Jason Christensen, a volunteer staffer, witnessed this type of activity routinely.

"You didn't have to be a brain surgeon to know what was going on," he said. "It was always whispered, 'Whose son is he? How much of a scholarship is he getting? How does that work?' People freaked out the first time they heard about it. Then it became second nature."

A woman close to the bid committee said everyone knew not to wear their best watches to dinner. If an IOC member admired it, you were expected to give it to him or her.

Welch's lawyer Tom Schaffer summarized the committee's philosophy this way: "If you are part of this family, and if you need something, we'll take care of you."

Beyond cash payments, Welch and Johnson got the children of IOC voters jobs in Utah companies and paid college tuition and rent. They took IOC members to the Super Bowl. Meanwhile, the bid committee handed out guns, dogs, draperies, beds, skis, Nintendo games, perfume and a violin. It set up medical appointments so two IOC members could get Viagra and even gave one IOC member a vibrator.

All gifts were supposed to be kept hush-hush, though Welch did create a line item in the budget called the "NOC program," an acronym meaning National Olympic Committees. He described this as humanitarian and educational aid to other countries, meant primarily for athletes.

Welch flew around the world ingratiating himself with the IOC elite and their families. In return for their hospitality, he invited some to his home for Christmas, not letting his children open any gifts until the guests arrived. He even raided one of his children's college trusts to loan $30,000 to an IOC member.

Welch's next-door neighbor — Jon Huntsman Sr. — watched the fawning over IOC members with disgust. While almost everyone in the community supported Welch and his drive to win the Olympics, Huntsman started having second thoughts. He had kicked in $100,000 to the effort to land the 1998 Games, but that was when Utah's economy was struggling. By 1994, the state had recovered, and Huntsman no longer saw the Olympics as such a good idea.

In an appearance before the Salt Lake Rotary Club, just nine months before the IOC awarded the 2002 bid, Huntsman stunned city leaders by saying the Olympics weren't worth the headache and might saddle the state with debt. He wished the Games would be held elsewhere and called for a public vote.

"What I am saying is not popular, but I believe it is the right thing to say. This conversation also is the last time I will address the issue," Huntsman told the crowd of business executives. "It now is up to political leaders, the media and the public to further analyze the issue, but somebody had to break the ice."

Welch gave a measured response, saying he had had some of the same financial concerns as Huntsman, but that they had been addressed. He promised the Games wouldn't lose money. Then Frank Joklik, chairman of the bid committee's executive board and a man who previously managed one of the nation's largest copper mines, struck back in his own speech at the Rotary Club.

"To say we no longer need the Olympics because our economy is now in better shape misrepresents the Olympic movement, which was never intended to be merely a machine for economic growth and job creation," Joklik said, even though that was the argument the state made in its previous four attempts to win the Games.

Despite his vow to stay quiet, Huntsman didn't. He called a popular talk radio show and slammed the state for directing so much energy at attracting an athletic competition when it should have been trying to woo companies to relocate.

The stinging criticism from his high-profile neighbor wasn't Welch's only problem. In early 1995, he separated from his wife, Alma.

"This process put a great deal of stress on our family," Welch told a pack of reporters. "You can't spend 18 hours a day focused on the effort without affecting the good balance in a relationship. In January, Alma and I decided to be business partners. Ten days later, she told me, 'You're not even a good business partner.' "

All of her husband's time and attention went into the Olympic bid, and Alma had had enough. Worse, she couldn't stand that he wasn't there for their six children. Welch missed his son's championship rugby game and a daughter's high-school graduation. When his oldest got married, he flew in the day before the wedding and flew out immediately afterward.

Welch tried to repair his family life, but not until after the IOC vote in June. Just as in 1991, Utah flew a huge delegation to the meeting in Budapest, Hungary, and Salt Lake City staged a big public party around city hall. Delta Air Lines ran through the same checklist as four years earlier, with firetrucks ready to spray a celebratory water arc.

Most observers saw Salt Lake City as a lock to get the 2002 Games over Quebec City; Ostersund, Sweden; and Sion, Switzerland, but Welch wouldn't accept premature praise, saying only: "We are comfortable with the fact that we have done all we can do, win or lose."

Salt Lake City won the IOC vote by more than a 3-to-1 margin and did it on the first ballot, a victory of historic proportions.

The crowd around city hall exploded into a flag-waving frenzy. Delta finally got to fire its water cannons, but only after city and state leaders held a tear-filled testimonial in Budapest. Johnson broke down. Welch's eyes welled up for a solid two minutes before he was able to speak. Alma was by his side for support despite their personal troubles.

"There's nothing like coming home having accomplished the goal you set out to do," she said when their flight landed back in Utah.

Welch felt vindicated. This was a high point in his life. No longer head of the bid committee, he now was president and CEO of the Salt Lake Organizing Committee. SLOC had seven years to prepare for the Games, with Welch as its triumphant leader.

That is, until it all went bad two years later.

The Welches never fully reconciled and yet they never divorced. They lived apart but remained connected, a volatile arrangement that turned nasty in July 1997, when Alma found out about another woman in Tom's life. The ensuing argument turned into a tussle when she tried to get her hands on the gifts and letters her husband intended to give to this other woman. Their 11-year-old son, witnessing the fight in the family garage, called the police.

Alma told Officer David Rowley that Welch threw her into a wall and placed her in a headlock, wrestling her to the floor. Welch said his wife was prone to exaggeration and that he only sat on the trunk of the car to stop her from getting in. Rowley could see bruises and small cuts on Alma's arms, legs, neck and chest. When she calmed down, Alma told police she didn't want to press charges, but Rowley was undeterred. He arrested Welch, then 52.

A few days later, Welch showed up at a SLOC board meeting, acting as though nothing had happened, and then jetted to Africa for a safari with one of his sons. While on the exotic trip, he got word that city prosecutors had brought domestic battery charges against him. It became international news.

Rushing back to Utah, Welch held a news conference, where he denied assaulting his wife and said he never had a sexual relationship with the other woman, though he acknowledged they were close. He hoped he could stay on as SLOC president. But Welch had badly miscalculated the public firestorm. Four days later, under pressure from leading Utahns and the IOC, he cut a deal. He would resign as president but would stay on as a consultant and receive a sizable severance for his years of service.

"I have concluded that the costs and stresses imposed upon the organizing committee, my children and me by the unfounded charges and allegations which have been widely reported in the media are simply too high," he announced, displaying little emotion while reading from a one-page statement.

Alma said he "made the right decision" and then added: "He is a good man. It is a good time for all of us to surround and support Tom and give him the time and space he needs for himself."

Welch pleaded no contest to the misdemeanor and accepted a deal from SLOC that would pay him a $1 million severance.

Joklik, the Austrian-born former mining CEO, stepped in as acting president of SLOC, while the organizing committee hunted for a new leader. Joklik was Catholic, stoic and soft-spoken, a contrast to Welch, who was a member of the state's predominant LDS faith, with a garish and temperamental personality.

SLOC created a five-member committee to determine who would take the job full time. Joklik was the clear front-runner, but he wasn't the only candidate. Despite his father's well-publicized Olympic skepticism, Jon Huntsman Jr. threw his hat into the ring, saying he would take the position without pay.

"I have been encouraged to look at it by some members of the board," Huntsman Jr. said. "Without compensation and in the spirit of volunteerism, I would be interested in serving if asked. It would come at a high price in terms of walking away from everything I'm doing now, but it's important enough. The Olympics are coming, and we have to make them the best ever."

At the time, in late 1997, Huntsman was president of the Huntsman Cancer Foundation and vice chairman of Huntsman Corp., a former ambassador and a Republican heavyweight in the state. But the board ended up feeling more comfortable with Joklik, who for the past five years had served as chairman of the organizing and bid-committee boards.

Huntsman didn't know it at the time, but the snubbing was a stroke of luck. He would be safely insulated from the coming media inferno.

The Salt Lake Organizing Committee had become bitterly divided between supporters of Welch and backers of Joklik and Dave Johnson. Welch believed Joklik and his old protégé Johnson had leaked information about his domestic-violence charge to the newspapers.

In such a toxic environment, Welch's former secretary, Stephanie Pate, decided she needed a change of scenery. She took a job at US West, a telecommunications company and sponsor of the 2002 Games.

In the fall of 1998, Ken Bullock, executive director of the Utah League of Cities and Towns and a chief agitator on the SLOC board, invited Pate and her new boss Dave Watson to lunch at an Asian restaurant. There, Bullock and Watson pressed Pate for any dirt she might have on Johnson or the bid committee. Watson scoffed that he wanted to see Joklik's "little heart burst."

Pate told them about a letter she had kept that mentioned a tuition payment for Essomba's daughter Sonia. Bullock's eyes got big. He wanted that letter, and he badgered her to hand it over. A week later, Pate met Bullock in a parking lot in downtown Salt Lake City and gave him a file. Bullock said he confronted Johnson about the document, but denies that he was the source who handed it over to a reporter.

Chris Vanocur, then a political reporter for the ABC-TV affiliate in Salt Lake City, won't say how he obtained the Essomba letter on Nov. 23, 1998, but it wasn't hard for him to confirm its contents. A quick Internet search showed that Sonia Essomba was the daughter of a prominent IOC member, and Frank Zang, a spokesman for SLOC, readily admitted that the bid committee paid her tuition.

Two days before Thanksgiving, Vanocur went on the air, holding up the leaked correspondence and saying: "This is the letter Olympic folks probably didn't want us to get."

The letter from Johnson was on SLOC stationery, stamped "Draft," and dated Sept. 17, 1996, more than a year after Salt Lake City won the Olympic bid. In it, Johnson tells Sonia Essomba: "Under the current budget structure, it will be difficult to continue the scholarship program with you. The enclosed check for $10,114.99 will have to be our last payment for tuition."

Zang argued the program was humanitarian assistance from citizens of a wealthy nation to someone from a poor one. Nothing more.

"Sonia never would have had the chance to pursue her own academic endeavors in the United States without this assistance," he said.

SLOC promised a full accounting, and more than a week later said it had paid more than $400,000 in tuition assistance for 13 people, six of whom were relatives of IOC board members, and that the payments started shortly after Salt Lake City's painful bid loss in 1991. To Stephen Pace, a vocal Olympic critic in Utah, the tuition help "looks like, walks like and quacks like a bribe."

Welch, then a SLOC consultant, was dismissive of Pace and the critics. "You know how important the Cameroon IOC member was? Not even a factor," he said, ignoring the fact that, next to Europe, Africa had the most IOC votes. The story might have simply petered out if not for the candid comments of one IOC member who long had been frustrated with what he considered corruption within the Olympic family.

"Certainly, it's a bribe," said Marc Hodler, the longest-serving member of the IOC's executive board. "I'm terribly sorry that Salt Lake City, as by far the best place to hold the Winter Games, had to use certain methods to get the vote. That's too bad. If there's a city in the world that didn't need that, it was Salt Lake.

"It was one thing if Salt Lake had spent its money on promising young African athletes," he said. "But if it is connected to the voting, of course it is corruption."

International reporters turned what had started out as a debate over tuition assistance into a full-fledged hunt for bribes. And they found plenty of smoking guns. Reporters identified men marketing themselves as IOC "agents," who for $500,000 or more would help a city lock up a bid. Among such agents was Ganga, and reporters soon discovered the free medical care SLOC arranged for his family. Once put on the defensive, SLOC didn't hesitate to throw Welch and Johnson under the bus. Kelly Flint, the organizing committee's lawyer, told Hodler: "Everything was done by Tom Welch, and he was not there anymore. We know nothing, nothing, nothing."

But Hodler didn't blame Welch or Salt Lake City. He pointed the finger at the IOC and the system it created for picking host cities.

"Salt Lake City was the victim of blackmail and villains," he said.

While dramatic, Hodler wasn't wrong. Investigations spawned by the Essomba letter eventually would find that Nagano, Sydney and Atlanta, among other Olympic cities, handed out expensive gifts in exchange for votes. But none of them got the searing, caught-in-the-act attention that Salt Lake City did, in part because SLOC kept orderly files on all of its dealings with IOC members, while other cities, such as Nagano, destroyed their records.

Jon Huntsman Sr., Utah's highest-profile Olympic critic, piled on, telling reporters that the bid committee's lavish spending had devastated the state's credibility.

"I would say it is a sad day for Utah," Huntsman said. "We were sending out reasonably inexperienced people with large amounts of cash in their pockets to try to figure out ways to attract people to Utah.

"Everything about it was simply wrong. The activities that surrounded the Olympic bid committee never passed what I would call a smell test. It was out of control almost from the very beginning."

The scandal got a second wind when the FBI launched a criminal probe. Olympic sponsor US West held back a $5 million pledge, and evidence surfaced that SLOC gave cash directly to IOC members. Under intense pressure from the U.S. Olympic Committee and Gov. Mike Leavitt, Joklik agreed to step down, fire Dave Johnson and quash Welch's $10,000-per-month consulting contract. A couple of other SLOC employees involved in the bid were placed on administrative leave.

Joklik, who said he knew nothing about the inappropriate payments, agreed to stay on until SLOC picked his successor.

In a grim, funereal news conference, Leavitt said Joklik was falling on the sword to make it "absolutely clear that the actions of a few do not reflect the values, moral expectations or standards of behavior of this community and state. We deplore it, and we revolt at being associated with them."

Leavitt called it "a systematic cover-up," and just about every other Utah bigwig involved in the bid process fingered Welch and Johnson. Johnson stepped aside but refused to say he did anything wrong.

"Our mission statement was to influence IOC members' votes and to obtain enough votes to win," he said. "At no time was there a quid pro quo, so it wasn't a bribe. It was a secret ballot. Even if an IOC member said he was going to vote for you, you never knew if he would."

Welch also spoke up, saying the bid committee knew of the tuition payments, and that the knee replacement for Ganga's mother was a life-or-death case because of an infection.

"I'd been in her home — if you want to call it a home — and she shared with me what she had," he said. "So when a friend was hurting and we're telling the world we have the best medical facilities in the world, I helped. And I'd help again."

Welch argued SLOC's activities were similar to that of any business.

"You support your friends and their causes, and that's what we tried to do. But as far as trying to buy somebody — no way."

Speculation about who would replace Joklik began just moments after he departed. Through a spokesman, Jon Huntsman Sr. and his eldest son said they were not interested, while, behind the scenes, Huntsman Jr. once again offered to lead the Olympics without pay, and his father pushed his candidacy. The board also took a strong look at David Checketts, a Mormon who was then president and CEO of Madison Square Garden in New York. Taking over the scandal-ridden organizing committee had some obvious attraction.

"You can come in and be the hero," said attorney Randy Dryer, a SLOC executive-committee member, noting the job had "that white-knight allure."

Construction magnate Alan Layton said the board should pick "someone with an understanding of Utah, our culture, community values and our heritage." But he insists his comments weren't directed at his old BYU college buddy Mitt Romney. His wife, Leslie, asked Layton if it was a job Romney may be interested in and he said: "Oh, honey, it's not that big."

What Layton didn't know was that Robert Garff, chairman of the SLOC board and an old Romney family friend, already had begun lobbying Leavitt to consider Romney. And developer Kem Gardner had called Ann Romney a few weeks before Joklik resigned, hoping to persuade his old friend to swoop in and save the Olympics.

Romney dismissed the feelers. He had felt no particular sense of pride when Utah won the bid, and he didn't care much for Welch.

The two met for dinner back in 1995 at Gardner's request. They went to La Caille, one of the Salt Lake Valley's fanciest restaurants. Afterward, Welch insisted on bringing Romney to his home in the foothills to see a statue of an eagle. Welch liked the statue so much he placed it in the center of a picture window and lit it up so the few people who ever drove by his remote neighborhood couldn't miss it.

"Everything about Tom seemed made for show. I suppose I attributed the same motives to the Utah Olympic effort, an opportunity to put on a show," Romney recalled. "I couldn't help but reflect back on that dinner when, much later, I first heard word of the ensuing scandal."

The allegations "sickened" Romney, and not just because he thought SLOC's gift-giving was improper. He also felt the sleaze had unfairly splashed onto all Mormons.

"There seemed to be an implied association of the scandal with the standing and character of the state, and further, with the Mormon church," Romney later would write. "Those who thought us Mormons to be too goody-two-shoes felt confirmed in their suspicions. I remember thinking what a shame it was that the entire community was being given a black eye by the seemingly unscrupulous actions of a flamboyant few."

Ann Romney told her husband he had a chance to influence that perception. Gardner could help him take the Olympic mantle and turn the scandal into success. She used his faith and his desire to perform public service to nudge him, reminding him how restless he was at Bain.

The Romneys made a ski trip to Utah that January, but they didn't spend much time on the slopes. Romney held a series of get-to-know-you visits with SLOC board members, either at their offices or at the Alta Club. He wooed them and wowed them. Romney had deep Utah ties and yet was an outsider. He had proven business acumen, a history of saving troubled companies and plenty of experience in the public eye. He seemed the perfect fit.

A few weeks later, Romney returned to Utah to meet with the governor. The two had exchanged pleasantries at an LDS general conference meeting before and had talked on the phone, but this would be their first in-depth conversation. They boarded the state's Beechcraft King Air plane in mid-January for a quick trip to Los Angeles, where Leavitt was scheduled to speak to a technology company about relocating to Utah. The flight gave them time to talk. A policy wonk who loves lists, figures and big game-changing projects, Leavitt speaks Romney's language. Romney, though, wasn't sure where he stood after the encounter.

"He grilled me for about two hours," Romney said, "and at the end of that he gave no indication if he was impressed with what he heard or not."

When they reached their destination, Leavitt took the podium while Romney hobnobbed with a few SLOC folks, who had tagged along for the trip, and easily won them over. On the return flight, they gave Leavitt a big thumbs-up sign and, as best they could in a small twin-propeller plane, cordoned off the back, with its comfy couch seats, so the governor and Romney could hold Round Two of their discussion.

During that private conversation, Leavitt gave Romney a rundown of the personalities involved in the organizing committee and more details on the momentous challenges that loomed. Romney said he would accept the job if offered. Leavitt said he wanted to offer the job to Romney. But there was a problem: SLOC never had established a process for choosing its next leader. Some board members chafed at what they saw as Leavitt ramming Romney down their throats.

News outlets touted Romney as the leading contender and noted that Huntsman and Checketts also appeared on the short list. It was exactly the kind of public speculation Leavitt hoped to avoid. None of these three proud, accomplished candidates wanted to have his name associated with a position he wouldn't get.

Leavitt felt he had to interview Huntsman and Checketts. The board liked Checketts' business background and his understanding of the sports world. Had Romney declined the job, he may well have been next in line.

Huntsman? Not so much.

"We just didn't see Jon Jr. as having enough substantive experience," said a SLOC board member. "The word on Jon was that he didn't finish anything. He didn't finish high school. We just thought of him as a rich kid. ... The judgment was probably unfair when you look at the way his life turned out."

Another board member said: "They just were not sure if he was serious enough about it."

Some SLOC officials worried Huntsman, often mentioned as a potential congressional candidate, would use the high-profile post to further his political goals in the state. Romney had political ambitions, too, but not in Utah.

Other board members noted that a Huntsman-led SLOC undoubtedly would bring his wealthy and influential father into the fold, ending the sporadic sniping from the state's most prominent Olympic critic.

Romney was annoyed the board was even having these conversations or that Leavitt was entertaining other candidates. He thought he had the gig in the bag.

"I had to call and explain that, all appearances of due diligence aside, I was not one to have my name bandied about — with all that that would mean for my relationship with Bain Capital — only to be passed over for the job," he said. "They either wanted me or they didn't. If they didn't, they should say so outright. If they did, I would accept."

He secretly accepted the job in early February 1999 and made arrangements to leave Bain Capital. His friends began talking him up publicly, saying he was a guy who turned around troubled companies for a living and would do the same for the Olympics.

"He would be a tremendous choice. He's one of the sharpest, most capable people I've ever met," said Darral Clarke, a professor at Brigham Young University and a Romney mentor at Harvard.

"When I first heard his name was being bantered about, I thought, 'We'd be incredibly lucky to get him. We couldn't do any better than Mitt,' " said

Fraser Bullock, a former colleague at Bain and a fellow Mormon who had moved back to Utah and eventually would take a job at SLOC.

Huntsman Sr. called Romney to see how serious he was about taking the Olympic job and found that Romney was all in.

"I can pull Utah out of the mess," Romney told Huntsman. "I can save Utah."

Huntsman's reaction: "I nearly choked on my Altoids. I told him that Utah did not need a savior. What it needed was a leader with vision and good business sense. Romney was brash and arrogant during the conversation, and his political ambitions were apparent. It was not a pleasant conversation."

At that time, Huntsman didn't know that Romney's selection was already a done deal, but he soon would, and his frustration would swell exponentially.

In explaining the hire, Leavitt said he needed a person "who could stand on the international stage and be viable and respected. A person who could turn the Olympics process itself around from just a dollar-and-cents point and then a person who could raise and reignite the Olympic spirit again in Utah. And I think we got the right guy."

Romney didn't want to publicly take the job until SLOC had aired as much dirty laundry as possible about the bid scandal. He waited until after the committee released its 300-page report, which went gift by gift through the bid process, placing blame at the feet of Welch and Johnson, though it insisted no laws were broken. At this time, a fifth of all IOC members were under suspicion of taking inappropriate gifts. Before long, 10 would lose their jobs.

"The first thing I needed to do," Romney said, "was to draw a clear, bright, heavy line between what had happened before and what was going to happen in the future."

He orchestrated a first-day media blitz that would reinvigorate the organizing committee and signal to the world the dawning of a new day. The plan called for Leavitt to address the scandal, announce changes to SLOC, which he negotiated ahead of time with Romney, and then turn over the room to the shiny new CEO.

A Leavitt aide bungled the plan when he told Alan Layton: "Mitt has asked that you be taken off the board."

Romney's old college friend was stunned and wounded. Romney, in fact, did want Layton off the SLOC board, along with two other members, because their companies were financially benefiting from the Games. He wanted to head off conflict-of-interest allegations. Layton's construction firm had a $29 million contract to build part of the speedskating oval.

"When Alan came in to see me, he looked terribly hurt," Romney said. "He felt like his friend had betrayed him. I explained the reasoning behind the decision. I talked about how important it was to put the Olympics back on secure footing. But it was very painful for him. I felt terrible, too."

Layton and the other ousted board members felt unfairly linked to the bribery scandal. They never were accused of wrongdoing or involved in the gift giving.

"It was an emotional day for me, because I had worked really hard for several years between the bid and the organizing committee," said Layton. He hated the timing, but knew SLOC needed a boost, and he backed his old buddy. "To be told, 'We didn't want you to be around,' it was emotional, but it was right. I recognized that and I stepped aside."

The rest of the day — Feb. 11, 1999 — went according to script.

Leavitt appeared before the board and reporters from around the globe, declaring: "We cannot change history. Today we will move boldly and decisively for a new beginning."

He announced that SLOC would start holding open meetings and make its records available for inspection. He said the organization would create new tough ethics guidelines, and he publicly booted the three board members with conflicts of interest. A fourth member resigned because he was a main player on the bid committee when the scandal occurred.

SLOC's house appeared as clean as it was going to get. Leavitt ushered Romney, then 51, into the room, calling him "a franchise player." A standing ovation greeted him. When the board voted him president and CEO, he said: "Where were you when I needed you? I wish I had a few of these voters in 1994," a joking reference to his failed Senate campaign.

Romney promised "the highest levels of ethical conduct" and fiscal prudence. He deferred his $285,000 annual salary until the Games closed three years later and said he wouldn't accept a penny unless he left SLOC debt-free.

In interviews after the meeting, he described how his love of the Olympics came from his friend Bob Richards, a distance runner at BYU who pursued a spot on the 1968 Olympic team as a steeplechaser. Richards trained by working summers on an Idaho ranch, baling hay, but he missed the Olympic trials because of illness.

Romney said he was thinking of Richards when he took the job, not about being a "white knight" or the possibility of a future in politics.

"The Olympics is about sport, not business," Romney said. "The Olympics is about the athletes, young people aspiring for greatness, not the managers."

He said he wouldn't use the SLOC post as a springboard to run for a Senate seat in Utah, which relieved Sens. Orrin Hatch and Bob Bennett. And he warned the board he wouldn't stomach any future scandals.

"I would expect any of you who cast a shadow on the Olympics to step aside," he said.

Romney accomplished his goals that first day. He distanced himself from the past scandal and made himself the face of the future. The only real criticism came from Jon Huntsman Sr., who called the CEO search a "sham" and complained his son had been used as a pawn. He argued that Romney accepted the job three weeks before the public announcement and that Huntsman Jr. and Checketts were interviewed only to give an appearance of legitimacy to the selection process.

Huntsman Jr. found out he was rejected via a perfunctory note from SLOC. He received no call or visit explaining the situation.

"We were pretty much faxed a notification that 'by the way, we found somebody and we are discontinuing the search,' or something to that effect, and I thought that was the height of classlessness," Huntsman Jr. said. "They use your name and they float it in articles as if it is some sort of competitive process and then you find that you are just being used in the end."

Huntsman family members felt burned, and their anger would cause Romney trouble. Leavitt already had been on the receiving end of that fury when he called Huntsman Sr. to explain the Romney pick. A nearby Leavitt aide could hear Huntsman Sr. screaming through the phone. Huntsman vented to others, too.

"He was pretty bent out of shape," recalled Ted Wilson, the former Salt Lake City mayor who had been involved in that first Olympic recruiting meeting with Tom Welch 14 years earlier.

Adding salt to the wound, Leavitt asked Huntsman Jr. to sit on the SLOC management committee. He refused. What about a spot as a special Olympic ambassador? Huntsman Jr. wasn't having it.

"I told him to screw off two or three times," he said.

Huntsman Jr. did send a letter to Romney, whom he never had met, wishing him well in the new post and reminiscing about playing tennis with Mitt's father as a child.

"I wasn't that good of a tennis player, but I was impressed by this older guy who was always in motion," Huntsman recalls. "I said something to the effect of if you're anything like your old man, you'll do a great job."

Huntsman Sr. later would downplay his frustration, saying it was directed more at state leaders like Leavitt. But the way Romney came to lead the Olympics marked the first serious fissure in the relationship between the two families and something that Mitt privately would remark upon a decade later when he and Huntsman Jr. squared off as presidential contenders.

The Huntsmans and Romney knew the man who led the Olympics would step into a national spotlight. The political benefits were obvious, and yet Romney insisted he took the Olympic job with no thought of his future.

"I had no plans to parlay the experience into political advantage," he wrote after the Games. "I gave very little thought at all to what I would do afterwards. Many people can't believe that. They think that I had calculated the political benefits. But honestly, I had no idea. I saw no political connection at all. The idea of going to Utah as a way of helping me run in Massachusetts was nuts. If I wanted to run, I would have stayed in Massachusetts. And I had no appetite for staying in Utah for a political career."

There's plenty of evidence to counter Romney's claim that he gave no thought to the political ramifications.

Rick Reed, who had advised Romney during his Senate run, wrote a letter urging him to take the Olympic post specifically because it would be a great launching pad for another political bid. Romney told Reed that his advice was crucial in making his decision.

Garff, who first raised Romney's name with Leavitt, said it was understood that Romney had aspirations.

"It was serendipitous," Garff said. "Mitt wanted to leapfrog from the world of business to public service, and this was a perfect opportunity for him to propel himself into the national spotlight, which I believe was all part of his overarching plan of his life."

And just two days after he became SLOC's president, Romney actively hinted at another run in Massachusetts, while refusing to rule out a campaign in Utah. He even spelled out his positions on abortion and gay marriage, the two major sticking points in his Senate run and issues that would dog him well into the future.

"It's hard to say what is going to happen three years down the road," he said. "But the reason we are keeping our house in Belmont is that we intend to go back and make that our home again. And there may well be a political future there."

Leavitt waited about a month before he tried again with Huntsman Jr. and got closer to smoothing things over with the scion of one of Utah's most influential families. The governor asked Huntsman if he would like to become chairman of Envision Utah, a public-private partnership that tries to guide long-term development in the state. Huntsman accepted the volunteer post, working to limit urban sprawl and enhance transit development.

"You can't look out over the valley and not appreciate the importance of growth," Huntsman said. He was referring not just to the increasing population in the densely urban Salt Lake Valley, but also to planned construction, much of it Olympic related. On the massive to-do list were a rebuilt 10-lane freeway, a light-rail line, a massive five-star hotel and hundreds of smaller projects to spruce up streets and expand access to mountain resorts.

"This is one of the greatest exercises in democracy I've ever seen," Huntsman said. "No one can claim this is centralized planning or Big Brother stepping in."

This position allowed Huntsman to build more ties in the state, but he never used it to interject himself into the planning of the Games. He instead signed on to help Texas Gov. George W. Bush's presidential campaign in the state, while his father supported Elizabeth Dole, his friend from the Nixon administration.

Huntsman Jr. dabbled in presidential fundraising and worked for his father's company. He also gave new thought to a long-harbored desire of Mary Kaye's: adopting a child. She specifically wanted a girl from China, an idea hatched while visiting that Taiwanese orphanage 12 years earlier.

They even came up with a name — Gracie Mei Huntsman. Mei means beautiful in Chinese.

But many arduous months passed before the couple received a life-altering call from the adoption agency. A little girl, only a few months old, was found abandoned in a vegetable market in Yangzhou.

Jon and Mary Kaye flew to China shortly before Christmas to get their new daughter and encountered a scene far more difficult than Mary Kaye had experienced in St. Anne's back in Taiwan. There were 150 girls reaching out, hoping to be picked up.

"It was heartbreaking," Mary Kaye said.

When they landed back in Salt Lake City, they found another group with arms extended — the Huntsman children. They all wanted to hold their new baby sister.

A few months later, some Utah Republicans, led by state Sen. Al Mansell, tried to prod Huntsman to run for Congress against sitting Republican Rep. Merrill Cook, whom the party establishment wanted gone.

Huntsman weighed the offer, but ended up passing, hoping to instead land a spot with team Bush. He was among those considered to become the new president's ambassador to China, and he had the support of eventual Secretary of State Colin Powell. But he never really had a chance.

In February 2000, Huntsman gave $2,000 to Bush's toughest rival, Sen. John McCain, in part because Huntsman loved the Arizona senator's call for tougher campaign-finance laws. Huntsman previously had given to Bush, but the latest donation was a slight that wouldn't be forgotten.

Karl Rove, Bush's political mastermind, summoned Huntsman to the White House for a terse conversation in which he grilled his visitor about the donation to McCain and questioned why the new president would give such a prestigious spot to someone who wasn't loyal.

"It was a quick and unhappy encounter," Huntsman said. "I went my way and I left him to do his political work."

Bush wound up appointing Clark T. Randt Jr., an expert in China and one of the president's fraternity brothers. The new administration put Huntsman on timeout, but he wasn't sidelined for long.

Presidential advisers asked if Huntsman wanted to be ambassador to Indonesia during a period when Jakarta was experiencing a spike in terrorism. He declined. How about deputy trade ambassador? Huntsman said yes to a job where he would work for his old friend Robert Zoellick and negotiate trade pacts with Asia and Africa.

Huntsman received the presidential appointment on his 41st birthday. He resigned from Envision Utah shortly thereafter. The Senate unanimously confirmed Huntsman on the first Friday in August, and with that, his family, including Gracie Mei, headed back to Washington and far away from the glaring spotlight of the 2002 Winter Games.

Ann Romney was in Utah for the new SLOC leader's big first day on the job, playing the role of the supportive, happy spouse. But she was in pain. For those first few weeks, she stayed close to their Park City mansion on Rising Star Lane, battling a flare-up of her multiple sclerosis that sapped her emotionally and physically.

"I was in my worst state when we first came here for the Olympics," she said after the Games. "It was really rough. It was a very hard adjustment for me. I was very sick and I didn't know anyone."

She found a retired reflexology expert in nearby Heber City who agreed to take her on as a patient, and she slowly put her life back together with the help of her husband, some new friends and her favorite horses.

"There have been studies shown that people who have MS for some reason respond well to riding horses, and they're not sure quite why that is," said Romney's son Tagg. "The big factor for her was being able to put her heart and soul in something and to connect with them. ... So much of that helped pull her out of the depression that she was in, just having the disease."

Ann would say she came to Utah in "a deep, dark hole" and that she had to learn to crawl out inch by inch. But she did learn.

"MS has been my best teacher," she said, "even though it's been an unwelcome teacher."

While Ann crawled out of her pain, Mitt dug into the Olympic budget he inherited with the intent of taking it apart and rebuilding it.

"He loves emergencies and catastrophes," Ann said. "He would never have considered doing it if it wasn't a big mess."

It was.

There were three years until the Olympic flame would reach Salt Lake City, and Romney knew that left no time to spare. The Games had a $1.45

billion budget but only about $1 billion in identified revenue. Organizers hadn't locked up a new sponsor in months, and because of the scandal, some previously pledged ones were thinking of pulling out. A security plan was barely in its infancy. Meanwhile, six active investigations were slogging into the bribery allegations, and the media blitzkrieg had left the staff and the community dumbstruck.

"We were in a psychological zombie-land; the whole community was walking around dazed," Romney said, acknowledging he felt a bit overwhelmed himself.

"The tsunami of financial, banking, legal, government, morale and sponsor problems following the revelations of the bid scandal swamped the organization," he said. "It was the most troubled turnaround I had ever seen."

There's plenty of debate about how dire it really was. The community never wavered in its support of the Games. Frank Joklik had completed a highly detailed plan for every aspect of staging the Olympics, providing a turn-by-turn road map for the Romney team to follow. The mountains were still as close to the city as ever. And the IOC never withheld funding or threatened to cancel the Games or award them to another city.

Every Olympics seems to run into drama, and Romney had 36 months to overcome the obstacles in his path. But those who had worked for years to bring the Games to Utah and who saw the event as a way to market Salt Lake City were panicking when Romney arrived. They looked to him as a savior.

"It was a mess in a public-relations sense," Garff said. "The momentum, everything we had been working for, was skidding."

Romney's first action was to hunt for cost savings. In his first few weeks, he slashed $98 million from the budget, in part by reducing the Olympic signs that were planned to adorn the city. No cut was too small. He wanted to send a message that the Salt Lake City Games wouldn't be extravagant, drawing a sharp contrast to the bid committee's exploits. He stopped holding board meetings in rented hotel ballrooms and put an end to the free catered lunches. Instead, he ordered pizzas and sold slices to board members for $1 apiece. If they wanted a soda, that would be another $1. The move shaved $250,000 from expenses.

He also needed to reassure big Olympic donors that he had righted the ship. Few were as influential as David D'Alessandro. The CEO of John Hancock had committed $50 million to the Winter Olympics but had since called the IOC sponsorships "radioactive" because of the scandal.

Romney wasted no time wooing back D'Alessandro, an old acquaintance who held court on the 59th floor of Boston's Hancock Tower. Moreover, with his blessing, Romney was able to help lock down other corporate sponsorships from companies with far less Olympic history.

The two men also confided in one another.

"If this doesn't work," he told D'Alessandro, "I can come back to private life, but I won't be anything anymore in public life."

D'Alessandro had his own theories on Romney's motivation, and they involved much more than his friend's personal reputation.

"I think he took it because he felt that the Mormons were in trouble," D'Alessandro offered. "He never said that, but I think he saw the scandal as a stain on his religion. But I don't believe he understood what he was getting into."

Romney did understand that the Salt Lake City Olympics were still a punch line, and he decided to change that by making himself the face of the Games and rehabilitating the organization — smiling news conference by smiling news conference.

He embarked on 11 national media tours during his tenure, building relationships with the most influential print and broadcast journalists on the Olympic beat. He ensured reporters were there when he tried Olympic sports such as hockey, curling and bobsled. Two years out, he invited Katie Couric of the "Today" show to Park City to watch him rocket down the bobsled track on a skeleton sled with a small camera strapped to his back.

He asked Jimmy Shea, the eventual gold medalist in the new event, to coach him. In skeleton, athletes zip down the track face first, their heads just inches from the ice. They navigate turns with a subtle tilt of their shoulders or hips. Romney took 18 runs to get good enough to start from the top, where he was assured of going at least 70 mph down the twisty tunnels of ice. The first time he did it, he instinctively dug in his feet and tore a hole through the shoes he borrowed from Shea.

When the "Today" cameras rolled, Romney made a smooth run. He wouldn't place in the real competition, but it impressed Couric. She asked him if he was "completely nuts," and he said, "maybe a little."

Romney tracked public opinion, whether letters from crazy people, most of whom wrote to savage his LDS faith, or more legitimate Olympic skeptics. He tried to curry favor with Stephen Pace, the acerbic and witty head of a group called Utahns for Responsible Public Spending. Romney even asked Pace for one of his "Slalom and Gomorrah" T-shirts.

"His first day in Utah, he called me and started blowing in my ear," Pace said. "It was very clear what he was doing, but it was a very smart gesture after the people before him had treated us very contemptuously."

Romney kept a copy of every edition of The Salt Lake Tribune and the Deseret News, the two dailies in Utah's capital. The stack reached 6 feet high.

"SLOC would have credibility and integrity if I did. SLOC would be seen as being open, responsive and accessible if I was," he said. "But any time someone at SLOC came across as confused, evasive or contradictory, that would be associated with me."

He couldn't do it all himself, so Romney hired Fraser Bullock, his old buddy from Bain Capital, to be the chief operating officer, responsible for drilling down in the organizing committee's budget. Romney also leaned on Utahns. He asked them to contribute an additional $100 million to help close the budget gap. Romney asked his friend Kem Gardner to lead the fundraising effort.

These two enlistments infuriated Jon Huntsman Sr., still seething from the way his son was bypassed. This time he didn't scold Leavitt or take his complaints directly to Romney — he talked to The Salt Lake Tribune.

On Bullock's hiring, Huntsman Sr. said organizers (read Romney) were "caught in a combination of cronyism and broken promises."

"They seem to have a lot of difficulty, when there are plum positions, to give them to somebody other than a friend or colleague," Huntsman said. "And that's not the way you build a business, and it isn't the way you get credibility. We've got a chairman who is active LDS, now we've got a present CEO who is active LDS. They claim they're going out and really scouring the world to find the best person, so Mitt brings in one of his cronies to be the COO. Another broken promise. Because we've got three LDS folks who are all cronies. Cronyism at its peak. They told the world and told Salt Lake that we're going to go out and find the most professional, the best, and to have some diversity — spiritual and ethnic. Diversity in the Olympic Games is what it's all about. These are not the Mormon Games."

He didn't stop there. Huntsman also panned the fundraising drive in the state, and he put the blame squarely on Leavitt.

"The governor has to make his position clear. He can't have it both ways. He's either got to say, 'No, we promised the people we wouldn't come to you with these burdens and these serious challenges,' or 'Yes, I think it's the only way we can escape financial distress.'

"It is wrong for the governor to allow this. It ought to be corrected before people start redirecting their charitable contributions."

Huntsman, insisting his tirade wasn't sour grapes, then unloaded on Romney personally, saying he's "a man of very fine character," but "also a plus and minus."

"He's politically driven. He's probably the best politician next to Bill Clinton. He's very, very slick and fast-talking and a knowledgeable guy. Mitt makes everybody feel better, but at the end of the day, where are we? Where are we in terms of fulfilled promises and commitments and integrity and the support of the public and the involvement of the public?

"I just want to see our community respected and admired by the world. I want to see our people united and happy about our heritage," Huntsman said. "We're quite a divided state and a divided city over the Olympics. It's not a healthy situation. Most people have basically written it off because it's like the Clinton administration. They just want to see the day when this ends and we can be united as a community again."

Utah was the only state in the 1992 presidential election where Clinton came in third, trailing even independent Ross Perot, so the comparison was meant to provoke a fight. But Romney and Leavitt had no stomach to take on this outspoken billionaire in a public mud fight.

"The world needs public-spirited citizens to devote themselves to all kinds of causes," Leavitt said. "Mr. Huntsman is a fine example of this. He is to be congratulated for his generosity. Others find satisfaction and value in devoting their financial resources to other causes. The world needs them all."

Romney gave an even more sugary response, calling Huntsman a hero for his financial contributions to Utah charities.

"Who could possibly measure up to Jon Huntsman's personal standard in that regard? I know of no one who has been more generous to this state," Romney said. "I go by the adage that you don't have to be larger than life to be a hero, just larger than yourself."

He refused, however, to back away from asking Utahns to donate to the Games. And he explained away Fraser Bullock's hiring by saying, "Clearly, when you have a state that is roughly half Mormon, you're going to find some Mormons on our staff."

Less than a week after Huntsman's scathing public rebuke, Leavitt, Romney and Garff drove up to the gleaming Huntsman Corp. headquarters for a private meeting. It lasted 2½ hours and involved dozens of detailed financial reports, with the trio trying to convince Huntsman Sr. that their plan made sense economically. In the end, Huntsman agreed to stop criticizing their efforts as long as Leavitt and Romney wouldn't pressure Utahns to contribute to the Games.

Romney argued that whether bidding for the Olympics was wise or not, Salt Lake City was on the hook and attacking the organizers was hurting an event forever tied to the city and state Huntsman loved.

"I pressed my view that our highest duty now was to stage them with excellence. We owed it to the athletes and to our country," Romney said. "It became clear that we really weren't that far apart. In fact, before it was over, Jon agreed to host a fundraising function for us."

Huntsman called a news conference. This time he said Romney's financial plan was "tangible and doable." He made a plea for unity, while making it clear he didn't intend to donate any money to the Games, though he might give some to the Paralympics.

"Many citizens are not excited and not enthused and, like myself, seriously question these Games. I would say to you, 'We need your help,' " Huntsman said. "There are still many things that can go wrong, but above all else, we need to be unified as a community. Let's go get them and make this thing work."

He apologized to Romney, saying his jabs were based on a previous conversation between the two of them that he "misinterpreted."

"And I made a mistake in judgment. I have nothing but the highest regard for Mitt Romney, an unusual and capable leader, one of the most uniquely qualified people in America today."

Romney accepted Huntsman's apology.

"I am touched by his sentiments with regard to me personally," he said. "As one of the lions of the community, when Jon speaks, people listen."

Romney would continue to cultivate a relationship with Huntsman and, six months later, the industrialist came through with a fundraising dinner gala on the top floor of the Huntsman Cancer Institute in honor of those who donated at least $1 million to SLOC, a list including Kem Gardner and Bain Capital. In a surprise, Romney announced he would personally contribute $1 million to the Games, a move that essentially meant he was paying SLOC for the privilege of organizing the competition. Not to be outdone, Huntsman Sr. announced he too would join their club, but he wanted his $1 million to go to the Paralympics, which follow the Games.

As these mega-donors enjoyed their fancy meal, Romney announced a plan to honor them in a special Olympic Legacy Park. He envisioned a wall naming the biggest donors and a fountain in the shape of SLOC's snowflake logo, nestled between a Starbucks and a Barnes & Noble at the city's newest outdoor mall. The Gateway, which sits west of downtown Salt Lake City, was developed by his dear friend and SLOC fundraiser Kem Gardner.

"We didn't want to do it. We did it as a favor to Mitt," Gardner said about the Olympic park.

The Boyer Co., where Gardner was an executive, fronted $5 million to build the plaza and spraying fountain, which attracts children in the summer like moths to a light. Gardner's company used the plaza to win tax incentives from the city and tapped $1.5 million in federal funding for housing at the mall that he rented to Olympic sponsors.

On top of that, Romney made an end run around the SLOC board to hand the tourist destination to his friend.

Salt Lake City's fiery new mayor, Rocky Anderson, said he thought any Olympic park should be in the heart of downtown, while Ken Bullock, an outspoken SLOC board member (not related to Fraser Bullock), said he was "just astounded" that Romney would publicly announce the project without seeking approval first.

"As nice and philanthropic as The Boyer Co. is, it is not [Romney's] prerogative to go around making unilateral commitments," Bullock said. "If this [park] is supposed to be for the people, it would be nice to have some public input, through the organizing committee and the city's elected leaders. ... I mean, what are the rest of us here for?"

Romney got his way, and the legacy park spotlights the wealthy, including Huntsman Sr. and Romney, who gave to the Games, and the volunteers, though it doesn't include the names of any athletes who competed or the medalists who triumphed. Those names appear elsewhere, outside the football stadium at the University of Utah, which housed the Opening and Closing ceremonies. Romney refused to include the names of Tom Welch and Dave Johnson in any Olympic park, saying it "would send the wrong message to the citizens of the world about the ethical standards of our community."

Romney made great strides toward rebuilding public confidence in the organizing committee and the Winter Olympics, but he never would fully shake the specter of the bribery scandal. The Justice Department made sure of that.

A federal grand jury returned a 15-count indictment against Welch and Johnson in July 2000. The duo refused to accept any plea bargain despite private urgings from Romney and Sen. Orrin Hatch, who tried to persuade them to take a reduced sentence to save the Games from future embarrassment.

"Mitt called and said he thought it would be best for the Olympics and for everyone's benefit," said Sydney Fonnesbeck, a former Salt Lake City Council member and friend of Welch's. "He said they would slap Tom's hands and it would be over."

Fonnesbeck thought Romney's request was out of line, and she refused to bring it up with Welch. Gardner, though, set up a conference call in which Romney made his pitch directly to Welch, a move not appreciated by Welch's attorney.

The pressure didn't work. Welch and Johnson wanted a trial despite the prospect of prison if convicted.

Two other men already had pleaded guilty to tax fraud in connection with the scandal: Alfredo LaMont, a U.S. Olympic Committee employee, who conspired to keep the gift giving secret, and Salt Lake City businessman David Simmons, who hired an IOC member's son and used bid-committee money to pay him.

Welch and Johnson appeared at their arraignment as if they were big shots, not defendants. Johnson joked with reporters, while Welch introduced himself to federal prosecutors. To avoid prison, they needed to convince at least one juror that others knew of the gifts and that they weren't trying to benefit personally from their actions.

SLOC didn't think they broke any laws and neither did George Mitchell, a former Senate majority leader and ambassador hired by the U.S. Olympic Committee to investigate. The Mitchell report stated: "It strains credulity to believe that so many responsible citizens could participate in such a long and highly public campaign to influence IOC members and spend so much money in the process, but that only Messrs. Welch or Johnson were aware of the improprieties surrounding these activities. Rather, it appears that an 'everybody does it' attitude took hold and many good people in Salt Lake City got swept up in what was seen as a good civic effort."

Romney said he was pulling for Welch and Johnson to be cleared, even though he personally blamed Welch for the scandal and tried to stop SLOC from paying their legal fees. Whether planned or not, the drawn-out fight over those fees — which SLOC eventually paid in full — helped delay the trial until the end of 2003, more than a year and a half after the Games. The move saved Romney from the nightmare of a TV split screen with figure skating on one half and Utah's governor on the witness stand on the other.

The Justice Department's case exposed salacious details, including how Welch's personal secretary, Stephanie Pate, unwittingly ignited the scandal that brought down her boss. It did not get close to proving that Welch and Johnson acted alone or lined their own pockets. U.S. District Judge David Sam eviscerated federal prosecutors for putting on a shoddy case and dismissed all charges.

"Several times during the history of this case I have heard counsel for the United States represent themselves as the protectors of our moral values here in the state of Utah and protectors of the sacred standards of the Olympic charter. How commendable and noteworthy. But when considered in light of the government's evidence in this case, how misplaced," Sam said. "The Court has determined that enough is enough and brought this misplaced prosecution to conclusion."

The judge — who happened to be a former LDS missionary companion of Sen. Orrin Hatch — also offered a personal apology to Welch and Johnson.

"How I regret that you were deprived of fully enjoying the fruits of your tireless efforts to bring the Olympics to our great state and to join in the celebration of the Games and all that went on during that time. I can only imagine the heartache, the disappointment, the sorrow that you and your loved ones suffered through this terrible ordeal. My hope is that you will now be appropriately recognized and honored for your efforts."

Welch hasn't received much credit or honor for his efforts, but he did get SLOC to pay him the $1 million in severance he agreed to when he stepped down as CEO. Johnson received $200,000.

"The legal process is not for the weak or the faint of heart," Welch said after Sam dismissed the case. "But the process works. It's painful and costly for those involved, but it works."

Romney argued that it didn't work.

"Of course, not being convicted of a crime isn't vindication of wrongdoing, and not all unethical behavior is criminal," he wrote in his book "Turnaround." "Even when criminal conduct occurs, it may be difficult to prove — and that's with effective prosecutors. I believe those who pursued Welch and Johnson were inept."

Richard Wiedis, the lead prosecutor, believes he lost the case because some witnesses "went south" and supported Welch and Johnson on the witness stand. He found Romney's slap to be ridiculous.

"Mitt Romney, as far as I know, was never in the courtroom, didn't review any of the evidence and never asked the prosecutors for a summary of their case," he said. "I don't see how he was in a position to make a judgment as to the competence of the prosecution team."

SLOC officials planned a big show to unveil the Olympic torchbearers, and they could think of no better place to do it than New York City's Battery Park, where Lady Liberty would stand behind them holding the nation's most famous torch. Their plan was to hold the event on Sept. 11, 2001, but a budget snafu forced Romney to reschedule his travel plans — sending him to Washington.

He was appearing on a Salt Lake City radio show by phone when the reporter cut him off to announce that a plane had crashed into the World Trade Center. Romney hung up. He turned on the TV in the office of Cindy Gillespie, SLOC's lobbyist, and called Ann. They said little to each other as they watched the buildings burn and then fall.

Romney's daze ended when the Pentagon was hit, and Gillespie said that if they didn't leave soon, they may get stuck in downtown Washington. They jumped in her BMW convertible and headed toward Virginia, a path that took them past the Pentagon and through a haze of black smoke from the wreckage.

"It didn't smell like burning jet fuel or a house fire," Romney said. "It smelled like nothing I had ever smelled before. Like war."

Gillespie drove him to a hotel in Alexandria, where Romney tried to process what was happening, the realization that the nation had come under at-

The Games begin • 125

tack, that thousands had been killed and, eventually, what that meant for the Olympics.

"Mitt wondered inwardly whether we could even hold the Games," Ann Romney said. "He wouldn't say it publicly, but that was his nagging fear."

Reporters started calling within a few hours, but Mitt didn't want to make a statement. It didn't feel right talking about the Olympics only hours after the towers collapsed. By that night, he changed his mind, releasing a short statement that in part read: "As a testament to the courage of the human spirit, and as a world symbol of peace, the Olympics is needed even more today than yesterday."

He wrote an email to his staff: "In the annals of Olympism and the history of Utah, this may stand as one of the defining hours. I am confident that we will perform with honor."

Like much of the nation, the SLOC team swam through the emotions of despair and fear, determination and patriotism. When Romney returned, he gathered hundreds of Olympic staffers in an outdoor courtyard and gave an impassioned speech about the ability of the Games to transcend terrorism and display the strength of this wounded country. Attendees called it his most presidential moment. People cried and cheered and sang "God Bless America."

The first order of business: a complete review of the security plan, a joint venture of federal, state and local law enforcement. Officials met to discuss adding new barriers to the athletes' village and the potential of shutting down Salt Lake City International Airport once the Games began. They considered adding more federal agents on skis patrolling the mountains. The governor canceled a public celebration and Salt Lake City considered doing the same. It took time to find the right balance, but in the end the revised plan would require more than $34 million in new federal money.

Utah had done remarkably well securing federal backing in the past. With the help of Sen. Bob Bennett, a member of the Appropriations Committee, the state already had received more than $1 billion for new highways, light rail, housing and security. As Bennett racked up these successes, Sen. John McCain had accused Utah of overreaching, turning the Games into a boondoggle.

"What the Olympic Games, supposedly hosted and funded by Salt Lake City, which began in corruption and bribery, has now turned into is an incredible pork-barrel project for Salt Lake City and its environs," McCain said on the Senate floor on Sept. 19, 2000. "I do not understand how we Republicans call ourselves conservatives and then treat the taxpayers' dollars in this fashion. This is terribly objectionable."

He was talking about the funding that made it through Congress, not the requests that had been rejected. Those items included armored personnel carriers, new sewer systems for cities far from the events, and a hydrofoil to save people if a plane crashed into the Great Salt Lake.

When Romney came on board, he met with McCain to smooth things over and found the Arizona firebrand to be angered more by the IOC's lack of financial support and the requests of some local governments than by SLOC's spending. But McCain remained an obstacle in those pre-Sept. 11 days.

Sen. Ted Kennedy, Romney's one-time Massachusetts rival, turned out to be a big help in getting federal support throughout the process, as was the Democratic administration of President Bill Clinton. And, it turned out, President George W. Bush championed the Salt Lake City Games — even more so after the Sept. 11 attacks.

Less than a month after the terrorist strike, Sen. Orrin Hatch organized a summit in which the White House, Congress, the military and intelligence agencies discussed a new security plan and how to fund it. The day before, Romney again visited McCain's office to see if he would face continued resistance. McCain cut him off before he even asked the question.

"He told me that he believed it was important to America that the Games go on and important to the world that the nations come together in a show of peace," Romney said. "He made it clear there would be no problems from him when we came to Congress for the funding necessary to keep the Games secure."

Romney encountered no roadblocks from anyone. The federal team decided that Utah's airport could remain open, except during the Opening and Closing ceremonies. The security plan bolstered, Romney turned his attention back to the psychological damage of the terrorist attack.

"It's been much more somber since Sept. 11, so I don't know that we will have the same kind of exuberant, celebratory feeling for the Olympics that other cities have enjoyed," he said. "But we are what we are, and the nation is experiencing the mood it's experiencing. In some respects, the Olympics take on a more profound meaning now than they might have in a more giddy time."

Every Olympics begins in Greece.

A Greek actress, dressed as an ancient priestess and surrounded by tunic-draped women, harnesses the sun's rays with a special mirror to ignite the Olympic flame in the sacred Temple of Hera, among the ruins of ancient Olympia.

Nov. 19, 2001, was cloudy, so the actress had to give the sun a little help with a lighter. The priestess then reached out her lighted torch and touched it to the one held by Greek cross-country skier Lefteris Fafalis, decked out in a white uniform. He was the first of more than 11,500 torchbearers who would bring the flame to Salt Lake City by foot, car, train, ship, plane, horse-drawn wagon, snowmobile and dog sled. But first it burned for two weeks in the white marble caldron at Panathenian stadium in Athens, where the Games were revived in 1896.

From there, the flame traveled to Atlanta, the last American city to host an Olympics, and then torchbearers carried it through 46 states, with special stops in the cities attacked on Sept. 11. Each torchbearer held the flame for about five minutes before passing it on to the next, a long, slow journey that brought the fire to Utah on Feb. 4, this time carried by Ute Indians through Delicate Arch, the crown jewel of Arches National Park.

Romney wanted many torchbearers to be everyday people nominated by their families and friends as heroes, and most of them were, but SLOC also let every $1 million donor have a chance to carry the Olympic flame. Jon Huntsman Sr. took his turn on the day of the Opening Ceremony, clutching the torch near Utah's Capitol and carrying it down a hill. He joked that he was a klutz and worried about dropping the sleek metal shaft, but he held firm. The experience burned away any residual resentment. He was downright giddy by the time he passed the flame to the next runner.

"That was so much fun," he said. "The Games are going to be extremely beneficial."

Huntsman had planned to fly to Hawaii and skip the Olympics, but he went to the Opening Ceremony instead. When the Games ended, he sent the Romneys to Hawaii on his corporate jet as a thank you.

Romney previously had announced that no SLOC employee could run the torch, but he did hold an event in which each staffer could get his or her picture taken with it. To stay consistent, he said he wouldn't run the flame, either, even though he had given $1 million. Instead he would pick his hero: Ann.

When she arrived in Salt Lake City in early 1999, she was so weak that Mitt planned to install an elevator in their Deer Valley home. She regained much of her strength with the help of Fritz Blietschau, the retired reflexologist, and Margo Gogan, a close friend and her dressage instructor. Ann would get so involved in the world of dressage, an equestrian sport, that she later would own a horse that competed in the 2012 Olympics in London.

But during the Salt Lake City Games, she had not yet gained the stamina she would display on the presidential trail. Jogging the torch down a tree-lined street was a huge accomplishment, which she achieved with some family help.

"It was an amazing thing," she said, "to have my children helping me to hold my arm up, and my husband was at my elbow, running with me and running the torch into Salt Lake City, as his hero."

"It was a more emotional moment for us than was apparent to others," Romney said. "Among my children and me, there was not a dry eye."

That night, Mike Eruzione and the 1980 "Miracle on Ice" gold-medal-winning U.S. hockey team lit the Olympic caldron as eight athletes carried an American flag salvaged from the World Trade Center into the emotional Opening Ceremony. Romney gave a three-minute speech, honoring the families and coaches who helped the athletes fulfill their potential and saying: "You skate, you ski and our hearts quicken with your dream. We find ourselves hoping for you, praying for you."

With that, the 2002 Winter Olympic Games began. They lasted 17 glorious days and went off largely as planned: no major security disasters; happy crowds greeted by friendly Utah volunteers; and just about every seat at every event filled.

The Olympics gave Utahns a shot of pride that hasn't dissipated to this day. As a testament to how well the Games went, the only major scandals involved some questionable judging in figure skating and a kerfuffle over whether Romney uttered the f-word during a traffic snarl.

During the Games, Romney bounced from one venue to another, accompanied by his 22-year-old Olympic assistant Spencer Zwick, who later would become a key cog in his presidential campaigns. The trips weren't to watch the world-class athletes as much as to thank the staff and volunteers. Traffic came to a frustrating standstill on one trip up to the ski slopes of Snowbasin, about 35 miles north of Salt Lake City, and it didn't move for a good 30 minutes. Romney, Zwick and his driver took to the road's shoulder to find out what the holdup was. They found Shaun Knopp, an 18-year old volunteer traffic officer from Colorado, who stopped a bus because it didn't have the right color placard, even though all aboard had shown him their official credentials.

Knopp wouldn't let the bus go, and the road was too narrow for it to turn around. Romney started screaming at the volunteer, who eventually got traffic moving.

"I expressed my frustration, including a jab or two of un-Mormon-like language," Romney said.

"Who the f--- are you and what the f--- are you doing," Romney supposedly said. "We got the Olympics going on, and we don't need this s--- going on."

Romney vigorously denied saying it, telling reporters: "I have not used that word since college, all right? Or since high school."

Weber County Sheriff's Capt. Terry Shaw, who oversaw security in that area, backed Knopp and demanded that Romney apologize. He did, but many in the law-enforcement community viewed it as halfhearted.

"There were a lot of people in public safety who were extremely angry," said Peter Dawson, an intern in the Olympic communications center. "The general consensus was 'I hope he doesn't need any help from us, because we aren't going to respond very quickly.' "

The 2002 Games, once besieged by an international bribery scandal, now weathered a brief flurry of stories about whether Romney used a curse word when scolding a volunteer police officer. He could accept that. Especially as the world heaped praise on the Games and the money rolled in. SLOC reaped a $100 million profit, enough to set up a fund to help support Utah's Olympic venues for decades to come.

Throughout his Olympic tenure, Romney dealt with speculation about his political future. Utahns, like his buddy Kem Gardner, tried to get him to plant his flag in Utah, while Massachusetts Republicans made sure he knew he was needed back home.

President Bush nominated Massachusetts Gov. Paul Cellucci to be the ambassador to Canada in 2001. In his place stepped Lt. Gov. Jane Swift, the first woman to serve as the Bay State's governor. Swift gained national attention when she had twins while in office, but it wasn't long before she became politically wounded in scandals involving her use of the state helicopter and an inaccurate marriage license. GOP leaders asked Romney, weeks before the Games began, to consider a run, saying he might be the only one who could keep the seat in Republican hands.

Politically cleansed by the Olympic flame, Romney couldn't resist. His return to the campaign trail launched a debate about how much credit he deserved for the success of the 2002 Games, a back-and-forth that persisted throughout his political career.

Romney joined SLOC at its lowest moment and then dropped expectations even further. He heaped criticism on Tom Welch and Dave Johnson and made sure everyone knew he had to fill a $379 million budget gap. He cut environmental and youth programs. He trimmed the budgets of flashy events like the Opening Ceremony, only to restore their funding when it was clear he'd have the cash. By doing so, he made the Games' success feel even bigger than it turned out to be, and his advisers pushed a narrative that he saved the Olympics from the brink of bankruptcy. He touted himself as a turnaround artist.

He had many supporters, among them Dick Ebersol, NBC's point person on the Olympics.

"I have no doubt whatsoever, as the representative of the chief investor in the Salt Lake City Olympics, that Mitt Romney was single-handedly responsible for those Games being the immense success they were," he said. "The list of people who could have pulled it off began and ended with Mitt Romney."

Mark Lewis, SLOC's marketing director, put Romney's contribution in sports terms.

"I'm not saying other people didn't play a role," he said. "When you say Tom Brady leads the [New England] Patriots to victory, that doesn't mean you're not complimenting the linemen, but there's only one Tom Brady. Mitt was Tom Brady. Without him, this wouldn't have gotten done."

But even some of Romney's biggest boosters would argue that the Olympics never were in as grave a state as some suggested, and that includes SLOC Chairman Robert Garff, who had urged Leavitt to hire Romney.

"I never thought there was a time when the Salt Lake Organizing Committee was in danger of failing in its duties," Garff said.

The scandal hobbled the organization, but it forced the IOC and the U.S. Olympic Committee to revamp their practices and to see that the Games were a success. After the Sept. 11 attacks, safeguarding the Olympics was on the U.S. government tab. And, in Utah, having the support of the LDS Church meant having an army of eager volunteers, including returned Mormon missionaries fluent in dozens of languages.

"Any well-trained chimpanzee could have come in and had a successful Olympics," said Doug Foxley, a Salt Lake City lobbyist who later would back Jon Huntsman Jr. for president.

Ken Bullock, executive director of the Utah League of Cities and Towns, and the man who poked and prodded all of SLOC's leaders, has been unrelenting in his criticism of Romney. He notes that Romney is the first organizing-committee president to OK a set of Olympic pins about himself, including one that says "Hey, Mitt, We Love You!" and another of a baseball glove that says "Mitt Happens."

"What's offensive to me is he made it about him and not our community and not our state. People should remember the Games, not the individual," Bullock said. "He was part of the success of the Games. It's not to say that he should not be recognized for a significant contribution, but I don't believe for a second that he could have done what Tom Welch did. Tom had the passion and the vision and the commitment to travel around the world to go get the Games."

Welch, who moved to California, had this to say about the man who received the Olympic credit that he felt was robbed from him:

"Mitt's objective was to look as good as he could, to wear the white hat," he said. "He viewed everything in terms of how he could promote himself and his legacy, even at the expense of others. He showed a mean side, as well as a competent side."

Leavitt, who forged a lasting friendship with Romney, was asked whether the Games would have been worse off if he had hired someone else.

"It's tough to prove a negative," he said. "But I think if you search Olympic history, you'll have a hard time finding a better-executed Games."

chapter six

Capitol gains

No terrorist attacks. No ticketing snafus. Sure, the figure-skating judges added a hint of scandal, but that only heightened international interest. The Winter Olympics came to a fantastic fireworks-laden conclusion and goodwill overflowed. Utah and its residents burst with pride, the nation experienced some post-9/11 catharsis and the athletes from the good ol' USA claimed 34 medals, topping all nations but Germany. The biggest winner of all, though, would turn out to be Mitt Romney.

Even before the Games ended, Republican bigwigs in two states tussled over the right to crown him governor or senator. The hopeful dismantled by Sen. Ted Kennedy in 1994 relished his revived political standing and, from time to time, would throw out tidbits to keep his fans salivating.

"I have to be honest. I will survey the political landscape in Massachusetts and in Utah," Romney said in mid-2001, adding that he wouldn't waffle for long. "It smacks of opportunism to move from race to race, place to place, party to party."

There's little evidence Romney ever really considered running in Utah, and for good reason. Massachusetts, his home for three decades, is more populous and politically vibrant. It's the state of John Adams and John F. Kennedy.

Utah? It's the state known for Mormons and, now, the Olympics. Making an easy political decision even simpler were the missteps of Massachusetts Gov. Jane Swift.

Fined $1,250 for using state employees as babysitters and accused of taking personal trips on the state helicopter, Swift suffered repeated, sustained blows to her reputation. Even before these eyebrow-raisers came to light, Swift wasn't well-loved or feared. She wasn't a made-for-TV campaigner or a world-class fundraiser. Few Republicans came to her defense during the pummeling. Her political standing suffered so badly from missteps involving everything from highway tolls to the severance package of her chief of staff that her party actively sought to replace her.

Barbara Anderson, a well-connected anti-tax crusader in Massachusetts, called Romney, leaving him this message: "I know you're really busy now with the Olympics, but when you're finished, please come back and save Massachusetts."

The state's Republican chairwoman, Kerry Healey, even took a secret trip to Salt Lake City to urge Romney to challenge Swift. Romney demurred. He previously had vowed not to run against Swift, but that was before the draft-Romney campaign began.

Ann Romney said her husband had been "getting a lot of pressure to come back [to Massachusetts] and run for governor. I mean, really, a lot of pressure."

He did what any data-devoted politician would do: He commissioned a poll. Romney wasn't so worried about winning his party's nomination; he wanted to see if he could beat a Democrat in such a liberal state. His poll said he could do so with unexpected ease. Quietly, since he was still running the Olympics, Romney started building a campaign team and developing a strategy. He informed Bain Capital he wouldn't be returning.

The Paralympic Games, which Romney also led, wrapped up March 16, 2002. The next day he flew to Boston, where a pack of reporters waited for him at the airport. A new Boston Herald poll showed Romney with an astounding 75 percent to 12 percent lead over Swift for the Republican nod.

Romney deflected reporters' questions, saying he was happy to be home. And, yet, his intentions were clear, even if he never actually told Swift that he'd challenge her. His advisers rented a big hotel ballroom to make an announcement. They didn't end up using that space. That's because, two days after the Romneys returned to the commonwealth, Swift held a tearful news conference to say she would not seek her own term as governor, a job she held for a little less than a year.

Swift said she couldn't run a campaign, be governor and take care of her three young children the way she wanted, a decision she reached after a "candid discussion" with her husband and advisers. She didn't end her statement with the old political saw that she wanted to spend more time with family. She instead addressed her liabilities.

"It's obvious to anyone what the challenges were that were ahead of me politically. You all can do the math. You can do the cold political analysis," said Swift, then the nation's youngest governor at 37. She said she would support Romney, though there were plenty of hard feelings behind the scenes. "I believe that this is in the best interest of our state, as it will allow the Republican Party's best chance of holding the governor's office in November."

In reaction, Romney walked out of his Belmont home to meet the reporters camped in his driveway. With Ann nearby, he talked about his business experience and how it would help Massachusetts before he finally cut to the chase.

"Lest there be any doubt, I'm in," he said. "The bumper stickers have been printed. The website is going up tomorrow morning. The campaign papers are filed today."

This wasn't the same Romney who got trampled by Kennedy eight years earlier. He emerged more confident, nimble and aggressive, ready for the combat of modern-day politics. The Romney team almost immediately produced ads defending the candidate against anticipated charges he was a heartless corporate raider.

"I learned in my race against Sen. Kennedy, don't be so naive as to just sit back and say, 'Oh, I'm going to be positive while they're negative,' " Romney said. "That doesn't make sense."

He tapped Kerry Healey, the GOP chairwoman who had secretly recruited him, to run as lieutenant governor and had his son Tagg oversee her end of the campaign.

Romney also wasn't going to let money be an obstacle. At the same time he built a formidable fundraising machine, he repeatedly dipped into his own pocket for bursts of cash. By the end of the contest, he had kicked in $6.3 million to the effort.

In the early days of his campaign, much of the activity focused on his recent Olympic success. He hired close aides from SLOC, such as Spencer Zwick, his personal assistant, who would become his chief fundraiser. Just two months into the race, Romney returned to Utah for two fundraisers: the first hosted by former nemesis Jon Huntsman Sr. at Huntsman Corp. headquarters and the second by Gov. Mike Leavitt. That summer, when articles in the Boston press suggested Romney overstated his Olympic record, Romney's team asked Salt Lake City Mayor Rocky Anderson to cut a TV ad. Anderson, a liberal former Democrat who in 2012 ran for president on a third-party ticket, stood before a portrait of JFK to tout Romney's fiscal responsibility and management skills.

In his standard six-minute stump speech, Romney mentioned the Games eight times, though he also threw in folksy lines about how much better Massachusetts was than Utah, a place he referred to as "back there."

"I have to tell you, I'm really more comfortable at home here in Massachusetts ... than even back there with the Olympics," he said to adoring Republican delegates gathered in the Boston suburbs of Newton and Lynnfield. "You come back to Massachusetts and say, 'You know, we have things going for us here that the rest of the country would die for.' "

Romney had a mojo envied by the rest of the field. Reporters labeled him a juggernaut, and People magazine named him one of the 50 Most Beautiful People, gushing that his "too-perfect Ken doll" looks could be a liability. Old buddy Tom McCaffrey told the magazine that while Romney's "family looks like a Gap ad, which makes us all a bit cynical," he's a man of "immense credibility and character — which shows in his face."

"Nothing embarrasses Mitt more than when someone says he's good-looking," said Cindy Gillespie, SLOC's lobbyist.

The fawning lasted for weeks, and Romney had cleared the GOP field, but he had five Democratic candidates to contend with, including former U.S. Labor Secretary Robert Reich. These Democrats started picking at Romney, and what better place to start than with a comment that would make the man blush.

In his big kickoff event, a reporter asked Reich what he feared about Romney. The 4-foot-11 candidate's deadpan response: "His looks."

That wasn't Reich's only zinger; he downplayed Romney's résumé by saying: "The Olympic-size challenge that we face in this state is more than a matter of organization and efficiency."

State Treasurer Shannon O'Brien, a leading Democratic candidate, took the same tack, saying: "I respect what he's done at the Olympics ... but we can't afford to bring in someone who is a novice at state government."

The Democratic candidates prodded Romney over whether he used the "f-word" in castigating an Olympic volunteer, and they pounced all over a letter he sent to The Salt Lake Tribune after an article appeared about his political opportunities.

"I do not wish to be labeled pro-choice," Romney wrote in that July 2001 letter to the editor.

That came as a surprise, since his spokesman Charles Manning told The Boston Globe during Romney's Senate run: "Mitt has always been consistent in his pro-choice position."

Romney's Utah buddy Kem Gardner brushed aside the flip-flop, arguing that Romney was "waffling" to appease Massachusetts voters. "That upset him to be characterized as pro-choice," Gardner said after Romney's letter appeared in The Tribune. "He has told me he is not pro-choice."

Romney said he favored adoption and personally opposed abortion, but would protect women's legal right to choose. His finessed answer didn't satisfy his opponents or even some of his supposed supporters. Swift, the outgoing governor, told the Boston Herald that Romney needed to clear up the "confusion" over his stand. The Boston Globe ran an editorial that questioned whether Romney's position depended on his audience, asking: "Does a change in venue bring a change of position?"

As the campaign continued, Romney tried to clarify his stance. In one TV interview, when asked if he would "preserve and protect" a woman's right to an abortion, he said: "I make an unequivocal answer: yes."

He wrote: "The truth is, no candidate in the governor's race in either party would deny women abortion rights. So let's end an argument that does not exist and stop the cynical, divisive attacks made only for political gain."

The abortion question flared repeatedly during the race, but didn't overwhelm it. Neither did the other big social issue of the time: civil unions for gay couples. Vermont had OK'd them in 2000, and in reaction Ann Romney and her son Tagg signed a petition calling for a constitutional amendment to ban gay marriages and civil unions in Massachusetts. Mitt didn't back a constitutional amendment, and it appeared he didn't support civil unions, either. But, as with abortion, his position ended up somewhere in the middle. He tried to court the gay vote by supporting a list of domestic-partner benefits, including health care and inheritance. "All citizens deserve equal rights, regardless of their sexual preference," his campaign site said. His team handed out fliers at the gay-pride parade on pink paper that read "Mitt and Kerry Wish You a Great Pride Weekend!" He tied gay rights to his father's support of civil rights in the 1960s.

"At a very young age, my parents taught me important lessons about tolerance and respect," he said. "I have carried these lessons with me throughout my life and will bring them with me if I am fortunate enough to be elected governor."

Romney's opponents worked to capitalize on his confusing stances on social issues, but they knew they would need something bigger to derail his candidacy.

Democrats feared Romney. He had the charisma, looks, riches, reputation and name ID to keep the "corner office" in Republican hands. And the polls showed him with a big lead. That may explain why Democrats threw a Hail Mary in the first quarter of this game, a full four months before the party even picked its nominee.

In early June, three activists argued Romney's name shouldn't appear on the ballot because, under Massachusetts law, candidates must be an "inhabitant" of the state for seven years before seeking office. And Romney, they argued, didn't meet that standard in part because he had filed his income taxes as a part-time resident one year and as a Utah resident for two years, and Utah tax assessors listed Romney's Deer Valley mansion as his primary residence.

That contradicted Romney's claims that he always had paid taxes as a Bay State resident. After the challenge reached the State Ballot Law Commission, Romney acknowledged that, in April, shortly after announcing his run for governor, he filed amended returns for 1999 and 2000.

Stung, Romney swatted at the challenge as if it were a pesky bee.

"Any effort to try to remove me by hook and crook and trick and legal machinations is going to end up failing," he declared.

Almost instantaneously, a Utah tax assessor apologized and said the whole dispute amounted to an error made by an overzealous employee in her office. Barbara Kresser, the Summit County assessor, said after reviewing the files, a staffer made the command decision to switch the status of Romney's $3.8 million log-and-rock mansion from a vacation home to a primary residence.

"He never asked for it," she said. But Romney did benefit from the assessment, and he didn't correct it.

In Utah, vacation homes are taxed at a higher rate than primary homes, and Romney saved $54,600 because of the switch. There's no question that during the Olympic years, Romney lived primarily in his Deer Valley home, which sat on nearly 11 acres and boasted stunning views all around, mountains on one side, a popular fishing reservoir on the other. The issue centered on whether he gave up residency in Massachusetts.

The Democrats' lawyer, Joseph Steinfield, pointed to an April 2000 story in the Deseret News in which reporter Lisa Riley Roche wrote that Romney had declared his Utah home his primary residence for tax purposes. Steinfield wanted Roche to appear at the hearing, and the Ballot Law Commission issued a subpoena. The Deseret News fought the request, and the two sides reached a compromise. Roche agreed to sign a sworn statement that Romney said his primary residence was in Utah and that he never had asked for a correction after the article appeared. She signed the statement the same week Romney appeared as a witness before the commission, a session that dragged on for two days. Asked about Roche's story, Romney said he didn't recall what he'd told her.

"I don't know," he said, "because I've met with that reporter at least 100 times over the past three years."

He also seemed to undercut the idea that an assessor made an error.

"It would not surprise me that I would claim Utah as my primary residence for tax purposes, because that's exactly what I have done," Romney said in his testimony, where he also repeated his willingness to send a $54,600 check to Utah. "I'd be happy to pay it if I owe it."

Under questioning by Steinfield, Romney gave other responses that Democrats felt bolstered their case that he failed to meet Massachusetts residency requirements to run for governor. He had obtained a Utah driver license, opened bank accounts and had tax bills for other homes sent to his Deer Valley address. He voted in Massachusetts only during the presidential primary and general election in 2000, missing several local elections.

Romney's attorney John Montgomery seized on that point. His client voted in Massachusetts' GOP primary, favoring George W. Bush over John McCain. Romney never had voted in Utah. He also left his birth certificate, photo albums and prized family possessions in his Belmont home.

During the week of the hearing, his campaign launched TV ads showing Romney strolling through his Belmont neighborhood as he says: "I've lived, voted, raised a family and paid taxes for 30 years," then he calls the commission hearing "ridiculous, dirty politics" by Democrats who "are suing to push me off the ballot because I spent three years in Utah working on the Olympics."

Romney told reporters that Democrats' claims were "a lot of sound and fury signifying nothing. I guess if you don't have the facts on your side, you bore everyone to death."

The commission apparently agreed, issuing a unanimous ruling in Romney's favor. Members saw the Olympics as a short-term assignment and found Romney's testimony "credible in all respects."

While four Democrats sparred in a competitive, expensive primary, Romney picked up trash, cooked sausages and stacked bales of hay — all for the benefit of TV cameras. To shake off perceptions that he was an elite executive far removed from the challenges of everyday folk, Romney hosted "workday" events in which he did regular jobs of regular people. He spent a day at Fenway Park, dishing out sausages to Red Sox fans. He volunteered in an emergency room and on an asphalt-paving crew. He helped feed the elderly at a nursing home and spent a day as a child-care assistant, which he later declared was the hardest job he tried.

Romney even stood on the back of a garbage truck as it made its way through a Boston neighborhood.

"I wasn't a particularly good garbage collector. At one point, after filling the trough at the back of the truck, I pulled the wrong hydraulic lever. Instead of pushing the load into the truck, I dumped it onto the street," Romney wrote. "Maybe the suits didn't notice me, but the guys at the construction site sure did: 'Nice job, Mitt,' they called. 'Why don't you find an easier job?' And then they good-naturedly came down and helped me pick up my mess."

Construction workers weren't the only ones who gave Romney grief over the publicity stunts.

Shannon O'Brien, the state's first female treasurer, emerged as the winner of the Democratic primary. "Massachusetts doesn't need a governor who thinks getting in touch with working people is a costume party," she said in her acceptance speech in mid-September.

That about summed up O'Brien's campaign strategy. She wanted to hit Romney hard and often. A Yale-educated former state lawmaker, O'Brien comes from one of Massachusetts' most famous political families, and she knew what it took to win in November.

She spent $4.5 million to win the Democratic nomination, a slog that left her campaign cash-poor. To make up ground quickly, she pounded Romney, challenging his trustworthiness and reigniting the abortion debate, though she had her own vulnerabilities on the issue. As a state lawmaker in the 1980s, she had opposed abortion except in cases of rape, incest or to protect the mother's health, then changed her mind and became an outspoken pro-choice supporter.

O'Brien's pummeling may have softened him up, because three weeks into the seven-week general election, Romney's polling had him as a 10 percentage-point underdog. His team didn't attribute the drop to the Democrats. Instead, his advisers thought Romney's own campaign made the candidate look too good to be true. One such example was an ad called "Ann," in which Romney professed his love for his wife. It ended with Romney and his sons, all shirtless in their bathing suits roughhousing on a dock, trying to push one another into the water. The Boston press immediately ridiculed the spot.

Romney's chief strategist, Mike Murphy, said voters were cynical about the candidate, handing O'Brien an opening that she was deftly exploiting. Murphy gave Romney an ultimatum: Change course drastically or fire him. Romney decided to stick with his guy and agreed to launch negative attacks against O'Brien. The most effective one showed a basset hound, assigned guard-dog duties, lazily watching thieves take bags of cash from the state treasury and loading it into a van labeled Enron. The ad referred to a drop in state pension funds tied to the post-Sept. 11 stock-market crash, which happened while O'Brien was treasurer and her husband had a lobbying contract with Enron, a failed energy company that lost billions in investments.

An enraged O'Brien called the spot "as disgraceful as it is inaccurate," and she countered with one that followed the 1994 Kennedy game plan. Her new ad featured a Kansas City steelworker laid off after Bain Capital purchased a plant. O'Brien's ad didn't work.

"It was the Ted Kennedy punch, but it was gone," said Michael Travaglini, deputy treasurer under O'Brien. "The Olympics had made Mitt a real celebrity. That carried significant weight, and it made him more credible."

Romney kept up the pressure by agreeing to more debates. His hope was that O'Brien's constant barrage of criticism would turn off voters. It also provided openings to remind the public that he wasn't part of a cronyism-riddled government.

Those debates tended to revolve around a handful of issues, including abortion and the death penalty. Unlike his multiple-choice position on abortion, Romney had a clear stand on the death penalty — he favored it; O'Brien opposed it. The other big issue was a local one. The $14.6 billion Big Dig highway project had become an embarrassment of mismanagement, busted budgets and missed deadlines. Both candidates said they were the ones who could put the project and state finances back on firm footing. Romney returned to his save-the-Olympics strategy. He vowed a $1 billion spending cut as a step toward eliminating the red ink and promised to use his ties to seek more help from Congress.

"We need to do a better job getting money from Washington," he said in a televised speech. "I was successful in doing that in organizing the Olympics, got record funds from the federal government. I'll do that here."

Religion never became an issue in the 2002 Massachusetts governor's race — an anomaly in Romney's political career. But O'Brien did poke Romney on his wealth, demanding he release his income-tax returns, as she had. He refused, just as he would a decade later during his presidential pursuit.

The race tightened and in the last debate, both sides made unforced errors. O'Brien endorsed a plan to allow girls as young as 16 to get an abortion without talking to their parents, a position unpopular with voters. Romney twice called O'Brien's constant jabs at him "unbecoming," a phrase she argued was sexist. The Boston Globe and Boston Herald ran front-page stories about his use of the word. Romney tried to salvage the comment in an interview with The New York Times, saying "unbecoming" could refer to people of either gender. He almost immediately called the reporter back to try a different tack.

"The most familiar usage of that term is 'conduct unbecoming an officer,' which is a military term and in that context it is overwhelmingly male," Romney explained.

Despite the misstep, the polls were encouraging. Romney's 10-point disadvantage disappeared and a Globe poll released four days before the election had the race within the margin of error, with O'Brien at 41 percent and Romney at 40 percent. As the Election Day results streamed in, the tide shifted to Romney, and he claimed a 5-point victory, buoyed by big support in the suburbs around Boston, a bastion of independent voters.

"We took on an entrenched machine and we won," Romney declared in his victory speech at the Boston Park Plaza Hotel. "Tonight we sent a loud and clear message. That message is that it's time for a new era."

The triumph washed away the residue of his 1994 defeat and allowed him to follow in his father's path. The Romneys both ran as moderates, and both were elected governor at age 55.

Willard Mitt Romney became the Bay State's 70th chief executive on Jan. 2, 2003. The Boston Globe dubbed him the CEO governor, an apt nickname. In his inaugural address, Romney said behemoth organizations from the military to corporations to governments had to become more nimble to survive. He promised to reinvent Massachusetts government even as he tackled what he saw as a fiscal disaster, with the state spending more than it was taking in.

"We are facing a financial emergency. There is no easy way out of this mess. We must take immediate action," a stern Romney said from his new Beacon Hill perch, surrounded by portraits of some of the nation's most iconic patriots. "I'll face our fiscal crisis head on."

Romney said only essential programs would get funding in his administration and warned the cuts would hurt. He also promised "to meet the highest standards of ethical conduct" and protect civil rights "regardless of gender, sexual orientation or race." And he hit on one of his regular campaign themes: his vow to take on the state's patronage system in which friends and family of the powerful landed plum jobs.

"The spirit of Massachusetts is the spirit of leadership," he proclaimed as he ended his 17-minute address to a standing ovation from those in attendance, the vast majority of whom were members of the other party. Romney met with those state lawmakers in the ornate Senate Reception Room, where he told them how it was going to be.

"My usual approach," he said, "has been to set the strategic vision for the enterprise and then work with executive vice presidents to implement the strategy."

That style helped him turn Bain into a venture-capital giant and the Olympics into a success. He thought it could revolutionize state government, too. The problem with this strategy is state representatives and senators don't generally see themselves as executive vice presidents whose jobs are implementing the governor's strategic vision.

"Here is a person who is well-intentioned and competent but unclear on the basic concept," said Andrea Nuciforo Jr., a state senator for the western part of the state.

The Democratic Legislature provided a valuable initiation on the workings of state government. In the first budget showdown, Romney scored a victory by avoiding any major tax hike, then used line-item vetoes to erase the spending plan of scores of items he found superfluous. The Senate held a marathon session that lasted until almost midnight in which a supermajority overturned almost every Romney veto. A Senate leader jokingly called for the meeting to end "in the memory of Mitt Romney."

"The Legislature had really killed this notion that he was going to run the place and we were there to execute his wishes," Nuciforo said.

Romney might have realized the limits of his powers, but he got enough of what he wanted to be satisfied. The surviving deal plugged a $650 million deficit, an accomplishment Romney would tout for years. In his retelling, he usually left out a few nagging details, such as that tax collections were higher than projected and he raised $331 million by broadly increasing fees on everything from marriage licenses to home purchases to driver licenses.

Still, Romney staved off the fiscal crisis he warned about and lived up to his reputation as a "turnaround artist." What he didn't do was improve his relationship with the Legislature. Unlike past GOP governors, he spent almost no time hobnobbing with the people he needed to pass his legislative agenda. Paul Cellucci played bocce with lawmakers. William Weld made unannounced visits to their offices. Romney cordoned off an elevator for his private use and stationed a guard so no lawmaker would wander in as he traveled from floor to floor. He never learned the names of the lawmakers who scurried around on the other side of the Statehouse and often called people by the wrong title.

"It was very irritating to lawmakers," said John O'Keefe, whose job was to maintain legislative relations for the new governor. "It was hard to explain."

The truth is Romney isn't a social animal. He didn't hang out with his Bain partners and he didn't let loose in Utah either. He's all business. His social life revolves almost exclusively around his family. Romney was chummier with a small band of legislative Republicans, but even those interactions were rare.

"Mitt Romney is not a schmoozer — that is not him," said Rep. Bradley Jones Jr., the GOP's House minority leader at the time. "That is what people expect, but it was not going to happen."

Romney met weekly with the legislative leaders and expected them to corral the rest of the members, while he held larger press events.

"His theory of government was 'I'm going to the bully pulpit, which is the press, and beat you so you succumb to my position,'" said Salvatore DiMasi, the House speaker who in 2011 was sentenced to an eight-year prison term on corruption charges.

Senate President Robert Travaglini said he never tried to horse-trade with Romney because he didn't see the governor as having any interest in the common currency of politics. Even so, Travaglini did compliment Romney before reporters.

"He forced all of us to bring our A game to the table," Travaglini said. "Say what you will about the man, to some degree he initiated the action and direction on reform."

That included the nomination of judges and state appointees in which Romney sought to ensure greater diversity and selection based on skill and experience rather than political connections. He talked about it on the campaign trail, in his inaugural address and during his first years in office.

"I wanted to change the environment in Massachusetts," he said. "I don't think that government is about doing favors for people. I think it's doing the right thing for the folks we represent."

After barely a month in office, Romney announced a new way to appoint judges, creating a nominating commission meant to strip politics from the system. He also banned potential nominees from giving political contributions and campaigning for the job. It appeared to work. The Republican governor's early appointments were loaded with Democrats and independents. Later, though, he changed course, weakened his own commission and started appointing more Republicans, including some with close political ties to him and other state heavyweights.

"They were trying to change the process," said Howard Kahalas, a lawyer who served on the commission. "Before, they didn't care about politics, and then it became business as usual."

In November 2003, the Commonwealth's Supreme Judicial Court issued a ruling that was anything but business as usual. The court, in a 4-3 decision, gave the state six months to start performing same-sex marriages. Romney denounced the edict as a move by "activist judges" and supported a federal gay-marriage ban, reversing a position he took during his campaign.

He tried to sway the Legislature to ban gay unions, but that went nowhere. So he took what actions he could. He eliminated the Governor's Commission on Gay and Lesbian Youth, a group that mostly fought teen suicide, and he derided the ruling in just about every forum possible, calling his state "San Francisco east." Two years later, he told a South Carolina GOP group that some gay couples "are actually having children born to them."

Romney also took his case to Congress, appearing before a Senate committee and advocating for federal supremacy on the issue of marriage by bringing up, of all things, the past polygamy of Mormons in Utah.

"There was, a long time ago, a state that considered the practice of polygamy [legal] and as I recall the federal government correctly stepped in and said, 'That is not something the state should decide,' " Romney said. "We have a federal view on marriage; this should not be left to an individual state."

Later, in his presidential runs, Romney would argue just the opposite: that marriage should be a decision of the states, free of federal interference. In 2004, he simply was grasping for a way to stop a new practice with which he disagreed. But he made no headway in Washington, just as he was stymied back home.

If he couldn't get the Massachusetts Legislature to move on gay rights or much else, the governor decided to replace the Legislature. In an audacious move, the normally risk-averse Romney recruited 131 Republican candidates to challenge sitting Democrats in 2004. It was the biggest Republican slate in more than 10 years, and Romney threw himself into the campaign. He crisscrossed the state, staging fundraisers and campaign events for his favorite candidates. He helped his party raise $3 million to send mailers, some of which ripped Democrats on hot-button issues such as sex-offender laws and immigration.

Making Republican gains in Massachusetts is hard anytime, but Romney's drive coincided with the 2004 presidential race, and the Democratic nominee that year was none other than Sen. John Kerry from the great state of ... Massachusetts.

§§§

The way Jon Huntsman Jr. tells the story, it wasn't his idea to run for governor of Utah, and it didn't come from his politically influential father, either. His three oldest daughters hatched the plan because they were tired of his constant trips to Asia and Africa as a deputy trade ambassador. So, in 2003, they staged a political intervention.

"My daughters sat me down after 2½ years and said, 'We'd like a dad back,' " Huntsman said. "They were just kind of moving into their high-school years, legitimately wanted to have the family together again, and they were the ones who suggested I consider running for governor of Utah. ... I thought it was a crazy idea."

That simplistic retelling washes Huntsman of any political ambition. It also brushes past the electoral realities in Utah. For starters, there's a reason GOP officials tried again and again to recruit him to run for Congress. On top of that, Gov. Mike Leavitt, who bypassed Huntsman in hiring Mitt Romney to lead the Olympics, had served three terms, and most political insiders didn't expect him to go for an unprecedented fourth.

By late 2002, Huntsman's name was on the not-so-short list of expected

Republican candidates and his boss, U.S. Trade Ambassador Robert Zoellick, urged him to run. Huntsman officially resigned from his federal post March 25, 2003, the day before his 43rd birthday. The first question he faced from reporters: "So, you running for governor?"

"My first and foremost priority is reconnecting with the family and getting back to corporate life," Huntsman responded. "On the political side, I happen to strongly support Mike Leavitt, and I still don't know what he's going to do. I wouldn't want to hazard a guess until such time he's determined what his future is going to be."

Huntsman returned to Utah and rejoined the family company as the CEO of Huntsman Family Holdings Co., which oversaw all of the family business's North American enterprises. He quietly assembled a political apparatus and kept his name in the public as Utah's GOP establishment watched the intricate mating ritual between Leavitt and the Bush administration.

Utah's governor flew in June to D.C., where he met with White House officials to discuss the Environmental Protection Agency, which was in need of a new leader. Huntsman said if Leavitt took the gig, he would run for governor. At the same time, he was having his own back-channel conversations with the White House about becoming the ambassador to India, though the talks never progressed far.

That August, Bush nominated Leavitt as EPA administrator and the floodgates in Utah opened. In the following weeks, Utah's House speaker, the head of the Board of Regents, a former U.S. representative, a state senator and a prominent county commissioner rushed into the race.

Huntsman joined the group Sept. 10, 2003, declaring that it was time to take "a fresh look at things."

"I can't look my kids in the face without worrying about the challenges and opportunities the next generation of Utahns are going to face," he said. "We're beginning fundamentally a new era — a post-Olympics era."

Huntsman's team settled early on that their best strategy would be to sell their man as a well-connected outsider, someone far removed from the Leavitt administration and yet a world-wise player who could turn Utah into a cosmopolitan state.

Behind it all sat Jon Huntsman Sr.

He had pulled strings to get his son into Sigma Chi and into the Reagan White House. He lobbied but failed to get him the Olympic gig. He wasn't about to sit on the sidelines during a race for governor. Huntsman Sr. personally interviewed Jason Chaffetz, a charismatic and eager executive at a prominent beauty-products company who was looking for a chance to break into politics. Chaffetz ended up becoming Huntsman Jr.'s campaign manager and later used the experience to help launch his own political career; he's now a member of Congress. Huntsman Sr. also called in Doug Foxley, one of Utah's most connected lobbyists, and asked him to serve as a senior campaign adviser, the "adult in the room" who could help when things got tense.

For those involved in the campaign, it became clear that Huntsman, like Romney, was largely a loner. He preferred spending his time with family than a network of friends and associates. Unlike Romney, who hired aides from Bain and SLOC, Huntsman didn't have a team of trusted advisers to bring into the effort. The insular Huntsman campaign nestled into a dormant area of the gleaming Huntsman Corp. headquarters, where aides developed a strategy that correlated closely with the aborted gubernatorial campaign his father had planned some 16 years earlier.

Huntsman would sell Utah to businesses seeking to relocate from tax-heavy states such as California and would seek to cut spending in a "top to bottom" review of government. His first and last priority would be job growth.

The staff and the vision may have hewed close to that of his father, but Huntsman's style was far more zen than Huntsman Sr. could ever muster. He didn't worry about the rough and tumble of politics.

"Nothing ventured, nothing gained," he said. "The worst that can happen is we lose."

Huntsman's entry forced the other contenders to swallow hard. They were facing the son of an industrial and philanthropic titan, and a family with deep ties to the Mormon hierarchy. The Huntsman name was gold, and it gave the candidate an instant edge.

"He had 94 percent name ID the day he started," complained candidate Nolan Karras, who led the Board of Regents, which oversees the state's colleges and universities. "I had people say to me, 'I'd like to vote for you, but my mother just got out of the Huntsman Cancer Institute. I've just got to vote for Jon.' "

Huntsman acknowledged the benefits of his name, but he also was sensitive to the drawbacks. He knew when many Utahns saw him, they thought of his father and his father's vast fortune. And while he did funnel $20,000 into his campaign early on, he didn't want people thinking he was trying to buy the office.

"If we can't raise money from individuals," he said, "we ought not to be in the race."

Talk of his family's wealth so irritated Huntsman that he considered making silver spoon pins to hand out as a joke.

"We certainly had a lot more than most other average families, and I plead guilty to that," Huntsman said. "But my upbringing was a lot more normal and grounded in reality than a lot of people would probably think."

He told of living in a basement fourplex in San Diego, where Huntsman Sr. was in the Navy, and of following his father as he delivered eggs for Olson Farms.

"We weren't born into a family business," Huntsman said, "even though the perception sometimes is you've got the silver-spoon syndrome."

Huntsman Sr. became president of Dolco when Jon Jr. was 7. When he made his first big stock deal for $8 million, his oldest boy was 14. Jon Jr. was 22 when his father created Huntsman Chemical and in his 30s when Huntsman Sr. became a billionaire.

Beyond wealth was the issue of influence. Opponents launched a whisper campaign suggesting the father was the puppet master, that every break the son ever received came from his dad's connections. Huntsman didn't want to push aside his father or suggest they weren't close, but he had to assert that he was his own man.

"I bounce ideas and thoughts off him occasionally," Huntsman said. "He never forces his will in any shape or form on this campaign. ... There is no Svengali effect in our relationship."

As a first-time candidate, Huntsman tried to shift the discussion away from his family's prominence and toward his positions on issues. Early on, he vowed to eliminate the sales tax on food as part of a wider tax-reform plan. He promised ethics reform, including a cooling-off period for former state officials who wanted to be lobbyists, more frequent campaign finance reporting and a two-term limit on governors. The issue that attracted the most attention was school choice, tapping public money to help parents send their children to private schools.

"There is a place for a tailored tax tuition-credit approach that is means tested," he said, speaking words the state's right wing yearned to hear. The Legislature repeatedly had debated such tax breaks, but Leavitt always threatened a veto, saying the move would undercut public schools.

Huntsman's tentative embrace of school choice, while also touting that all of his children were in public schools, sought to head off claims from his Republican opponents that he wasn't conservative enough.

He became an instant top-tier candidate, but he didn't scare away anyone from the wide-open race. Actually, more candidates kept crowding in, among them Fred Lampropoulos, the outspoken CEO of Merit Medical, a medical-device company. He was the other wealthy candidate, having already spent more than $1 million on radio and TV ads to boost his name identification. His biggest obstacle was his multiple marriages, which turned off some conservatives in the party.

Next was Karras, the man Huntsman Sr. had asked to be his running mate in his ill-fated 1988 run. Former Gov. Norm Bangerter, the man Hunts-man Sr. challenged back then, introduced Karras to reporters and then Karras immediately criticized Huntsman's plan to remove the sales tax on food as unaffordable.

Huntsman, Lampropoulos and Karras were all seen as candidates tied to Salt Lake County, by far the state's most populous area. To win, a candidate also has to do well in the more conservative Utah County, home to LDS Church-owned Brigham Young University. The first straw poll took place there and favored House Speaker Marty Stevens and Utah County Commis-sioner Gary Herbert. Huntsman was a distant third, followed by Lampropou-los and Karras.

The jockeying for position was in full force when one last heavyweight entered the ring: Gov. Olene Walker, the candidate Huntsman most feared.

Leavitt's resignation made Walker the state's first female governor, and her late decision to run created a race with some similarity to the Romney-Swift showdown in Massachusetts. But the scandal-free Walker wasn't going to be pushed aside as easily as Swift had been, not with an approval rating above 80 percent.

"It is hard to fight against Grandma," said a Huntsman campaign adviser. "She is so nice. She is the first woman governor. She is a sweet lady, and it's hard to drive home a point on economic development when she is smiling and patting you on the back."

Other candidates tried to find tasteful ways to jab at the governor, most of which involved her continued opposition to school choice and her ties to the existing administration. Huntsman stuck to his talking points. He was the future; the rest of the field was the past.

When Walker announced her run in March, Huntsman said she came into the race with the "shackles of incumbency."

"People are looking for something new," he said. "Rightly or wrongly, she is going to get hit with the Leavitt legacy — the good and the bad — and she'll have to defend that."

Her late entry left her hobbled in other, more practical ways. Her oppo-nents had locked up the most experienced political operatives and scooped up huge amounts of cash. They had spent far more time getting their friends and supporters to run as delegates, and, under Utah's nominating system, those delegates were remarkably powerful.

About 3,500 Utah Republicans, elected as delegates in neighborhood meetings in late March, gathered in early May at the party convention to winnow the field from nine candidates to two. In that frenzied six weeks, the candidates and their surrogates traveled the state speaking at GOP dinners and small county conventions, honing their stump speeches and getting to know one another.

Huntsman would appear at some — suave and worldly, articulate and engaging. At others, he'd send his parents, who at times were a little more blunt than the campaign would have liked. Huntsman Sr. would note he flew to rural county conventions in his company jet, the same one he often loaned to the president of the LDS Church. The other candidates would just roll their eyes. At another gathering, Huntsman's mother, Karen, glibly noted that certain people should make their grandchildren a bigger priority than their political careers, a direct shot at Walker.

Huntsman absorbed a few jabs as well. In a debate in southern Utah, Lampropoulos posed a question to the former ambassador. As Lampropoulos recalls, it went something like this: "I'd like Mr. Huntsman to tell us how much employment has Huntsman's worldwide operations actually created in Utah. And while he's at it, please explain to us all how he personally had anything to do with it."

Huntsman Corp. was a big employer in places such as Texas and Ohio, but it had only about 30 employees in Utah at the time, and most of that gleaming Huntsman Corp. building sat empty.

Huntsman deftly ducked and said how proud he was of his family and the business they had built.

After the back-and-forth, Huntsman Sr., who went to every candidate debate, confronted Lampropoulos in a public hallway and a shouting match ensued. Huntsman Sr., his face flushing, called Lampropoulos' swipe "a low blow."

"Jon was upset at that and he told me so," Lampropoulos said, " ... and I didn't like it."

A few days later, Huntsman Sr. called to apologize.

" 'You know, Fred, we have great passion for our family and our children. We sometimes get a little carried away,' " Huntsman Sr. said, according to Lampropoulos. "I accepted the apology and every time I saw him after that it was nothing but cordial and good dialogue."

Gary Herbert was used to being popular, and as the state GOP convention drew near, he found he had all kinds of new friends. The man, with a background in real estate, has an easy manner and an always-handy smile. It's hard to find anyone in Utah politics who has a bad word to say about him. He also had stronger ties in the conservative bastion of Utah County than anyone in the race.

Huntsman saw opportunity there. So did Karras. But Huntsman got to Herbert first, enticing him with the offer of a meaty policy portfolio as lieutenant governor and a true governing partnership. Herbert said he would think it over.

Then, on an April day loaded with political events scattered throughout the state, Herbert accepted a ride on the Karras campaign's twin-engine plane, where the two candidates talked about a potential alliance. The conversation appeared to go well. Herbert was spotted on Karras' plane again the next day.

Herbert played the field deftly, but without deceit. He told Karras that Huntsman was wooing him and he was leaning toward accepting the offer. He finally did just that. About two weeks before the convention, Herbert and Huntsman appeared before a phalanx of TV news cameras to make the announcement.

"This represents a significant shift in the campaign dynamics," Huntsman said. "This team is the Republican Party's best hope for victory in November."

Herbert said he would be the "nuts-and-bolts guy," while Huntsman would handle the big picture. The only policy issue they had a public disagreement on was Huntsman's plan to eliminate the food tax, but the two quickly found an accommodation, with Huntsman promising he wouldn't tamper with the local share of revenue without finding a replacement source of funding.

Lampropoulos' campaign responded by releasing information Herbert had given in a canvass of state delegates. Asked about his first choice at convention, Herbert picked himself, with Karras as his second choice.

But a group of five polls showed few rated Karras so highly. Those delegate surveys placed Huntsman in a narrow lead, followed by Lampropoulos and Walker. Karras was back in the pack of second-tier candidates.

A few days after he missed out on bringing Herbert on board, Karras made a splashy announcement of his own, naming Enid Greene, a former congresswoman, as his running mate. It was a bold, albeit risky choice that drew considerable attention. Greene had a strong following, but she was known for a scandal that cost her her House seat.

Greene's then-husband and chief of staff, Joe Waldholtz, was accused of bouncing checks and of illegally funneling $2 million from Greene's wealthy father into his wife's campaign. He went into hiding as federal investigators searched for him, creating a national soap opera that ended with Greene filing for divorce and holding a five-hour news conference during which she tearfully denied any knowledge of her husband's deceit. Waldholtz ended up serving prison time and Greene left office tarnished. In the intervening seven years, Greene, a former aide to Gov. Norm Bangerter, worked to rebuild her credibility within the party.

"The big risk for me was that I would be put aside because people say, 'You can't win.' So we thought we needed to make a statement, and we're doing that," Karras said. "She brings a huge amount of strength to me — she's from Salt Lake County, a woman, experience in federal issues, worked in the governor's office and has a legal background."

Greene said she emerged from her scandal a wiser person, and Huntsman didn't second-guess her. Instead of raising her past tangles, Huntsman praised Greene, then the Utah Republican Party's vice chairwoman.

"She is very well respected by delegates," he said. "She has had enough opportunity to outgrow any challenges she had before, and I believe the Republican Party has forgiven her."

Karras had a decent political résumé, and adding Greene to the ticket helped with delegates, but it didn't give him an immediate bounce in the polls, all of which continued to predict a three-way race among Huntsman, Lampropoulos and Walker. In the days before the convention, Karras kept up his last-ditch campaigning, sometimes going door to door and, when delegates weren't home, he would take a selfie with a Polaroid to show he was there and leave it as a memento.

"I don't have the advantages of a household name and I don't have a famous father," he said. He also didn't have the cash of the other candidates.

Huntsman raised $870,000, of which nearly $165,000 came from his family or Huntsman Corp. Lampropoulos spent nearly $2.2 million, almost all of it his own money. When asked to justify how much he poured into a Republican convention race, Lampropoulos responded: "It's my money and this is America."

He kept on spending right up to convention eve, where he tried to attract delegates to a catered party that featured a Beatles tribute band. Huntsman held a pork-and-beans barbecue with a country band at Huntsman Corp. Walker drew people to the University of Utah's football stadium for her own dinner featuring a popular local band. Karras, like many of the other candidates, had no free dinner-and-music event.

The delegates, the candidates and their entourages descended on a cavernous concrete convention hall in a suburb of Salt Lake City the next morning. Elaborate booths allowed for last-minute politicking, and then the show began. Each candidate gave a short speech before the delegates voted.

No one could top Huntsman's show. He had former Sen. Jake Garn, an astronaut, signing autographs on a picture of himself next to a space shuttle. And, in a video, he had President George H.W. Bush endorsing his former ambassador to Singapore. Huntsman Sr. had lined up the presidential backing at a Texas chemical convention earlier in the year.

To no one's surprise, Huntsman Jr. emerged from the convention in first place. The shocker was that Karras was just 85 votes behind him. In the instant-runoff system, Walker came in fourth and her supporters largely backed

Karras as the next best choice, propelling him into the GOP primary.

"We knew we were surging," said Karras, his normally sober expression replaced with a big grin. "We didn't know how much."

As Karras soaked in his unexpected second-place finish, Huntsman Sr. approached him, shook his hand and whispered: "Congratulations, I knew I picked the right man 16 years ago."

Walker took her loss in stride, noting how moderate she was compared with the Republican delegates, who criticized her on private-school vouchers and were ready to move on from the Leavitt years.

"There are a lot of extremely conservative people here," she said earlier in the day. "I mean ... extremely."

She refused to endorse either candidate, a position she held throughout the election, and some of the Republican governor's children publicly supported Scott Matheson Jr., the Democratic nominee.

The state's Democrats tried to paint the GOP conventioneers as out of touch with mainstream Utahns, using Walker's ouster as Exhibit A. State Sen. Gene Davis said: "They got rid of a woman who supports education, a woman who supports the bipartisan workings of state government." But that critique failed to recognize that the two other moderate candidates — Huntsman and Karras — were the ones who emerged from the convention.

"It produced two candidates who are traditional, Reagan Republicans," Huntsman said. "To call us right-wing radicals is very inadequate."

After the initial contest, the campaigns hit reset. Karras was thrilled to be in a primary, but he knew he was an underdog. He didn't see Jon Huntsman Jr. as his opponent; he was up against the Huntsman mystique.

"I don't think there's any question I'm running against the family," he said just days after the convention. But turning that strength into a Huntsman liability was delicate. Karras tried to approach it indirectly by saying his campaign was one of "substance over style." His team made an ad noting that Karras had paid off his modest mortgage, while Huntsman had $2.5 million left to pay on his home, though Karras shied from using it. Too edgy.

While the Karras campaign was probing for soft spots, it took a kick in the shorts. City Weekly, Salt Lake City's alternative newspaper, had a story calling Karras a "radioactive" candidate because of his close ties to Khosrow Semnani, a controversial political figure who started a low-level radioactive waste dump in the state. The story included details of a cozy fishing trip to British Columbia enjoyed by Karras and Semnani.

It was true. Karras managed Semnani's investments, and the story came as Semnani's company, Envirocare (since sold and renamed EnergySolutions), was seeking authority to store hotter radioactive waste, something Huntsman had vehemently opposed.

Karras' team feared the City Weekly story and made a move to blunt its impact. Spencer Stokes, a bald, dapper bulldog of an operative, called a Salt Lake Tribune reporter and offered a scoop on Karras' ties to Semnani, hoping a quick story would allow them to say that the City Weekly piece was old news.

It wasn't the only hand Stokes played, though this one went over far better than his second.

Karras and Stokes were convinced that the Huntsman camp had fed the story to City Weekly through Doug Foxley, the lobbyist Huntsman Sr. hired to advise his son, and a man known to enjoy his own fishing adventures in the northern wilds. Foxley, a Huntsman neighbor, also had a widely known distaste for Semnani.

Foxley had served as a political mentor to Stokes, helping him win a Weber County County Commission seat and later helping him line up clients when he moved into lobbying. Stokes called his old friend and left a heated voice mail accusing Foxley and Huntsman of going negative and threatening retribution.

"Just tell Jon Sr. to be warned that if you guys decide you are going to go negative on Nolan, hell hath no fury," Stokes said. "We have a lot of s--- on Jon Huntsman Sr. and Jr. that we've not used, but if he is going to play that game, we will play that one, too."

Foxley, who denies any connection to the City Weekly piece, found the voice mail amusing. He played it for a business partner and then went about his routine. A few days later, he decided Huntsman Sr. may like to hear it. Foxley made an appearance at Huntsman Corp. and played Stokes' tirade for the big boss. Predictably, Huntsman Sr. was irate. He ordered an employee to record a copy of the message, thanked Foxley for bringing it to his attention and then stewed over it. He later called Foxley and said he planned to release the tape publicly, a move Foxley signed off on, though he knew it would end his friendship with Stokes.

Chaffetz, who regularly spoke for Huntsman Jr. at the candidate's request, summoned the state's major political reporters to Huntsman headquarters and brought them into his office one at a time, playing the tape for each. He gave them a prefab statement from Huntsman Jr., who was nowhere in sight.

"The threat against my family cannot stand. These type of scare and intimidation tactics have no place in Utah politics. I am particularly outraged that my own father, who is not a candidate, was targeted and threatened by someone in my opponent's camp."

What was Karras' reaction to the whole mess? "I could have wrung Spencer's neck.''

But that is not what he said on that May afternoon. He had his campaign manager, Steve Starks, take the heat.

"He renounces the statement and wants voters to know that he's committed to staying above the mudslinging," Starks said. "But the point here that people are missing is that they have gone negative and Spencer's plea was a plea for them not to go negative."

Stokes emerged sheepish and tried to explain away the episode as a dispute between blunt-talking political veterans.

"I'm embarrassed by this, and that's what he wanted to do was embarrass me," Stokes said. "What you have here is two people who have very frank conversations and very frank voice mails over the years. If I played you every voice mail [Foxley] left me, he would be embarrassed, too."

Stokes' threats referred to the information KUTV and Rick Shenkman dug up back in 1988, along with some salacious and unproven rumors. But by releasing the voice mail, the Huntsman camp essentially inoculated itself from such criticism, and Karras ordered Stokes to trash his file of dirt on Huntsman.

"It served a very useful purpose in the way I handled it," Huntsman said later in the race. "I don't think you're going to see shenanigans on either side of this campaign, and I think that's a good outcome."

Throughout the contest, Huntsman trotted out signals that he was a regular guy — from his old denim jacket to his frayed leather belt. He ate peanut-butter-and-jelly sandwiches with supporters and made stops at roadside taco carts. He rode motorcycles and played his keyboard. He got his concealed-carry gun permit. People who know Huntsman say while all of this may have been calculated, it wasn't fake. He may be the son of a fabulously wealthy businessman, but he loves rock concerts and motocross.

Huntsman's advantages in the battle for the all-important GOP nod were numerous and weighty. He was cooler and better-known. He had more campaign funds and was a more polished speaker.

Karras, then 59, decided he had one chance: Play up his more expansive résumé, noting his time in the Legislature, on the Board of Regents and as a self-made businessman, which turned him into a millionaire. He unveiled a new campaign slogan: "Experience money can't buy."

Huntsman offered a two-pronged response. He tied Karras to Leavitt and the old guard, and he constantly used some version of the refrain: "I've been at the highest levels of government and the highest levels of business."

As primary election day drew near, Karras was doomed, and he knew it.

To make matters worse, beloved LDS Church President Gordon B. Hinckley agreed to attend the dedication of the Huntsman Cancer Institute, a high-profile event that occurred the day before voters went to the polls. Karras tried to put on a good face as he marched headlong into a 66 percent to 34 percent drubbing.

After the victory, Huntsman and his father sneaked away to Henrys Fork of the Snake River in Idaho. For eight hours, they chatted and relaxed as they caught and released cutthroat trout.

The general election became the battle of the juniors. Huntsman's Democratic opponent, Scott Matheson Jr., is the first son of the late two-term Utah Gov. Scott Matheson and a member of the state's only family that could contend with the Huntsman aura. Matheson's brother Jim also would be on the ballot that November, seeking and winning a third term in Congress.

No Democrat dared challenge Scott Matheson Jr. for governor, so he sat watching the Republican battle from the sidelines as he prepared his general-election strategy. He hadn't expected Huntsman to enter the race, and when he did, he hadn't expected him to best Walker. By the time Huntsman was headed to an easy primary victory, Matheson's people knew they were in trouble. A pre-primary poll from The Salt Lake Tribune showed Huntsman ahead of Matheson, 49 percent to 35 percent.

"Voters are going to look at each candidate carefully and make an independent judgment. Because of that, I like my chances," Matheson said. "As hard as it may be, I am actually quite excited in the challenge to accomplish it. If elected, it means I would have a very broad-based foundation of support from which to govern."

That statement reveals a lot about Matheson's thinking and his approach to politics. At the time, he was the dean of the University of Utah's law school, a former U.S. attorney and a Rhodes scholar. He is now a judge on the 10th Circuit Court of Appeals. An exact, methodical man, not prone to emotional displays or spontaneity, Matheson spent considerable time dissecting each issue. When a reporter asked him what made him tick, he went into the tank for a full 45 seconds before coming up with a tentative answer that began: "Well, what makes me tick? I guess I'd have to say a lot of different things make me tick, if I understand what 'tick' means."

Huntsman aides respected the Matheson name, but they didn't fear Scott Matheson Jr. as a campaigner. Their plan was to be nice, accommodating and, well, boring, hoping to ride their edge to an easy win in November.

The two candidates differed on only a few issues. Huntsman supported at least a limited experiment with private-school vouchers, while Matheson opposed them categorically. Huntsman focused almost exclusively on economic development, while Matheson zeroed in on public education.

Also on the ballot that November was a state constitutional amendment banning gay marriage. Huntsman supported it, though he would reconsider that position in the years to come. And even in 2004, he was softer on the issue than many in the state. As a nod to gay Utahns, Huntsman said he would back a bill offering reciprocal benefits for "people with mutual economic interests," an idea that never went anywhere. Matheson opposed the gay-marriage ban from the outset, even though he understood it would be an unpopular stance in conservative Utah.

While clearly the underdog, Matheson refused to go on the attack.

"Taking shots, that was just not the kind of person or candidate he was," said Mike Zuhl, Matheson's campaign manager. "He strongly believed he should articulate his views and allow voters to make their choice."

But Huntsman didn't walk through this general election without absorbing a few hits, personally and politically.

David B. Haight, Huntsman's maternal grandfather and a leading Mormon apostle, died in July at age 97. Huntsman recalled taking long walks with his grandfather in which Haight would discuss public policy. Haight also made a point to visit Huntsman in Singapore shortly after he became the ambassador there.

"He taught me the importance of not forgetting one's roots," Huntsman said a few years before Haight's passing. "He loves everything that life has to dish out. He takes it all, analyzes it, always with a positive heart."

The next week, The Salt Lake Tribune published a piece it called "Huntsman Paradox," which contrasted Huntsman Sr.'s incredible contributions to cancer research in Utah with his chemical plants in Texas, which released emissions that neighbors blamed for all kinds of health maladies, including cancer. It wasn't a story about Huntsman Jr. or his run for governor, but the campaign worried about the public's reaction to the piece.

"Philanthropist. Chemical plant owner. Jon Huntsman is both. He is a complex man, yet one who sees himself in the simplest terms: He does good. Period," the story read.

Roughly 900 neighbors of one Texas plant joined a class-action suit against Huntsman's company and two employees, holdovers from when Huntsman bought a plant in Port Arthur and the company pleaded guilty to criminal charges under the Clean Air Act.

Huntsman Sr. insisted he had cleaned up the troubled plant, and of those who challenged his chemical operations, he said: "I really don't kind of blame them because as a kid growing up, you know, we didn't have anything and I kind of resented wealthy people."

The only time the story mentioned Huntsman Jr. was when Huntsman Sr. alleged the lawsuit against his company was a form of "extortion" timed to coincide with his son's run for office. The class-action suit dragged on for years and later was neutered by an appellate judge who said the families didn't have the technical evidence to verify their claims. The case remains alive and Huntsman Corp. remains a defendant, but nothing has been filed in years.

The article sent Huntsman Sr. into a rage. He called The Tribune's publisher to complain, bought a full-page ad to rebut the story and wrote a letter to the editor calling the piece "a cheap, dishonest shot."

"It is obviously political season," he wrote, "and the good Democrats at The Tribune are once again out to destroy anything good that comes from Utah."

Huntsman Sr. didn't stop there. He got a small newspaper in Beaumont, Texas, called The Examiner to write a page 1 story that featured a picture of The Tribune's front-page story under the banner headline "Misled." The story claimed a Tribune reporter gave a source $200 in a check to fabricate a story about Huntsman. The reporter named in that story never met the source nor traveled to Texas to research the story with the other two reporters who worked on the piece.

Throughout the hubbub, Huntsman Jr. stayed quiet and steered clear of his father's efforts to impeach The Tribune's profile. He was no fan of the piece, but he didn't bring it up in the campaign. Neither did Matheson, and the article had no apparent impact on the race. Neither did a late media blitz by a liberal group that capitalized on the class-action suit to slam Huntsman in a news conference and a robocall campaign that reached more than 100,000 homes. Matheson said he had nothing to do with that effort, and Huntsman believed him.

The two rivals conducted a remarkably civil general election, focused on high-minded policy debates over taxes, education and whether to move the state prison.

On election night, Huntsman amassed 58 percent of the vote and took the stage among a crowded room of Republican revelers at the Salt Lake Hilton to say that he was "humbled by your support in making us the next governor of the greatest state in America." Utah voters had also overwhelmingly approved Amendment 3, banning gay marriage and any marriagelike benefits to same-sex couples in the state.

As a sign of how just how collegial the gubernatorial campaign was, Matheson walked one block to the GOP celebration and embraced Huntsman and his family, congratulating him on the victory.

§§§

The feeling wasn't so genial in Massachusetts. The dominant Democrats were disappointed that President George W. Bush eked out a victory over Sen. John Kerry. Still, Kerry carried his home state by 26 percentage points, and his Bay State coattails doomed Mitt Romney's bid to add more Republicans to the Legislature. His party actually lost two seats in the House and one in the Senate. It meant that out of 200 legislative seats, the GOP held just 27. The outcome embarrassed Romney and left Massachusetts with the most lopsided Legislature since 1867. The effort also damaged Romney's already-tenuous relationship with Democrats.

As one liberal operative said: "He put his personal reputation on the line — and he lost."

chapter seven

From friends to foes

Even in the middle of his quixotic quest to Republicanize the Massachu-setts Legislature, Mitt Romney found time to go on a book tour. "Turn-around," his autobiographical take on his Olympic experience, reached stores in mid-2004, and he bounced across the country to promote it — and himself — to the nation at large, creating even more buzz about a potential run for the White House. As part of his tour, he returned to Salt Lake City and held a series of book signings, including an exclusive event at Huntsman Corp. headquarters.

Jon Huntsman Jr. had sewn up the Republican nomination by then and was well on his way to joining Romney in the club of governors. Still, Hunts-man's team thought it couldn't hurt for the candidate to rub elbows with one of the most beloved men in Utah and raise a little money at the event.

That gathering, staged in a state-of-the-art auditorium in the mammoth and mostly empty building, was the first time Huntsman Jr. and Romney met face to face. Sure, Huntsman Sr. had had plenty of interactions, not all of them pleasant, with Romney, but Huntsman Jr. hadn't. Part of it was the age difference. Romney was closer to Huntsman Sr. (a nine-year gap) than to Huntsman Jr. (a 13-year gap). And after Romney landed the Olympic gig, Huntsman Jr. wanted nothing to do with the Salt Lake Organizing Committee. All of that was in the past now.

The Romneys and Huntsmans were buddies, and Mitt and Jon Jr. were about to start running into each other regularly. Romney headlined a Lincoln Day dinner for Salt Lake County Republicans in which he poked fun at Massachusetts and heaped praise on his "home away from home."

"Being a Republican governor in a blue state is like being a cattle rancher at a vegetarian convention," he joked.

While Republicans ate stuffed chicken and drank alcohol-free red punch, Romney talked about the need to strengthen the military, bolster the economy and promote family values — in other words, he sounded like a man eyeing an office beyond the one in Boston.

"America cannot continue to lead the family of nations around the world," he said, "if we fail to lead the family here at home."

Huntsman Jr. had introduced Romney at the $100-a-plate event, calling him one of the GOP's most impressive leaders.

"He is principled. He is brilliant. He has boundless energy. In fact, the only flaw I can find is that he attended BYU," Huntsman said, a nod toward his years at the rival University of Utah.

Huntsman Sr. heaped even more praise on Romney in his own book "Winners Never Cheat," released in April 2005. In this collection of business advice, he cited Romney as an example of someone making the wise choice of taking a job with meaning over one that paid better.

"It is not uncommon for people to forgo higher salaries to join an organization with strong, ethical leadership," Huntsman Sr. wrote. "A good example of this is Mitt Romney, governor of Massachusetts, who returned integrity to the scandal-ridden 2002 Winter Olympics. That classic show of leadership was infectious all the way through the Olympic organization to the thousands of volunteers. As a result, those Games came off as the most successful and problem-free in recent Olympics history."

Romney, in turn, was one of 17 people who wrote blurbs for Huntsman Sr.'s book cover. "Over the years," it read in part, "Jon's extraordinary business achievements have been matched by a sense of charity that continues to touch countless lives. I am privileged to call him a friend."

The Huntsman-Romney love fest continued when Romney returned to Salt Lake City for a Republican Governors Association fundraiser in April 2005. He signed books, donated money to BYU and met with business leaders to talk about the education system. But the highlight of Romney's visit was a high-level meeting with Huntsman Jr. and close advisers. Seated around a conference table at the Grand America, the city's most opulent hotel, Romney asked Huntsman to help his nascent 2008 presidential campaign. Huntsman said he would, though the conversation wasn't formal or precise, with Romney using wiggle words about his "team" without actually mentioning what that team was trying to accomplish. But people in the room thought it was clear enough: Huntsman was backing Romney.

If it wasn't clear then, it certainly was the next time Huntsman huddled with Romney a few weeks later in a suite at the lavish Wynn Las Vegas hotel. Huntsman, accompanied by his wife, told Romney that he wanted to be the first governor to endorse him and asked to be included in the campaign's strategy sessions. Romney demurred, saying he had yet to decide if he would run, but that he would welcome Huntsman's support if he did.

Huntsman underlined the commitment during a Deseret News editorial-board meeting. He told the board he had written a white paper on China for Romney "because he asked," adding that he'd spoken to his friends in the national-security and foreign-policy world on Romney's behalf.

"I've told [Romney] that I'd help in putting together a national-security team," Huntsman said. "I've talked to some people in Washington, D.C., about keeping their powder dry.

"I'll do whatever I can. Mitt would make an excellent candidate. I'm probably the only governor who has come out this early."

It's hard to read those comments as anything but an endorsement, and yet Huntsman would argue in the years to come, when their relationship was not so chummy, that he never fully committed to supporting his distant cousin. His team would note that there was no public announcement of a Huntsman endorsement for Romney.

"We had conversations, and he didn't want to talk very openly in our meetings. It was always 'what if' and 'maybe I'll be doing this,' " Huntsman recalled. "I don't think we ever got to the point where he explicitly said, 'I'm running. Here's my team and, you know, you need to be part of my team.' "

§§§

Huntsman wasn't really focused on Romney in early 2005. He was trying to figure out how to be governor. He took the oath of office using the Bible of his late grandfather, LDS apostle David Haight, on Jan. 3. Since the Capitol was under construction, the ceremony took place in the gold-leaf-adorned home of the Utah Symphony, and it included all of the necessary pomp and then some.

Huntsman attracted dignitaries from Taiwan and China. His former boss, U.S. Trade Representative Robert Zoellick, attended as well. The Mormon Tabernacle Choir performed, and a Utah National Guard field artillery unit gave a 19-gun salute (which was taped a week earlier and played on video). Huntsman saluted his teary-eyed father and stood before the crowd, declaring himself "an agent of change."

"I stand before you," he said, "with a burning desire to prove an often-forgotten point — that public service is noble, honorable, and in need of greater trust and confidence by you."

Huntsman pledged to wield whatever political capital he had to boost the economy, increase teacher pay and expand roads and amenities. To drive home his point, he turned to his dad.

"My father, one of the great entrepreneurs and philanthropists of this state, taught me that capital, monetary or political, is to be used to benefit others," Huntsman said. "I intend to continue that tradition."

He also continued a family tradition that few ever knew about.

Shortly after the Huntsmans moved to Utah in the early 1970s, the exclusive Alta Club snubbed Jon Huntsman Sr. while accepting his brother Blaine as a member. Huntsman Sr. believes Dean Olson, his old nemesis, or his ties to the Nixon White House were to blame. Annoyed, he decided if the Alta Club, a hub for political and business dealings, was going to blackball him, then his family would reciprocate.

When Huntsman Jr. became governor, the club, as is customary, offered him a free membership.

"I turned them down every time, just to live out that commitment," Huntsman Jr. said. "We all held true to that."

Tradition and change were the two keys in Huntsman's early days in office.

Less than a week after his swearing-in, he sent Jason Chaffetz, his former campaign manager and newly installed chief of staff, to fire 33 employees in the state's economic-development office, a move some described as heartless, but illustrative of how hands-on Huntsman would be in selling the state to domestic and international businesses. He wanted his people in these key roles. He then dumped the state's federal lobbyist, saying he had enough personal ties to handle the job. Huntsman didn't waste any time replacing department leaders. All of these steps took place in the few weeks before the state Legislature convened.

Each session starts with the governor's State of the State address. With the Capitol still a construction zone, Huntsman dragged grumbling lawmakers 145 miles south to the sandstone Territorial Statehouse in Fillmore, the central Utah city his ancestors helped build.

"My whole family tree is represented there in Fillmore," he said wistfully. "It's where I learned how to drive a car, learned how to shoot a gun."

In this address, he demanded action on tax reform for corporations, along with term limits and ethics reform for the governor and state lawmakers. In a nod to conservatives, he expressed an openness to diverting state funds to help parents send children to private schools.

With the exception of that last item, Huntsman's agenda landed with a thud in the Legislature. The mostly Republican members (unlike the Democrat-dominated Statehouse Romney confronted in Massachusetts) rejected his tax plan and ignored his calls for ethics reform. Lawmakers also launched an effort to gut the governor's budget-writing power. Huntsman sent an aide to confront House Speaker Greg Curtis, saying the new governor "felt like a bride who was delivered divorce papers on her honeymoon."

The Legislature backed off a bit. Lawmakers agreed with Huntsman to ban hotter radioactive waste from entering Utah and to pump more money into tourism promotion. On school choice, the Legislature passed a limited voucher pilot project for children with special needs.

Throughout the 45-day legislative session, Huntsman was rarely seen, the result, at least in part, of a strategic decision not to confront lawmakers right after he took office. Instead, rank-and-file legislators often met or talked with Chaffetz, and their messages didn't always reach the governor. Lobbyists, Republican insiders, even some Huntsman department heads hit the same wall. By June, some were grousing publicly. Others in the governor's office took notice.

A few weeks later, Chaffetz, a former BYU field-goal kicker, fell off a ladder after absorbing an electrical shock from a faulty outlet. The impact shattered his heel, resulting in a painful recovery that entailed a lengthy leave from the governor's office. Although Chaffetz tried to handle some business from home, his absence allowed Huntsman and the rest of the team to envision the office without their outspoken chief of staff. The governor sent a letter to lawmakers urging them to go through a different staffer to contact him, acknowledging the poor working relationship many of them had with Chaffetz.

A traditional chief of staff is a powerful player who remains behind the curtain. That wasn't Chaffetz. Shortly after he hobbled back into the office, Huntsman politely told him it was time for him to move on and gave his chief a few months to find a landing spot.

Chaffetz's first thought was elected office. He contacted GOP bigwigs to see what they thought about his chances against Democratic Rep. Jim Matheson. After getting input from political insiders, he decided against it. He looked at being the chief spokesman for the family that owns the Utah Jazz basketball team. Word of that job interview got out, forcing Huntsman's team to acknowledge a staff shake-up.

The office announced Chaffetz would leave in a month and that Neil Ashdown, a far more traditional aide, would assume the role of chief of staff.

Chaffetz insisted he wasn't fired, though others in the office say that is semantics. He also argued he didn't block access to the boss; rather, he carried out Huntsman's wishes. "We have always had an open door," Chaffetz said, "and provided great access to the governor in the style and manner in which he wanted it executed."

Huntsman sent out a perfunctory note wishing Chaffetz the best and promising to help him find a job. Chaffetz ended up creating his own consulting firm as he sought the right opportunity to re-enter politics, eventually winning a U.S. House seat in Utah.

§§§

As Huntsman tried to find his footing, Romney raced into one of the nation's stickiest social problems: health care.

It was his second big gamble. He took it just weeks after the first one — to put Republicans in the Legislature — flopped and annihilated what was left of his relationship with state Democrats. Instead of lying low, Romney pressed ahead with a Boston Globe op-ed in which he vowed a major health-care overhaul. It was a savvy, albeit risky, move.

Insuring the uninsured may have been the only issue that could persuade Democratic lawmakers to put down their pitchforks. If it worked, Romney would notch a legacy achievement that would earn plenty of national attention. But his advisers warned of potential pitfalls, since Republicans were and remain largely wary of bringing more government into the medical-industrial complex.

Romney chose to go for it. Before his splashy Globe piece appeared, he sent an advance copy to Sen. Ted Kennedy, a national heavyweight on health-care issues.

"Everyone expected Kennedy to come out screaming, but he said, 'This looks pretty good, and if he's willing to work for this, let's work with him,'" said Stacey Sachs, Kennedy's health-care adviser. "People wanted to be against it because it was Romney's, but because Kennedy came out in favor, they had to bite their tongues."

Kennedy reasoned that Congress was unlikely to act on the issue quickly, so states should try to tackle it.

Romney's team had studied the issue for months, concluding many of the uninsured could afford basic plans and many others were eligible for Medicaid but just didn't sign up. The question was how to get these groups to act. Their solution came from the Republican counteroffensive launched in the 1990s, when President Bill Clinton tried but failed to reform health care. All state residents would be required to buy insurance or enroll in Medicaid. If they didn't, the state would fine them. In health-care jargon, this is called an individual mandate.

Years later, Romney would join the Republican Party in angrily opposing such a mandate on a national scale when President Barack Obama included it in the Affordable Care Act. But, in 2005, Romney called it the "ultimate conservative idea."

"No more free riding, if you will, where an individual says, 'I'm not going to pay, even though I can afford it.' "

His plan would create an online store to sell insurance, and he would expand an existing fund to help the poor afford coverage.

With an outline in place, Romney delivered his plan to the Legislature's top two Democrats, House Speaker Salvatore DiMasi and Senate President Robert Travaglini, and then sat back and waited.

"Romney knew his best chance to get it passed was to be not too visible in the process," said Alan Macdonald, a business leader involved in the negotiations.

Letting the Legislature work its will made sense politically, but it also put two men at the helm, and they clashed. It started as a simple policy disagreement, with DiMasi wanting a tax on businesses that didn't cover their employees and Travaglini seeking a narrower health-care bill. The dispute ballooned into a battle between entrenched business interests, a fight between the House and Senate and a power struggle between two Democratic alpha dogs.

Romney wanted a deal by the end of 2005. He didn't get one. The state then missed a mid-January deadline set by the federal government involving millions of dollars in Medicaid money. Time was slipping away.

The governor decided to make a grand gesture in hopes of nudging the negotiations. He wrote a letter to the two men saying "the plane is circling and we have to land it." He personally delivered it to their homes — on a Sunday, no less. DiMasi wasn't there, but Travaglini opened the door wearing a sweatsuit. He invited Romney into his home, and the two chatted for a few minutes.

"How often does the governor ring your bell on a Sunday morning?" asked Travaglini, impressed by the gesture.

Still, the standoff dragged on for weeks, leading to a confrontation between Romney and DiMasi. The House speaker later said it was the most forceful he had seen the governor.

"He did everything he could to put pressure on me to change my position on the business assessment," DiMasi said. "I tried to walk out, and he wouldn't let me go out the door. I actually opened the door and he said, 'No, no no. Get back in here.' "

On March 1, a group of business leaders negotiated a truce, agreeing to a $295-per-employee assessment — everyone decided not to call it a tax — for businesses with more than 10 workers that didn't offer insurance. The next evening, DiMasi and Travaglini took their wives to a nice Italian dinner, where they cleared the air and blessed the compromise.

When the legislative leaders unveiled the final bill, Romney took center stage, declaring: "Today, Massachusetts has set itself apart from every other state in the country. An achievement like this comes once in a generation."

It was the beginning of his prolonged victory lap. The House and Senate overwhelmingly approved the reform, dubbed Romneycare, setting up an elaborate signing ceremony in mid-April 2006.

Big banners in an old-fashioned font said "Making History in Health Care." They flanked a stately desk in the middle of the hallowed space of Faneuil Hall. A fife-and-drum corps, outfitted in tricorner hats, led dignitaries to their spots behind Romney, who emerged to a long, enthusiastic ovation.

"This is a politician's dream, you've got to admit," Romney told the crowd. He jokingly thanked famed movie director Cecil B. DeMille for organizing the spectacle. Behind him stood the key players, with Kennedy occupying the coveted photo spot just over Romney's left shoulder.

"My son said that having Sen. Kennedy and me together like this on the stage, behind the same piece of landmark legislation, will help slow global warming," Romney said. "That's because hell has frozen over."

"My son said something, too," Kennedy offered. "And that is when Kennedy and Romney support a piece of legislation, usually one of them hasn't read it."

Seriously, though, Kennedy called the measure "an achievement for all the people of our commonwealth and perhaps for the rest of America, too," foreshadowing the health-care debate that Obama would lead three years later.

Romney used 14 pens to sign his signature bill. With the last mark, he shouted, "It's law!" He wasn't as gushing about its prospects, though, as Kennedy.

"I have to admit that I'm very, very proud of having been part of this process," Romney said after he signed the bill. "But I have no way of guessing whether it's going to be a help or a hindrance down the road. Time will tell."

Shortly after the signing, Romney vetoed a few sections he considered untenable. They correlated with parts that national Republicans disliked, including the business assessment he defended when the legislation was introduced. The Democrats rolled their eyes and promptly overturned Romney's line-item vetoes.

Signing the bill into law wasn't enough. Romneycare needed a signoff from the federal Department of Health and Human Services for it to work, because the state proposed keeping an expanded Medicaid program. The HHS secretary at the time happened to be Mike Leavitt, Utah's former governor and Romney's Olympic partner. Leavitt gave a final nod to the Massachusetts plan in July 2006, although his endorsement was lukewarm.

"I don't know if what Mitt Romney did is a conservative idea or a liberal idea," Leavitt said at the time. "But it is clearly an innovative idea."

It also was an idea Romney realized would be forever tied to his tenure as governor. In mid-2009, well after his first presidential run fell apart, Romney returned to the Massachusetts Statehouse to unveil his official portrait, painted from a photo by artist Richard Whitney. It depicts a serious-looking Romney half sitting on a desk. He's wearing a blue suit and a conservative striped tie. His hand rests on his left leg and his wedding ring is parallel with a small framed picture of his wife. Between his leg and that picture of Ann is a folder of official papers with a caduceus, a symbol of the medical profession, embossed on the cover.

"As long as the symbol was there, that was important," Whitney said. "He wanted to be remembered for that."

As the fight over health reform raged in December 2005, Romney made an announcement that surprised almost no one — he wouldn't seek a second term as governor.

"It's almost as though he had his eye on higher office very early into his governorship. I think it ended up hurting his performance as governor and the fortunes of the party in general," said Richard R. Tisei, a former Massachusetts House minority leader who didn't support Romney's run for the White House.

Tisei had it right.

Romney advisers started meeting with campaign operatives in Washington, D.C., just six months into his term. About that same time, then-Sen. Bob Bennett of Utah sent Romney a memo with one message: You don't need to decide whether to run for president yet, but you need to decide if you want the option.

It was sage advice, and Romney took it.

"I didn't know if I wanted to run; I didn't know what would happen," Romney recalled. "But I knew I didn't want to foreclose the possibility."

While still leading Massachusetts, Romney sought the chairmanship of the Republican Governors Association and used that post to traverse the country throughout 2006, introducing himself to officials in key states, glad-handing donors and burnishing his profile. He also set up Commonwealth PACs in several states, including Utah, raising money by the fistful, gaining the attention of political consultants he would need.

Folks back in Massachusetts couldn't help but notice his extracurricular political activity, and they didn't particularly like it.

DiMasi used the traditional St. Patrick's Day political roast in 2006 to poke Romney over his out-of-state efforts. He gave Romney a fake Oscar, saying: "For a great job of acting like you really enjoyed being governor of Massachusetts." The Democratic House speaker then noted that Romney never drew a salary for his gubernatorial work. "I guess it's true what they say, you get what you pay for."

A New York Times review of Romney's public schedules revealed he spent at least 417 days out of Massachusetts during his term in office. About 70 percent of those days were spent on personal or political business unrelated to his official duties. He was a regular at Super Bowls and spent considerable time at vacation homes in New Hampshire, a presidential primary state, and Utah. He visited 38 states and took foreign trips to Afghanistan, Iraq and Guantánamo Bay, along with Greece, China, Japan and other nations.

"I thought he gave up on his job," said Phil Johnston, chairman of the Massachusetts Democrats. "Romney was quite popular at the beginning of his tenure. The relationship between him and the Massachusetts electorate really soured."

Eric Fehrnstrom, one of Romney's closest aides, rejected such criticism, telling The Times: "Democrats who are carping about Mitt Romney's travels also defended Mike Dukakis when he campaigned for president as a sitting governor. Their complaints come across as more than a bit hypocritical."

He may have had a point. Massachusetts residents seemed open to having a Republican lead the state, but they were far less excited about having him lead the nation. Gone was moderate Romney, replaced with a more conservative version of the man they elected.

"I think there's really a Romney One and a Romney Two," said Marty Linsky, a former Republican state legislator and a lecturer at Harvard. "Romney One really worked very hard to try to do what he thought was in the best interests of the commonwealth; Romney Two worked very hard to position himself to run for president of the United States."

Linsky added: "People felt they didn't know who he was. The only way to make sense of his trajectory was that he was only about himself."

At the end of 2006, his final full year as governor, Romney's approval rating had fallen to 39 percent.

§ § §

Utah's mostly conservative lawmakers streamed into Salt Lake City in early January 2006, ready for a month and a half of legislating. Gov. Jon Huntsman was waiting for them, having no interest in a repeat of his meek performance during his first year in office.

He allied himself with House Speaker Greg Curtis on a plan to reduce the sales tax on food. He buddied up to Senate President John Valentine to push a flat income-tax proposal. He prodded the two leaders into a celebratory news conference, and a few days later boasted of his ability to shape the process by threatening to veto bills.

When differences emerged, he pitted the House and Senate against each other, rather than allowing them to gang up on him as they did in his first go-round.

In the end, he got half what he wanted. The Legislature cut the food tax by nearly 50 percent, though it would take him another year to strong-arm a flatter income tax into place.

His sudden aggressiveness surprised legislative leaders, who thought they had taught Huntsman his place in 2005. They complained he made tactical errors that doomed his wider tax plan.

"The one mistake I think the governor made was he asserted himself this session," Curtis said. "It is a fine line between exerting yourself and totally frustrating those who you are exerting your pressure against and having a backlash. I think he crossed the line."

Huntsman shrugged off the defeat, displaying newfound self-confidence and a determination to lead his way.

"I'm just a simple dweeb that is pretty forthright and honest," he said.

Huntsman always had fashioned himself a maverick, even if he didn't use the word. He wanted to be a person who floated between Utah's religious divide and the standard partisan splits. He gravitated to similar political personalities. At a governors meeting early that year, he ran into Sen. John McCain, a likely 2008 presidential contender from Arizona. Huntsman asked him to headline Utah's 2006 Republican Convention in May. McCain agreed, but he had a request of Huntsman, too. He wanted the charismatic governor to join him on a fact-finding trip to Iraq.

Huntsman was one of three governors who went with McCain and five other members of Congress on the short visit, where they met with the Iraqi president and later the U.S. commander. These politicians carried a message of impatience with the war, delivering it on a particularly violent day. Dozens of people were reported killed in a series of gunbattles between sectarian militias.

The next day, Huntsman celebrated his 46th birthday by mingling with U.S. troops in Fallujah, an Iraqi city that saw more than its share of violence. The trip allowed Huntsman and McCain to get to know each other, and they bonded over their foreign-policy interests.

McCain came to Utah two months later, telling activist Republicans about his time as a Vietnam prisoner of war, pledging to fight wasteful spending and arguing in favor of a compromise on illegal immigration. He also framed the Iraq War in starkly moral terms.

"We must win in Iraq. We cannot fail. If we lose in Iraq, they're coming after us. We will fight them somewhere else — like here," he said. "It's all part of a gigantic, titanic struggle between good and evil."

McCain ducked any comments about Romney's potential presidential run, though their rivalry would turn out to be the titanic struggle within the Republican Party in the months to come.

Huntsman also sidestepped any talk of presidential politics, though he obviously was chummy with McCain and relishing the role of chaperone to one of the party's biggest names.

Two months later, while Huntsman was on a regular lobbying trip to Washington, McCain summoned the Utahn to his office. Skipping the small talk, McCain asked Huntsman for his endorsement. The maverick also want-ed Huntsman to be a campaign co-chairman. Huntsman paused, caught off guard by McCain's bluntness. Then he said yes.

"He knew it was going to be a bombshell locally, and he knew outside the state of Utah no one was going to care," said a Huntsman confidant, thinking about Mitt and the Mormon connection. "He said, 'I'm going to take a hit for this, but I think this is the right thing to do. I'm going to do it.' "

Utah's governor believed McCain was the right man when it came to foreign affairs, his pet issue, and he disliked Romney's pandering to the right wing. Huntsman also felt taken for granted by Romney. He had written Rom-ney the white paper on China and heard nothing back. He would offer help and get no response. Huntsman told Romney allies of his frustration and warned that he may bolt. Still, he heard nada.

"He just assumed that all the nice boys in Utah would just sort of hang around and wait for future guidance and light," Huntsman said.

One of his close advisers believes the split could have been avoided.

"If Mitt had really involved [Huntsman] in the campaign, I think he would have said yes to Mitt early on. He would have stayed loyal to that. If someone asked, he felt he was ready to commit."

McCain asked.

Huntsman broke the news to his staff, many of them Romney admirers. They recognized that a big majority of Utahns swooned over their Olympic savior with deep Mormon roots, and they knew Huntsman's father planned to continue to back Romney as a key member of his national finance team. They braced for the inevitable backlash.

Later in the week, McCain aides announced that they had snagged Huntsman's endorsement. Huntsman ducked the news media, instead send-ing out spokesman Michael Mower to say the governor and McCain "share common viewpoints on many important issues, such as those impacting the

Western states, and have similar viewpoints on international issues." He also said the endorsement wasn't a slight against Romney, who a year earlier was his good buddy.

Romney, his family and his advisers saw it differently. Romney learned about what he viewed as a clear betrayal from The Washington Post and immediately reached out to an adviser in Utah with ties to Huntsman. Mitt was incredulous and Ann seethed.

Mitt Romney knew Huntsman had been irritated, but how could he take such a drastic action? How could he do so without even the courtesy of calling? Romney saw the McCain endorsement as downright cowardly.

Spencer Zwick, Romney's go-between with Utah's political elite, vented to Chaffetz, who had left Huntsman's office nine months earlier. He also sent missives to at least two Huntsman aides, one of which said: "Not even a phone call."

Huntsman never phoned Romney to explain his decision, but Romney sure called Huntsman. Their terse, angry exchange — including Romney's accusation that Huntsman's grandfather would be ashamed — marked the break in the relationship between not just two competitive politicians, but also these two families.

Above: In this informal family portrait from 1962, George Romney (far right) sits on the couch playing with granddaughter Jody Keenan, while Mitt Romney (center) looks on. (file photo, The Salt Lake Tribune)

Right: Michigan Gov. George Romney and his wife, Lenore Romney, in 1967. Lenore, once a movie star, would make her own unsuccessful run for political office. (file photo, The Salt Lake Tribune)

Left: Mitt Romney shook hands with commuters during his 1994 Senate run against Sen. Ted Kennedy, D-Mass. He expected to lose, but doing so hurt more than he anticipated. (Joe Ragash, The Salt Lake Tribune)

Below: Ann Romney points to a photo of her husband as a young man as she talked about how the two fell in love during the 2012 Republican National Convention in Tampa, Fla. (Trent Nelson, The Salt Lake Tribune)

Left: Mitt Romney took a break from the 2012 campaign to speak at an event marking the 10-year anniversary of the 2002 Winter Games in Salt Lake City. (Rick Egan, The Salt Lake Tribune)

Above: Mitt and Ann Romney made a 2012 campaign stop at Hires Big H Drive-in in Salt Lake City. Will Huntsman, one of Jon Huntsman Jr.'s sons, was among those in the crowd. (Leah Hogsten, The Salt Lake Tribune)

Right: Josh Romney, one of Mitt Romney's five sons, talked to supporters in Utah during the 2008 primary. (Steve Griffin, The Salt Lake Tribune)

Below: At the close of the 2012 Republican National Convention, Mitt and Ann Romney were joined onstage by Rep. Paul Ryan, R-Wis., his running mate, and Janna Ryan. (Trent Nelson, The Salt Lake Tribune)

Left: Mitt Romney posed with Greg Whiteley, the director of the documentary "Mitt," at the 2014 Sundance Film Festival. The movie resulted in a rush of good publicity that led Romney to briefly consider a third presidential campaign. (Scott Sommerdorf, The Salt Lake Tribune)

Right: Jon and Karen Huntsman spoke at a news conference in 1987 shortly after the FBI saved their son James from a kidnapper. (Rick Egan, The Salt Lake Tribune)

Below: Jon and Karen Huntsman cut the ribbon during an expansion of the Huntsman Cancer Institute in 2007. (Ryan Galbraith, The Salt Lake Tribune)

Above: A young Jon Huntsman sat in President Richard Nixon's seat in the Cabinet room of the White House in 1971. (Courtesy photo)

Left: Jon and Mary Kaye Huntsman left the Utah Capitol in August 2009 shortly after the swearing-in of new Gov. Gary Herbert, who stands in the background with his wife, Jeanette. (Francisco Kjolseth, The Salt Lake Tribune)

Below: Gov. Jon Huntsman accepted the food stamp challenge in 2007. He brought Mary Kaye and their adopted children, Gracie Mei, 7, right, and Asha, 1, in basket, to hunt for inexpensive food. (Al Hartmann, The Salt Lake Tribune)

Above: Gov. Jon Huntsman mingled with legislators after his 2009 State of the State address. Later that year, President Barack Obama nominated Huntsman to become the U.S. ambassador to China. (Al Hartmann, The Salt Lake Tribune)

Below: Abby Huntsman, then 19, and Gracie Mei Huntsman, then 6, work on homework in the Utah Governor's Mansion in 2005. (Francisco Kjolseth, The Salt Lake Tribune)

Above: As Jon Huntsman explored a presidential campaign in 2011, he visited with Debra Chouinard at Robie's Country Store in Hooksett, New Hampshire. (Max Bittle, The Salt Lake Tribune)

chapter eight

Making the leap

As Mitt and Ann Romney strode out of the golden-domed Massachusetts Statehouse and down the stairs in his final hours as governor, fans lined the sidewalks and a 19-gun salute breached the brisk, quiet night. In the Bay State, the "lone walk" by outgoing governors is a tradition dating to the 1880s.

Romney completed the stately tradition with head held high, even though he was far from universally loved by that time.

"He was basically never here. ... I don't think he's done anything for the state. ... You can have him back in Salt Lake," lifelong Bostonian Roberta Kilduff said on a chilly morning inside the Faneuil Hall Marketplace in 2006. Utah, she suggested, should "have another Olympics."

Going backward wasn't part of Romney's playbook. He already had saved the Games; now he intended to save the country.

He created a presidential exploratory committee just days before the lone walk and gave himself barely a month to put the finishing touches on a campaign plan, snag more endorsements, shoot commercials and grant strategic interviews before his big announcement. And he needed to raise money. Lots of it.

The campaign wanted to make a splash and announced the "National Call Day," his inaugural presidential fundraiser. The spacious hall in the Boston Convention and Exhibition Center looked like a high-tech startup: 40 white-linen tables ᴬrranged in horseshoes, each with an IBM laptop and phone and staffed by some 350 eager supporters, including Missouri Gov. Matt Blunt and eBay CEO Meg Whitman.

Before the first phone call, the crowd — and some journalists stuck behind the rope line — saw a motivational video about Romney's career, including pictures of him with President George W. Bush at the Olympics. A narrator described Mitt in good ol' Boston slang as "wicked smart" in helping Massachusetts residents get health-care coverage without a tax hike.

Romney, in a dark suit as usual, emerged to the Goo Goo Dolls' "Give a Little Bit" and rallied the assembled troops.

"You guys today are my hope," he said, standing on a platform in the center of the room. "What you are doing is going to make all the difference in the world."

Romney made the first call, which had the feeling of a tee-ball swing rather than a big cut in the big leagues. He called his sister Lynn Romney Keenan in his hometown of Bloomfield Hills, Mich., but could hardly get a word in as his sibling heaped on the praise.

"This is an exciting day, isn't it?" she asked, before launching into a litany of Romney accomplishments.

Romney didn't even get to finish his request for $2,100 before Keenan excitedly said, "Of course."

The event was billed to show off Romney as a top-tier candidate and warn the rest of the field he was serious — and able to raise serious cash.

It also had the feeling of a "This Is Your Life" episode. Friends from his Mormon ward in Boston, Bain Capital, the Olympics and Utah loomed large in the room. Longtime buddy Kem Gardner, a Salt Lake City developer, was there, as well as Utah lobbyist Bill Simmons and Mormon authors Linda and Richard Eyre.

Utah Lt. Gov Gary Herbert made calls for Romney from the convention center despite the fact his boss, Jon Huntsman Jr., was backing Romney's rival. "It's not a hard sale in Utah because people know Mitt Romney," Herbert said in dialing for dollars from his home state.

Also present: Huntsman's brother David Huntsman, who joked that the divergent endorsements made for interesting family discussions but that he was a Romney guy.

"We're excited about what he's doing; we believe in his message that he has," David Huntsman said. "He's a true leader. He's been successful in everything he has been involved in."

Among donors contributing that January: Jon Huntsman Sr., his wife,

Karen, and their son David. Each gave the maximum $2,300.

In his 1994 Senate campaign against Ted Kennedy, Romney had railed against big money flowing into political campaigns.

"I don't like the influence of money, whether it's in business, labor or any other group," Romney had said. "The kinds of demands being placed on the economics of running a campaign suggest an increasing power on the part of monied interests, and I think it's wrong and we've got to change it."

That was then. This was now.

At day's end, Romney's team announced it raised $6.5 million in pledges, far more than the low-ball goal of $1 million set by his aides.

Asked if he would chip in himself, Romney responded that would be "akin to a nightmare." In fact, he already had primed the pump with $2.4 million of his own cash and eventually would "loan" the effort $45 million. The candidate never planned to and never did repay himself.

With the Romney rollout ready to go, the soon-to-be candidate jetted to his native Michigan for his campaign kickoff. Romney's choice of locations: the Henry Ford Museum in Dearborn, where he parked himself between a new Ford hybrid car and a Rambler made famous by his father's American Motors. He penned his 20-minute speech himself, playing largely off his father's work in the auto industry and his own business acumen.

"It is time for innovation and transformation in Washington. It is what our country needs. It is what our people deserve," Romney said on that cold Feb. 13. "I do not believe Washington can be transformed from within by a lifelong politician. There have been too many deals, too many favors, too many entanglements ... and too little real-world experience managing, guiding, leading. I do not believe Washington can be transformed by someone who has never tried doing such a thing before, in any setting, by someone who has never even managed a corner store, let alone the largest enterprise in the world."

He also touted himself as doer.

"It is time for hope and action," he said. "It is time to do, as well as to dream."

Romney had his own dream, and he was doing something about it. He could picture himself behind the Resolute desk in the Oval Office, just as Hollywood could picture him there: chiseled jaw, broad shoulders, complemented by a dollop of gray at his temples to add an air of distinguishment.

He hadn't always been sold on running. After his dad's experience and his own loss to Kennedy, he didn't want to run only to fail.

His father was the gold standard against which he often weighed himself.

"My dad is my life hero," Romney said. "I probably would have never thought about politics, it would have never crossed my mind, had I not seen him do it. He's the real pioneer."

Romney didn't make the ultimate decision to run until Christmas 2006 at the family's mansion in the Utah mountains. As later shown in a campaign documentary — complete with Romney sledding head first down a hill with his grandkids and shoveling snow off the porch — he gathered Ann and the kids in the cavernous living room to talk about it.

"If people really get to know who you are, it could be a successful campaign," said the youngest son, Craig.

"I don't think you have a choice," said Tagg, the eldest. "I think you have to run. Look at the way your life has unfolded, and you're gifted, you're smart, you're intelligent, but you've also been extraordinarily lucky, and so many things have broken your way that you couldn't have predicted or controlled. It would have been a shame not to at least try, and if you don't win, we'll still love you."

They went around the room. It was unanimous.

Romney would enter a GOP field with some venerable party stars as well as some rabble-rousers and dark horses. John McCain, of course, was the front-runner, having finished second to George W. Bush in 2000. He was widely known, could raise money, knew foreign policy and his independent streak charmed TV pundits. As a former prisoner of war in Vietnam, the Arizona senator also packed solid credentials on the fighting in Iraq and Afghanistan.

New York Mayor Rudy Giuliani was termed America's mayor for his calming leadership after the Sept. 11, 2001, terrorist attacks. Everyone knew his name, and he could garner crossover votes. In his second run — the first as a Libertarian — Rep. Ron Paul knew how to fire up his conservative base, and his supporters were die-hards, even if the Texan congressman stood little chance of winning.

Mike Huckabee wasn't a household name, but he was a Southern governor, a position that could swing the early heartland states. He also came across as folksy, a Republican version of his Arkansas predecessor, Bill Clinton.

Then there was the B team: Rep. Duncan Hunter, perennial candidate Alan Keyes, Rep. Tom Tancredo, Sen. Sam Brownback, former Wisconsin Gov. Tommy Thompson and TV actor and ex-Sen. Fred Thompson. The latter's campaign, which promised a big buzz, hit with a thud, leaving the wannabe candidate asking for applause at his own sparsely attended event.

Handicappers saw the race this way: McCain vs. Giuliani, followed by long shots Romney and Huckabee and, far behind them, everyone else. Those rankings seemed common sense and didn't leave much space for a Romney nomination.

Romney and his team viewed it differently, eyeing an opening for a Republican candidate who wasn't McCain. After President Bush's poll ratings had slid, the GOP needed a standard-bearer from the outside to rescue Washington.

"We felt like McCain's not that guy," said a former top Romney aide. "Romney had the great ability to be the antidote" to McCain's insider status.

McCain's people mobilized quickly to brand Romney a flip-flopper — a strategy that had worked against Democrat John Kerry in 2004. Kerry's vote for — and subsequent vote against — the Iraq War provided loads of fodder for Republicans, as had an aloof style that left him looking rich and above the average American. Romney was to face the same fate. At several events, anti-Romney folks handed out cheap flip-flops as reminders; one activist went so far as to don a porpoise outfit nicknamed "Flip Romney."

The tactic worried Romney advisers. They knew McCain had material from Romney's runs for Senate and governor, namely on gay rights and abortion. A video of Romney defending abortion rights surfaced early on, and his campaign struggled to tamp it down.

"At the beginning of the campaign, people didn't know much about Mitt Romney," said his campaign manager, Beth Myers. "But if they did know him, that's what they knew about him. Our challenge was to make sure they got to know more."

Democrats wanted in on the action, too. The Democratic National Committee blasted out 15 news releases against Romney over a few months, more than were aimed at McCain or any other GOP hopeful. Romney's aides welcomed the attacks in a way; it showed their man was a top contender, and they used the attention to help rake in cash.

Jon Huntsman Sr. was a big help. He wrote 25 letters a day seeking support for Romney from wealthy family members and acquaintances. Romney won the first Federal Election Commission report contest, logging $20.6 million in donations (and an additional $2.35 million from himself). It was almost double McCain's bottom line.

In one of his first big appearances, Romney wowed the far-right audience at the Conservative Political Action Committee gathering in Washington, receiving a level of adulation missing in subsequent visits. The annual event draws big-name speakers from the conservative movement and scores of activists, many in their early 20s, to give them rock-star treatment.

It's kind of the anti-Woodstock, where Ann Coulter is the conservatives' Grace Slick and Obama plays the Nixonian role of villain. The crowd is also bustling with future Henry Kissingers. It's not unheard of to see college students debating the intricacies of Middle East politics, even if they're simply regurgitating talking points.

"It's time to take government apart and put it back together," Romney declared to the delight of the crowd.

Of the 1,705 votes in the event's straw poll, Romney grabbed 21 percent, more than Giuliani, Brownback and McCain, who, sensing it wasn't his crowd, skipped the confab altogether.

As spring rolled on, Romney tossed out ads to introduce himself to early-state voters.

The Republican primary season consists of an orchestrated series of skirmishes that makes little sense in the larger scope of things. First up are the caucuses in Iowa, a nearly homogeneous state of white, rural voters who care about farming and ethanol and the impact of federal subsidies as much as they do about faith and good looks. Then comes the debut primary, New Hampshire, also a rural state of nearly all white voters. Third is South Carolina — proud owner of the First in The South primary — where there's greater diversity of race and issues.

Despite the relatively tiny numbers of voters involved, these three contests are vital. A candidate who notches one or two victories there, before heading into Florida and Michigan, can dominate the attention of media and donors. That translates to momentum going into Super Tuesday, when a slew of big states, including California, New York and New Jersey, head to the polls on a single day.

Romney's strategy was straightforward: Win Iowa and New Hampshire and funnel that head of steam to roll to the nomination.

It worked — for a while.

Romney's early ads cost precious dollars in the fledgling campaign but fueled interest and gave him much-needed exposure leading into the first two contests. Another public-opinion survey, this one the almost-laughable straw poll in Ames, Iowa, was a big target for Romney until it became clear McCain and Giuliani weren't going to play ball there.

Ames is the sort of faux bellwether that draws much attention for no logical reason. Candidates front almost everything but sunscreen for voters. They bus them in, feed them barbecue and ply them with concert tickets. Romney walked away with a win that carried a price tag of about $2 million.

"Change begins in Iowa and change begins today," he said, happily accepting the 32 percent victory.

Ames did produce one surprise: Huckabee. The former Arkansas governor topped Sam Brownback, the Kansas senator who was expected to score big with conservatives. That twist should have worried Romney's people more than it did.

In New Hampshire, WBZ-Boston unveiled a poll showing Romney up 10 points over McCain, whose campaign was starting to fracture, and 9 points higher than Giuliani, who hadn't caught fire as many had assumed.

McCain's inevitable nomination appeared less and less inevitable.

Mid-2007 saw a mass exodus from the Arizona senator's senior staff as finances dried up. The team, so convinced of its invincibility, was hemorrhaging cash, leaving it with only $2 million by July after having raised $26 million. And the undertaking was $2 million in debt. The national media tasted blood in the water.

"Sen. John Edwards began what he's calling his poverty tour today," joked Jay Leno. "He's visiting people who have no money and no hope. His first stop: John McCain's campaign headquarters."

Campaign manager Terry Nelson resigned, as did deputy Reed Galen and political adviser Rob Jesmer. Chief strategist John Weaver was out, too. Half the staff was axed.

Weaver, an ever-present political pro who knows as much about where the bodies are buried as political spin, had been a McCain loyalist for years. The alliance came long after the tall, skinny Texan had partnered in the 1980s with guru Karl Rove before the two had an irreconcilable split. The two GOP masterminds faced each other in 2000, when Bush waged a nasty campaign against McCain, annihilating any remaining shred of camaraderie.

Drummed out of the GOP side of the business after Bush's 2000 victory, Weaver had gone to work for the Democratic Congressional Campaign Committee and the Democratic Party-aligned Association of Trial Lawyers of America. He returned to Republican politics in 2008 to help McCain win, but when things went south, he fell on his Texas-size sword.

"We had a spending problem, a message problem. ... That's nobody's fault but mine," Weaver said. "We began the campaign believing our own BS, and I'm very guilty of that."

It was so bad that McCain thought about dropping out, though advisers later stressed that wasn't a serious consideration.

Romney and his top aides disagreed on whether to write off McCain; one senior staffer offered that they should finish him: "He's not dead yet; let's stomp on him."

Romney, though, wanted to focus on Giuliani, his bigger concern at the time. The strategy backfired when every other candidate in the crowded GOP field ganged up on Romney.

With the ex-Massachusetts governor in the cross hairs, McCain was able to quietly regroup. He staked out hard-line positions on the war in Iraq, a touchy subject that he previously dodged. His remaining campaign team took the little money it had and rounded up veterans to drive across the country advocating against withdrawing troops from the war. They dubbed it the "No Surrender" tour, and it restored the political oxygen — news coverage — that McCain needed to survive.

While the rest of the candidates battled one another, McCain toughed it out. Veteran GOP consultant Charlie Black bluntly summed up the strategy: "Be the last man standing."

At a debate at the University of New Hampshire, McCain found the right opportunity to join with the pack and turn on Romney.

Romney previously said he favored shifting U.S. forces into a support role in Iraq after Bush's troop surge had been successful. Now, during the debate, he said the effort had "apparently" worked.

"The key is, we don't start pulling back troops; we don't go into a support mode until we are successful with this surge and we are providing the security and the stability that we anticipate for this country."

The comment gave McCain his opening.

"Governor, the surge is working," McCain said in a tone less father-to-son than foreign-policy-professor-to-dimwitted freshman. "The surge is working, sir."

"That's just what I said," Romney countered.

"It is working. No, not 'apparently,' " McCain lectured, flaunting his Vietnam POW hero status. "It's working. It's working because we've got a great general. We've got a good strategy."

Debate host Chris Wallace, a Fox News personality, helped McCain reload for another shot, asking the senator whether he still stood behind his crack that Romney's plan for immigration reform would be to "get his small varmint gun and run the Guatemalans off his lawn," a reference to accusations that Romney hired undocumented immigrants for yardwork at his Belmont, Mass., mansion.

"I thought it was a pretty good line," McCain said to laughs from the audience — all but the Romney family. "I wish I would have written it myself."

McCain was on the upswing and focusing all his efforts on the Granite State. The Straight Talk Express soon would be everywhere there. Huckabee, meanwhile, was on the rise in Iowa, meaning Romney was confronting two strong rivals on two fronts — the two states on which he had counted.

The former Massachusetts governor needed a Diet Coke. His campaign needed to hit back and hit hard.

"John McCain, an honorable man," an announcer intoned on a new Romney spot in New Hampshire. "But is he the right Republican for the future?"

McCain wanted amnesty for immigrants and to give them Social Security benefits, the ad charged.

Romney press secretary Kevin Madden sent out two emails to reporters with the subject line "What the …??!!" They included stories on Huckabee still making paid speeches and a string of foreign-policy gaffes. While The Boston

Globe wrote a story on Romney's positive campaign, that same campaign was ensuring the news media caught wind of anything that cast "Huck" in a negative light.

Huckabee then stepped in it himself.

His campaign, sensing a tightening race, tossed together an ad calling Romney "dishonest," slamming him for an increase in fees and taxes in Massachusetts and noting that he left office with a big deficit. Huckabee planned a news conference to unveil the spot only to decide at the last minute that he didn't want to air it. He said he wanted to keep a positive tone going forward.

He aired it anyway — to reporters at the news conference and on several TV stations in Iowa. It was, in essence, Huckabee claiming the high road while strolling straight down the low road.

Romney called Huckabee's now-you-see-it-now-you-don't move "confusing" and "puzzling" at a campaign stop in Independence, Iowa, but tried to stay nice in his on-air buys, sticking to his themes of turning around the country as he had the Olympics.

In Iowa, it all came down to Jan. 3, 2008. Caucuses across the state brought out farmers and business owners, homemakers and executives. Immediately evident were a lot more Huckabee signs than Romney ones. Voters followed suit.

More than 120,000 people turned out, and exit polls showed three-fifths of them self-identified as evangelical Christians. A Baptist minister from the South naturally appealed to that demographic much more than a Mormon from the North.

Huckabee grabbed Iowa with 34 percent to Romney's 25 percent.

The only person happier than Huckabee may have been McCain, plotting his own Romney defeat in New Hampshire. He phoned the Iowa victor to congratulate him.

"Now it's your turn to kick his butt," Huckabee said.

Romney's team had chartered a JetBlue Airbus A320 to New Hampshire, and reporters had already signed up to ride along. Many wished they had stuck with Huckabee.

His hair uncharacteristically disheveled, Romney boarded after all the journalists were safely tucked in back. The onboard movie for the three-hour flight, "The Comebacks," about a misfit football team that eventually wins the big game, was not a prophetic pick by the Romney team.

Venturing into McCain Country, Romney dubbed himself a "silver-medal" winner. The orchestrated welcome in the hangar of the Portsmouth International Airport attempted to pump up spirits with thumping rock music. Veteran political consultant Tom Rath was dancing onstage. It was 4 a.m.

"Wow, you guys are crazy! What a welcome! What a welcome!" Romney said, hoarse and standing on the bed of a Ford F-350 pickup. "Have you guys just gotten up or are you going to bed — which is it?"

They had stayed up, watching the painful results from Iowa. Nevertheless, they had prepared a hero's welcome and were determined to put on a good face. So was Romney. After a short speech, he greeted the crowd and someone handed him a medal on a red, white and blue ribbon. It was gold and said, "Winner."

New Hampshire isn't Iowa. New Hampshire voters strike a more libertarian tone, far less focused on social issues. They don't like taxes. They don't like Washington. The state's motto, borrowed from its most famous Revolutionary War hero and emblazoned on license plates, is "Live Free or Die."

As Romney barnstormed across the Granite State, his focus shifted.

"This isn't the time for us to shrink from conservative principles," he intoned in an ad airing three days before the primary. "It's a time for us to stand in strength. America must remain the world's superpower."

New Hampshire, though, is like Iowa in that winning the contest means glad-handing voters. As the old joke goes, in the early primary states, undecided voters just haven't met the candidates enough times.

In his first few hours in the state after Iowa, Romney, sleep-deprived but pushing forward, stopped at The Golden Egg diner in Portsmouth to greet the early birds. He wanted to discuss the pending primary, but the gaggle of reporters still wanted to talk Iowa.

Romney came into that first contest as an unknown, the past governor of the "bluest of the blue states," he reasoned, and he was unable to market himself as well as Huckabee.

"Had I been a Baptist minister, I perhaps could have chosen a different path, but that wasn't the path that's available to me," Romney said, raising the issue of religion as a cause of his Iowa demise. "He took one that was available to him, worked it extremely well, turned out people extremely well and I congratulate him on a well-run campaign."

Romney didn't want to talk about Huckabee; his sights were now locked on McCain, a difficult target, given that the Arizona senator had camped out in the state for the past month and already had the 2000 primary win in his résumé. Romney's campaign issued a series of releases called the "Straight Talk Detour," a takeoff on McCain's Straight Talk Express.

Sen. Barack Obama had won Iowa's Democratic caucuses by marching to the drums of change, and Romney saw an opening. McCain had served in the Senate for 21 years by then; he was Washington. Romney's advance people hung a new sign in the William B. Cashin Senior Activity Center in Manchester and aimed a spotlight at it. As New Hampshire voters entered the room, they couldn't miss the warning: "Washington is broken."

The race had tightened. WMUR's poll that Saturday showed McCain at 33 percent and Romney at 27. The top two candidates would have a final chance for a smackdown at the ABC News/Facebook/WMUR debate at Saint Anselm College. The setting: six of the top candidates sitting at a roundtable like a circular firing squad.

This time, Huckabee seemed to be helping McCain whack Romney.

"You know, Governor, don't try and characterize my position," Romney said, after the ex-Arkansas chief executive tried to criticize him on the Iraq war.

"Which one?" Huckabee asked to laughter.

McCain seized the opportunity to pile on when Romney said he was inaccurately quoted in The Associated Press about immigration reform.

"You're always misquoted," McCain said.

"It was — that does happen from time to time," Romney countered.

"When you change issues — positions on issues from time to time, you will get misquoted," zinged back McCain.

When Romney tried to cement his message of change, McCain couldn't resist one more hit.

"I just wanted to say to Gov. Romney, we disagree on a lot of issues, but I agree you are the candidate of change," McCain said.

Ouch.

The debate had been bruising for Romney, but he had one thing to celebrate: He had won the Wyoming caucuses! Sure, Huckabee took Iowa and McCain was leading in New Hampshire where all the national media attention was trained, but, hey, Romney had won eight delegates from the least populous state in the nation.

He was, of course, the only top-tier candidate to have visited the Cowboy State (and three of his five sons had dropped by, too). But still, Romney had eight more delegates than McCain. He took a victory lap at Varick's sports bar, touting his win in the Western state.

Election Day arrived Jan. 8 for New Hampshire, and Romney's team tried to tamp down expectations. His aides sent out talking points during the early afternoon to assist surrogates. One item: "Is it over if he loses in New Hampshire?"

"Well," the memo advised as an answer, "Gov. Romney has a strong base of support across the country. He is not a one-state wonder, but the full-spectrum conservative that the Republican Party needs. He got the silver in Iowa, won Wyoming and will have a strong showing here tonight."

Seeing the surge of independent voters leaning toward Obama, Team Romney was hoping that shift would undercut McCain's support.

It didn't happen.

GOP voters favored Romney slightly over McCain, but independents loved the self-styled maverick, putting him over the top by 5 points.

Romney's strategist tried to put a brave face on the back-to-back defeats. In a memo circulated by the campaign, data-cruncher Alex Gage noted that with seconds in Iowa and New Hampshire, Romney now had more votes than any Republican hopeful. His message of change was gaining momentum, he would be the best candidate against any Democrat in the general election and he was the only GOP contender who would be competitive in many states.

Next up: Michigan, Romney's native state and where his dad served three terms as governor. It would be his easiest win, as many expected. Not only did he have the best brand in the state, but also his message about turning around the economy was welcomed.

Romney dubbed his tour across the state "Change Begins With Us."

"I don't know about the Washington politicians, but I can tell you this: If I am president, I will not rest until Michigan is back," he told the Detroit Economic Club. "Michigan can once again lead the world's automotive industry. But it means we're going to have to change Washington. We're going to go from politicians who say they are 'aware' of Michigan's problems to a president who will do something about them."

Ironically, his prescription for what ailed Detroit would go from a positive in 2008 to a negative four years later. But in this first go-round, Romney earned 39 percent of the vote, his first solid victory, though when you counted Wyoming it was his second "gold medal" — as he reminded Leno in an appearance on "The Tonight Show" three days later.

"Big chins and perfect hair," joked a Romney aide in advance of the network appearance. "Makes for some great late-night TV, apparently."

In typical Romney style, he quipped to Leno that he starts his day with a bowl of granola and a three-mile jog and ends it by changing from his dark suit into something more comfortable, like a light suit.

A day later, Romney, propelled by a large Mormon population, took the Nevada caucuses. Another gold medal.

"The people of Nevada voted for change in Washington," Romney said, continuing to embrace that whole hope-and-change motif that was carrying Obama on the Democratic side.

South Carolina, though, was the same day and sucked up almost all of the media attention. Romney didn't really try there, and for good reason: McCain and Huckabee had polled so much better. McCain ultimately won, by single digits.

There was now a front-runner, and it wasn't Romney.

On to Florida, likely the most competitive of the early contests. By this time, the economy was tanking and Romney was touting his ability to rescue the Olympics and save companies as he did at Bain.

"With the nature of the challenges America faces, economically and in foreign policy," Romney told a crowd at a Coral Gables restaurant, "it would be vastly beneficial to this country to have a leader who's actually had a job in the private sector."

Florida, though, was McCain's.

Giuliani, who had made his big stand in the Sunshine State, gave up and flew to California to endorse McCain before Super Tuesday. California Gov. Arnold Schwarzenegger and Texas Gov. Rick Perry backed McCain as well.

On top of that, McCain swept nine of the states while Romney took seven. While that count sounds like a close race, it didn't tell the real story. McCain won the big states and 600-something delegates. Romney had 274, total. Mathwise, the race was over.

Romney knew it and discussed with aides bowing out with class. By now, it was just Romney and Huckabee trailing McCain, and Romney figured it'd be best to look magnanimous and also punch Huck a bit for not lining up behind the eventual GOP flag bearer. After all, in the Republican Party, the man coming in second gets to go to the front of the line the next time around. Romney figured he could pull out of the race while knocking the Democratic front-runners, Obama and Sen. Hillary Clinton, at the same time.

He ended his campaign in February 2008 at CPAC, a year after his triumphant first appearance before the influential Republican crowd.

"Last year CPAC gave me the send-off I needed," he said. "At the time, I was in single digits in the polls, and I was facing household names in the Republican contest. As of today, more than 4 million people have given me their vote for president."

That's the glass-half-full version. He eventually got to the half-empty part.

"If I fight on in my campaign, all the way to the convention, I would forestall the launch of a national campaign and make it more likely that Sen. Clinton or Obama would win," Romney said. "And in this time of war, I simply cannot let my campaign be a part of aiding a surrender to terror. ...

"I hate to lose," Romney continued. "My family, my friends and our supporters — many of you right here in this room — have given a great deal to get me where I have a shot at becoming president. If this were only about me, I would go on. But I entered this race because I love America, and because I love America, I feel I must now stand aside, for our party and for our country."

A week later, Romney endorsed McCain in Boston at what was formerly known as the Romney for President Headquarters. They hung a giant U.S. flag in the building's entrance and hid the spare Romney signs. Aides who had worked so furiously to prop up the ex-governor and tear down McCain stood off to the side, straining to smile.

"I am pleased to introduce a real American hero, the next president of the United States, Sen. John McCain," Romney said.

As he spoke, the campaign's money folks were busy figuring out how to refund millions to Americans who had given to Romney's not-gonna-happen general election.

But there was still a glimmer of hope for Romney: He could be named McCain's running mate.

Romney didn't just fade away. He became McCain's surrogate. Wherever the Straight Talk Express couldn't make it, the runner-up went.

He spoke at the Nevada GOP convention and the one in Maine. He flew to Pennsylvania, Colorado, Oregon and Texas. He hit his "home states" of Michigan, Utah and Massachusetts — not to mention appearances for down-ticket candidates in Texas, Virginia, Florida and Washington state.

Romney's willingness to help impressed McCain. He could talk about the economy with confidence, something that escaped the GOP nominee. It seemed for a while everyone was writing about how McCain would pick Romney as his vice-presidential nominee. Such chatter filled hours on TV talk shows.

Those same pundits named other potential running mates such as Minnesota Gov. Tim Pawlenty, independent Connecticut Sen. Joe Lieberman, Secretary of State Condoleezza Rice and Utah Gov. Jon Huntsman Jr.

Like all good veep hopefuls, each muted expectations.

"We're not going to join the parlor guessing game over who is going to be John McCain's running mate," said Romney spokesman Eric Fehrnstrom. "That is not what Gov. Romney is focusing on."

But it was the position he wanted — and he might have landed it had McCain not forgotten how many homes he himself owned. The economy was tanking and when Politico reporters asked, McCain couldn't remember how many homes he and his wife, Cindy, had.

Choosing Romney, who had four houses, would have meant the GOP's dynamic duo were homeowners a dozen times over — not the best face of the party as regular Americans sank underwater in their own mortgages.

That McCain and a few trusted aides had picked little-known Alaska Gov. Sarah Palin was so secret that McCain's advance team set up the podium for the announcement expecting the choice to be Romney. They were told to lower it.

Romney stayed true to his word and backed the McCain-Palin ticket. At the Republican National Convention in St. Paul, he took the stage the night before McCain would accept the nomination.

The convention, which took over the Twin Cities, already had suffered a blow from Hurricane Gustav. It's hard to party when a massive storm is killing people in Haiti, Cuba and Jamaica and hammering U.S. cities along the Gulf Coast. Republicans canceled the first day of festivities, adding an air of gravity to what was supposed to be the GOP's big celebration. The show had to go on, though, and the sea of red, white and blue, the McCain-Palin signs and the confetti and balloons were ready and waiting. Thousands of exuberant delegates filled the floor of the Xcel Energy Center and stretched into the nosebleed seats.

The crowd rose to its feet when Romney strolled out, overshadowed by a large video screen projecting a red field with the McCain campaign logo dead center. He had to wait several minutes at the podium until the cheering ceased.

"President McCain and Vice President Palin will keep America as it has always been — the hope of the world," Romney said, tweaking his standard stump speech about himself to help out the party.

It was Huntsman, for years the stalwart McCain guy, who would land a better speaking role: introducing Palin just as the hype around her was taking off.

Huntsman had spent the convention shuffling between interviews on radio, TV and newspaper roundtables, catching an unfortunate cold that left his voice hoarse and gravelly — kind of a mix between Bobcat Goldthwait and a young boy going through puberty. It was not the best moment to have a national platform and an audience of millions.

Palin is "a hockey mom, a hunter, a hard-hitting reformer, and, quite frankly, she's not afraid in a little town called Washington to kick a few fannies and raise a little hell," Huntsman said, nominating her as McCain's running mate. It must have stung a bit for this seasoned diplomat, who could talk ad nauseam about China-U.S. relations, to be endorsing a one-term governor who couldn't recall what newspapers she read or what wars the U.S. was fighting.

Huntsman played the good soldier, though, and brought the audience to its feet with chants of "Sarah! Sarah! Sarah!"

Palin proved to be a disaster on the trail and not the kick the McCain campaign needed to bring out the vote. Obama, with newly minted vice presidential candidate Joe Biden, rolled to a historic victory.

Romney went back to his home in Belmont, braced to become the party's standard-bearer in four years. Huntsman, too, returned home, to Utah — at least for a while.

chapter nine

A diplomat in China

In early 2008, Jon Huntsman Jr. was a re-election lock before he even filed for a second term as Utah's governor. A Salt Lake Tribune poll showed him with 78 percent support from voters.

His previous three years had been scandal-free with hefty economic growth, a boost in education funding and a major overhaul of the tax code. The Huntsman brand was stronger than ever.

In fact, the governor spent time during his own campaign traversing the country to pitch another candidate: presidential hopeful John McCain. The move didn't go unnoticed in Utah. At his monthly news conference in April, he was asked about eyeing higher office.

Huntsman responded with a nondenial denial. "Well, since I don't seem to be headed to that position, why would I have any such conversation?"

A few months later, he gave a similar response when his name was floated as a possible McCain running mate.

"Anyone with a pulse is kind of being talked about, and that's kind of the way these things go, they become free-for-alls," Huntsman said, "which my kids think, and my dogs in particular think, is really pretty humorous."

Again, was there no "no" in there.

Huntsman kept to his mantra: He was running to serve Utah. He loved his job. His family didn't want him to jump.

"I'm in the best position already," he said.

When the dust from the election had settled, the Obama-Biden ticket had rolled over the McCain-Palin team nationally, while in Utah, Huntsman had demolished his Democratic challenger.

The wheel of fortune, though, was still turning for the re-elected governor.

U.S. Ambassador to China Clark T. Randt Jr. resigned his long-held post when George W. Bush's term ended, leaving a plum spot for Obama to fill.

Enter Jeff Bader, a senior Obama adviser who had worked with Huntsman in the trade representative's office under the first President Bush.

Huntsman, Bader assured Obama, was the "best qualified person for the job, given his experience in the region, fluency in the language and culture, and knowledge of critical issues affecting the region."

Yes, he was a Republican. Yes, he had backed McCain in 2008. And, yes, he had been buzzed about as a potential 2012 presidential candidate. But what better way to neutralize a possible rival than to send him halfway around the world?

The candidate of hope and change already had said he wanted to "think outside the box," and at one point said he wanted to mimic Abraham Lincoln's effort to appoint a "team of rivals" — top aides who wouldn't just be yes men and women.

Bader's push — coupled with lobbying by Senate Majority Leader Harry Reid, a friend of Jon Huntsman Sr. — persuaded Obama.

Awaiting a flight in Detroit en route to Chicago, Huntsman's chief of staff, Neil Ashdown, got a message that his White House counterpart, Rahm Emanuel, wanted to chat with the governor. Ashdown thought it might be about bird flu, then believed (incorrectly) to be a pandemic threat.

Huntsman found a quiet spot in the airport to phone Emanuel and emerged from the call with an ashen face.

"The president wants to see me," he later informed Ashdown. "He wants to talk to me about China. I think he wants me to be the ambassador."

Huntsman wasn't inclined to take the job initially, though it had been his lifelong wish.

Four days later, en route on a Utah trade mission to Israel, he and Mary Kaye made a quiet stopover at the Oval Office. Obama sat them in comfy couches around a wooden coffee table.

"I need you to be the U.S. ambassador to China," Obama told Huntsman bluntly.

The governor decided he couldn't say no. He didn't suspect until later that it might be an attempt to sideline him from the 2012 presidential race.

One of his first calls after accepting the job went to political consultant John Weaver, a former McCain strategist. While unofficial, and on the down low, Weaver and Huntsman had spoken multiple times about what the political scene in 2012 might look like, and if Huntsman might be a possible presidential candidate against Obama.

Weaver, a tall, lanky Texan, saw an opening for the GOP with a Huntsman candidacy, and he was already sketching out in his mind how the Utah governor could win over the Republican base. Huntsman's call ended any conversation.

"I apologize for wasting your time," Huntsman said. "We'll see what happens when I come back. I don't know when that will be."

Family members insisted it wasn't an easy decision for Huntsman.

"This is something that was very tough for him," brother Peter Huntsman recalled. "He feels very dedicated to fulfilling his role as governor. At the same time, look at the world's history, and the role that China plays in that, and it's immense."

Huntsman took off for Israel to keep up appearances but cut short a visit to Greece to return for the announcement. It was so hush-hush, so rushed, that he hadn't even alerted Lt. Gov. Gary Herbert.

"Are you sitting down?" Huntsman asked the soon-to-be-governor-in-waiting the Friday before Obama made it official.

"The lieutenant governor doesn't have any idea what's happening," Herbert chief of staff Joe Demma said at the time.

Huntsman already had been contemplating a future presidential run, and resigning his governorship to work for a Democratic president prompted some soul-searching. But the president was persuasive: The country needed Huntsman in Beijing.

In the Diplomatic Room of the White House, with his wife, his parents and his children standing to the side, Huntsman Jr. tried to stress the "country first" theme that a few years later would become his presidential campaign slogan.

"I grew up understanding the most basic responsibility one has is service to country," he said. "When the president of the United States asks you to step up and serve in a capacity like this, that to me is the end of the conversation and the beginning of the obligation to rise to the challenge."

Obama tried to help, too.

"I hope the good people of Utah will forgive me," he said, "and understand how proud they should be of their governor for his willingness to answer his nation's call."

It was the beginning of what would turn out to be a short-lived friendship.

"I am grateful for the graciousness and kindness you have shown me and my family — particularly your confidence in my ability to represent you in China," Huntsman said in a handwritten note to the president. "Mary Kaye and I will begin our journey tomorrow — leaving behind a state we love — but anticipating an extraordinary experience in Beijing. You are a remarkable leader — and it has been a great honor getting to know you."

Huntsman underlined "remarkable," a bit of punctuation that would come back to bite him on the 2012 campaign trail.

China had fascinated Huntsman since he was a child.

When his father worked for President Nixon, Jon Jr. often tagged along on Saturdays to the White House, where he recalled once carrying a bag for then-Secretary of State Henry Kissinger to a waiting helicopter. Turns out, Kissinger was embarking on the first high-level visit of a U.S. official to mainland China in decades.

That was simultaneously the first chapter in a new era of U.S.-China relations and the start of Huntsman's lifelong enchantment with Asia. He began studying the language and culture and reading book after book about it.

He later would serve his Mormon mission in Taiwan and return to the region as U.S. ambassador to Singapore under President George H.W. Bush. He was, at the time, the youngest ambassador in modern times. As was often the case, his father's intervention helped propel his son's career trajectory.

Then-Sen. Jake Garn of Utah told the White House he wouldn't support a treaty Bush wanted to push through. Shocked, White House aides called to ask why and reported back to the president that Garn, prompted by Huntsman Sr., wanted an ambassadorship for his son.

"Ambassador to Singapore?" Bush said, according to a Utah Republican who recalls the episode. "Appoint him now."

It's unclear if Huntsman Sr. had anything to do with his son's later appointment to be America's envoy to China — though Harry Reid's lobbying might indicate so — but he played the role of proud papa just before Obama announced the new posting. In the appropriately named China Room, Huntsman Sr. recounted for the president the story of his little boy carrying Kissinger's bag.

"When you leave," Obama retorted, "I'll get Dr. Kissinger to carry your bags to the plane."

The China ambassadorship was Huntsman Jr.'s dream job. It was something else for his family.

"It is not necessarily a fun place to live, but the work was fascinating," said a former aide to Huntsman in China. "It was more difficult on his family than it was on him."

Everyone who worked in the embassy — from the cleaning crew to the diplomats — needed top-secret security clearance. Mary Kaye didn't have such a clearance, and neither did the Huntsman daughters who went to Beijing.

"[Mary Kaye] couldn't just come and go," said the former aide. "She couldn't go to his office. She couldn't be involved. She was just living in this terrible pollution. It was dark and dreary, and she couldn't be involved. It was the same for the kids; they were cut off from their dad."

Abby Huntsman, the second eldest, recalled the isolation of being stuck in a foreign land with all eyes on you.

"We could still wander around, but we were pretty much followed," she said. "They tracked where each of us was at all times. But you knew that, so there was a real lack of privacy, when it comes to conversations."

The ambassador would return home in the evenings, unable to say much about how his day went, other than that he had had good meetings. But the experience also helped bring the Huntsman clan together.

"It was also a memorable time for our family because of the privacy issue," Abby Huntsman said. "We really bonded over that."

Between high-level meetings, the ambassador was able to escape and show his kids around various parts of China; he spoke fluent Mandarin and was adept at the culture.

The family came to the gig with a plan to move on after two or three years; it wasn't a long-term commitment.

For the most part, Obama's people seemed happy with Huntsman's performance.

A White House official said Huntsman was an "effective" team player during most of his time in Beijing. When Chinese officials wanted to take Huntsman to the woodshed — over some U.S. action or the latest flap over Taiwan — he would hop on his Forever-brand bicycle and pedal to the scolding instead of showing up with an entourage in a convoy of black SUVs.

In Obama's only visit to China, Huntsman was the key staffer, introducing the president to Chinese leaders and even posing on the Great Wall for the obligatory souvenir photo.

"As one observer and someone who takes this relationship seriously, as the on-site manager, I was very, very proud of our president," Huntsman told reporters at the Beijing Marriott City Wall hotel.

The ex-Utah governor was even more effusive in his assessment of the president after Obama returned to the United States to criticism over his failure to make progress on human rights, clean energy, nuclear weapons and a host of other issues.

"I've got to say some of the reporting I saw afterward was off the mark," Huntsman said. "I saw sweeping comments about things that apparently weren't talked about, when they were discussed in great detail in the meetings."

Obama's big goal with China — beyond the more difficult and unreachable ones such as securing Chinese assistance in dealing with North Korea and Pakistan — was to increase U.S. exports. That goal was met while Huntsman was holding down the Beijing compound.

The ambassador also achieved something else during his tenure: celebrity status. Jumping on a loaner Harley-Davidson for a ride around Shanghai, he became a target for Chinese paparazzi. Mary Anne, his eldest daughter, was reportedly picked up for a date by the son of a Communist Party official in a red Ferrari. And the Huntsmans' adopted daughter Gracie Mei had become a "hometown hero" in the more wealthy prefecture of Yangzhou.

"I can tell you that because I've traveled with Gracie to Yangzhou," Huntsman said. "And the mayor came out and half the town of 5 million people came out to greet her when she was there. And it was the most emotional journey I've ever taken. And as a gift to her, they basically put her on a postage stamp."

She was 11 years old.

Relations also were good between Huntsman and Obama at the time. In the words of a senior administration official, the ambassador "worked really well as part of a team."

But hints began appearing that America's envoy might be thinking about his next dream job. In a sitdown with Newsweek, Huntsman showed that he had his eye on a bigger position than the one in Beijing.

"You know, I'm really focused on what we're doing in our current position," he said. "But we won't do this forever, and I think we may have one final run left in our bones."

Huntsman may have regretted uttering those words when they set off a chain of events leading to a White House bid. "It swirled out of control," said a former aide.

John Weaver, who had shelved any idea of a Huntsman candidacy, given that his first choice of a candidate was now an Obama appointee, saw the Jan. 1, 2011, Newsweek cover story, headlined "The Manchurian Candidate," and the subsequent buzz; it was like spotting the bat signal. He began creating a campaign while Huntsman was still taking orders from the White House.

With Zions Bank CEO Scott Anderson as the principal officer, the Horizon PAC launched in Utah in January, setting up a fund for Huntsman fans — such as Huntsman Sr. — to toss in cash to help set up what would become a full-blown presidential campaign.

The PAC's website initially featured a big "H" bracketed by "maybe" and "someday." It later switched to a spectrum-colored logo and some cryptic text that wiped across the screen, teasing the idea that "maybe someday we'll find a new generation of conservative leaders."

No one bought the charade.

Back in China, Huntsman took a stroll one Sunday to the Wangfujing shopping district of Beijing with Gracie Mei and Mary Kaye. He donned his signature leather jacket and seemed to be surprised when someone recognized him.

"You guys don't know me. Really?" Huntsman said in Mandarin as he eyed the large crowd gathered in the square.

It wasn't just a big sale that drew hundreds of people. Anti-government protesters had chosen the spot to make their voice heard. It was the last place in the world for America's top diplomat in China to be spotted.

Huntsman confidants stressed that the ambassador happened onto the demonstrations purely by accident. Warned by a staffer, Ashdown called Huntsman to tell him to steer clear of Wangfujing, where demonstrations were being staged, but it was too late. "I know," Huntsman responded, "I think I just stumbled onto one."

Huntsman and the State Department downplayed the incident. The ambassador just wanted to go shopping. But the White House was, to put it mildly, surprised.

"There wasn't a split," an administration official later explained. "We certainly shared all the views of the situations, right. We didn't know he was going to do certain things. So I think in some instances, particularly toward the end, we weren't aware that he was going to attend a rally. Would have been good to know that and coordinate it."

A different type of coordination was going on in New Orleans around the same time.

Weaver, who would go on to be the campaign's chief strategist, pulled together Team Huntsman. Some shook hands for the first time; some were longtime buddies; many never had even met the man for whom they would devote the next nine months of their lives.

Mr. B's Bistro on Royal Street is in the French Quarter but a stark contrast from the grain-alcohol hurricane cocktails and bead throwers on Bourbon Street. The barbecue shrimp, fried oysters and gumbo are famous — even in a city where everyone serves those dishes.

Weaver took his seat at the head of a long, skinny table, sipping a screw-driver — the Huntsman team's signature drink — and talking about a candidate who could rise above the oddball field lining up on the Republican side. Since this was a team assembled by the Horizon PAC, the group had met at the restaurant on its own. These conversations, carefully following legal advice, started with, "In my own free time …" before Huntsman's name was ever mentioned.

But word was out. It was clear Huntsman would return to America as a presidential candidate.

It was, therefore, an awkward scene when Chinese President Hu Jintao visited America and held a news conference with Obama, while Ambassador Huntsman sat on the front row. Obama knew the question about his potential rival was coming and responded by showering praise on his envoy.

"I couldn't be happier with the ambassador's service," Obama said. "I'm sure that he will be successful in whatever endeavors he chooses in the future. And I'm sure that him having worked so well with me will be a great asset in any Republican primary."

It was a tone Obama would take with Huntsman going forward: Kill his campaign with kindness.

Obama attended his first Gridiron Club dinner as president in 2011, ready to jab at the White House hopefuls lining up against him.

As much as he admired Haley Barbour, Mitch Daniels and Tim Pawlenty, Obama said, "I'm a little biased towards my dear, dear friend, Jon Huntsman.

"In fact, I was just telling the Des Moines Register, nobody has done more for my administration than Jon Huntsman. As his good friends in China might say, he is truly the yin to my yang. And I'm going to make sure that every primary voter knows it. If there's a fish fry for Jon Huntsman in Cedar Rapids, guess who's going to be at the grill. Barack Obama. If you see me on the streets of Nashua, [N.H.], wearing my parka and waving a sign, give me a honk for Huntsman. The next GOP nominee for president. Love that guy."

Huntsman handed in his resignation Jan. 31, effective at the end of April. He phoned reporters the day he delivered his letter, speaking off the record and denying that he was already planning a White House bid.

He returned to China to wrap things up while Weaver signed on veteran adman Fred Davis as well as communications director Matt David and spokesman Tim Miller.

Huntsman's last day in office coincided with the annual White House Correspondents Association dinner, or nerd prom, as it's known in Washington. He and Mary Kaye had snagged seats with Bloomberg — sitting with New York Mayor Michael Bloomberg, Treasury Secretary Timothy Geithner and White House adviser Valerie Jarrett — while The Salt Lake Tribune invited Weaver to join its table with Obama's former campaign manager, David Plouffe.

Huntsman showed up while a Tribune reporter was walking into the event with Weaver.

Weaver and Huntsman said a quick hello when "introduced" by the reporter, but Weaver then encouraged Huntsman not to chat with hundreds of reporters around.

"Governor, please keep walking," he advised.

Huntsman was still bound by diplomatic rules and couldn't talk about the campaign.

Weaver later appeared at The Tribune's table and shook hands with Plouffe. It was a delicious pairing of political hacks. Weaver was hoping he would be going up against Plouffe come November 2012. Plouffe would prefer that Weaver's guy quickly flame out.

Obama made sure to mention his rivals when he took the podium to deliver his comedy routine for the evening.

"My buddy," Obama said, "our outstanding ambassador, Jon Huntsman, is with us. Now, there's something you might not know about Jon. He didn't learn to speak Chinese to go there. Oh, no. He learned English to come here."

Huntsman's distant cousin wasn't present in the cavernous banquet hall, but he didn't go unmentioned.

"There's a vicious rumor floating around that I think could really hurt Mitt Romney," Obama joked. "I heard he passed universal health care when he was governor of Massachusetts. Someone should get to the bottom of that."

After the dinner, the Huntsmans headed out, taking a brisk, one-block walk across Connecticut Avenue to their new home he barely had seen. Weaver & Co., meanwhile, headed upstairs to the hotel bar.

Rounds flowed as Weaver held court from his perch at the power position of the roundtable, his back to the wall with a view of the tuxedo- and gown-clad crowd swarming the pub. Eager young aides flirted with nearby women as much as they talked politics. Just after midnight, Weaver slipped out of the room to take a call.

Huntsman wanted a meeting at 8 a.m. There was no time to waste.

Weaver told the group that they were expected to be at the Huntsman residence early the next morning, news that only fueled more rounds until the bar closed at 2 a.m. The next morning, they would stagger across the street to meet the man they wanted to be president.

chapter ten

Late to the party

Two schools of thought emerged on whether Jon Huntsman would run for president: those who thought it was game on and those who assumed it was idle chatter. Some saw it as a sure bet; others dismissed it as mere beltway banter. One side had worked for months to lay out a campaign, ready to launch on the word "go." The other was thinking, well, it's too late, let's hold off for another few years.

Huntsman straddled the two.

The Sunday morning after the White House correspondents' dinner was illuminating to all. Huntsman's home, which he bought in July 2010, was a red-brick Federal-style row house, most recently the living space for the contestants on Bravo's "Top Chef." The reality show featured the magnificent kitchen and the intimate courtyard in many shots, often as the retreat for the participants in the frenzied competition to unwind. In the space where chefs once aspired to a TV-launched career, now resided a politician unsure of his ambitions.

Weaver showed up first, with bagels and coffee, along with Susan Wiles, who would be the incoming campaign manager. The rest of the gang — spokesman Tim Miller, communications director Matt David and his deputy,

Jake Suski — stumbled in, still reeling from the night before. Pleasantries exchanged, they moved to the dining room in the rear of the house to sit around a dark-wood table, one of the few pieces of furniture in the newly acquired, bare-walled home. Most of Huntsman's possessions were floating somewhere in the middle of the Pacific Ocean on their long journey to the new home.

A former aide said Huntsman had clearly thought about his political future, dissecting his strengths and weaknesses like a man ready to hit the trail. The crew asked a lot of questions. What would he want to run on? Was he ready for the long slog and the intense pressure? What about the fellow elephant in the room: Mitt Romney? What would he say about their relationship?

"He had really good answers," the ex-aide later recalled, offering a gut-check assessment that Huntsman was 90 percent in.

Huntsman, sitting aside Mary Kaye, was still recovering himself from the night before — but for a diff'rent reason. He had just left Beijing, living a "siloed life" as he called it, as stringent as the military and where policy trumps politics. His introduction back to the states was this lavish, celebrity-filled dinner and the buzz that followed him as he walked around the ballroom.

"I was maybe living in naive land, but I was somewhat surprised at the level of interest in a race," Huntsman said later on. "Washington is kind of a fairy land of sorts where people create their own sense of reality."

Huntsman was shocked — shocked — at the narrative ginned up by political insiders and pundits about his plans. Now there was this team of people sitting in his home planning a rollout of his presidential campaign with ideas about targeting states, positioning, strengths and weaknesses and more. He was cautious but interested.

"Thank you all for an interest in our cause," he declared at the outset, unsure yet of what that cause would be. "I don't know if this is ever going to be real, but I'm willing to at least test the market and see what's there."

Questions rolled out from the advisers-for-hire. Huntsman, ever the diplomat, thought through them and offered careful answers.

In Republican circles, having worked for Obama isn't a good thing, the guests noted, so how are you going to blast the guy who hired you? How would you expose the underbelly of the Obama administration's actions?

Huntsman, whose political races in Utah previously took on positive notes, as is the case in a small, GOP-dominated state, was taken aback.

"I can't do that. If you're looking for somebody to do that, that's not me," he made clear, a point that would haunt his future campaign.

The Romney question prompted a different response. There was a reason Huntsman, a distant cousin, felt a need to jump in against a strong front-runner.

"I thought [Romney] had compromised himself with his move to the right. The Romney of Massachusetts, as governor, I thought, was the ideal model for national success, truly," Huntsman later recalled. But Romney's "move inexorably to the right on a lot of issues, I think left a huge opening in the market for somebody who was willing to stay consistent on issues that they have stood for, whether popular or not popular."

Huntsman wanted to talk about his own successes as governor and stay true even if his message wasn't as popular as Romney's, which had undergone serious revisions on abortion, gay rights, health care and other issues.

"I thought there had been that element of authenticity that was lost in that transition for Mitt," Huntsman says.

He was open to a test run, to see if his own authenticity would provide a path; he wasn't full in, but he wanted to float a White House trial balloon.

That distressed some in the Weaver camp who weren't expecting such a tepid response. They had spent months planning a Huntsman bid, translating the signals they had received from Mary Kaye to Weaver, in addition to some talk between the consultant and Neil Ashdown, Huntsman's longtime right-hand guy. It wasn't overt about a presidential run, more of the chatter that one keeps to stay relevant; at least that's what Mary Kaye and Ashdown thought.

"We thought we had a winning candidate and a winning campaign," said a top campaign adviser. The organizing meeting in "New Orleans was well-orchestrated and organized. I would call that one of the high points of the campaign. Everything worked pretty well until Jon came back. And that's when things kind of went down the tubes."

One thing was sure: The campaign structure was in place. A spokesman, a strategist, a speechwriter, an ad guy, people on the ground in the early states. The pyramid was built, just waiting for a candidate to top it.

Months earlier, Weaver had taken a cue from Huntsman's coy-but-telling response to Newsweek about a possible political run, and set about hiring folks for a national race. No expense was spared.

Before Huntsman stepped off the plane from China, the Utah-based Horizon PAC had raised more than a million dollars and was throwing cash at consultants, who were essentially the soon-to-be candidate's "campaign in waiting." Weaver's Network Cos. snatched up $350,000 by April 25. South Carolina's Richard Quinn took in $80,000. Adman Fred Davis picked up $68,000. And Wiles Consulting — run by Susan Wiles and Lanny Wiles, who would be his advance man — pulled in $67,000.

Three prospective aides split $63,000 to get the movement rolling before they even had met the prospective candidate. And there was no question who was bankrolling the effort: the Huntsmans.

Huntsman's immediate family members, including his parents and brothers, ultimately chipped in more than three-quarters of a million bucks to the Utah PAC, which had no limits to the sums it could accept.

Huntsman Jr. had no idea the level of cash funneling his way — he read about it in the newspaper. He hadn't contributed a dime, but the money was there, fueling his introduction.

Three days after he was free of the administration's reins, his team made its first official move toward a race, filing documents with the Federal Election Commission to form "H PAC," touted as a placeholder for a full-blown campaign.

"This is a paperwork step," spokesman Tim Miller said. "He's doing the organizational things required by campaign-finance law. When he wants to make an announcement, he will make an announcement."

Huntsman wasn't going to form an exploratory committee; there wasn't time.

Weaver had made calls to arrange him as the commencement speaker at the University of South Carolina and at Southern New Hampshire University, a way to muster easy publicity — and in early primary states — without having to answer questions from reporters.

"Give back — as much as you're able," Huntsman told the hundreds of graduates in Columbia, S.C., a prescient message on which he later would campaign. "Work to keep America great. Serve her, if asked. I was, by a president of a different political party. But in the end, while we might not all be of one party, we are all part of one nation, a nation that needs your generational gift of energy and confidence."

The Washington Post and The New York Times were on hand. Politico had a scribe there, too. It wasn't your usual gaggle of news hounds at a commencement speech. In fact, Supreme Court Associate Justice Sonia Sotomayor hadn't drawn that media crowd the night before for her speech.

Huntsman was the in guy, for now. The political chatter was deafening. The former U.S. ambassador sought, at the same moment, to toss out his credentials and make clear his unique standing.

"The way I saw it from overseas, America's passion remains as strong today as ever," he said, dressed in the Gamecocks' garnet robe and sprinkling his speech with a few "cool" and "awesome" mentions. And he had to — just had to — reference his high-school wannabe band.

"Wizard didn't make it, but I'll never regret following my passion," Huntsman said, offering his own hopeful advice. "Be you, remember others, embrace failure, find someone to love, give back, [and] never forget to rock 'n' roll."

The GOP field by then already had a mix of characters: some solid, others sure to fade away. But it was early, and as Mitt Romney played the cool candidate — steering clear of the too-early entrance — the game was on.

At the same time, and in the same state, Huntsman was playing coy, Fox News was welcoming candidates for the first debate of the 2012 season. The former Utah governor wasn't invited, and those diving in headfirst weren't even sure who he was.

"I've met him once in my life, so I don't know much about him," said former Pennsylvania Sen. Rick Santorum.

"I've certainly heard of him," chipped in former New Mexico Gov. Gary Johnson, "but I really don't know anything about him."

Herman Cain, the former chief executive of Godfather's Pizza, was stumped as well. "I don't know him well, and I don't know a lot about him."

Neither did South Carolina Republicans. At the GOP's state convention, the same day as Huntsman's commencement address, 408 delegates voted in a straw poll of potential presidential contenders; Huntsman nabbed four.

New Hampshire likewise didn't know Huntsman, but he was on his way to changing that.

The commencement address at Southern New Hampshire University was only one of several events slated for the former Utah governor. Riley's Country Store, Robie's Gun Shop, a VFW hall and a few house parties awaited him, but his first meet-and-greet was in Hanover at Jesse's Steaks, Seafood & Tavern, where the Huntsman entourage was welcomed by giant moose antlers adorning the entrance.

Huntsman's new staff didn't know much about him, whether he could excite audiences and dazzle on the stump. They had never really seen him speak.

"We literally realized a couple days out we didn't have a stump speech," recalls another senior aide. "He said, 'Guys, I got it,' went into the diner and literally we had no idea what he was going to say — scariest feeling in the world. [But] he was great. He was fantastic."

The same day, ABC News' George Stephanopoulos scored the first big interview with Huntsman, still only a few weeks back in the country and without time to draw up big talking points.

Stephanopoulos wasted little time to reach the tough question: People say you don't have a chance, that you worked for Obama. How do you respond?

"I worked for the president of the United States," Huntsman shot back. "The president asked me, the president of all the people. And during a time of war, during a time of economic difficulty for our country, if I'm asked by my president to serve, I'll stand up and do it."

"So you'd do it again?" Stephanopoulos asked.

"I'd do it again. Of course."

Huntsman aides were proud of their choice; they thought he hit it out of the park.

"That was probably the highest moment on the campaign from the perspective of senior staff," said that aide.

Abby Huntsman, the second eldest daughter who had remained in China as her dad transitioned back to the states, was shocked to see the unfolding campaign upon her return. She thought he might think about it but take a slow approach, even wait for a few years.

"I will say my dad, up until that point, he didn't want to run. He didn't really talk about it. And anytime you'd bring it up to him, [like] 'You're moving back; what are you thinking?' He would say, 'I don't really want to think about it right now. I'm in China, this is what I love to do.' He didn't really want to leave China, but it was hard on the family, the pollution and the young girls — my mom was worried about that."

Those closest to Huntsman felt a bit stunned at his sudden thrust into the political spotlight, and Abby wasn't the only one who didn't understand his quick move to join the 2012 field.

"I was very surprised. I didn't see it coming," says a close Huntsman aide. "I thought it was ridiculous. The other guys were raising money for four years. He had nothing."

The talk before this had been about 2016. Huntsman didn't even know the landscape. While he was in China, dealing with Communist leaders and international relations, the tea party had poked and needled the GOP until politicians felt the inevitable urge to surrender. The right wing essentially owned the Republican Party. Huntsman, a guy who had worked for the Democratic president the tea party revolted against, wasn't necessarily the ideal candidate the new folks in charge wanted.

But his mind was made up. He scored endless media attention as the non-tea-party moderate — intelligent, experienced, with the looks and the pedigree to take on the rough road ahead.

Visits to the early states done — positive coverage so far — Huntsman returned to the hardwood dining table for a "go, no-go" conversation with his family. There were definite negatives to jumping in, but positives as well. He was happy, even surprised, with the attention he was getting.

"I had enough of a feel of the marketplace, knowing it would be tough, or totally undoable," Huntsman recalls. "But that we had certain issues that were worth discussing during that cycle."

As usual with politics, though, the media darling that Huntsman was before he was a candidate quickly turned as reporters started digging into his record. His campaign sought to out a few of the potential skeletons early on to void gotcha moments.

Matt David, then the communications director, dispatched a staffer to Utah to dig through the governor's archives, then boxed up in a building near the state Capitol. It was mostly dry stuff — schedules, announcements, draft news releases — but there were two letters that were gold to opposition researchers.

"Dear Mr. President," the hand-scrawled note on official gubernatorial stationery read. "I am grateful for the graciousness and kindness you have shown my family — particularly your confidence in my ability to represent you in China. …

"You are a remarkable leader," Huntsman ended the note to Obama, underlining the adjective, "and it has been a great honor getting to know you."

The other letter — one that even Huntsman had forgotten — went to former President Bill Clinton, praising him for his brilliance and hoping for a meeting at one point.

"I must report that Sec. [Hillary] Clinton has won the hearts and minds of the State Dept. bureaucracy — no easy task. And after watching her in action, I can see why. She is well-read, hardworking, personable and has even more charisma than her husband! It's an honor to work with her," Huntsman wrote just before he left the governor's office.

David, sensing the urgency to inoculate his candidate, wanted to leak the letters to the news media early and homed in on a place where he thought no one would suspect a handout from the Huntsman people: the right-wing outlet The Daily Caller.

The online news outlet bannered the headline "Jon Huntsman's love letters," and reporters scrambled to find out where they came from to get their own copies. The Democratic National Committee said it didn't have the letters. A White House aide called to say off the record, it didn't come from 1600 Pennsylvania Ave. "Have you asked the Huntsman people?" the aide asked.

There were more questions about Huntsman's record: He had backed civil unions, a stance that wouldn't sit well with the GOP base. As governor, Huntsman had supported taking funds from Obama's stimulus act and aligned with economist Mark Zandi, who had advocated for a trillion-dollar package from Congress to help end the limping recession.

Huntsman also had joined then-California Gov. Arnold Schwarzenegger to sign on to the Western Regional Climate Action Initiative to combat greenhouse gases. The cap-and-trade idea didn't sit well with conservative, open-market types.

"Until we put a value on carbon, we're never going to be able to get serious about dealing with climate change," Huntsman said during a 2008 gubernatorial debate.

And while he ran for office in 2004 on a promise to provide vouchers for private-school students, when it came time to defend a new state law, he disappeared. Utah voters eventually killed it.

Patrick Byrne, a businessman who considered school choice his only major Utah issue, was Huntsman's biggest donor not named Huntsman. He felt so burned by the former governor that when Huntsman considered a run for higher office, Byrne wrote a scathing editorial for Politico, which ended by saying: "Having once been his largest donor, and having had substantial personal involvement with him, the possibility that he might be elected this nation's president is something I now consider unthinkable."

Huntsman's answer to critics labeling him a RINO (Republican In Name Only) because of those positions was almost a side slap against Romney's evolving spots.

"Well, first of all, I don't change on my positions," he told Stephanopoulos during that New Hampshire interview.

By that time, Romney was soaring. He already had been mostly vetted in 2008 by the news media — though he took an occasional hit (for example, for saying that, as a wealthy millionaire, he was unemployed) — and had raised more than $18 million by the end of June 2011. He had a veteran team, loyal and strategically placed. He had learned his lessons from 2008.

Romney's announcement, on a bright sunny June 2, went off flawlessly. Unlike in 2008, when his backdrop was his father's automobile company roots, he chose the Bittersweet Farm in Stratham, N.H., for a chili cookout, complete with hay bales, tractors and a barn with a large American flag.

He pitched himself as a turnaround artist and then lit into Obama, who Romney said hadn't lived up to his 2008 promise of economic recovery.

"At the time, we didn't know what sort of a president he would make," Romney said. "Now, in the third year of his four-year term, we have more than promises and slogans to go by. Barack Obama has failed America."

Romney, who had ditched the tie to appear less formal, shook some hands after the speech and jumped in line to help serve the chili. He was all smiles.

Huntsman, meanwhile, faced a struggling fundraising operation. He had to ante up $50,000 before his announcement to keep the engine running — despite saying he didn't want to self-finance. He told reporters at the time he had to "prime the pump," though apparently it was a dead well. It was the first of his many infusions.

"I had no choice," Huntsman recalls. "When you look at the numbers and in the first month or two, just to keep things going, you have to write out a check and take out a loan against your home ... when that started happening, that was an indication we were moving in a direction of counterproductivity on the financial side."

The campaign had enough cash — or at least thought it would be there eventually — to plan Huntsman's rollout. First up was Fred Davis, the ad guy whose job it was to raise Huntsman's name ID from essentially zero.

Davis wasn't a typical political consultant. His longer locks, his affinity for sports cars and his home in the Hollywood hills didn't scream Republican, but he was the one who could break the mold of button-down politics and bring a new image to a candidate.

He did it for Carly Fiorina, the former Hewlett-Packard CEO running for Senate from California, by grazing some demon sheep in a spot that can be described only as unconventional. Or his attempt to quell the feeding frenzy that followed Delaware Senate candidate Christine O'Donnell's comments that she once dabbled in witchcraft by creating ads with her proclaiming, "I'm not a witch."

Davis wanted Huntsman's introduction to be groundbreaking as well, a tease campaign that took a big, wide step away from the usual flag-waving, America-is-great ads or the I-did-this-for-you, vote-for-me spots. Huntsman needed something different.

So Davis rented a helicopter and hired a pilot, obtained a permit from the Navajo Nation and borrowed Huntsman's motorcycle and gear to film a rider zipping along dirt tracks — jumping over bumps and kicking up some dust amongst the sagebrush — with southern Utah's iconic Monument Valley in the background. It wasn't LBJ's daisy/nuclear bomb political spot, but it was certainly out of the ordinary.

"Mr. Huntsman is trying something different in GOP politics: a campaign based almost entirely on atmospherics," wrote The Wall Street Journal's Neil King. "It is, in many ways, the political version of a Ralph Lauren product launch."

The ads began — online only because there wasn't enough cash to splash them anywhere else — the week before Huntsman's announcement.

"In six days: Did not become famous with his band Wizard."

"In four days: Has seven children, one from India, one from China."

"Tomorrow: The candidate for president who rides motocross to relax."

In case there was any confusion, the ads ended with the line, "Paid for by Jon Huntsman."

Of course, there was no Jr. or Sr. tag, but it was clear who the candidate would be.

Weaver picked an announcement spot that he thought would attract prime coverage: Liberty State Park in New Jersey. Huntsman had no ties to Jersey, but he had worked as a young staffer for President Ronald Reagan, who announced his 1980 general election from the same location. The famous photo from that campaign launch is Reagan, in a white shirt, sleeves rolled up, pointing at the flame that sits atop America's most famous statue.

Weaver wanted that for Huntsman. After all, could you really beat the idea of bringing up your Reagan ties in front of the Statue of Liberty, bracketed by American flags and your tight-knit family?

Things did not go as planned. Reporters who showed up early were handed press badges proclaiming them part of the "John Huntsman for President Announcement Tour." When the misspelling of the candidate's first name was pointed out, staffers snatched them back, but not before an ABC News reporter tweeted out the image.

The crowd was slim — easily outnumbered by journalists. Minutes before the event was to begin, a bus arrived that had started in the wee hours in Washington and driven through Philadelphia picking up willing college Republicans.

An organizer, sporting a Utah Jazz shirt as a cape, high-fived the newcomers — mostly young men and a few women — as they exited the bus. A young Huntsman staffer saw they weren't moving fast enough.

"Guys! We're about to start this live shot," he shouted, "and we need everyone to run."

It was overcast — not the sunny, blue-sky backdrop Weaver had envisioned — but it wasn't raining. A staffer gave the expected two-minute heads-up to the TV camera crews when someone in the back yelled out. "Wait! We have no power!"

Fred Davis, the ad guy, had warned the organizers they needed two generators, one for the show and one to be ready. Due to cost concerns, only one generator was ordered, and it had died.

Former Texas Rep. Tom Loeffler approached the podium, now with a dead microphone, while Davis sought out the staffers huddled around the sputtering generator. Miraculously, a minute before Huntsman was to appear, it sparked to life and power returned to the camera stand, the microphones, the custom-made music that Davis had used in the motorcycle video that was ready to appear on the TV screens just offstage.

Huntsman then started his long walk across the grassy park to the stage, holding hands with Mary Kaye and Gracie and flanked by the rest of his kids. After the tease campaign that had preceded the rollout, the audience half-expected him to arrive on a motorbike. Instead, he stopped at the stairs, kissed Mary Kaye and stepped up alone.

Huntsman's father, Jon Sr., stood offstage beaming. It was June 21, 2011, his 74th birthday. "A father couldn't ask for a better birthday gift," the elder Huntsman said.

"Today, I'm a candidate for the office of president of the United States of

America," Huntsman declared. The audience cheered. The generator stayed on.

He then touted his record as Utah governor, his time in China, his service to the nation and, remaining true to his vow to run a positive campaign, he even had nice words for the man he wanted to oust from office.

"I don't think you need to run down anyone's reputation to run for president. Of course we'll have our disagreements. I respect my fellow Republican candidates. And I respect the president. He and I have a difference of opinion on how to help the country we both love. But the question each of us wants the voters to answer is who will be the better president, not who's the better American."

At least, Huntsman's team thought, he didn't mention Obama's name during the 14-minute speech. Not that many Americans saw it. Five minutes into the address, CNN's Kyra Phillips cut away to a commercial break, MSN-BC's Chris Jansing already was seeking feedback from pundits and Fox News was on to commercials.

Not that the networks had the best view anyhow. The media platform was too high, leaving most cameras pointed down at Huntsman so that his background was not the famed symbol of America but a Circle Line tour boat docked on Liberty Island.

Still, Huntsman was in, officially, and ready to jaunt to New Hampshire for another introduction to the Granite State, this time with a large contingent of media in tow. Reporters were rushed to the bus to head to Newark's airport, where upon arrival a Port Authority squad car escorted the entourage to a plane with Arabic writing on the side.

After some confusion, the reporters were shuttled to another plane that would be headed to Portsmouth, N.H., and not Saudi Arabia. At a packed Exeter Town Hall later, Huntsman gave a similar speech before jetting back to Jersey. It wasn't the kickoff he wanted.

"I was furious," Huntsman recalled. Two of the top people — campaign manager Susan Wiles and advance man Lanny Wiles, who had held that spot for Reagan at one point — soon were let go, though it wouldn't become public for a month.

Campaign aides knew it was bad. Really bad. If they couldn't pull together a scripted, made-for-TV moment like the announcement, how could they run a campaign that needed to pivot in the rough-and-tumble race? But there wasn't much that could be done immediately. The pop-up team was already locked in place, and there was no time to start fresh.

"If the Titanic is sinking, you don't talk about the paint on the cabin doors," said a former Huntsman senior aide.

Huntsman's entrance was met with sneers from the Romney folks. To them, they had a little-known competitor who had just left the Obama administration and thought he could topple the heir apparent.

"It was an annoyance," said a top Romney aide, "like a gnat."

chapter eleven

The Mormon question

M itt Romney was incensed.

The interview should have been easy: Drop in, spout some stump-speech lines, answer a few softballs. WHO Radio in Des Moines, Iowa, is a 50,000-watt talk-radio station that appeals to the kind of voters Romney needed in October 2007. The station aired conservative heavyweights such as Rush Limbaugh and Sean Hannity, and had once, in the 1930s, employed a young upstart named Ronald Reagan.

Romney, late for the interview, rushed into the studio in a crisp white shirt and blue tie, all smiles when host Jan Mickelson introduced him. That was the high point of the interview.

Mickelson, a self-proclaimed libertarian pro-lifer who hosted the No. 1 morning show in the Hawkeye State, quizzed Romney about Roe v. Wade and other firebrand GOP issues. Then the host wondered if Romney should have been excommunicated from the LDS faith for being pro-choice previously. Romney tried to explain, but time ran out.

"I don't like coming on the air and having you go after my church," he charged.

"I'm not going after — I agree with your church," Mickelson said.

"I'm not running as a Mormon," Romney responded, "and I get a little tired of coming on a show like yours and having it all about Mormon."

"I don't mind it being about that."

"I do. I do."

"I agree with the ethics of your church, for Pete's sake."

"So do I," Romney said, standing up, pushing his chair in and trying to control his rage.

Mike Huckabee was the former governor of Arkansas. Tim Pawlenty led Minnesota. John McCain was the maverick senator from Arizona.

Mitt Romney was the Mormon.

No matter his business résumé or his Olympic cred, it seemed on the campaign trail the only adjective attached to him in news stories — and even water-cooler conversations — was his faith. Most Americans have heard of Mormons, even if most don't know what they believe, wrongly think they are polygamists or deem them non-Christian. And polls were clear that a Mormon candidate had only a slightly better chance of winning the White House than a Muslim or an atheist. It's a tough place to start from if you're running for president already worried about charges of being a flip-flopper and the ex-governor of a liberal state.

Even in the modern political age — when a candidate could come back from sex scandals and corruption charges — the Mormon religion was serious baggage. The reality was that despite its members' wholesome lifestyles and straight-out-of-"Leave It to Beaver" families, the Mormon tag could hamstring a national campaign.

Romney, a fifth-generation Mormon who was as devout as any church apostle, knew this well from his 1994 Senate run. He was already an underdog scrambling to keep up with the pack, and it didn't help that a sizable number of Americans said they would never vote for a Mormon.

The faith factor hounded him during that first presidential run, especially in Iowa, where Protestant evangelicals ruled. Romney wanted to talk about government overspending, about returning to constitutional principles, about America being the "shining city on top of the hill," as he liked to paraphrase a famous Reagan line. At the WHO radio studio in Des Moines, Mickelson wanted to talk Mormon doctrine.

"I have to get back on the air. But I want you to know I take this stuff real seriously," Mickelson said.

"Well, I don't," Romney said, facetiously. "For me, all this stuff is frivolous. Pfft. C'mon. I'm running for president."

"Just — just relax," the host countered.

It was a candid moment for Romney, who had attempted to keep the focus on policy, on red-meat issues, not diverted by curiosity about what church he attended. He and his team were quick to tell anyone who asked that he was not running to be pastor in chief. But Mickelson had gotten under his skin, and, unbeknownst to Romney, the whole exchange was captured on video.

"Nobody was more surprised than I that he folded up so quickly," Mickelson later said. "I had no idea he was going to come unglued like this."

Romney aides were surprised, and angered, that the station had videotaped what they thought was an off-air discussion. But they also sensed an opportunity. Back at 585 Commercial St. in Boston, Team Romney's headquarters, national press secretary Kevin Madden and communications director Matt Rhoades watched the video and immediately began farming it out to reporters covering the campaign.

"We have to own this," Rhoades said. "This is feisty."

The video was going to circulate, so the Romney folks figured they should spin it their way: Romney looking tough in the face of an offensive line of questioning. It was a rare move by Romney aides, who generally steered clear of Mormon stuff.

Religion is always a touchy conversation, and in his presidential bids, Romney found himself in the awkward role of trying to define himself while also defending a faith so strange to so many people.

The LDS Church has fought, essentially, the same PR battle as it comes of age, growing in size and influence but still dogged by misconceptions about its true beliefs and its polygamous past. Today's LDS Church claims more than 15 million members worldwide, a small blip in the population of 7 billion. But its tremendous growth in the 20th century rocketed the once-obscure band of faithful into the mainstream.

The church can boast of 16 Mormons in Congress, as well as among the lofty ranks of judges, celebrities, artists and CEOs. The Tony-winning musical "The Book of Mormon" — albeit a spoof by the creators of "South Park" — sold out on Broadway and went on tour. But for all the publicity and growth, ignorance about Mormonism remains pervasive.

Mormons who have lived outside the Mormon Belt — the largely LDS region in and around the Rocky Mountains — often face questions about how many wives they have, whether they really abstain from alcohol or about secret rituals performed in their members-only temples. Beyond the questions are the jokes, some barbed, because making fun of Mormons seems to be socially acceptable.

The church tried to combat some misconceptions with a multimillion-dollar ad campaign tailored to explain to the masses that Latter-day Saints are like everyone else. The spots featured people of various ages, races and nationalities doing something normal and ending with the tagline, "I'm a Mormon."

Romney never appeared in the ads, which ran just before his second run at the Oval Office in 2012. The church stressed the campaign had nothing to do with the candidate, but there was no doubt he was becoming synonymous with the faith. If the LDS religion was a basketball team, Romney would have been the mascot. His first presidential race already had offered an opportunity for Americans and the world at large to meet a Mormon.

One thing was clear from the outset: Romney wasn't going to distance himself from the religion he had been born into, had served his whole life and profoundly believed.

High above Boston Common, the Ritz-Carlton offered picturesque views of the golden-domed Massachusetts Statehouse. Romney had a suite and a mission: Persuade some GOP leaders from early presidential-contest states to come to his aid. He was hoping to sign on Iowa's Doug Gross, a veteran political consultant, as his state chairman. Despite all the policy and political strategy questions, Gross went straight to the heart of a concern he had.

"I'm not changing my religion," Romney declared.

"I'm not asking you to," responded Gross, who eventually joined the campaign.

But deciding to sidestep the religion question doesn't mean questions won't be asked.

He faced an onslaught of queries about church founder Joseph Smith, about polygamy, about bans on coffee and tea and why, as some feared, he believed in a different Jesus than other Christians.

Though it may have seemed like it from the media coverage — covers of Time, Newsweek and others framed Romney as The Mormon — Romney wasn't the first Latter-day Saint to jump into presidential politics. Some previous LDS candidates saw their faith as a help, while others viewed it as a hindrance.

The first Mormon to run for president was the first Mormon: Joseph Smith.

Smith had written letters to contenders for the White House in 1844 asking each what he would do to tamp down the government persecution of his followers as they were forced from state to state. Front-runners Henry Clay, John C. Calhoun and Lewis Cass responded but didn't endorse the federal help Smith sought; neither President Martin Van Buren nor Vice President Richard M. Johnson wrote back at all. Smith decided if he was going to get a president to help, he'd need to win election to the office.

The Council of Fifty, then a church governing body, endorsed Smith on

Jan. 29, 1844. A week later, the church newspaper, the Nauvoo Neighbor, published a long editorial, "Who will be our next president?", with the answer: "General Joseph Smith," a nod to his newfound spot as leader of the Nauvoo Mormon Militia.

Smith's approach — one that would have been laughable in the present day — was to dispatch the church's volunteer missionaries to visit every state to woo voters, as well as potential converts. Ten of the faith's 12 apostles also campaigned for him, arguing that he would end slavery by compensating owners, finance the government through tariffs, create a national bank and bring Oregon and Texas into the union.

His eight-page campaign pamphlet didn't mince words. He wanted to cut Congress in half and make it mandatory that politicians fulfilled their campaign vows.

"We have had Democratic presidents; Whig presidents; a pseudo-democratic whig president; and now it is time to have a president of the United States," Smith wrote. "And let the people of the whole union, like the inflexible Romans, whenever they find a promise made by a candidate, that is not practiced as an officer, hurl the miserable sycophant from his exaltation."

He signed it "a friend of virtue and a friend of the people."

His campaign was short-lived. He was murdered by a mob while incarcerated in the Carthage, Ill., jail for, ironically, inciting violence.

It would be another 124 years before a second Mormon made a serious bid for a major political party's presidential nomination. George Romney's approach was very different.

With the Vietnam War raging and civil-rights protests spreading, a politician's faith wasn't that big a deal.

The political press (the boys on the bus) were more focused on policy — especially on Romney's confusing Vietnam stance — than on his Mormon beliefs. Much as his son would later, the elder Romney didn't spend a lot of time talking about his faith on the campaign trail. But he still faced questions, sometimes hostile ones.

Knowing full well the anger toward his faith over black males being denied the Mormon priesthood at the time, Romney traveled in February 1967 to Atlanta's Morehouse College, a historic all-male black school, for a speech and then opened it up to questions from the audience. The initial queries focused on the war, and Romney was annoyed.

"Can't we get on to something else?" he asked, scanning the basketball court lined with folding chairs. "I want a question from a woman."

It would be a fateful request. Anna Grant, a professor of sociology, stepped forward, introducing herself as someone who studied the Mormon faith and found that its followers were taught anthropological untruths that would lead them to believe blacks were inferior to whites.

"I must confess," she spoke into the microphone, "that I don't feel too comfortable about the fact that the Mormon position has not changed ... and that you feel that the church does not preach a racist doctrine. I know you cannot change Mormonism, but I just wonder how you can be as comfortable in your beliefs as you have indicated."

The audience rocked with applause. Romney leafed his fingers through the white hair at his temples.

"I appreciate this question being asked," he said, "because I know from your reaction that it's a question you're interested in." From the crowd were laughs, and then silence.

"It is not true that my faith preaches a racist doctrine. Now it is true that a Negro cannot hold the priesthood in my church."

Romney's fist slammed the podium.

"But I have been raised from childhood with the firm belief that the Declaration of Independence and the Constitution of the United States are divinely inspired documents, and as a result of my background I have fought in my private life and in my public life to eliminate social injustice and racial discrimination."

Grant wasn't satisfied. "He's just saying what his personal position is, but he can't explain away his religion. ... A man of his importance can use his influence to change doctrines."

Grant wasn't at Romney's next event, a speech at Atlanta's Rotary Club, where black waiters served food to the white businessmen. The program didn't start until the servers left the room.

Romney arose and brought cheers when he criticized the centralization of power in Washington but earned silence for his next charge, a warning of sorts against discrimination.

"I believe it would be a tragedy to the South and to the people of this nation to support a third party, particularly one based on the presumed right of a state to decide whether or not it will extend to all men the rights which they have been endowed by their creator."

Romney wasn't done with his lecture.

Most of the "impoverished, diseased and dirty people in the world are colored" and our "enemies will turn their envy against us unless we make our practices equal our principles."

The meeting ended with "The Star-Spangled Banner." The only one in the room singing the lyrics, softly but noticeably, was Romney.

The question about blacks and the LDS Church would not go away.

"People don't understand this church position," Romney said at a news conference in Lansing, Mich., when quizzed about whether his civil-rights push was in direct conflict with his Mormon beliefs.

"I'm not going to undertake to discuss and argue the church's position," he said, "because I'm not serving or I'm not seeking to serve or I'm not planning to seek to serve in any capacity that would involve [anything] other than my status as an American citizen."

That said, while he didn't want to go line by line through the Book of Mormon with the press, he wasn't shy about who he was. If he was going to church, then by God, the press could come, too.

Romney, on his initial trip to sway voters, began in Alaska, which entered the union a strong Democratic state and began flipping only years later. He and his wife, Lenore, were, of course, teetotalers, but the 40 reporters traveling on the junket were not. On the Northwest Airlines flight from Detroit to Seattle to Anchorage, the flight attendants were lax on the two-drink-per-passenger limit, leaving a raucous press section in the back of the plane.

The drinking continued in the frozen north, where bars stayed open until 4 a.m. and reopened two hours later. The Baltimore Sun's Jules Witcover recalled that not all the journalists availed themselves of the liberal drinking laws, but enough did to keep the press "well-oiled."

Perhaps sensing the trailing journalists needed a moment in church, or maybe just because it was Sunday, Romney invited them to join him and his wife at a Mormon service in Anchorage.

The Romneys were seated on the dais of the new LDS meetinghouse while reporters were escorted to the front pews. The couple sang with gusto the opening hymn, "Now Let Us Rejoice," about the day "when all that was promised the Saints will be given."

George Romney, even with the scribes a few feet away, was blunt about his faith, more than his son would be years later, quoting from Smith's revelations in the Mormons' Doctrine and Covenants. Comfortable in the setting, Romney headed straight to the concern that had dogged his campaign: the fact that black men were denied entry into his faith's priesthood. He hated the racial discrimination that was so prevalent in America, but also spoke up against civil-rights riots that had taken place.

"[Can] the urgent need to correct social injustice justify defiance of law? I believe personally that God has given a very clear statement on this point," he said, quoting a Mormon scripture: "Let no man break the laws of the land, for he that keepeth the law of God hath no need to break the laws of the land."

"We must deal with social injustice with respect for law," he added. "We must do both."

The Washington Post's David Broder and scholar Stephen Hess wrote the comprehensive book about the 1968 race a year before the election and featured Romney as a top-tier candidate. They set out to educate an American populace that knew little about Romney's church.

"More than being merely American, Mormon doctrine is patriotically American, reflecting a kind of romantic nationalism peculiar to the 19th century. ... These people whose beliefs and practices are so idiosyncratic, and who actually took up arms against the United States government, are also as hyper-American as a rodeo or county fair," the authors wrote. They eschew alcohol, coffee and tobacco, give 10 percent of their income to their faith and don't curse.

"Romney says 'gosh,' 'by golly' and an occasional 'aw, nuts,' " Broder and Hess reported, telling readers about a time when Newsweek quoted Romney saying he calls his best friends "sons of bitches."

In a letter to the magazine's editor, Romney denied he'd said such a thing and wouldn't even use the "vulgarism," as he described it. "Use of such a phrase is contrary to my beliefs and my nature," he said.

In his final stretch of the campaign, Romney reached out to his Mormon network for help. One couple opened up their home in Janesville, Wis., to host him for a cottage meeting, clearing out their furniture and lining the carpet with plastic sheeting.

"Please don't smoke," the hostess chided a reporter. "This is a Mormon household."

The greatest crisis facing the nation at the time was, Romney declared, "the decline in religion, morality and patriotism."

Romney's run crashed before the first primary in New Hampshire, but he never blamed his faith. An aide on that 1968 campaign years later dispatched a note to Mitt Romney, outlining 20 reasons why his father had lost.

"One of them was not because he was Mormon or people didn't understand the Mormon church or whatever," Mitt Romney recalled.

It would be nearly 40 years later when the younger Romney would get to find out for himself whether his faith would be a hurdle. In the meantime, other Mormons took a shot at the highest political post in the land.

The witty, "fiercely" liberal Congressman Morris Udall of Arizona would run for president in 1976. He was a Mormon by birth — splitting forever with the faith over blacks being denied the priesthood — but he still faced repeated questions about the church and its attitude toward race.

The 6-foot-5 former basketball player set out to show that his honesty and rugged integrity would win out over folksy Georgia Gov. Jimmy Carter. It was a time of national reflection after the Watergate scandal had rocked Americans' confidence in their elected leaders.

Udall took stout liberal positions — he wanted to break up big oil, set up a national, single-payer health-insurance program, kill tax loopholes and make business pay higher taxes.

He finished second in six Democratic primaries as his liberal positions were thought too extreme by many in his party. His last stand came in Michigan, where Udall had hoped to halt Carter's momentum.

But Coleman Young, Detroit's first black mayor, was a Carter man, and he tried to sink Udall's chances. Young told a gathering of black Baptist ministers that they had to choose "between a man of Georgia who fights to let you in his church and a man from Arizona whose church won't even let you in the back door." It didn't matter that Carter's church didn't allow black members and that blacks could attend Mormon churches, the damage was done.

Even though Udall had broken with the LDS faith 30 years earlier over its policy toward blacks, Young refused to apologize. Udall lost the Michigan primary by three-tenths of a percent.

Sen. John McCain later would recall how Udall poked fun at the political system by describing "the difference between a cactus and a caucus. A cactus has its pricks on the outside."

Udall, who had lost an eye as a child, also noted in a book he wrote called "Too Funny to Be President" how his presumed faith in the LDS Church, coupled with his other qualities, doomed his race.

"I'm a one-eyed Mormon Democrat from conservative Arizona," he said. "You can't find a higher handicap than that."

The next major Mormon candidate to seek the Oval Office was a politician of a different stripe. Conservative Republican Sen. Orrin Hatch was, as he would later acknowledge, the longest of long shots for the 2000 presidential nomination. He announced his bid in July 1999 while most other candidates, including Steve Forbes, John McCain and Texas Gov. George W. Bush, had been campaigning and raising cash for years. Knowing he had little chance to win against the widely known and well-heeled Bush, Hatch repeatedly said he was only running in case Bush stumbled.

But the Utah Republican made a serious effort, campaigning to reduce taxes, abolish the Internal Revenue Service, protect Social Security and Medicare and stand up for Second Amendment gun rights. As one of the nation's highest-profile Mormons, Hatch was bound to be asked about his faith. He even tried to head off questions shortly after entering the race as rumors spread in political circles that he believed he was divinely called to run.

"If I had a revelation, I'd tell you," Hatch said. "I've never spoken to God."

But not too long into the campaign, he nearly lost his footing on this sometimes-slippery line separating politics from religion.

The "White Horse Prophecy" is one of those pervasive legends for Mormons, holding that in the latter days, a Saint will be called upon to save America from ruin. When that time comes, the lore goes, the Constitution will be "hanging by a thread." Mormon youths were once taught the tale, even if church leaders disavow it.

The story stems from a disputed prophecy recorded in a diary entry of a Mormon who had heard the yarn secondhand from men who were with Joseph Smith when he supposedly revealed it.

"You will see the Constitution of the United States almost destroyed," the diary entry quoted Smith. "It will hang like a thread as fine as a silk fiber."

This Mormon champion, astride a metaphoric "white horse," according to the so-called prophecy, would have the power to rebuke the "nations far off, and you obey it, for the laws go forth from Zion."

The LDS Church denounces the tale, noting that it was written down 10 years after Smith's death. A church spokesman pointed to a quote from the faith's sixth president, Joseph F. Smith, who called the prophecy "ridiculous."

Hatch should have known there are some words Mormons running for office shouldn't utter anytime anywhere. But during an interview with Doug Wright, conservative host of a popular radio show in Salt Lake City, the veteran politician got carried away on one of his rants against Democrats.

"They tolerate everything that's bad, and they're intolerant of everything that's good," Hatch said. "Religious freedom is going to go down the drain, too. I've never seen it worse than this, where the Constitution literally is hanging by a thread."

Oops.

A Hatch spokeswoman later clarified that the senator doesn't spend "one iota of time" thinking about the prophecy.

Coming late to the game, Hatch needed a ready supply of supporters on the ground in Iowa for that state's important first-in-the-nation caucuses. For that, he reached out to the 16,000 Mormons in the Hawkeye State.

In a late July meeting at the home of a Mormon couple, Hatch spoke of his need to turn out the vote for the upcoming Ames straw poll. Outside that room, it seemed few voters thought Hatch had a shot.

"Not in Iowa. Someplace in Utah, maybe. I don't know, is he a Mormon?" said Don Newquist, a rental-property owner. "Tell him to go back to Utah. George W.'s already got it wrapped up here. Everybody knows that."

Nearly 24,000 people voted in the poll. Bush walked away with 7,400 votes; Hatch, a humiliating 558.

Hatch brought up the back of the pack, in polls and in fundraising. He started a campaign for people to donate $36 to his effort, a nod to the $36 million that Bush had raised. It was "Orrin's Skinny Cat Campaign," as he liked to call it.

Hatch's campaign opened an office in a Des Moines strip mall but didn't have the money to go on TV or radio and certainly had no ground game in the states that followed. Few people called themselves Hatch voters.

A December debate allowed Hatch to pull a good zinger out of his holster against Bush. The Utahn lavished praise on the front-runner and eventual victor but noted that Bush had only had four years "in a constitutionally weak governorship."

"Frankly, I really believe that you need more experience before you become president of the United States. ... Just think — just think — Ronald Reagan picked your father," he told Bush, "because he had foreign-policy experience. Somebody suggested the other day you should pick me because I have foreign-policy experience. They've got it all wrong. I should be president. You should have eight years with me and boy, you'll make a heck of a president after eight years, I'll tell you."

The audience laughed, but Bush stayed firmly in the lead and Hatch foundered. Unlike Udall or George Romney, the Utah senator bluntly blamed his faith for his campaign's lack of traction.

"Bigotry has raised its ugly head here in Iowa," Hatch said. "I thought bigotry and religious intolerance had gone out when John F. Kennedy was elected the first Catholic president. But it hasn't. Not by any means."

Not only did Hatch consider his faith a hindrance, but he also said his fellow Mormons were of little help. He received no Mormon surge, no outpouring of cash from his the LDS faithful — which Mitt Romney would later enjoy in an extended and generous flow.

"They are just not political and that's the problem," Hatch blurted at one point. "If I had to depend on my fellow Mormons, I would not have come this far."

Jon Huntsman Sr. had backed Elizabeth Dole, the wife of former Sen. Bob Dole, with whom Huntsman had worked during his time in the Nixon White House. Only when Dole pulled out did Huntsman throw his support behind Hatch. That was as big a Mormon boost as he would get.

Brian Duffy, cartoonist for the Des Moines Register, poked fun at Hatch's campaign on caucus day, portraying the Utah senator outside the starting gate while everyone else was nearing the finish line.

Hatch was stoic when he stopped by the media center to talk to reporters. He knew it was over but donned a brave face.

"We're planning on going up to New Hampshire," he declared, despite the conventional wisdom he was out. "I hope we can continue to go forward. And if we can, that'd be great. If we can't, well, I won't be the first one who filed too late and wasn't able to get it done."

He finished last among the six GOP candidates in Iowa, pulling 1 percent, or fewer than 900 votes.

He wasn't even in the state for the bad news, deciding instead to return to Washington. A record snow — one of those storms that shut down the government in D.C. but would be a normal Tuesday in the Midwest — struck that night, delaying Hatch's plan to withdraw by one more day.

Pulling the plug on the failed campaign, Hatch noted that he told his wife, Elaine, that perhaps the snowstorm was a sign from God that he should continue on. His wife was blunt.

"No, Orrin," she said, "the Iowa caucuses were the sign from God."

As Mitt Romney geared up for his 2008 White House run, his advisers knew his faith would be an issue. A PowerPoint presentation attempting to look at the concerns Romney would face called it the Three M's: "Mormon, millionaire, Massachusetts."

"There is a perception out there that there is this rich guy from a liberal state who's got a funny religion," said his campaign manager, Beth Myers.

The team planned to mimic George Romney's mantra: He was running as an American, not a Mormon. Voters were electing a president, not a pastor. Voters didn't care what faith a candidate was as long as he had faith.

Romney wondered aloud whether there was "some tiny slice of people for whom that's a major issue. Of course," he said, answering his own thought, "it may be an issue for some, but it's not a factor in the final analysis."

He miscalculated. The slice was far from tiny.

In fact, as recently as 2007, nearly a quarter of Americans said they wouldn't vote for a candidate who was Mormon even if he was their party's nominee and was well-qualified, according to a Gallup poll. That was up from 17 percent when the same poll was taken during George Romney's run in 1967. A more startling number came in yet another Gallup poll that found 66 percent of Americans didn't believe the nation was ready for a Mormon president. Romney needed help, particularly from Southern evangelical leaders who could perhaps soften his religion-based opposition.

Mark DeMoss, an Atlanta public-relations consultant who had strong ties in the evangelical community, signed on to the campaign in 2006, saying he would work without pay to quell any suspicions that he was being bought off. His first initiative was inviting big-name born-again Christian leaders to Romney's Belmont, Mass., home.

It was an impressive guest list: the Rev. Jerry Falwell, the Rev. Franklin Graham (son of the legendary Rev. Billy Graham) and Richard Land, head of the Southern Baptist Convention's Ethics & Religious Liberty Commission. Romney wasn't trying to sell them on Mormonism; instead he wanted to convince them, leaving doctrine aside, that he was a solid, God-fearing candidate who deserved to be heard on policy issues. He pitched well.

DeMoss added the cherry on top, saying it was "more important to me that a candidate shares my values than my faith, and if I look at it this way, Mr. Romney would be my top choice."

Madden, Romney's press secretary, fielded question after question about Romney's religion, as though it were something alien to the world of politics. Does the candidate wear funny underwear? How many wives does he have? Does he pray to Joseph Smith? Does he drink Diet Coke?

It was insulting, Madden recalls, but the requests kept coming as political hacks from across America and around the globe plunged into their newfound fascination with ferreting out weird Mormon tidbits.

"When they'd ask me the question," Madden recalls, "I'd ask them to take the word Mormon out and insert the word Jew, Catholic, African-American and then say, 'Tell me that isn't a bigoted angle.' "

Sometimes it didn't matter; it was just too juicy to report — or fabricate — something about Romney and his faith.

"Former Massachusetts Gov. Mitt Romney pops into Pennsylvania for a quick visit later today, but you'll be hard pressed to see the GOP presidential candidate or his 17 wives," read an item on the Pennsylvania Patriot-News' website. "The Morman [sic] candidate is scheduled to hold a media availability at Philadelphia International Airport in the morning. ... There's yet another opportunity to spy one of his wives at another fundraiser at the home of Megan and Jim White in Devon."

Andrew Sullivan of The Atlantic posted a picture of Mormon garments — specially crafted underwear worn by devout members as a symbol of their commitment to their beliefs — with no thought that it was offensive to millions of LDS faithful.

"So Mitt Romney will never have to answer the boxers or briefs question," Sullivan wrote. "But will he tell us whether he wears Mormon underwear at all times, including when asleep?"

It wasn't just the media. In Iowa, a county chairman for McCain addressed a gathering of Republicans and read to them an article alleging the LDS Church helps fund the terrorist group Hamas, and likened Mormons' treatment of women to the Taliban. Al Sharpton suggested those who believe in God would defeat Romney. Aides to former New York City Mayor Rudy Giuliani and Sen. Sam Brownback forwarded emails with anti-Mormon rhetoric.

"The only thing Christianity and the LDS Church has in common is the name of Jesus Christ, and the LDS Jesus is not the same Jesus of the Christian faith," the email from the Brownback staffer to fellow activists said. Brownback and Giuliani later apologized to Romney and the church.

All Romney could do was roll his eyes and trudge forward.

On an early testing-the-water trip to New Hampshire, at Lowe's general store in Randolph, a tiny town on Route 2, the proprietors wanted Romney to try their new green-tea drink.

"Ooh," he said, standing near the coolers, amid the dust-covered cans and $8 bottles of syrup, "I don't drink tea." Romney was kind, offering it to an aide who wasn't Mormon. No one noticed, and Romney didn't want to explain.

It was part of his strategy when it came to handling the faith question: Don't try to differentiate yourself from others.

"I found people who are faithful in virtually any denomination to have the same core values, and by that I mean they love God, they love their fellow men and women and see them as children of the same creator, they love their country, they recognize a need to serve their community and to serve their fellow man and they recognize their own weaknesses and try and improve on themselves. My faith, like other faiths, has made me a better person as other faiths have made other people better people."

Translation: I'm just like you.

"I think what is at the core of the American desire is to have a person of faith lead the country," he continued. "They want someone who believes in a creator, someone who believes in a greater purpose to life than just the here and now, and the selfishness of their own life, but I don't think that the American people, in the final analysis, have shown that they care about the doctrinal differences between different faiths."

It was clear Romney had thought out his responses to questions of his faith. He didn't want to lecture about the Mormon afterlife or hold forth on baptisms for the dead.

"My goal is not to affiliate in any way my campaign with any other organization, whether it's my faith or anyone else's," he said. "I want to get as much support as I can from every possible person in this country who supports my effort and whether they're Presbyterian, Catholic, Mormon or Jewish, I want their help."

He had solid evidence to show that he wouldn't govern with a strong Mormon hand. When he was Massachusetts' governor, the Legislature repealed a prohibition on alcohol sales on Sundays, and he readily signed the bill into law. "I believe that, in our state, allowing the sale of alcohol is good for the consumer," said the teetotaling chief executive. "That isn't saying that I disagree with my church. I simply did what I thought was in the best interest of the state, which I was elected to serve."

Romney would later say: "I could serve alcohol in the White House."

As many questions as were aimed at the candidate about his faith, on the flip side, the LDS Church was deluged by requests from reporters. It was a fine line for the Utah-based church, too.

If it responded too aggressively, the church, which touts its neutrality in partisan politics, would risk appearing as though it was promoting Romney. But if it was too aloof, the church, which spends millions of dollars and untold energy carrying its message to the world, would miss a huge opportunity.

The nerve center of the church's PR operation is on the second floor of the grandiose Joseph Smith Memorial Building, formerly the Hotel Utah in downtown Salt Lake City that had hosted dignitaries including Presidents William Howard Taft and Woodrow Wilson. The gray-and-white cubicles that replaced the hotel rooms match the various spokespeople for the faith, many of whom are men in gray slacks and white shirts. There are some 35 people in this press shop — in addition to others in Los Angeles, Washington, New York City, London, Frankfurt and Moscow.

The charge that went out to the church's mouthpieces: Respond to inquiries and promote the faith. Questions about Romney should go to the Romney campaign. It wasn't unlike the 2002 Winter Olympics, which Romney led and which opened a window for the church to trumpet its message.

"The current situation is similar to some degree, but there is a higher level of interest, especially from overseas," said the church's media- relations director, Michael Purdy. "The difference, I suppose, is that some of the recent interest is politically motivated and that creates challenges for us. We are happy to address questions about the church but do not want to weigh into the politics. Some don't want to separate the two."

Indeed, as the platoon of PR folks read over the stories posting from across the world, you could hear audible guffaws.

"We can't even recognize our church in the news reports that attempt to describe our beliefs and practices," Purdy added.

That said, rank-and-file Mormons didn't necessarily follow the same instructions as the paid representatives. In late 2006, emails surfaced from Romney's Utah consultant, Don Stirling — who had worked for him on the Olympics rounding up local sponsors — saying that top church leaders were consulted on a plan to build Mormon support for Romney's presidential run. Stirling said in a Sept. 8 email to the CEO of LDS Church-owned Deseret Book, Sheri Dew, that Jeffrey R. Holland, a member of the Quorum of the Twelve Apostles, had informed President Gordon B. Hinckley and his counselor James E. Faust, a former Democratic state senator, about an effort to mobilize Mormons on Romney's behalf.

"According to [Romney friend Kem Gardner], Elder Holland has been designated/assumed the role of coordinating these matters," according to Stirling's email, obtained by The Boston Globe. "Elder Holland surfaced the idea of using BYU Management Society and its locally based organizations as a starting point to rally and organize the troops on a grass-roots level. Elder Holland subsequently surfaced the idea with Presidents Hinckley and Faust, who voiced no objections."

Stirling's email also invited Dew to meet at church headquarters with Holland, Gardner, Romney's son Josh and an official from the BYU Management Society. A second email indicated Romney himself was aware of the push and suggested adding author Richard Eyre to the discussion.

"Gov would like to have Rick Eyre join that meeting as a source of names throughout the country, which is probably a pretty good call," Stirling wrote.

Around the same time, two deans from BYU's Marriott School of Management sent an email to 150 supporters and alumni on their BYU accounts seeking help for Romney's bid.

The leak made a big splash and would be the last to draw such a clear-cut link between the LDS Church and the campaign of the country's most prominent Mormon.

In the short term, the LDS PR machine went into defense mode.

A church spokesman said Stirling had mischaracterized church leaders' involvement. "We have no responsibility for what others may write, and what they may think," said Michael R. Otterson, managing director of the faith's public affairs. A Romney PAC aide quickly said Stirling was overenthusiastic and overstepped his bounds with the emails. Stirling, likewise, fell on his sword and said he mischaracterized the effort.

The BYU deans were told to cease political activities but weren't disciplined, while Dew eventually gave Romney the maximum $2,300 contribution.

Years later, the LDS Church would ban its full-time leaders from making political donations, but not before two members of the Quorum of the Seventy slipped checks to Romney in advance of the deadline. One of those donations, totaling $2,450, came from W. Craig Zwick, a church official who also happened to be the father of Romney's finance director, Spencer Zwick.

So Mormons were helping Romney, but Mormonism was still hurting him. Journalists, advisers and even the candidate himself pondered a move to cauterize the wound.

Mormons weren't the only faith to face critical questions over a prominent adherent running for national office. In 1960, then-Sen. John Fitzgerald Kennedy's Catholic faith had become an issue in his bid for the presidency. People wanted to know whether, if he was elected, the pope would control him. Only about a quarter of Americans identified themselves as Catholics; a schism persisted between the world's largest Christian denomination and Protestant religions.

"The single biggest obstacle to his election was his religion," said Ted Sorensen, a Kennedy speechwriter and a Unitarian. "You should have seen the hate mail that came in, both from rednecks and from liberal intellectuals who should have known better."

A leading Protestant minister from Dallas had declared that the Roman Catholic faith "is not only a religion, it is political tyranny." The president of the Southern Baptist Convention added, "No matter what Kennedy might say, he cannot separate himself from his church if he's a true Catholic."

Kennedy chose the lions' den to tackle the issue head on — a JFK biographer said the setting had the "earmarks of an inquisition" — at a meeting of the Greater Houston Ministerial Association. Sorensen said Kennedy needed to "state his position so clearly and comprehensively that no reasonable man could doubt his adherence to the Constitution."

The Crystal Ballroom of the Rice Hotel in Houston was packed with men in suits; cigarette smoke hung in the air.

"Contrary to common newspaper usage, I am not the Catholic candidate for president," Kennedy said. "I am the Democratic Party's candidate for president, who happens also to be a Catholic. I do not speak for my church on public matters, and the church does not speak for me."

Kennedy noted that if America allowed a religious test for office, it wouldn't always be Catholics screened out.

"For while this year it may be a Catholic against whom the finger of suspicion is pointed, in other years it has been, and may someday be again, a Jew — or a Quaker or a Unitarian or a Baptist," Kennedy said. "It was Virginia's harassment of Baptist preachers, for example, that helped lead to Jefferson's statute of religious freedom. Today I may be the victim, but tomorrow it may be you — until the whole fabric of our harmonious society is ripped at a time of great national peril."

Kennedy was right, and now it was Romney's turn.

Richard Land, the Southern Baptist Convention's political guru, is a big man who holds tremendous sway with his followers. Time magazine called him one of the most influential evangelicals in the country. During Romney's bid, he became the go-to expert for the question: Are Mormons really Christians?

Land didn't answer directly. Instead, he would say, Mormons were the "fourth Abrahamic religion" — essentially, that the LDS faith was a branch of faith like Judaism, Christianity and Islam. But he also knew, as Kennedy had said, that Virginia Baptists had faced persecution, and Land believed strongly in a separation of church and state.

At the meeting in Romney's pinkish colonial home in Belmont early on, Land had urged Romney to speak directly about his faith, as Kennedy had done. He even brought a copy of JFK's speech and suggested that time was of the essence. Romney promised to think about it.

There was no shortage of opportunities for Romney to make such an address. He could have done so when he spoke to religious broadcasters in Florida or when he gave the commencement address at the Christian Regent University, or he might have taken advantage of an invitation to the Religion Newswriters Association. But he didn't.

Aides knew such a speech could go either way: It could help put to rest the pervasive questions, endear faithful voters and nab some national media attention. Or it could cement the candidate as "The Mormon," distract from his efforts to talk about policy, even alienate a base of GOP voters he critically needed.

"There really isn't a 'current strategy,' " an aide wrote in mid-2007 when asked about planning for the faith speech. Advisers could discuss the pros and cons all they wanted, but the decision was purely Romney's. "We all await the Guv's guidance on this."

Meanwhile, Mark DeMoss kept up his outreach on behalf of the campaign to the evangelical crowd. At that Florida meeting of the National Religious Broadcasters Convention in February 2007, where Romney declined to speak, DeMoss tackled the Mormon question.

"You see, I had been hearing that evangelicals would not support a Mormon for president, even though we've worked closely with them for 30 years on a host of issues of importance to us, and that thinking bothered me," he told the crowd in Orlando. "After all, I would not want people to say, 'I could never vote for an evangelical — those people are crazy.'

"I have an answer to the question 'Could I ever vote for a Mormon?'," he continued. "It depends on who the Mormon is! The question should not be 'Could I vote for a Mormon?' but rather, 'Could I vote for this Mormon?' Or 'Could I vote for that Southern Baptist, or this Methodist, or that Catholic?' After all, there are Mormons Mitt Romney would not vote for; and there are Southern Baptists I would not vote for."

Romney was more than just a Mormon; he had been a lay LDS leader, a bishop and a stake president — in charge of several congregations — during the late 1980s and early 1990s. He was considered a good listener and an innovative manager, even going so far as to work around some bureaucratic edicts from Salt Lake City to help fellow members. He allowed divorced men to stay on as leaders, rather than remove them, as church policy said at the time. He didn't punish some Mormon writers and activists who had spoken out at a time some church leaders engaged in purges of critical voices.

This wasn't something Romney wanted to discuss, though.

At Regent University, a school founded by evangelical luminary Pat Robertson, Romney didn't mention his Mormon faith. He instead exhorted the graduates to venture into the deep waters — a metaphor for giving more of yourself to faith and public service — and leave the shallows of selfishness.

He did, though, test the waters on his Mormon faith a bit later in 2007 at the Family Research Council's Values Voter Summit, a confab of the politically active pro-life, conservative crowd. It was only the second time the FRC had held the convention, but it drew every GOP candidate.

"By the way," Romney said, "a few of you may have heard that I'm a Mormon. I understand that some people may think they couldn't support someone of my faith. That may be because they've listened to Harry Reid."

The audience chuckled — well aware that Reid, the Senate Democratic leader, was Mormon, too — and then applauded Romney's point.

"Actually, I'm pleased that so many people of so many faiths have come to endorse my candidacy and my message."

The hits on his Mormonism, though, kept coming.

John McCain and his 95-year-old mother, Roberta, appeared together on MSNBC's "Hardball With Chris Matthews," where the host pressed the two on whether they thought Romney had done much "heavy lifting for America" through his government service and leading the Salt Lake City Olympics.

"As far as the Salt Lake City thing, he's a Mormon and the Mormons of Salt Lake City caused that scandal and to clean that up — it's not even — it's not a subject," Roberta McCain declared.

Her son smiled during the remark and added, with a tinge of laughter, "The views of my mother are not necessarily the views of mine." Candidate McCain, sensing this could be a problem, later added that Mormons are "great people" and that "it should never be a consideration and I know that [Romney will] be judged on his record."

Thanksgiving that year brought Romney's family to his Belmont home, where he sought the advice of his most important sounding boards. Romney felt it was time to speak out about his faith, and his family agreed.

The timing was clear. Huckabee had passed Romney in the Iowa polls and was airing a television ad that targeted evangelicals.

"Faith doesn't just influence me; it really defines me," Huckabee said in the spot. "I don't have to wake up every day wondering, 'What do I need to believe?' "

The words "Christian leader" floated across the screen in all caps.

Romney's advisers gave the candidate mixed messages. Some said it was "not a good idea — it draws too much attention to that issue," while others, noting the candidate had done 400 town-hall events, said, "Have you ever been to one where somebody didn't ask the [Mormon] question?"

Romney decided to confront the issue on his own terms, on a field of his own choosing.

"He'd always said, 'At some point, I know I want to do this,' " an adviser said.

Former President George H.W. Bush previously had offered his library in College Station as a forum for Romney, and lobbyist Ron Kaufman, a close confidant of Romney, was dispatched to make the deal. Bush agreed, though he made it clear it was not an endorsement.

Romney aides wanted to announce the decision through the Drudge Report, but when they couldn't reach Matt Drudge, they decided to give the scoop to Time magazine's Mark Halperin.

Thursday morning was a bit crisp for a Texas December. Satellite trucks lined up outside the George H.W. Bush Presidential Library, their cables streaming along the sidewalk and into the auditorium. Advisers stressed this was not going to be a Mormonism 101 lecture — nor would it be a sermon. Romney wasn't going to explain his faith's signature scripture, the Book of Mormon, or call attention to doctrinal differences. He wasn't going to preach, either.

He was going to talk about faith in general.

From a podium sporting his presidential library seal, Bush introduced the speaker as a "great man," and then Romney, in a blue tie and dark suit, took the stage flanked by eight American flags. His handpicked audience applauded.

"Freedom requires religion just as religion requires freedom," Romney said. "Freedom opens the windows of the soul so that man can discover his most profound beliefs and commune with God. Freedom and religion endure together, or perish alone. Given our grand tradition of religious tolerance and liberty, some wonder whether there are any questions regarding an aspiring candidate's religion that are appropriate. I believe there are. And I will answer them today."

Romney referred to Kennedy, who had answered critics of his faith just 90 miles from the spot where he stood.

"Like him, I am an American running for president. I do not define my candidacy by my religion. A person should not be elected because of his faith nor should he be rejected because of his faith. Let me assure you that no authorities of my church, or of any other church, for that matter, will ever exert influence on presidential decisions. Their authority is theirs, within the province of church affairs, and it ends where the affairs of the nation begin."

He vowed, if elected, he would serve no one religion, no one group, no one cause except that of the American people. "There are some for whom these commitments are not enough. They would prefer it if I would simply distance myself from my religion, say that it is more a tradition than my personal conviction, or disavow one or another of its precepts. That I will not do. I believe in my Mormon faith, and I endeavor to live by it. My faith is the faith of my fathers — I will be true to them and to my beliefs. Some believe that such a confession of my faith will sink my candidacy. If they are right, so be it. But I think they underestimate the American people. Americans do not respect believers of convenience. Americans tire of those who would jettison their beliefs, even to gain the world."

He was bold, humble and faithful, all at the same moment. His campaign was quick to shoot around reviews from friend and foe.

"Mitt Romney, who sure looked presidential, explained effectively that he is a man of faith who is committed to America's values," wrote Kate O'Beirne of the conservative National Review.

"For the first time in this campaign, and it has been long already, I heard greatness this morning," said MSNBC's Chris Matthews.

"It was a magnificent speech, splendidly delivered, it was moving. ... I don't know how he could have done it better," said Pat Buchanan, whose sister was a Mormon convert. "I mean, I was very moved."

In one fell swoop, Romney had rallied the religious right to his defense.

"Gov. Romney's speech was a magnificent reminder of the role religious faith must play in government and public policy," reacted evangelical author James Dobson. "Whether it will answer all the questions and concerns of evangelical Christian voters is yet to be determined, but the governor is to be commended for articulating the importance of our religious heritage as it relates to today."

The speech even earned a response from President Kennedy's brother Sen. Ted Kennedy, who once used Mormonism as a weapon against Romney.

"Each of us, whether public official or private citizen, is entitled to our own private religious beliefs. But, as elected officials, we have taken an oath of office to uphold and defend the Constitution. What President Kennedy said in 1960 is equally valid today — 'I do not speak for my church on public matters, and the church does not speak for me.' "

Privately, Romney's faith played a big role in helping him endure the rough times. Just before he was called to the stage for the final New Hampshire debate in 2008, the candidate and his family waited in the hotel room and knelt in prayer. His elbows rested in a wooden chair; Ann's hands were clasped on her knees.

"We pray that thou would understand our desires in doing this are pure, and that we are grateful for our blessings," Ann Romney said, as the family circled her, "and have a desire to serve thee and to bring greater light to this Earth. We pray that if it be thy will, that our desires may be made manifest through the Holy Ghost and through thy spirit to make this a possibility. [This] is our prayer in the name of Jesus Christ, amen."

Mitt hugged her and headed to the bomb-throwing. "These aren't tears of sorrow," Ann said. "These are tears of gratitude."

As the primary results piled up the next day, Romney winced.

"Ooh, that's not good. That's not good," Mitt said, knowing he had been tarred with two equally black marks. "OK. The flipping Mormon. I can't fix the Mormon side, or I won't fix the Mormon side," he quickly corrected himself. "The flipping side … "

"And that would hurt the flipping side," an aide joked, noting that taking on the flip-flop concern would only promote it further.

Less than a week after Romney's big faith speech, rival Huckabee, a former Baptist minister, asked a New York Times reporter about Mormon beliefs.

"Don't Mormons believe that Jesus and the devil are brothers?" Huckabee asked. It was true, in Mormon doctrine, that God was the father to all and all beings created by him, even Lucifer, were his spirit children, but Huckabee's backhanded message to evangelicals was clear: Romney believes Christ and Satan are family.

By the end of December, Huckabee aired a Christmas ad designed to send a message as bright as the red sweater he wore. WIth the candidate sitting beside a beautiful tree and with "Silent Night" playing softly in the background, the camera panned in such a way that the light formed an unmistakable cross. The none-too-subtle outreach worked, and evangelicals turned out for him as if for a church calling.

"Mike had a terrific base as a minister — drew on that base, got a great deal of support, it was a wonderful strategy that he pursued effectively," Romney told reporters after his Iowa loss.

Romney then encountered a true test of his faith.

Gordon B. Hinckley, the stoic Mormon leader who had worked to endear the church to the mainstream media and build an empire of temples, died. His funeral was set for Feb. 2, 2008. Super Tuesday, which could give Romney a lifeline or doom his bid, was three days away, but he put the campaign on hold and flew to Salt Lake City. In the front row of the church's cavernous Convention Center, built under Hinckley's watch, Romney joined other Mormon dignitaries, including Jon Huntsman, then Utah's governor.

"This is a personal visit," Romney spokesman Eric Fehrnstrom reminded reporters.

Romney failed to make any headway Feb. 5, when 21 states voted to pick their nominee. The 2008 campaign was over, but Romney was known now, and he'd have another chance.

"When this is over, I'll have built a brand name," he said. "People will know me. They'll know what I stand for: The flipping Mormon."

Mitt and Ann Romney looked comfy on the large couch on the set of ABC's "The View" in early 2011, but Barbara Walters was about to dive into The Question.

"I want to bring up something that could cause you and has perhaps caused you some problems if you run, and that is the fact that you're a Mormon," Walters said. "We have televisions shows with Mormons with multiple wives and such, which perhaps doesn't do you any good."

Romney went back to the stock response.

"The great majority of Americans understand that this nation was founded on the principles of religious tolerance and liberty, so most people do not make their decision based on someone's faith. But you don't worry about that."

As the 2012 campaign geared up, Romney was asked time and again whether he would give another speech about his faith. No. He'd been there, done that. When opportunities came to address it, he didn't mention the word Mormon.

"My path to conservatism came from my family, my faith and my life's work," he said in February 2012. "My 42-year marriage to my wife, Ann; the life we've built with our five sons; and the faith that sustains us — these conservative constants have shaped my life."

At Liberty University, founded by the late Jerry Falwell, Romney talked about God, about the need for faith, but he didn't mention his own.

"People of different faiths, like yours and mine, sometimes wonder where we can meet in common purpose when there are so many differences in creed and theology," he said. "Surely the answer is that we can meet in service, in shared moral convictions about our nation stemming from a common worldview."

It wasn't by accident that he didn't use the word Mormon or talk specifics about his faith. The Romney family and advisers had decided to steer clear of any talk about his religion, calculating there was nothing to gain by it.

"It was just so hard last time that they were exceedingly careful this time," said an adviser. "I can't tell you how many times [the campaign] gets people calling and saying, 'We want to know what he thinks about blacks and the priesthood, or polygamy.'

"I think part of it was, 'Look, we're the front-runner this time,' " the adviser added. "Why get into this discussion?"

Again, though, supporters of rival campaigns wanted very much to have the discussion.

Robert Jeffress, senior pastor at the First Baptist Church in Dallas, introduced Texas Gov. Rick Perry at a conservative gathering in Washington, calling Perry a "proven leader, a true conservative and a committed follower of Christ." After the speech, Jeffress let loose.

"Rick Perry's a Christian. He's an evangelical Christian, a follower of Jesus Christ," the pastor told reporters. "Mitt Romney's a good moral person, but he's not a Christian. Mormonism is not Christianity. It has always been considered a cult by the mainstream of Christianity."

With Romney determined not to engage on the issue, it was Huntsman who stepped up to the challenge.

"The fact that, you know, some moron can stand up and make a comment like that — first of all it's outrageous," Huntsman said. "Second of all, the fact that we are spending so much time discussing it makes it even worse."

He added that religion should be off the table, and surrogates needed to know that.

"This kind of talk, I think, has no home in American politics these days," he said. "Anyone who is associated with someone willing to make those comments ought to stand up, distance themselves in very bold language, and that hasn't been done. And Rick ought to stand up and do that."

Perry quickly distanced himself from the remarks.

Despite the Mormon-is-the-new-mum's-the-word stance, Romney still tried to find time to attend church wherever in the country he was. He was spotted, on occasion, reading the Bible or Book of Mormon on his iPad.

When Romney clinched the nomination after a grueling primary season and the Republican National Convention neared, he finally was more comfortable talking about Mormonism. The primaries, filled with evangelical voters, were over and now the campaign needed to humanize Romney. Faith, even of a Mormon flavor, could help.

Neither the Romneys nor the campaign flinched when an Associated Press reporter joined the family at an LDS chapel near the Romney vacation home in Wolfeboro, N.H. Inside, Mitt Romney sat next to Ann, and his grandkids filled out the rest of the row. Some 30 Romneys took up a lot of space. Some of the kids grew restless, and Romney offered some colored cereal from a Ziploc bag.

As the sacrament, or communion, closed, Romney's family sang all the verses to "America the Beautiful." The AP story offered a glimpse into the faithful family, but it wasn't one that the Romney campaign organized.

It would be different a month later. A pool of reporters followed Romney almost everywhere he went, even church. The reporters again feasted on images of Romney and his brood singing hymns, taking the bread and water of sacrament, but there were no special shoutouts to the man who soon would be the Republican nominee, no prayers to help him.

It was at the Tampa convention where Romney's faith was on full display. Ann Romney capped the first night, offering the delegates and the national television audience the heartfelt story of meeting her husband, rearing their five boys and being diagnosed with multiple sclerosis. She also became the first one on the stage to utter the word "Mormon."

"When Mitt and I met and fell in love, we were determined not to let anything stand in the way of our life together," she said. "I was an Episcopalian. He was a Mormon."

Ann talked of the countless hours Mitt spent helping others.

"I've seen him drop everything to help a friend in trouble," she said, "and been there when late-night calls of panic came from a member of our church whose child had been taken to the hospital."

Grant Bennett knew that side of Romney well. He took the stage two days later to talk about the time he was in the bishopric, the lay clergy that led an LDS ward and that Bennett referred to as assistants to a pastor.

"As we began working together, Mitt asked, 'How early can I call you in the morning?' I said 6 a.m. I regret my answer — for several years, Mitt became my alarm clock."

On a typical morning, Bennett recalled, Romney phoned to say a woman in the ward had tripped and bruised her hip and to ask for Bennett's help checking in on her. Mitt offered members rides to the doctor, visited shut-ins, shoveled snow and raked leaves.

"Mitt challenged each of us to find our life by losing it in service to others. He issued that challenge again and again," Bennett said. "The church itself was a marvelous vehicle for extending that challenge."

Fellow Mormons Pat and Ted Oparowski came next, bringing the audience to silence as they spoke of son David's diagnosis with non-Hodgkin lymphoma. Romney would visit the 14-year-old in the hospital and learned that he liked fireworks. On the next visit, when David was back home, Romney brought a box of "Big Time Fireworks" that were so powerful they couldn't be set off in the city. Toward the end, David learned that Romney was a lawyer and asked him to write his will. On a yellow legal pad, Romney scrawled out that David's skateboard, model rockets and fishing gear would go to his best friends; his brother would get his treasured Ruger .22 rifle.

"How many men do you know would take the time out of their busy lives to visit a terminally ill 14-year-old and help him settle his affairs?" asked Pat

Oparowski. Romney gave David's eulogy as he was buried in his Boy Scout uniform.

It was the sort of conversation that Team Romney had avoided for so long, now squarely on display for the world. The campaign decided not to air the testimonials during prime time, when networks provided wall-to-wall coverage. But it was out there. Finally.

It was heartening for Romney and Mormons everywhere to see their faith in the spotlight — in a positive way. Shortly after the convention, the Romneys returned to their Wolfeboro home and, on Sunday, the Romney brood again piled into the Mormon ward there. J.W. "Bill" Marriott, a longtime friend of the family, rose to the podium to thank Romney for bringing favorable scrutiny to their faith.

"There has never been as much positive attention to the church, thanks to the wonderful campaign of Mitt Romney and his family," Marriott said. "Everybody is looking at us and saying, 'Are you as good as the Romneys?' Today we see the church coming out of obscurity, and we see that 90 percent of what has been written and said … 90 percent of it has been favorable," he said. "And that's a great tribute to Mitt and Ann."

§ § §

When Jon Huntsman returned to America from Beijing in early 2012, he headed to the University of South Carolina to offer the commencement address. It wasn't happenstance. His soon-to-be presidential advisers stood offstage as Huntsman, decked out in the garnet academic robe, struck a patriotic and optimistic tone.

"Give back — as much as you're able," Huntsman told the graduates in Columbia. "Work to keep America great. Serve her, if asked. I was, by a president of a different political party. But, in the end, while we might not all be of one party, we are all part of one nation, a nation that needs your generational gift of energy and confidence."

The fluent Mandarin speaker also showed off his linguistic skills, offering the traditional Gamecock chant, "Go, fight, win!," in Chinese and then in English.

The next day, a Sunday, Huntsman could have easily visited any of the half-dozen Mormon wards, or congregations, in or around Charleston, where he was staying. The Mount Pleasant ward met at 9:30 a.m., Charleston ward at 10.

Instead, Huntsman headed to Seacoast, a nondenominational megachurch that hosts worship service in its 100,000-square-foot facility and broadcasts to satellite spots in the region. He and his wife, Mary Kaye, joined then-Rep. Tim Scott, who is now a senator, at the service that featured a rock band and a leather-jacket-clad pastor, Greg Surratt.

Running for and serving as governor, Huntsman was labeled a Mormon; in Utah, no one really questions candidates or officeholders on how devout they are. He shocked the political establishment in 2004 by posing with a glass of milk at Burt's Tiki Lounge; Republicans in the state don't get photographed in bars. (Huntsman, for the record, had brought his own milk.)

At the same time, he was teaching an Aaronic Priesthood class in his Mormon ward and, when elected, occasionally dropped by an LDS service near the Governor's Mansion. But he also visited other services and even invited members of the state's Indian community to the mansion for annual celebrations of Diwali, the Festival of Lights.

Perhaps, too, there was a message being sent when, in 2008, Huntsman's office issued a statement on the newly chosen LDS prophet, Thomas S. Monson, and the governor made no mention that it was his own faith.

"I look forward to continuing my association with President Monson as he takes this new role," Huntsman said. "He is a compassionate leader who is committed to bettering his community, our nation and the world."

Huntsman raised his adopted daughter Asha with a nod to the Hindu faith. Daughter Abby Huntsman wed in the Episcopal-run National Cathedral, with the service officiated by the dean of the cathedral, the Rev. Samuel T. Lloyd III.

In 2011, a reporter asked Huntsman point-blank whether he was still a member of The Church of Jesus Christ of Latter-day Saints.

"I'm a very spiritual person," he said, "and proud of my Mormon roots." Pressed again, Huntsman sidestepped. "That's tough to define," he said. "There are varying degrees. I come from a long line of saloon keepers and proselytizers, and I draw from both sides."

That was a much different answer than Romney had given. As young men, both Huntsman and Romney had traveled abroad to share the Mormon message and convert others to the faith. But through the years, their approaches diverged. Romney dove into church service; Huntsman referred to himself as a cultural Mormon. Romney downed Diet Coke; Huntsman sipped Chardonnay.

A Newsweek cover illustration in June 2011 featured Romney, decked out in missionary garb, jumping, his hand on the Book of Mormon, and declared it was the "Mormon moment." The New York Times repeated the line. With Romney and Huntsman in the presidential race, HBO's "Big Love" and Broadway's "Book of Mormon" big hits, this was the time for the faith to enjoy the spotlight. But it was also an opportunity to show the nation that Mormonism was not the monolith it had long been perceived.

A poll showed that some 77 percent of Mormons said they attended church weekly; 67 percent considered themselves "very active." But it also found that 32 percent said not drinking coffee and tea was an important tenet of the faith but not essential. Nearly half said the same about R-rated movies that Mormons are counseled to avoid.

Nearly 70 percent of Mormons surveyed said religion is very important to their lives, they pray every day and attend a church service at least weekly. Some 2 percent said the faith isn't that important and about 30 percent fell somewhere in between. That latter category is likely where Huntsman fit.

Abby Huntsman, his second-oldest daughter, says her dad is one of the "most spiritual guys I've ever met," but he doesn't talk much about the Mormon faith. When living in Asia, Abby recalled going to various churches, the same as when he was governor.

"That's always been who he is," she said. "I don't think what he said nationally was anything different."

Keeping his faith private, though, has earned disdain from some Mormons who saw Huntsman's aloofness as offensive.

State Sen. Todd Weiler, a Mormon Republican like most members of the Utah Legislature, said Romney was more popular in the state than Huntsman, largely because of their disparate approaches to faith.

"Mormons believe that Mitt Romney is sincere about his faith and Jon Huntsman Jr. is a charlatan," Weiler charged. "He kind of pretended to be a card-carrying Mormon when he ran for governor, but it was all a ruse."

An indicator of the popularity gap: Just weeks into Huntsman's presidential outing, a poll showed Romney 50 points ahead of him in a state that overwhelmingly elected Huntsman governor twice.

"They want him to wear it on his sleeve and they want him to go out and preach the gospel wherever he goes," Abby Huntsman says, "and that's just never been him. Never."

For journalists, the idea of a nondevout Mormon became a fascination. Many asked whether they should call him a "Jack Mormon," a term used to describe a Latter-day Saint who perhaps knocks back a few beers but still believes. Some saw it as a strategy by Huntsman to cool potential problems with the evangelical wing of the Republican Party. To his family, it wasn't a shock.

Jon Huntsman Sr., who had served in a governing body of the LDS Church, said his son is someone "you want to sit next to" in a Mormon service or any other.

"I believe that all of our children have varying degrees of activity in the LDS Church and I'm proud of Jon; I'm very proud of his family," Huntsman Sr. said. "He's an extremely honest man; he has a wonderful marriage; he's maintained his marital vows; he's an outstanding father; he's a man of high moral principles. He has a sense of personal integrity. I could have asked for no greater son than that when it comes to religion and someone is a man of great faith. I wasn't the least bit disappointed."

Devout or not, the younger Huntsman remained dogged by the issue. Not even 24 hours into his official presidential bid, he flew into Columbia, S.C., popped on safety glasses and toured the Thermal Engineering Corp.'s plant, where workers were making infrared grills. He talked about a labor dispute, troop reductions in Afghanistan and his conservative problem-solving cred. A reporter wanted to know if he was Mormon.

"I believe in God," Huntsman responded. "Good Christian. I'm very proud of my Mormon roots."

Huntsman noted that his wife, Mary Kaye, was raised Episcopalian. "Spirituality is very important," he said.

No one was asking Newt Gingrich or Rick Santorum about being Catholic. But the Mormon question still appeared fair game. Romney had tried to assuage concerns about his LDS faith with his big speech, and while it may have swayed some voters, it didn't end the unrelenting questions about and references to the religion.

Nevertheless, two Mormons running for president in 2012, and gaining remarkable media attention, were clear signs of emerging acceptance for the faith.

"In '12, with Huntsman in the race, it was a shared burden," said a former Romney adviser.

Abby Huntsman laid it all out during an appearance on NBC's "Rock Center With Brian Williams."

Her break from the LDS Church came, she recounted, when her Mormon bishop had learned she was dating a guy who wasn't of the fold. He was worried for her.

"And at that point I said, 'Whomever I fall in love with I'm going to fall in love with. I'm not going to live in this bubble anymore. I just need to live my life for me.' He basically said, 'You're not going to have the blessings. Your kids will not be blessed if you end up marrying this man.' He's such a great guy and in my heart, I just — I get kind of emotional," she said, breaking up, "about it because for a bishop to tell me how I needed to live my life and that I would or would not be blessed because of it was very difficult. I know I'm one of many, many women who go through experiences like that. I walked out that door and I couldn't go back."

Friends texted, emailed and called Abby to thank her for speaking out. That was the good part.

"The other half was horrible. Horrible," Abby recalls of the tweets and emails. "I spent probably much of that next week in tears. … They were all Mormons, upset that I said the church needs to evolve, that it needs to open up and embrace the changes that are occurring in society. You know very strict Mormons, they don't do well with that."

Like her father, Abby plays up the good role that the Mormon faith has had on her life, the family values that she says made her a good person.

"But I still think there is this looking over the fence [attitude] with some people. There are so many incredible Mormons out there that are open-minded, that are fun, that don't judge, that [say], 'You live your life, I'll live mine.' But there's still, in any religion there's the very strict, strong [strain of], 'This is the only way to live.' "

She isn't the only Huntsman kid who made the move. After Abby joked during another TV interview that she would join the Democratic Party, her sister Liddy took to Twitter to defend her big sis.

"The day my sister becomes a Democrat, is the day I go back to the Mormon church," Liddy Huntsman wrote, adding the hashtag #Notinthislifetime."

Liddy married a Roman Catholic. Mary Kaye grew up Episcopalian; Abby considers herself Episcopalian. Jon III is engaged to a Protestant.

"We are a combination of a lot of religions," says Mary Kaye, who noted Jon Huntsman Sr. is accepting of the divergent beliefs of his son and grandchildren.

"Religion is to make people better," she adds. "Why not take the best you can of each, try to find the goodness, love and respect. … Put it this way, we are not anti-anything, we are not anti-Mormon or anti-anything, that is not how we are. … We gain from all the different aspects that make up our family."

Abby insists there are no hard feelings between how the Romneys approach their faith and how the Huntsmans do. She says the dual campaigns were good for the church; it opened people's minds and educated them about Mormons.

"My dad and Romney are both, I think, different but both pretty strong examples of having been raised in the church, just being good people," she said. "I think that was all positive."

The interaction between Romney and Huntsman on politics didn't remain as cordial.

chapter twelve

The showdown

Mitt Romney has a lot of "home" states: Michigan, where he was born; Utah, where he found the national spotlight and moved after his 2012 presidential defeat; Massachusetts, where he served as governor; and New Hampshire, where his vacation home made him practically a local.

That last one was key to his White House dreams.

In the 2012 race, political pundits expected Romney to win the nation's first primary. So did Romney. While still eyeing the bigger states, and the nation at large, Romney's aides knew their man needed to spend quality time among these politically independent Northeasterners. And so it was that Romney found himself in Amherst, N.H. — population 11,200 — on the Fourth of July, 2011, six months and five days before voters would trim the Republican field.

And so did Jon Huntsman.

Of course, Huntsman had more to gain by his visit, since no one really knew him. Where Romney was leading the polls — 35 percent of voters supported him that July, according to one survey — Huntsman barely registered. He was at 2 percent.

Amherst hosts one of those small-town Fourths with a parade that features firetrucks, a shiny new tractor, bagpipes, clowns, even oxen pulling a cart. Then there was the wall of Romney signs slowly making its way down Boston Post Road.

"Good to see you," a polished Romney said as he shook every hand he could.

Huntsman's entourage was sparser, a mix of black-and-red Jon 2012 signs and a few handmade ones.

Just before they started marching, Romney spotted his distant cousin and jogged over.

"Welcome to New Hampshire," Romney said.

"It's not Beijing, but it's lovely," Huntsman responded. "The air is breathable."

Huntsman publicly played it off as a nice gesture, just "wishing each other luck and being friends" — not the below-the-radar dig that it was from the longtime candidate-in-residence to the newcomer.

Friends? That may have been too strong a word.

While outwardly cordial to each other, especially with cameras snapping around them, the two were far from close. Huntsman not only endorsed Romney's rival in 2008, he came back from China in part because he saw the former Massachusetts governor as a weak front-runner. Romney saw Huntsman as an opportunist and just another GOP hanger-on, someone he would outmarch as the primary season dragged on.

The official Romney strategy was to ignore Huntsman just as Romney was ignoring the other Republican candidates, but first the Romney team set out to undercut Huntsman in his home state.

First up: Rep. Jason Chaffetz, whom Huntsman had plucked from relative obscurity to run his first gubernatorial campaign and then tapped to be his chief of staff. The go-getter parlayed his savvy media skills and red-meat speeches into a House seat, bouncing a six-term congressman, Chris Cannon, in 2008.

Chaffetz's endorsement of Romney would sting, the congressman knew. The former Huntsman confidant waited until he could call his former boss to relay the news that he thought Romney was a better candidate against President Obama. Chaffetz already had attended two Romney fundraisers, and Romney had repaid the favor. The two-term House member also knew which way the GOP wind was blowing.

"It's nothing against Huntsman; he's been very good to me," Chaffetz said. "I had this discussion with Jon last week. It was tough for me, but I was honest and candid that I'm going to support Mitt Romney."

That wasn't enough. The Romney camp also had lined up then-Attorney General Mark Shurtleff for an endorsement, a move that hurt as well because

Huntsman and Shurtleff had bucked the Utah establishment to back John McCain four years earlier.

That was just the tip of the endorsement iceberg. A day after Chaffetz's blow to Huntsman, the Romney folks released a long list of supporters in Huntsman's home state. It included Sen. Orrin Hatch, Rep. Rob Bishop, Lt. Gov. Greg Bell and a majority of state lawmakers.

"Throughout his life, Mitt has demonstrated that he isn't just qualified, but has the leadership needed to be president of the United States," Hatch said.

Romney loved that he was more popular in Utah than his opponent, who was twice overwhelmingly elected governor there, saying the endorsements "represent the deep level of support that I have enjoyed over the years in Utah."

The Huntsman side didn't want to comment on the endorsements but did quibble with the fact that state Rep. Paul Ray, listed among Romney's followers, hadn't actually backed Romney and was supporting Huntsman. It was Huntsman's only arrow.

How could Huntsman not own the state that re-elected him governor with 78 percent of the vote just a few years earlier? Perhaps it was his take on religion or that he left the governor's office to work for Obama, or maybe it was simply that Romney already had built such a strong following.

The former head of Salt Lake City's 2002 Olympics, who had never stood for office in Utah, nabbed 63 percent in a statewide poll of Republicans asked for their first pick for president; Huntsman got 10 percent.

When asked for comment, a Huntsman aide responded — off the record — with an expletive.

That wasn't all the bad news coming Huntsman's way. Shortly after the former Utah governor announced his bid, his son Will, who was about to enter the U.S. Naval Academy, joined with a group of friends to hit a presidential campaign event in Salt Lake City. Only this one was for Romney.

And Will didn't just hang in the back. He inched his way to the front of the rope line and, clad in dark sunglasses and a polo shirt with a crest of the U.S. Embassy of Singapore, flashed a "hang loose" sign with his pinky and thumb while a friend snapped a photo of him next to Romney. A freelance photographer caught the moment — and the Huntsman campaign off guard.

"Will wanted to see another campaign event," Huntsman spokesman Tim Miller said when shown the photo. "He was having fun, and it was not his intention to be disrespectful in any way."

Of course, that was the least of the worries of the newly formed Huntsman campaign.

Huntsman seemed to lack the fire to fight for the nomination, and aides were concerned.

"I don't think he has a speaking problem, enthusiasm or looks or intelligence [problems], he had a major motivational problem," recalled a former top aide. "It's really hard to run for president."

It's a grueling, night-and-day effort. People are beating you up left and right. It's difficult to attract the spotlight. Huntsman thought he was ready because he had run two campaigns in Utah.

"You think you've been through that running for governor of Utah?" the same aide snarked. "That's kindergarten, and this is the big leagues."

And the big leagues are expensive. Huntsman staffers expected to be rolling in money because their candidate was a millionaire and his dad was a billionaire. Between them, they knew a lot of wealthy folks. Lynn Forester de Rothschild, a Manhattan socialite who had switched from backing Hillary Clinton to supporting McCain in 2008, held Huntsman's kickoff fundraiser, reportedly collecting $1.2 million, though financial reports would later show little sign of that big haul.

Huntsman seemed good at glad-handing potential donors — once a diplomat, always a diplomat — but he struggled asking for money. He also didn't want his father fronting any cash or bugging his friends for donations.

Aides were shocked, even more so when Huntsman Jr. told them he wasn't going to pump much of his own money into the effort and that he wasn't as wealthy as people assumed. Initial indications were that he had stocked up some $70 million — the top end of what financial reporting documents said — but he was actually worth around $15 million, much of it tied up in real estate and other holdings. "That certainly was news to us," said a disappointed aide.

Top Huntsman strategist John Weaver envisioned a pop-up campaign, in which he would quickly set up headquarters, hire a big team and focus on New Hampshire, South Carolina and Florida. The plan hinged on a quick infusion of cash that just wasn't coming. Weaver plowed ahead anyway, setting up shop in Orlando, where Mary Kaye grew up. The notion was to tout her roots as part of the candidate's D.C.-outsider strategy.

"This is not a Washington-based campaign and not a Washington-based candidate," said campaign manager Susie Wiles, despite the fact that the Huntsmans' home was in a tony D.C. neighborhood.

The sixth floor of 255 S. Orange Ave. in Orlando was now Huntsman central. Rent was $66,000 a month, and the team had signed a contract for 18 months, without an early-termination clause. Customary campaign signs were taped to the wall. Paper signs announced each office's occupant, or simply that it was for Huntsman staff, since there was plenty of unoccupied space to go around. A sign on the women's restroom noted it was for HuntsWOman.

"I was being told to hire, hire, hire," one aide recalled. "A couple weeks later — late June and early July — we were upside down on the balance sheet."

Huntsman was dismayed at the fire hose of spending and annoyed that his top advisers thought he would just pour his own fortune into the bid and beg his buddies to throw more money his way.

His idea, he recalls, was to imitate former Wisconsin Sen. William Proxmire, who pulled $200 out of his own pocket to win his last two terms, just enough to pay the filing fee and return postage for donations he didn't ask for.

"I hate big money in politics," Huntsman recalls. "I think it's the cancer that's killing this country."

Even so, he dutifully hit the fundraising circuit in July, but found few willing to bite after his campaign launch fizzled.

"A lot of the donors, they want to know the pathway. It was particularly acute in '12: What is your message going to be to take down the president? How are you going to take him down? ... I wasn't the guy who was going to rip Obama to shreds, which is what a lot of the big funders wanted."

There are only so many big-money folks to hit up, and Huntsman figured out quickly the "chattering class in the money circles" didn't think he was the guy.

He grudgingly put in $2 million of his own money to prime the pump, as the team called it. It didn't help much. Nothing was working right.

"Then it became, 'OK, what do you do about this?' If you begin to fire people at the top, they will destroy you. That's just the way the game is played," Huntsman recalls. "And I didn't want to go down that way. I refused to get in a whizzing match with, you know, with some of the folks who were around the campaign, knowing full well what it meant."

That meant John Weaver, his chief strategist, was safe, but Huntsman let campaign manager Susie Wiles go. It was all about optics: When the ship isn't running right, you toss the captain overboard.

Weaver slid communications director Matt David into the manager role.

"Now the campaign is moving into phase two, which will be more aggressive from a messaging and tactical standpoint, and Matt is prepared to take that on," Weaver explained.

Huntsman, at the time, called it a "fine-tuning," brushing off accusations that his campaign already had failed.

"If the election were next week, that would be problematic," he said of his still-at-2-percent poll numbers. "If by October or November, we're not up to where we need to be, then I would be a little concerned. But no one's paying attention now except insiders."

Those insiders observed an interesting battle within the Huntsman camp.

At the candidate's request, Weaver ousted David Fischer, who had been an advance man for Ronald Reagan and a friend of the Huntsman clan for decades. Fischer, obviously ticked, went to Politico to lay out how badly the campaign was being run and dish dirt on Weaver and pals. The Huntsman folks determined to dirty Fischer first.

Real Clear Politics posted a story July 31 detailing how Fischer had been asked to leave when he caused distractions. An anonymous aide was quoted alleging Fischer was upset about staffers who smoked, sported tattoos or were gay.

"He acted like a hall monitor," an aide told the news outlet. "There was a cloud on morale down there [in Orlando]."

Fischer rejected the idea that he was antigay or despised smoking or tattoos — "Oh, my gosh, I couldn't care less if someone smokes or drinks," he said — but now he was even more angry and told Politico that he would go on the record and share personal emails between him and Huntsman.

The blockbuster came Aug. 4, 2011, and was pitched as an inside look at the dysfunction in the Huntsman operation.

"I look forward to a future of less drama, more money and increasing contrasts with my opponents. We can win this thing," Huntsman wrote in an email to Fischer after Wiles was forced out. "Goodness will overcome the temporary difficulties and early turf-protecting within the campaign," Huntsman wrote, adding to Fischer: "I love you like a brother."

Fischer described the campaign as disorganized, tense and loaded with problems the news media had yet to discover. More people had resigned than previously disclosed, and Weaver's management style was rife with "verbal abuse." He claimed Mary Kaye Huntsman and Jon Huntsman Sr. were furious and blamed Weaver. He also said the team was split into pro-Weaver and anti-Weaver sides.

"It's not an ego [thing]," Fischer said when asked why he was going public. "In fact, a lot of it is if the story gets told, I want the story to be, because Weaver's history in past campaigns is when they don't work out, for whatever reason, he attacks the candidate. And in this case, I am hoping that people at least focus on, well, what went wrong here? The strategy went wrong. The strategy didn't work. At least to this day it hasn't worked."

The campaign launched an angry counterattack.

"Dave Fischer tried to threaten the campaign regarding his participation in this story, and we refused to cooperate with him," said spokesman Tim Miller. "As a volunteer staff member, he attempted to usurp authority, asked inappropriate questions about junior staff and was rightly asked to leave by Gov. Huntsman. His statements about this campaign are untrue. The fact that he would be willing to undermine Gov. Huntsman in this way says everything you need to know about his character, his credibility and whether he has the governor's best interests at heart."

Fischer may not have been loyal, but he wasn't wrong, at least not about Weaver, as would become clear down the campaign trail.

As the infighting raged on, Huntsman had to prepare for his first presidential debate, the third held during this marathon primary season.

By then, the field was a motley cast of characters: Herman Cain, the former chief executive of Godfather's Pizza, and his 9-9-9 plan (9 percent business tax, 9 percent income tax and 9 percent sales tax); Rep. Michele Bachmann of Minnesota, the rabble-rousing tea-party darling; former House Speaker Newt Gingrich, who was trying to revive his dormant political career; ex-Sen. Rick Santorum of Pennsylvania, buoyed by the pro-life crowd; Rep. Ron Paul of Texas, adored by his libertarian base; and former Minnesota Gov. Tim Pawlenty, who had nearly been McCain's running mate in 2008 and played the nice guy in the GOP contest. Then there were Huntsman and Romney, the two Mormon boys with picture-perfect families.

Fox News, the Washington Examiner and the Iowa Republican Party were the debate hosts.

Not wasting any time with the newbie in the race, the moderators asked Huntsman about his support for civil unions, immigration reform and a more expansive stimulus package to boost the economy. They asked him about working for Obama. Fox News' Chris Wallace then asked a gut-puncher: "Some people have suggested that maybe you're running for president in the wrong party."

"Chris," Huntsman responded, "let me just say I'm proud of my service to this country. If you love your country, you serve her. During a time of war, during a time of economic hardship, when asked to serve your country in a sensitive position where you can actually bring a background to help your nation, I'm the kind of person who's going to stand up and do it, and I'll take that philosophy to my grave."

It was pure Huntsman, but not something that played to this crowd.

The real show was Romney, the perceived front-runner and the guy all of the candidates wanted to challenge. The hosts wanted to challenge him, too.

Fox News' Bret Baier asked Romney why he stepped in only at the last minute to bash a deal between Obama and Congress to increase the nation's borrowing power. Some columnists, Baier noted, had said Romney was in the "Mittness Protection Program." Would he have vetoed the deal?

"Look, I'm not going to eat Barack Obama's dog food, all right?" Romney said. "What he served up was not what I would have done if I'd had been president."

Pawlenty, needing a kick for his campaign, had whiffed at a chance in a previous debate to dig Romney with a word his campaign had coined for the mixture of Obamacare and Romneycare. He wasn't going to miss it this time.

"Obamacare was patterned after Mitt's plan in Massachusetts. And for Mitt or anyone else to say that there aren't substantial similarities or they're not essentially the same plan, it just isn't credible," said Pawlenty. "So that's why I called it Obamneycare, and I think that's a fair label, and I'm happy to call it that again tonight."

"I think I like Tim's answer at the last debate better," Romney joked.

Pawlenty later quipped that if anyone could find detailed plans on Romney's website about reforming Social Security, Medicare or Medicaid, Pawlenty would come over and mow their lawn.

"But in case Mitt wins, I'm limited to one acre. One acre," the candidate snarked.

Romney didn't take the bait. He stuck to his game plan: Look like the front-runner by ignoring the other candidates and direct all fire toward the president.

"Barack Obama won in 2008 on hope," Romney said. "I'm going to win in 2012 on solutions."

He couldn't duck another question on the nation's debt ceiling. The moderators asked candidates, by a show of hands, who would refuse any tax increase even if it was paired with a move to cut $10 for every $1 raised. All of the candidates raised a hand, including Huntsman, who immediately regretted it.

"If you can only do certain things over again in life," he said. "What went through my head was if I veer at all from my pledge not to raise any taxes … then I'm going to have to do a lot of explaining. What was going through my mind was 'Don't I just want to get through this?' "

Perhaps he was in shock, too, at the makeup of the GOP field.

"You stand up on the stage in the debate like we did the other night and [look] around and say, 'Whoa, where'd these folks come from? What an interesting assortment of characters,' " Huntsman would say at a fundraiser shortly after.

The Ames, Iowa, straw poll — that much-hyped faux test of candidates — took place two days after the debate, and it accomplished two things: It boosted Bachmann's candidacy and ended Pawlenty's.

Romney aides, seeing Pawlenty as one of their most formidable opponents, now became even more confident that this was their nomination to lose.

At the same time, Romney knew a win would take months, millions of dollars and an amazing amount of patience.

The Republican Party had changed the primary system, eliminating the winner-take-all contests for a proportional system, with the obvious result that the campaign likely would drag on. The GOP also sanctioned two dozen debates, each one an opportunity to make a gaffe or a chance to get forced into taking an extreme stance that would alienate general-election voters.

The whole process frustrated the Romney camp.

"You look at everything the party did to try to hamper the eventual nominee, they did it," said Josh Romney, one of the candidate's sons.

Of course, Huntsman wasn't the only late entrant into the race.

Texas Gov. Rick Perry jumped in the same day as the Ames straw poll ended Pawlenty's hopes. Unlike Huntsman, he immediately shot up in the polls. In late August, he was up 12 points over Romney.

Perry's reception proved that the GOP electorate wasn't in love with Romney and that party elders were concerned.

Suffering a dip in the polls, Romney headed to New Hampshire, where he hoped to rebound but instead found a testy welcome.

"I wish you would speak to the truth rather than say something that you think is a platitude, when in fact we do need the government to spend money," a woman told Romney at a town hall in Lebanon, citing government support of schools, police stations and for victims of natural disasters. The voter wouldn't yield to Romney despite his best efforts.

"Do you have a question? Do you have a question and let me answer it," Romney said, smiling. "You had your turn, madam, now let me have mine. ... Just hold on a moment. Just hold on."

Romney needed to face the crowds — whether hostile or friendly — and he responded by effusively praising those in attendance. "This has been fun, I'll tell ya," he said at the end of the event. "This is the most fun I've had in a long time. This is a great group. This is what's so fun about town meetings in New Hampshire. You guys care. You're informed."

As Romney hit a rough patch, Huntsman's troubled campaign started gaining attention and endorsements — from people they would rather not hear from.

Former Democratic presidential candidate Howard Dean said Huntsman was the "thinking man" of the GOP. Ex-President Jimmy Carter already had planted a big kiss on Huntsman's bid, saying he was "very attractive to me personally." And Bill Clinton, the archnemesis of the GOP before Obama: "I just kind of like him. And he looks authentic, he looks like a real guy — I mean a real human being. I like his family. He was a pretty good governor."

Soon, filmmaker Michael Moore, that liberal bogeyman, would add his backing, saying that of all the GOP candidates, Huntsman was the only one "that has sanity operating inside of him."

That didn't help Huntsman's conservative bona fides, and neither did his attraction to the world of high society. The fashion magazine Vogue requested an interview, and to sweeten the deal, one of the world's most famous photographers, Annie Leibovitz, would take pictures of the Huntsman clan. Leibovitz, of course, had photographed John Lennon with Yoko Ono hours before Lennon was killed, and is the go-to portrait artist.

"Then you have Annie Leibovitz show up at your home and, you know, I thought, I can't turn down Annie Leibovitz," Huntsman says. "When she shows up with a camera, you've got to pose."

"A few weeks into the race, Huntsman looks like a protest candidate — less a figure of the current Republican zeitgeist than a canny challenger to his party's orthodoxy," Vogue writer Jacob Weisberg chimed in. The article featured a serious-looking Huntsman, in a blue oxford shirt, his back to a bookshelf, as well as a shot of his family — minus the two sons at the Naval Academy — strolling hand in hand through a park.

The Huntsmans loved the photos. The party? Not so much.

His adman Fred Davis jumped ship to work on the Our Destiny super PAC that Huntsman's dad was largely floating. Without money in the actual campaign, Davis knew it was the only place he could get paid to make ads.

Huntsman also had fired his New Hampshire campaign manager, Ethan Eilon, and replaced him with Sarah Crawford Stewart, Pawlenty's former Granite State aide.

Huntsman and his top guy, Weaver, were becoming more distant.

Weaver "doesn't suffer fools," says an ex-Huntsman aide, who noted that Weaver is "one of the smartest guys I've met" but that he also charges a lot upfront, is hard to reach and, although he may have a brilliant campaign plan, he doesn't write it down.

"He's not a good communicator of what he's thinking," the aide said. "He changes his mind. He's a hard, hard guy to work with."

Huntsman, though, pressed on and took more shots at his rivals, using an interview with Bloomberg's Al Hunt to jab Romney and Perry.

Romney, Huntsman charged, doesn't have the "hands-on foreign policy experience" to be president, and he doesn't have the record of job creation the country needs.

"I prefer having a governor who is No. 1 in job creation as opposed to No. 47, someone who didn't raise taxes to the tune of $750 million a year," Huntsman said, comparing his record as Utah's chief executive to Romney's time in Boston.

As for Perry, well, his positions on climate change and evolution should be concerning, Huntsman said: "On science, he's out of the mainstream."

Huntsman's advisers were heartened to see their guy finally fight, and they persuaded him to turn to Twitter as another attention-grabbing technique.

"To be clear. I believe in evolution and trust scientists on global warming. Call me crazy," Huntsman's team tweeted out, a move mainly aimed at poking Perry's anti-climate-change rhetoric. Some 5,300 users retweeted it, and cable TV ate it up.

Huntsman wasn't just winning the attention of his opponents, he also was becoming a favorite of the Democratic National Committee — not because the party folks there wanted him to succeed, but he was tossing out such wonderful fodder for them to use. He was, essentially, the DNC's new surrogate. In an email to reporters with the subject line "Don't take our word for it …," the party committee noted several of the barbs Huntsman had thrown at his rivals so far:

• That the other GOP candidates had "zero substance" and were "too far to the right."

• That he wouldn't trust any of his rivals with the economy because they would have allowed the country to default by opposing the debt-ceiling deal.

• That the GOP has a "serious problem" in becoming the "anti-science party."

• And when asked about Romney's flip-flops, Huntsman responded, "If we talk about inconsistencies and change on various issues, we'd be here all afternoon."

Instead of backing off, Huntsman stepped it up. Asked about Romney's response to a question about the nation's debt, he said: "When you need to stand up, you take your position, you defend your position, you run a little risk in taking that position, you don't wait until the very end as Gov. Romney did, [where] you put your finger to the wind and basically come down on the safe side politically; I just don't think that's leadership."

But for all the media attention, Huntsman's campaign was broke. The $66,000-a-month Orlando headquarters was jettisoned, as was the too-expensive three-state strategy. And he was laying off staff in droves, including his closest Utah confidants. Neil Ashdown, the deputy campaign manager and Huntsman's right-hand guy for years, was gone, as was Greg Hartley, the campaign's deputy political director who had held the candidate's ear at one point.

His new strategy was a sleek, stripped-down play for one important early state — a repeat of McCain's successful 2008 primary comeback.

"I knew my only option then," Huntsman says, "was run as fast and as hard as you can to New Hampshire, work your heart out and if you do well there, you can reorganize."

The Huntsmans moved into Manchester's Hilton Garden Inn, just a block or so from Romney's New Hampshire headquarters. Huntsman's hotel included a patio that faced the Northeast Delta Stadium, where the Fisher Cats played. If he was lucky, on game days, he could return home after campaigning and catch the eighth and ninth innings from his room. The Cats, the double-A affiliate of the Blue Jays, were the Eastern League champions in 2011. Huntsman wouldn't be as lucky.

Instead of enjoying the national pastime, he got distracted by "The Donald."

Romney already had visited real-estate mogul Donald Trump, as had Perry and Sarah Palin. Depending on which side you believe, Huntsman sought a similar meeting — or didn't.

Huntsman spokesman Tim Miller tweeted that Huntsman wasn't wasting his time with "Presidential Apprentice. His focus is on real solutions to fix our economy." In an interview with ABC News, Trump responded that Huntsman's people had asked at least once for a meeting.

"I didn't call him back," Trump said, "not that I would."

Huntsman has "zero chance of getting the nomination," Trump tweeted. "Whoever said I wanted to meet him? Time is money and I don't waste mine."

The Donald, though, was set to meet with another of Huntsman's competitors, the former Godfather's Pizza CEO.

By mid-October, Herman Cain was topping Romney in national polls, he was earning the thrust of the cable show time, and his 9-9-9 plan was getting buzz. He had won a straw poll in Florida and then dominated another such contest in Illinois at a gathering of tea partiers called TeaCon. His blunt style was captivating for Americans already tiring of the long nomination process.

But at the latest GOP debate, this one at Dartmouth College in Hanover, N.H., Cain made it clear he knew Romney was still the one to beat. During his chance to ask a rival a question, he looked straight at Romney, conveniently to his left on the oblong wood table.

"The 9-9-9 plan that I have proposed is simple, transparent, efficient, fair and neutral. My question is to Gov. Romney. Can you name all 59 points in your 160-page plan, and does it satisfy that criteria of being simple, transparent, efficient, fair and neutral?"

The audience laughed. The candidates laughed. Even Romney chuckled.

"Herman," Romney responded. "I have had the experience in my life of taking on some tough problems. And I must admit that simple answers are always very helpful, but oftentimes inadequate." He didn't list all 59 points but rattled off a few.

Huntsman, too, tossed Romney a tough question, one that had more bite to it than Cain's.

"Since some might see you because of your past employment with Bain Capital as more of a financial engineer, somebody who breaks down business-es, destroys jobs, as opposed to creating jobs and opportunity, leveraging up, spinning off, enriching shareholders," Huntsman said, "since you were No. 47 [in job creation] as governor of the state of Massachusetts, where we were No. 1 [in Utah], for example, and the whole discussion around this campaign is going to be job creation, how can you win that debate, given your back-ground?"

"Well," Romney said, "my background is quite different than you de-scribed, Jon. So the way I'll win it is by telling people an accurate rendition of what I have done in my life. And, fortunately, people in New Hampshire, living next door, have a pretty good sense of that."

That wasn't the only clash between the Romneys and the Huntsmans that night. Huntsman's three eldest daughters, Abby, Mary Anne and Liddy — who, like the Romney boys, had begun to emerge as surrogates for their father — also got into it with Romney.

In response to Romney's debate vow that he would, once elected, label China a currency manipulator and go after the country for stealing intellec-tual property, they tweeted: "How does Romney know anything about Chi-na? He's only been there once and that was for the Olympics. Panda Express doesn't count."

Zing!

Around the same time, Cain's top aide, Mark Block, appeared in an on-line video touting how his boss would put " 'united' back in the United States of America."

"Tomorrow is one day closer to the White House," Block said, ending the video by taking a puff on a cigarette and blowing smoke toward the camera — not something that would typically, or really ever, end up in a campaign ad.

Huntsman's daughters, known as the Jon2012Girls, found it a perfect target for parody. The young women, all in their 20s, went to Urban Outfit-ters and bought fake mustaches — to match Block's stache — and filmed a no-budget spot in the courtyard of their parents' D.C. home. "Tomorrow is Friday, one day closer to the weekend," Liddy said, poking fun at Block's line.

"We are shamelessly promoting our dad like no other candidate's family has, but then again, no one's ever seen a trio like the Jon2012Girls," added Mary Anne. In a nod to Block's cigarette puff, the spoof ends with the three women blowing bubbles at the camera.

Huntsman couldn't stop laughing when he saw the video.

First the Panda Express jab at Romney and now this. The daughters were creating their own media buzz with snarky tweets that circumvented the campaign operation. They didn't worry about being too edgy. "That's probably why it has been so popular," Abby Huntsman said. "We all just kind of say what we think. People seem to like the honesty."

Campaign aides weren't too happy about that part, especially when the women recorded a parody YouTube video of Justin Timberlake's "SexyBack" song, saying they were "Bringing Huntsman back. The rest of them are a circus act," and then individually dinged the front-runners.

"The video was produced without authorization," an unnamed aide told The Washington Post. "The girls were asked by a number of campaign officials to not release the video. The campaign was not informed of the release of the video. The video does not have a disclaimer and is not a campaign product." The video came out a day after Huntsman's message was about the need to "stay focused on the issues that really do matter."

Not that Huntsman's team was above attacking another candidate on the down low. After a tip from a donor, Huntsman's researchers dug into Cain's past, uncovered two sexual-harassment claims and then tossed them — no fingerprints attached — to Politico.

"Herman Cain accused by two women of inappropriate behavior," the headline blared. A new allegation of a long-standing affair doused Cain's poll numbers, and he soon would quit the race.

Huntsman's attention remained largely on Romney, and he continued to hone his criticism, which focused on two topics: Romney's flip-flops and his lack of international experience.

Appearing via satellite from Salt Lake City on CNN's "Situation Room with Wolf Blitzer," Huntsman sported a purple tie and dark suit, the Wasatch Mountains towering behind him.

"You can't be a perfectly lubricated weather vane on the important issues of the day," Huntsman blurted out. "Romney has been missing in action in terms of showing any kind of leadership."

Blitzer facilitated another showdown at CNN's national-security debate in Washington in late November 2011, providing a chance for Huntsman and Romney to spar over the U.S. involvement in Afghanistan.

"Now, Gov. Huntsman, do you agree with Gov. Romney that the U.S. has to stay in Afghanistan at these levels?" Blitzer asked.

"No, I — I totally disagree," Huntsman responded. "I think we need to square with the American people about what we've achieved. We need an honest conversation in this country about the sacrifices that have been made over nearly 10 years. We have — we have dismantled the Taliban. We've run them out of Kabul. We've had free elections in 2004. We've killed Osama bin Laden. We've upended, dismantled al-Qaida. We have achieved some very important goals for the United States of America." What we need, the candidate added, are drones and intelligence officials and training, not 100,000 troops.

"Well, let me respond," Romney said, acknowledging the existence of his opponent.. "Are you suggesting, Governor, that we just take all our troops out next week or what — what's your proposal?"

"Did you hear what I just said?" Huntsman shot back. "I said we should draw down from 100,000. We don't need 100,000 troops. We don't need 100,000 troops in Afghanistan. ..."

But the commanders, Romney interrupted, are suggesting a timeline. "I stand with the commanders in this regard and have no information that suggests that pulling our troops out faster than that would do anything but put at — at great peril the extraordinary sacrifice that's been made. This is not time for America to cut and run."

Blitzer tried to move on, but Huntsman wanted one last point.

"Listen, I think it's important for the American people to know we have achieved some very important objectives in raising standards in Afghanistan and helping to build civil society," he said. "But at the end of the day, the president of the United States is commander in chief, commander in chief. Of course you're going to listen to the generals. But ... I also remember when people listened to the generals in 1967 and we heard a certain course of action in South Asia that didn't serve our interests very well. The president is the commander in chief and ought to be informed by a lot of different voices, including those of his generals on the ground."

The next day, The Washington Post featured Huntsman as one of the winners of the debate, though pundits praised Romney's "commanding performance."

The Jon Huntsman signs outside the community center in Atkinson, N.H., in October were obscured by snow.

Motorists maneuvered their cars into makeshift parking spots since the white mush had erased any semblance of order. Nearby flashing lights warned of a "snow emergency" as a heavy storm continued to blanket the New Hampshire hamlet on the Massachusetts state line.

Huntsman, sporting red fleece and checkerboard flannel, strode into the town hall and shook the hands of everyone there. All eight of them.

"This is truly the intrepid few," he declared as he took a seat at the head of the small conference room. "I didn't think anybody would be here."

Four months in and millions spent, Huntsman still was trying to weather the storm that followed his presidential launch.

"Campaigns are generally controlled chaos, even in the best of circumstances," he said at the time. "People win in a world of controlled chaos. You can either look at the negative side and say things might not always go as planned or you can say, 'Well, on the other hand, [you're] beginning to connect with the people of New Hampshire.' "

At least a few of them.

Gail Witham, whose family had lived in New Hampshire for 400 years, attended the Atkinson event. She was an independent voter who had never before backed a candidate but jumped at the chance to serve as the chairwoman for Huntsman's effort in her small community.

"I just feel totally convinced this is a man with integrity; he's stable, he's well-educated," she said. "It's not just because he put on a plaid flannel shirt."

Witham was a minority in the state: a Huntsman backer. While Huntsman had been elated in September to find himself at 10 percent in a New Hampshire poll, a more recent one had him down to 4 percent.

Romney, meanwhile, stood steady at 38 percent, some 18 points above his closest rival, Cain, who was about to drop out. Even though Huntsman had lasered in on New Hampshire, barely half the voters recognized him, the least of any GOP candidate.

At MaryAnn's Diner in Derry, a New Hampshire haunt that boasts pictures of Al Gore, Rudy Giuliani, Ron Paul and two of Mitt Romney, it was hard to find a voter who knew much, if anything, about Huntsman.

"At least he's one of the sane ones," said Charles Miller, of Derry, a self-described independent who often votes for Democrats. "Huntsman projects an intelligence that I find appealing."

But Miller probably wasn't going to vote in the Jan. 10 Republican primary, so that appeal wouldn't help the Huntsman cause.

A few tables over, Margie Anderson, of Kingston, was deciding among the 1950s-era menu items that vary between the tuna-sandwich Barracuda and the Big Bopper burger.

"I don't like the cut of his jib," Anderson said of Huntsman. "I don't think he espouses what I like," which is, she added, a candidate who "stops being so much a Republican or a Democrat and do what needs to be done."

Actually, that had been a big part of Huntsman's stump speech, but Anderson hadn't heard it. And in a state where even Huntsman acknowledges you need to shake a voter's hand 15 times to get his or her support, Anderson hadn't met Huntsman.

Huntsman's camp had no money for TV ads introducing him to voters, let alone digital spots to lure interested Googlers to his campaign website.

He had one hope left: the Our Destiny super PAC, largely funded by his dad. The group was finally — finally — going on air in New Hampshire to help the fumbling campaign.

"The president has failed. The economy is worse," intoned an actor. "The stock market is a wreck. Are we the next Greece?" another asked.

"Consistently conservative," the ad declared. "Two-term successful governor. Three-time ambassador." A few more accolades splashed on the screen. "Why haven't we heard of this guy?" an actor says at the end.

Huntsman hadn't seen the ad, but he was happy for something. "Any efforts will help," he said. "I don't know what it will consist of, but I'm grateful for any support that shows up."

The super PAC reported spending about $1.3 million around the time for "media buys." The PAC ad was introductory in nature: Hey, look at this guy. The Huntsman campaign went the small-dollar route, creating web videos hitting Romney that they hoped would go viral.

"Is the Massachusetts approach that was passed under Gov. Romney, is that a good model for the nation?" CNN host John King asks in a clip for the web video put out by Huntsman's team. "Well, I think so," Romney replies.

That's followed by Romney saying elsewhere that he doesn't think Romneycare is something the nation should do. Then Romney is shown backing an economic-stimulus package, followed by him saying he doesn't back Obama's stimulus plan. Another shot depicts Romney saying he doesn't support a timed withdrawal of troops in Iraq, and then arguing for a "series of timetables and milestones" for the same thing.

"You can't be a perfectly lubricated weather vane on the important issues of the day," Huntsman chimes in. "Whether it's Libya, whether it's the debt ceiling, whether it's the discussion around the Kasich bill in Ohio — where Gov. Romney has been missing in action in terms of showing any kind of leadership."

Another web spot took a more comical, if pointed, approach. It features a split screen: one one side Romney making apparently contradictory statements on issues such as abortion; on the other side, a small, wind-up, back-flipping monkey.

Near the end, Republican strategist Mary Matalin asks Huntsman about Romney's core. "It smacks a little bit of leading from behind," he responds.

Two punches thrown, and then the campaign went for a third, launching a website called ScaredMittless.com that featured a parody of Romney's logo and hosted articles on Romney avoiding the press with headlines like "Mitt's Vanishing Act" and "Don't Take It Personally Iowa; Romney's Avoiding Everyone." To add more heat, a clock counted how long it had been since Romney's last Sunday talk-show appearance (610 days at the time) and his last news conference (28 days).

After starting out so hesitant to say anything about Obama or his rivals by name, the new tactics revealed a more-desperate Huntsman, though he insists he was never as comfortable in attack mode as his advisers.

"It was more about ideas, and that was something that my campaign never understood about me," the candidate recalls. "They always figured the head-on, trench warfare was the way to do it, and I was of a different mold. So we always had a lot of conversations about the level of fire and I was always turning them down, to dump that video, to change their direction or at least minimizing their messaging to something that I could stomach."

But strategies change as campaigns progress — or don't progress, in the case of Huntsman's poll numbers. Now the trench warfare was winning out. It was a "natural evolution," he says, because when you get hit, you can't just retreat.

"And so you ratchet up according to whatever the level of warfare happens to be," he says. "So as we were organizing and more active in New Hampshire, and focused more on New Hampshire, that's where the incoming [fire] became more intense and the tricks that other campaigns would play and, you know, you get a little more whizzed off at the tricks that you've seen."

Romney saw another strong challenger fumble when Rick Perry forgot the third federal department he wanted to cut. It was the "oops" heard around the political world and the kind of error Perry wanted to avoid.

Then Romney had one of his own.

Perry insisted Romney was for the health-care individual mandate before he was against it, a point Romney adamantly denied.

"You know what? You've raised that before, Rick. And you're simply wrong," Romney shot back.

"It was true then," Perry said. "It's true now."

"I'll tell you what: Ten thousand bucks. A ten-thousand-dollar bet?" Romney offered.

Ten thousand dollars for a friendly bet?

Oops.

The Huntsman team took glee in Romney's gaffe, throwing up the website 10kbet.com, loaded with coverage of Romney's odd joke, and pointing out news releases from Romney's 2008 bid that showed he highlighted the Massachusetts reform as a "national model that would dramatically expand access to health care."

Romney tried to shrug it off — he joked that his wife, Ann, noted he was good at debating but not good at betting — and besides, the candidate had another emerging rival to watch.

With Cain out of the race, Newt Gingrich, the former House speaker, vaulted the front of the pack, earning new scrutiny. Opponents, including Romney's super PAC, took notice. It ran a blitz of ads, saying Gingrich had a lot of baggage, and it worked. Romney recaptured the lead.

In New Hampshire, the only state that mattered for Huntsman, the former Utah governor, after months of shoe-leather campaigning, saw his poll numbers at 9 percent and moving in the right direction.

Newt Gingrich, taking his turn at the front of the pack after the fall of Cain and Perry, hoped to keep his momentum as a cerebral Republican. He had been begging opponents to sit down with him and debate in the style of Abraham Lincoln and Stephen Douglas: no moderator, a timed period for remarks and rebuttals, and just a few topics.

Huntsman, sensing that any opportunity for press was a good one, signed on. What could be better than two policy wonks discussing policy in the wonkiest way possible?

"I can see my daughter nodding off over there, which means we've gone too long," Huntsman said an hour in. Gracie Mei, his 12-year-old, didn't seem as enthralled with the discussion of how America could capitalize on the Arab Spring revolutions. "She's also my senior foreign-policy adviser, so that's not a good thing."

There were no zingers. There was barely a pulse. But the two candidates praised each other for the civility and discussion.

"This is what we should have a lot more of because this is substantive," Gingrich said. "This is not a Hollywood game. This is not a reality show. This is reality."

So who won? "The winners would really be the American people," Huntsman declared. Not that many tuned in beyond the small audience at Saint Anselm College in Manchester. But to this day, Huntsman considers that conversation a highlight of his race.

"The only one that was worth our time," he recalls, noting that debate was the "most enjoyable and the most substantive."

"But what we heard after was that there was no blood on the floor. Where was the blood? Where was the sex and violence?" Huntsman says. "And so that kind of left me to conclude what I concluded for a long time and that is the media set expectations of the level of blood and violence that they want to see."

The media also like fun things, so Huntsman took his turn in the "Saturday Night Live" swivel chair of "Weekend Update" with Seth Meyers, who asked the former governor if he was alienating all the other states in favor of New Hampshire.

"I love all of America, from Dallas, Texas, to Manchester, New Hampshire," Huntsman said. "From the majestic Rocky Mountains to New Hampshire's scenic Lake Winnipesaukee. From the innovation of Silicon Valley to the affordable outlet malls in North Conway, New Hampshire."

Huntsman then asked Meyers, a New Hampshire native, if his parents were registered to vote. His mom is a Democrat, the comic answered, and his dad is an independent.

"Well, say hi to your dad for me," Huntsman said.

Romney, too, was up for a bit of comedy in December, appearing on the "Late Show with David Letterman" and rolling out his own top 10 list.

"What's up, gangstas, it's the M-i-double-tizzle," Romney recited as the No. 9 thing he wanted to say to the American people.

"I just used all my campaign money to buy a zoo with Matt Damon," Romney said as No. 4. No. 1 was an easy go-to laugh line: "It's a hairpiece."

But it was the No. 2 item that was less of a joke. "Newt Gingrich, really?" Romney deadpanned.

Not to be outdone, Huntsman scheduled an appearance two days later on Letterman, and the former band geek brought his keyboard skills. Letterman showed an image of Huntsman from his days in the high-school band Wizard, noting it was "rather incriminating."

"I thought I could make it big," Huntsman joked. "I wanted to be Paul Shaffer," he added, referring to Letterman's longtime bandleader. It was planned, of course, but Huntsman then jumped at the chance to play the keyboard aside Shaffer for a rendition of Chuck Berry's "Johnny B. Goode."

A Christmastime poll in New Hampshire showed Romney holding stubbornly at 39 percent, enough to win, but he hadn't gained support in months. That survey showed the sliding Gingrich and the rising Ron Paul tied with 17 percent. Paul — whose libertarian leanings (audit the Fed!) gained ground among New Hampshire's more independent-minded voters — had become the new concern for Huntsman and, to a lesser degree, Romney.

Huntsman had inched up to 11 percent, but a fourth-place finish would kill his run for sure.

After spending four months camped out almost solely in the state, Huntsman took a break from campaigning to return to Salt Lake City for Christmas, where he spent part of the day helping to serve the city's homeless at a shelter, as he had done for years as governor.

The Huntsman Sr.-funded Our Destiny super PAC took no such break.

Instead, it prepared an ad aimed right at Romney. The group spent $300,000 to reserve airtime in New Hampshire.

"Two serious candidates remain," a voice intoned, with images of Huntsman and Romney on screen. "One willing to say anything, be anything. One who can actually do the job.

"One state can stop the chameleon. Vote Jon Huntsman."

While the Huntsman machine was hammering away in New Hampshire, Romney rushed to the Hawkeye State.

His late December trip was only his eighth visit to Iowa that year. His low-key efforts were meant to signal how strong he could be without a big push. He relied more on the groundwork he laid in 2008.

"We started with a blank piece of paper four years ago," added state Rep. Renee Schulte, who backed Romney in 2008 and now was a state co-chairwoman. "We, of course, have kept all that data. So now this year, I still have the list and I still know all the people."

Santorum treated Iowa the way Huntsman was treating New Hampshire. It was everything to his long-shot bid. The former senator and his signature sweater vest traveled to all 99 counties in his gray 2006 Dodge Ram extended-cab pickup, often with just one staffer. He had persisted in meeting county party officials, touting nearly 400 such meetings. Santorum had little cash and a small operation compared with Romney, but he was scrappy and willing to spend a lot of on-the-ground time meeting voters.

Romney wanted to win Iowa but set the bar lower just in case.

"I don't have any predictions," he told reporters. "No expectations are set. We're hoping to do well everywhere."

Jan. 3, Iowa caucus day, brought months of effort to a head. Unlike other contests, where voters show up between 7 a.m. and 8 p.m., the caucuses all happen at night, at one place, in one meeting.

Romney and his family huddled in a room at the Hotel Fort Des Moines, watching as results rolled in. Romney was killing it in the places his folks had targeted, but there was a surprise creeping up. Santorum, boosted by last-minute momentum, captured a host of rural precincts.

At night's end, Romney appeared to eke out a win — by eight votes — over Santorum, though the former Pennsylvania senator saw that as a victory in his own right: The underdog, hardworking candidate essentially tied with the big-money heir apparent. It was the closest Iowa caucus result since at least the 1970s.

"Game on," Santorum told supporters.

Romney was gracious, offering congrats to Santorum while also claiming victory — "This has been a great victory for him and for his effort. He's worked very hard in Iowa. We also feel it's been a great victory for us here"

— but the front-runner kept his ultimate goal in mind, slamming Obama for failing to live up to his own hype.

"I will go to work," Romney said, "to get America back to work."

Perry, who landed fifth, told his supporters he was headed back to Texas to evaluate his options. Bachmann, who finished sixth, canceled her planned trips to South Carolina and soon suspended her campaign. Romney and Santorum got more than 30,000 votes in the caucuses. In seventh place, Huntsman, who had barely stepped foot in Iowa, wound up with 739.

New Hampshire became the center of the political world on the morning of Jan. 4. Candidates were zipping into the state, reporters in tow, looking for that one last bump before the Jan. 10 primary.

Romney had prepared a surprise for the occasion.

"It's with some nostalgia that I return to this place that I loved so well," said Sen. John McCain, taking the stage at a school in Manchester. "But I'm really here for one reason and one reason only, and that is to make sure that we make Mitt Romney the next president of the United States of America."

The endorsement helped Romney own the media coverage as he sought to steamroll the field. McCain, given his 2000 and 2008 wins in the state's primary, was beloved in New Hampshire.

It was a big blow to Huntsman.

Huntsman had backed the Arizona maverick early in 2008 to the surprise and angst of many Utahns, and, as a presidential candidate this time around, he at least hoped his buddy would stay neutral until after the first primary.

Publicly that day, Huntsman said he had "great regard" for McCain. "I love the man," he added, noting in the end voters don't care about endorsements.

"It's another example of the establishment piling on," Huntsman said. "And it seems the more the establishment piles on — [former Sen. Bob] Dole, McCain and all the rest — nobody cares. Nobody cares about this."

Privately, Huntsman cared. Very much.

"You know, for a guy who paid a huge price in my state to support you, the least you could have done — I don't care if you support Romney, that's great — but just to have given me the dignity of waiting until after the New Hampshire primary," he wrote in an email to McCain.

Mary Kaye was stronger in her response, calling the endorsement a "petty betrayal of a dear friend."

McCain sent a short response: "I didn't mean to offend. I hope your family is well."

With the primary fast approaching, the candidates — Romney, Huntsman, Santorum, Paul and Gingrich — lobbed darts in all directions, though most continued to be slung at Romney.

"The establishment is going to say, 'We've got your guy: Gov. Romney,' " Huntsman said at a town hall in Peterborough. "Nobody wants a coronation. Nobody in this state wants to be told for whom to vote."

They didn't have to be. Romney was walking and talking like a man awaiting that victory even if all of his rivals were teeing off on him.

Romney was unelectable nationally, Gingrich charged. He wouldn't "come anywhere near enough voters per state to become the nominee."

Doubling down, Gingrich rolled out his first TV ad, labeling Romney's economic plan "virtually identical to Obama's failed policy" and asserting that being "timid won't create jobs, and timid certainly won't defeat Barack Obama." Gingrich told reporters that Santorum wasn't presidential material. "In historical terms," he said, "he would be a junior partner."

Huntsman didn't escape the barbs, either. Noting that Huntsman kept touting how many events he had done in New Hampshire, Santorum agreed that may be true, but added, "He's cheating. He lives here."

Meanwhile, a self-described Ron Paul supporter, dubbing himself or herself NHLiberty4Paul, posted a YouTube video that earned the ire of the Huntsman and Paul camps.

The video — made to look like a Paul campaign ad — questioned "Jon Huntsman's values" and his religious conviction (including a photo of him and his adopted Indian daughter, Asha, with red bindis on their foreheads) and called Huntsman "China Jon," with an image of his other adopted daughter, Gracie Mei.

"American values? Or Chinese?" the ad asked. The video ended with a fictitious Huntsman in a Chairman Mao uniform and the words "American Values and Liberty — Vote for Ron Paul."

"If someone wants to poke fun at me, that's OK," Huntsman responded. "What I object to is bringing forward pictures and videos of my adopted daughters and suggesting there's something sinister there."

Paul's folks later sued in federal court to ascertain the identity of the video poster. "This is a classic case of dirty politics resulting from the unlawful use in commerce of an underhanded and deceptive advertisement designed to tarnish plaintiff's reputation," according to the complaint that later was dropped.

In the lead-up to the all-important primary, a YouTube video was nothing more than an annoyance. The real focus was two final, back-to-back debates. Romney tried to avoid mistakes; Paul sought to sway independents; Huntsman clawed to win over anyone who would listen.

The two-day tussle would prove to be the most vicious interaction between Romney and Huntsman during the primary season.

It was back to Saint Anselm College in Manchester for the candidates, and the whole crew was there, even Rick Perry, who had decided to soldier on. The debate was typical, some sniping, some squabbling over time and some zinging. For the most part, Huntsman was treated kindly.

"I congratulate Gov. Huntsman on the success in his governorship to make the state more attractive for business," Romney said after Huntsman rattled off a list of his accomplishments in Utah.

Huntsman didn't respond in kind, instead criticizing Romney for a low job-creation record as governor of Massachusetts. "It's part of his record, and, therefore, it's going to be talked about," Huntsman said.

Toward the end of what had become a routine for the candidates, Huntsman was asked about his vision for dealing with China.

"We've had challenges for 40 years. It's nonsense to think you can slap a tariff on China the first day that you're in office, as Gov. Romney would like to do," Huntsman said. "You've got to sit down and sort through the issues of trade like you do with North Korea, like you do with Iran, like you do with Burma and Pakistan and the South China Sea. They're all interrelated. And to have a president who actually understands how that relationship works would serve the interests of the people in this country, from an economics standpoint and from a security standpoint."

Perhaps it was Huntsman's daughters' tweet about Panda Express or the pro-Huntsman super PAC calling Romney a chameleon or the "perfectly lubricated weather vane," but Romney reached the breaking point.

"I'm sorry, Governor, you were, the last two years, implementing the policies of this administration in China," Romney fired back. "The rest of us on this stage were doing our best to get Republicans elected across the country and stop the policies of this president from being put forward."

Romney might as well have called Huntsman a socialist. China and Obama weren't the best words to be associated with in the Republican Party.

"It's important to note, as they would say in China," Huntsman responded, adding in a phrase in Mandarin and then translating for the audience: "that 'he doesn't quite understand this situation.'"

"What he is calling for would lead to a trade war," Huntsman said, returning to English. "It makes for easy talk and a nice applause line, but it's far different from the reality in the U.S.-China relationship."

The irritation between Romney and Huntsman was palpable for the rest of the debate. Weaver, Huntsman's strategist, took to the spin room afterward, pointing to Romney's attack as evidence the leading candidate feared a Huntsman surge.

"Here's a guy who usually tries to float above, and they're worried about their turnout here, quite frankly. They've taken this state for granted," Weaver said. "I think they're worried about our ground game."

Romney adviser Kevin Madden dismissed Weaver's comment.

"We take nothing for granted," Madden said. "We're absolutely focused on talking directly to [New Hampshire] voters to make sure they show up to support the governor on primary day."

The candidates returned to their hotels for a short night before the final New Hampshire debate in Concord the next morning.

"There was no sleep," Huntsman later recalled. "And there was a sense of anger that seeps in because you see how somebody took advantage of you totally. Although I'd not been that steeped in presidential politics and campaigning, I did feel very strongly that we were gaining momentum and therefore in the sights of opponents like Mitt, and I thought I'm not going to let that sit. That's a totally inappropriate slap. I went out and served my country because I felt it was the right thing to do."

That Sunday morning, the candidates were lined up onstage at the Capitol Center for the Arts, just down the street from the Statehouse, for their final chance to score some points. This time, Huntsman was ready, though it would take about a quarter of the hourlong debate before he got a chance to speak.

"Let me get to policy, Gov. Huntsman," said the moderator, NBC's David Gregory. "This is, by all accounts, an age of austerity for this country, a jobs crisis, also a spending crisis in Washington. I wonder what specifically you would do to say to Americans, 'These are cuts I'm going to make in federal spending that will cause pain, that will require sacrifice'?"

Huntsman didn't want to answer that question, so he took the time to say what he should have the night before.

"Let me say, first [of] all, with respect to Gov. Romney, you know, there are a lot of people who are tuning in this morning, and I'm sure they're terribly confused after watching all of this political spin up here," Huntsman said. "I was criticized last night by Gov. Romney for putting my country first. And I just want to remind the people here in New Hampshire and throughout the United States that I think …" — his remarks were interrupted by applause — "he criticized me, while he was out raising money, for serving my country in China, yes, under a Democrat, like my two sons are doing in the United States Navy. They're not asking who — what political affiliation the president is. I want to be very clear with the people here in New Hampshire and this country: I will always put my country first. And I think that's important to them."

Romney, given a chance to respond, didn't want to let up on Huntsman.

"We serve our country first by standing for people who believe in conservative principles and doing everything in our power to promote an agenda that does not include President Obama's agenda," Romney said. "I think the decision to go and work for President Obama is one which you took. I don't disrespect your decision to do that. I just think it's most likely that the person who should represent our party running against President Obama is not someone who called him a remarkable leader and went to be his ambassador in China."

"This nation," Huntsman snapped back, "is divided, David, because of attitudes like that." More applause rang out for Huntsman.

"The American people are tired of the partisan division. They have had enough," he continued. "There is no trust left among the American people and the institutions of power and among the American people and our elected officials. And I say we've had enough, and we have to change our direction in terms of coming together as Americans first and foremost and finding solutions to our problems."

Romney's campaign said after the debate that Huntsman's attacks against the front-runner spawned the verbal clash and senior adviser Eric Fehrnstrom doubled down, noting Huntsman wasn't a military general but a political appointee under Obama.

"Over the last two years, Jon Huntsman has been working to implement the Obama agenda," Fehrnstrom said. "Mitt Romney has been working to oppose it. ... It's fine if Jon Huntsman wants to serve in the administration of Barack Obama, but we don't think that's the right experience for the Republican nominee who needs to go up against him in 2012."

Huntsman campaign manager Matt David countered that the exchange was telling.

"It was a moment for [Huntsman] where he showed the people the biggest difference between Mitt Romney and Gov. Huntsman: When it comes to service, he's going to put country ahead of politics," David said. "If Mitt Romney is arguing that what [Huntsman] should have been doing is raising money for politicians, I think the voters of New Hampshire are going to reward Gov. Huntsman for putting his country first."

Huntsman, though, was now a target, and even Paul's son Sen. Rand Paul took a shot.

"I'm not sure he really has a constituency," the Kentucky senator said. "I don't think he's going to do very well."

Huntsman's team set out to build on the debate performance, ordering new signs that stole directly from McCain's 2008 message: Country First. They would appear in the final 48 hours of the New Hampshire primary chase. It was a last-ditch effort. Huntsman sensed his campaign finally was moving up.

"I feel a little momentum," he told reporters outside a packed house party in Bedford that Sunday night. "I feel a little surge. We're still clearly the underdog and because of that we have a lot of work ahead of us … and we're not going to stop until we reach the finish line."

Romney continued to make his final pitch to voters but uttered a gaffe that would come back to haunt him. The eve of the primary, the Nashua Chamber of Commerce held a breakfast in the ballroom of the Radisson Inn, and Romney had some big fans in the room. He was so confident in the crowd that he fielded some questions, including one about health-care providers. Romney offered his belief that the free market is the best answer.

"I like being able to fire people who provide services to me," he said. "You know, if someone doesn't give me a good service that I need, I want to say, 'I'm going to go get someone else to provide that service to me.' "

There was almost an audible gasp from the press corps huddled in the back. Did he just say he likes to fire people? Romney already endured criticism from GOP rivals and Democrats over his record at Bain Capital, where depressed companies he was trying to turn around sometimes laid off workers.

Romney later tried to spin his comments to reporters, but, at that moment, the campaign — or perhaps, depending on whom you want to blame, the hotel — sensed an urgency to ward off the press. After Romney spoke, the music in the ballroom blared so loudly it precluded any follow-up questions. Security asked the remaining reporters in the hallway to leave.

Aides informed Huntsman that Romney had just said he likes to fire people and urged Huntsman, on his way to a rally in Concord, to respond. Huntsman wanted context. "He really said that?" he asked. The aides didn't care about context. Just shoot back, they argued.

"That's what I hate about politics," Huntsman later recalled about that experience. "It's the sound bite of the hour just to keep the media machine going. I can't do that. I'm not a sound-bite person."

But Huntsman did find his voice that day.

"Gov. Romney enjoys firing people. I enjoy creating jobs," he told reporters, who smothered the candidate as he left his black SUV on Concord's Main Street. He went on to target Romney as being "slightly out of touch with the economic realities."

The Huntsman team, feeling upbeat, issued a memo to reporters spelling out how it saw the race turning out. Perhaps a bit of gleeful ignorance (or, more likely, posturing), the talking points were aimed squarely at Romney.

"The race will ultimately be a contest between Mitt Romney and an electable alternative to Mitt Romney," the document said. "That alternative will be Jon Huntsman or Rick Santorum but will not be decided until late spring, despite the wishes of Washington insiders."

Romney could claim a victory in New Hampshire — given his poll strength and his financial and home-state advantage — only if he won an outright majority on primary day. For Huntsman, his aides noted, his New Hampshire showing would trigger a "critical burst" of momentum headed into South Carolina and Florida. "He has not yet been well-defined in [those states] and his consistent conservative record will play well — particularly juxtaposed against Romney's record of flip-flops and abandonment of the South Carolina primary in 2008."

This race, Weaver said, "is not going to be decided after one caucus, one primary."

Huntsman was winning one unique sector of New Hampshire: the goat vote. Bill Higgins lives within walking distance to Dover's McConnell Community Center and relishes visits by presidential candidates. So does his goat.

Izak, the second goat Higgins has brought to meet presidential wannabes, often could be found in the 2012 race on a leash hanging outside candidate visits. The animal was sort of a symbol of New Hampshire's rural voting bloc and a nod to the notion that presidential hopefuls have to step off their soapboxes and mingle with everyone. Izak doesn't vote, of course, but his owner does, based on his goat's instincts.

"He's an independent. He represents independent voters," Higgins said. "I judge the candidates on how the animals react to them."

And Izak liked the taste of Huntsman. Literally.

In October, Huntsman met Izak, who wanted to take a closer inspection. The goat nibbled a bit at the candidate's signature jean jacket and then went in for a bite on his leg. Higgins called it a "taste-testing." It worked. Not that the goat endorsement was an important sign in the upcoming primary, but Huntsman was happy for what he could get.

"You know, I'm feeling it," he said a day before the primary. "Each passing hour, I'm going up, not going down. That's the trajectory that I think is going to be a surprise for people tomorrow night."

He made his final comments before voting began at the Exeter Town Hall, where he had visited first after announcing his bid in June. This time around, the crowd was overflowing, and the campaign had made sure to arrange a festive atmosphere with a Huntsman logo projected on the building and spotlights pointing the town's attention his way.

"Can you feel a little momentum in the air?" Huntsman asked at the microphone, surrounded by signs. "Every stop along the way today I heard the same thing: 'Something is happening out there.' I don't know what's going to happen tomorrow night, but I do know this: We're going to surprise a whole lot of people."

Confetti cannons shot above the crowd as Huntsman milked the moment onstage with his family.

A few hours later, just after midnight, the tiny town of Dixville Notch opened its polls in the grand tradition of the state. Nine people voted, and Romney and Huntsman each grabbed two. Three Democrats voted for Obama, and Gingrich and Paul got one apiece.

The Huntsman clan saw it as a good omen; the Romneys saw it as a sideshow.

As for election-night galas, Romney's camp had reserved a big space at Southern New Hampshire University's campus in Manchester. Huntsman's aides, who planned their party when their candidate was in fifth place, had rented out The Black Brimmer bar on Elm Street, also in Manchester. The two-level spot overflowed as reporters and supporters alike elbowed for room. As results trickled in shortly after 8 p.m., there was little doubt who would be on top. CNN projected Romney would win three minutes after polls closed.

Huntsman called his cousin. "Congratulations," he told him. "You're a good man, and you looked great with your family. We'll see you in South Carolina." It was unclear what Romney said in response, but he emerged onstage not too long after to a rousing cheer.

"Tonight, we celebrate," Romney told his people. "Tomorrow, we go back to work." More applause.

Romney had captured a little more than 39 percent of the vote. Paul nabbed 23 percent. Huntsman finished third with 17 percent, better than he registered in the polls. But was that enough to keep going, especially when he had banked everything on this state?

His family members — including Jon Huntsman Sr. and Karen — made their way onstage a little later in the night, followed by Huntsman himself. A large blue Huntsman sign dominated the stage, proclaiming, "Country First."

"I say third place is a ticket to ride, ladies and gentlemen," Huntsman declared. "Hello, South Carolina."

Both Romney and Huntsman had planned events in South Carolina in the following days. Only one of them would stick to the schedule.

chapter thirteen

A tepid endorsement

A fter delivering a one-two punch in Iowa and New Hampshire, Mitt Romney flew to South Carolina determined to level a knockout. He had begun taking on the aura of the presumptive nominee and hoped the other contenders would see the light.

"Romney comes in here 2-0 and, at least at this point, I don't see an indication that the anti-Romney factions are going to be able to come together enough," Republican consultant Chip Felkel said. "This is a game of perception and momentum, and he'll have both."

There can be a downside to being the front-runner, though, especially in a state like South Carolina, where social conservatives still were not aboard the Romney train.

"I don't want to be overconfident," Romney said in Columbia. But he had a reason to be pretty confident: a plump war chest.

The Romney camp announced that it had raised $56 million and was sitting on nearly $20 million in the bank. That didn't even count the well-funded pro-Romney super PAC, which was raising and spending millions to boost his bid.

But money wouldn't buy South Carolina's conservatives, and Newt Gingrich knew it. His first TV ad hit straight at a big issue in the state: abortion.

"What happened after Massachusetts moderate Mitt Romney changed his position from pro-abortion to pro-life?" a female narrator asked in the spot, filled with spooky music and an unhappy-looking Romney. "He governed pro-abortion."

And from Huntsman's super PAC? Silence.

But the former Utah governor pressed forward, as promised, speaking in a jammed, overheated room at the University of South Carolina's business school.

"People of this state don't want to be told for whom to vote," Huntsman told the crowd, carefully avoiding Romney's name. "They will not allow the establishment to tee up their favorite candidate. That's just not how the people of this state work."

He kept up his Country First theme, acknowledging that he did cross a partisan line to serve his country. "I did, and I wouldn't trade that for anything. If you believe in putting politics first, I'm not your guy."

But Huntsman had another, particularly embarrassing, obstacle: A TV comedian was polling ahead of him.

Stephen Colbert, a South Carolina native, told fans on "The Colbert Report" that he had been searching for a non-Romney candidate when he figured out the answer. "Oh, my God, it's me! It all makes so much sense. … [My] heart always leads me to me. And I am so not Mitt," the host said to cheers from his studio crowd. "But wait, wait, wait, that's crazy! These guys have been running for a year now. How can I ever compete with an established candidate like Jon Huntsman?"

Soon enough he declared: "I'm sorry, Gov. Huntsman," when one poll showed him edging Huntsman 5 percentage points to 4, "I guess the Colbert bump reflected off of you and bounced back to me. That happens in the rare instances when my guests are whiter than I am."

Huntsman laughed it off.

After all the setbacks, he did have one thing going for him: the endorsement of The State newspaper. In an editorial titled "Huntsman could bring us back together," South Carolina's largest daily said Huntsman was "more principled, has a far more impressive résumé and offers a significantly more important message" than Romney.

"What makes him attractive are the essential values that drive his candidacy: honor and old-fashioned decency and pragmatism," the paper wrote of Huntsman. "As he made clear Wednesday to a room packed full of USC students on the first stop of his 'Country First' tour, his goal is to rebuild trust in government, and that means abandoning the invective and re-establishing the political center."

Nice, but too little, too late. Huntsman knew — and had known for days — that his presidential run was over. Even if he poured every dollar into his bid and his father tossed in millions more and somehow got voters to take notice, he had little chance to win South Carolina, compete in Florida or top any contests going forward.

New Hampshire's third-place finish wasn't, after all, "the ticket to ride."

"I knew in the back of my mind, and I'd talked to Mary Kaye about the reality," Huntsman recalls. If he had scored a second in New Hampshire, the afterburners could have kicked on. They had folks in place who had helped Mike Huckabee in 2008.

"When we hit third, I knew that night," Huntsman says. "It was hard to stand before the group, after you'd just taken third — although people were pretty jubilant that we'd come from dead last to third — knowing full well that's probably going to be it."

He didn't want to announce his withdrawal then, believing it would be too tough on the campaign aides who had uprooted their lives for months and the volunteers who spent countless hours knocking on doors.

"I wanted to just make sure my thinking was sound, that there wasn't anything I was missing," he says. "I thought third just doesn't do it but let's give it [a little more time]. I think in fairness to our team, who were so excited about South Carolina, I just thought I just can't do that to them. Maybe over the next few days, there will be something that emerges that we don't see today."

Nothing emerged. The family talked it over and decided to bag it.

On Jan. 15, a Sunday, Huntsman and a few family members sat down for dinner at a Southern plantation home in Charleston to discuss how to wind down the presidential campaign. A New York Times reporter called Huntsman to ask for comment about dropping out. "Then all the phone calls started coming in," he says. The TV at the restaurant scrolled the news that Huntsman was out; he suspects a campaign aide — perhaps Weaver, who was not at the dinner with him — leaked it to The Times.

"We were sitting in the middle of dinner," Huntsman says. "I thought it was going to be a methodical rollout and we'd be prepared to control it, but there it came."

Across town, Weaver had assembled some 10 members of his team for dinner at a Southern restaurant — fish and biscuits and the like — when a food fight broke out. Perhaps a bit of revelry after working so hard only to find themselves without jobs. They tipped $100 before and after, but a manager still asked the group to leave.

The libation-fueled party continued at a nearby rooftop pool bar, where staffers jokingly tried to push one another into the water. No one took an unplanned dip, but a security guard suggested they leave that establishment as well.

Huntsman had a more contemplative night. He paid the dinner check and walked back to his hotel. Ryan Smith, his body man — the aide who carries a candidate's bags and keeps him on time — had already obtained Romney's phone number from his counterpart, Garrett Jackson. Huntsman dialed the number during his stroll, informing Romney of the pending announcement and endorsement.

The call lasted five minutes.

The two discussed the "state of the race," and Huntsman offered to help swing moderate blocs of voters in South Carolina and to record a robocall for Romney. He asked for nothing in return, and Romney offered nothing.

In some cases, a failed candidate asks for help paying off campaign debt in exchange for an endorsement. Huntsman didn't want that, and his campaign thought it was wishful thinking Romney would help anyway.

Huntsman aides already were scrubbing the campaign site and YouTube channel of any anti-Romney materials. ScaredMittless.com and 10kbet.com were pulled down.

They began dialing a phone tree of reporters to inform them of the decision and spin the news. "He is proud of the race he ran, but he is not going to stand in the way of the man who can beat Barack Obama," one aide said.

"Jon Huntsman should win," added another senior adviser. "He had the best qualifications, the best vision. He would have been our best candidate. It just didn't work out."

A Huntsman friend saw the end differently.

"Long story short, Jon and Mary Kaye are amazing people," the friend said. "They will not throw their campaign staff under the bus, but this could have had a much different ending."

The Huntsman campaign sent out notice at 12:42 a.m. that Huntsman would speak that morning at the Myrtle Beach Convention Center. Everyone knew what he would say, just not how he would say it.

The conference room was packed. Campaign manager Matt David and strategist John Weaver stood stage right as Jon and Mary Kaye Huntsman strode out, most of their kids awaiting them behind the podium. It had been 210 days since Huntsman entered the race near the Statue of Liberty. Now his backdrop was U.S. flags and his family trying to smile.

"Good morning, everybody," Huntsman said. "I'm delighted to be surrounded, first and foremost, by those I love and appreciate most." He thanked a few in the room, including his dad, who took a front-row seat for the sad moment.

But before uttering the words everyone was awaiting, Huntsman got something off his chest.

"Now, as candidates for our party's nomination, our common goal is to restore bold and principled leadership to the White House — leadership that will reignite our economy and renew the American spirit," he said. "Yet rather than seeking to advance that common goal by speaking directly to voters about our ideas to rebuild America, this race has degenerated into an onslaught of negative and personal attacks not worthy of the American people and not worthy of this critical time in our nation's history."

This was not your typical withdrawal speech. Huntsman used his last big media moment to stress a point: The race was "toxic" and wouldn't help the GOP cause until the candidates started talking ideas. But he also knew there were a few key words he had to utter.

"Today I am suspending my campaign," Huntsman said. "Ultimately, this election is about more than the future of one campaign or one party, it is about the future of our nation."

Huntsman wasn't excited to endorse Romney — he wasn't happy with the front-runner and still a bit livid about how he was attacked — but he also didn't want to be dogged for weeks about why he didn't line up behind Romney. He would say his rival's name once.

"I believe it is now time for our party to unite around the candidate best equipped to defeat Barack Obama. Despite our differences and the space between us on some of the issues, I believe that candidate is Gov. Mitt Romney."

Huntsman finished by noting his family had found a greater appreciation for U.S. democracy during his bid, saying thanks and promptly leaving the stage. A reporter lobbed a question referencing that days before, Huntsman had hit Romney for being detached from the real world.

"You still think he's completely out of touch," the reporter shouted from the back. Huntsman kept walking.

Romney's people paid little attention to it, though they weren't happy with Huntsman's comments preluding his pullout.

"If you looked at the endorsement, it looked like he was sucking on a lemon," said a Romney confidant. "I saw the clip later. It was kind of like a backhanded endorsement."

Romney's campaign issued a three-sentence statement.

"I salute Jon Huntsman and his wife, Mary Kaye," Romney said. "Jon ran a spirited campaign based on unity, not division, and love of country. I appreciate his friendship and support."

Huntsman knew the Romney team didn't care all that much about the endorsement.

"I mean for them, I think it was totally inconsequential," Huntsman would later say.

Weaver, who had planned Huntsman's campaign, was reluctant to own up to its failures.

"I'm not going to look back at one thing that went right or went wrong," he said. "At the end of the day, if you didn't win, you didn't win."

Huntsman didn't win. And, as it turned out, neither had Romney in the first contest of the GOP nomination quest.

The eventual final tally of the Iowa caucuses showed Santorum had 34 more votes than Romney. It didn't matter on the delegate count — the caucuses don't decide that — but it changed the storyline. Romney was no longer 2-0, and he wasn't the first nonincumbent Republican to win both Iowa and New Hampshire since 1976.

"The narrative that Gov. Romney and the media have been touting of 'inevitability' has been destroyed," Santorum communications director Hogan Gidley trumpeted in a news release. "Conservatives can now see and believe they don't have to settle for Romney, the establishment's moderate candidate."

Romney, for his part, called the results a "virtual tie."

The nomination suddenly felt less like an inevitability and more like a tossup.

Not only had Santorum belatedly won Iowa, but Gingrich was surging in South Carolina. Then Marianne Gingrich, his second ex-wife, threw out a bombshell in an interview with ABC News and The Washington Post, saying that he offered her a choice of an open marriage or a divorce when he admitted to having an affair with a woman he later made his third wife. He allegedly offered the choice two days before he gave a speech titled "The Demise of American Culture."

"How could he ask me for a divorce on Monday and within 48 hours give a speech on family values and talk about how people treat people?" Marianne Gingrich asked.

Two days before the South Carolina primary, CNN hosted a debate during which moderator John King cut right to the Gingrich stories. "Would you like to take some time to respond to that?" King asked.

"No, but I will," Gingrich said. "I think the destructive, vicious, negative nature of much of the news media makes it harder to govern this country, harder to attract decent people to run for public office. And I am appalled that you would begin a presidential debate on a topic like that."

Applause rang out.

"Is that all you want to say, sir?" King asked.

"Let me finish," Gingrich said. "Every person in here knows personal pain. Every person in here has had someone close to them go through painful things. To take an ex-wife and make it two days before the primary a significant question for a presidential campaign is as close to despicable as anything I can imagine."

Conservatives love to bash the media, and Gingrich played into it. "I am tired of the elite media protecting Barack Obama by attacking Republicans."

The audience lapped it up.

King tossed the question to Romney about whether the latest allegation was a concern for Gingrich's bid.

"John, let's get on to the real issues is all I've got to say," Romney declared.

A poll later showed that 55 percent of those who voted decided on their candidate in the last few days. Nearly two-thirds said the debates were one of the most influential factors in whom voters chose. Gingrich attracted support from tea partiers, evangelicals and young white men. That proved to be enough. He outpaced Romney by a full 12 percentage points.

Romney played the gracious runner-up.

"Tonight, I want to congratulate, of course, Speaker Gingrich and my fellow Republicans at a hard-fought campaign here in South Carolina," Romney said. "We're now three contests into a long primary season. This is a hard fight because there's so much worth fighting for. We've — we've still got a long way to go and a lot of work to do and tomorrow we're going to move on to Florida. It's a state that has suffered terribly under the failed policies of President Obama."

As the late journalist Tim Russert once said about the 2000 general election, it was down to "Florida, Florida, Florida," and Romney was prepared to unleash his big advantage there: cash.

Romney's campaign, and his supporting super PAC, spent heavily on television, radio and direct mail, nearly $10 million for ads bashing Gingrich, including charges he "cashed in" with his dealings with Freddie Mac while "Florida families lost everything in the housing crisis." The former House speaker and his backers couldn't compete on that level.

Romney hammered home the point in debates labeling Gingrich an "influence peddler" for working as a consultant to the failed mortgage lender.

Romney needed a big win, and he got it, racking up 46 percent of the vote to Gingrich's 32. Romney claimed all 50 delegates. The best news for the victor: An overwhelming number said he was the best candidate to take on Obama, by a 2-to-1 margin over Gingrich.

When Romney took the stage that night, he did so not only to claim victory but also to make clear that the nomination was his. He congratulated his opponents on a good fight but then focused all his attention on Obama.

"Don't worry, Mr. President, we remember exactly how we got here. You won the election," Romney said, noting that Thomas Paine once said that you lead, follow or get out of the way. "Well, Mr. President, you were elected to lead. You chose to follow, and now, it's time for you to get out of the way. I stand ready to lead this party and to lead our nation as a man who spent his life outside Washington."

Romney's aides were giddy.

"Newt doesn't control the board anymore," a Romney aide added. "The road just got very, very uphill for him."

Romney also won another cool prize out of Florida: Secret Service protection.

While Herman Cain had protection for a short period before he dropped out, Romney would be the only GOP candidate with government guards. The change — Romney had used private security to this point — came not because of a specific threat but because of the increase in crowd sizes as the primaries progressed. The Secret Service remembered too well the 1968 assassination of presidential candidate Robert F. Kennedy and didn't want a repeat.

While it was, of course, a nonpartisan decision, nothing speaks better to the air of inevitability than black-suited men and women with earpieces and a black SUV motorcade.

Huntsman had jetted off on vacation shortly after withdrawing but had returned and proved to be an annoyance to Romney — again.

Appearing on MSNBC's "Morning Joe," Huntsman declared that he was "not a surrogate for anybody" and that a viable third party in the presidential race would be a "healthy thing."

"We're going to have problems politically until we get some sort of third-party movement or some voice out there that can put forth new ideas," he said. "Someone's going to step up at some point and say we've had enough of this. The real issues are not being addressed, and it's time that we put forward an alternative vision, a bold thinking. We might not win, but we can certainly influence the debate."

The comments didn't sit well with Romney aides, who had expected that, if nothing else, Huntsman would sit quietly on the sidelines. They never expected him to go on the attack. After all, he had endorsed Romney — even if it was tepid.

Huntsman had said in that interview that Romney was the best remaining candidate to fix the economy.

But, he added, there are "a whole bunch of Americans out there that can't find a place politically." Huntsman included himself in that category. He wasn't saying he would run — "ain't gonna be me, by the way" — but that didn't mean there weren't plenty of people calling for him to emerge as an alternative.

Americans Elect was gearing up for an online primary to select a third-party candidate who could appear on ballots in multiple states and trump the Democrat vs. Republican stranglehold. In fact, the nominee would have to pick a running mate from the opposing party to balance the alternative ticket, according to the group's rules. Huntsman had been a prime target, even when he was still running as a Republican.

"I would hope he would do it, frankly," former New Jersey Gov. Christine Todd Whitman, a Republican and board member of the new party, said of the former Utah governor. "He's someone that I would support." Throughout his run, Huntsman was publicly clear that he was sticking with the GOP, even if the GOP wasn't sticking with him. But, behind the scenes, he had explored it.

"You can't help but have your mind wander toward a scenario where perhaps you can break out as an independent," Huntsman said later, "and then you sort of review history and see that a lot of folks have done that, but they haven't gotten very far."

While still a Republican candidate, Huntsman had huddled in the fall of 2011 with New York City Mayor Michael Bloomberg, who was continually touted as a top-tier independent for president. They discussed the options — "not that I was seriously considering but sort of a friendly banter," Huntsman recalls — and Huntsman decided it wasn't his best route.

After Huntsman left the presidential race, millionaire investor Peter Ackerman, who had founded Americans Elect in 2010, approached him about running. The group was on the ballot in 29 states and was planning a Web-based primary in March.

"They had everything but a messenger," Huntsman recalls. "They had this online primary that had been planned, they had built the framework, everything but the messenger. And so they showed up on our doorstep a few times with a few aggressive overtures about getting involved. But, at that point, I really had no interest at all."

Americans Elect never could find its messenger. The group folded well before Election Day.

A third party at the time may have been a good option for Huntsman, given the Republican Party's disenchantment with him.

One example: He had been scheduled to speak at a lavish spring gathering in Florida in 2012 for donors of the Republican National Committee, but party officials decided to disinvite him. RNC Chairman Reince Priebus didn't even tell Huntsman himself, dispatching a staffer to inform one of Huntsman's former campaign aides.

GOP officials said they were ostracizing Huntsman because he called for an alternative political voice, according to Abby Huntsman, the former candidate's second-eldest daughter.

"In fact, he has actually been uninvited to a lot of events," she said. "So the party that we see today is one of not inclusion."

Jon Huntsman was clearly upset at the snub, comparing the GOP to the Communist Party. "This is what they do in China on party matters if you talk off script."

He said he was approached by so many reporters on the subject because he seemed to be the only one speaking out about the wayward trajectory of the GOP.

"I felt like the lone voice in the wilderness because nobody else wanted to talk about it," he says. "I felt a bit like a pariah at times, but that's not a bad place to be. That's kind of where Huntsmans find themselves every now and again."

Beyond the pariah problem, Huntsman also was saddled with debt from his shuttered campaign. He has forked over $5.1 million to pay down all the bills that campaign aides had left behind. "I'm still taking care of it," Huntsman says. "Will be for a long time."

He doesn't talk with Weaver anymore — "Nothing against him; campaign's over," Huntsman says — but there is still some lingering angst over the bid that foundered upon launch.

He says he doesn't feel taken.

"No, I feel educated," Huntsman says. "Those who took the ride with us, I'll never have negative thoughts about because they believed in our cause even if they made a lot of money on it. And they were willing to go to war in our name and I'll always be grateful for that. And if one of them — you know, I hear from many of them on a regular basis, wanting a letter of recommendation, wanting this or that, and I'm always, always happy to do anything they want."

Huntsman's father maintains his son engaged the best advisers available when he parachuted into the race in spring 2011.

"Obviously there were better advisers with other candidates than what Jon Jr. had, but again, entering as late as he did, they did the very best they knew how," Huntsman Sr. says. "But clearly there were other advisers who had been working with other candidates for a year or two, and I think they probably had a better perspective of their candidates, knew them better, knew their strengths and weaknesses than perhaps Jon Jr.'s did."

Still, Dad has no regrets. The campaign allowed the country to get to know his son.

"He has such respect around the world, particularly around the United States, and has brought such a remarkable image to the name of Utah and to our family," Huntsman Sr. said. "I think it was worth every effort that Jon Jr. or I put into it, or others. Clearly he won a tremendous following and tremendous respect by so many people that will last with him forever."

Romney's remaining opponents didn't see the need to bow out anytime soon and for one main reason: super-wealthy backers who would try to bend the race their way.

While Romney headed to Palm Beach, Fla., to raise $1.5 million the old-fashioned way, the pro-Gingrich group, Winning Our Future, nabbed $5 million from casino magnate Sheldon Adelson. Mutual-fund executive Foster Friess tossed in $600,000 to help the pro-Santorum Red, White and Blue Fund. The outside money helped keep the primaries relevant even as Romney amassed wins in Maine, Arizona, Michigan, Wyoming and Washington.

On Super Tuesday, when 10 states would go to the polls, Romney sought to show his dominance. He claimed victories in the delegate-rich states of Ohio and Virginia, and he added Alaska, Idaho, Massachusetts and Vermont for good measure. By contrast, Santorum claimed Tennessee, Oklahoma and North Dakota, while Gingrich took his home state of Georgia.

Santorum was the next to bail. As the crucial Pennsylvania primary inched closer, the former U.S. senator from that state shelved his campaign. He did not endorse Romney nor mention his name. "We made a decision over the weekend that while this presidential race is over for me, and we will suspend our campaign today, we are not done fighting," Santorum said in a hastily called announcement in a small hotel meeting room in Gettysburg.

It took Gingrich longer to declare his "wild ride" over. His concession speech was less an endorsement of Romney than a Gringrich-style lecture on the perfect being the enemy of the good.

"This is not a choice between Mitt Romney and Ronald Reagan," Gingrich said. "This is a choice between Mitt Romney and the most radical leftist president in American history."

Huntsman, too, invoked the name of the great communicator and GOP icon — in explaining his decision to skip the party nominating convention in Tampa. It was the first one he had missed since 1984.

"I encourage a return to the party we have been in the past," said the still-smarting Huntsman, "from Lincoln right on through to Reagan, that was always willing to put our country before politics."

That's not exactly the kind of comment the GOP wanted as backdrop for its big show in Florida. Then again, there were a lot of things that would come out of the convention that weren't in the party's best interest.

chapter fourteen

Taking the silver

It was late, and Josh Romney was exhausted. The middle son of Mitt and Ann sat in his hotel room, staring at a muted TV tuned to the Discovery Channel, when a documentary filmmaker asked about the emotion-sapping months on the campaign trail.

"Ever once have you thought, 'This isn't worth it?' " the moviemaker asked.

Josh paused, cracking a faint smile. The documentary "Mitt" wouldn't air until the campaign was over, but the question still posed a challenge.

"Um, you know, it's hard for me to do these interviews because I'm so used to doing interviews with the media where I'm so trained, where I'm so trained to say, 'Oh, absolutely not.' "

He knew reporters and the public would parse any answer every which way and someone somewhere would jump up and shout, "See! See! He doesn't even want his own dad to be president!" So Josh offered two takes, one the regular, tried-and-true media answer, and the other what he really wanted to say and how he truly felt.

"The challenges we face as a country right now, to have someone like my dad with his experience, his knowledge and his vision for America, someone that can, you know, come in and do this, it's worth whatever it takes to get my dad into office," Josh Romney said.

"Translation," he added, chuckling: "This is so awful."

For months, he dealt with critics and friends alike jabbing at his father, a man he esteemed. He heard the jokes, suffered the barbs and through it all zipped from one city to the next giving the same stump speech, as if someone just hit reset. His dad had his gaffes, sure, but his experience and leadership should trump that.

"You know, is he perfect? Absolutely not. He's made mistakes. He's done things wrong but, for goodness' sakes, here's a brilliant guy who had his experiences turning things around, which is what we need for the country. I mean, it's like, this is the guy for the moment. And we're in this and we get beat up constantly. 'Oh, Mitt Romney's a flip-flopper, he's this, he's that.' It's like, man, is this worth it? This is awful."

That was 2008, near the end of the exhausting first leg of the presidential race — after visits to all 99 Iowa counties, rallies in New Hampshire and drop-ins in Nevada and Wyoming before Mitt Romney's chances eroded.

The family was drained. Soon the campaign would sputter out, even as advisers and friends suggested Romney would rocket to the front in 2012 if he tried again.

"If you're tempted," Ann Romney said at the time, "the answer's no; it's too much."

Four years later, after mustering the courage to face the onslaught again, Romney finally had won the coveted GOP nomination, reaching a political pinnacle that had eluded his father.

"We finally got there," Mitt Romney declared as Texas primary results rolled in to put him over the 1,144-delegate threshold. "It's an honor and a privilege, an honor and a privilege" — he repeated it for emphasis — "and a great responsibility. And I know the road to 1,144 was long and hard, but I also know that the road to 11/06, Nov. 6, is also going to be long, it's going to be hard, and it's going to be worth it because we're going to take back the White House and get America right again."

It was nearly June 2012, and Romney had swept contest after contest on his way to the magic number. The demands on the candidate were unending, the press pool constantly hounding and the scrutiny crushing. Still, there were highlights.

Josh Romney, who left his real-estate business to help his dad on the stump, jetted into Ohio to hit a tea-party rally. It wouldn't have been friendly territory months before, but the crowd of nearly 500 welcomed the Romney son. The leader of the local tea party took the stage and noted he had campaigned against Mitt Romney. He didn't want him as the party's nominee. But then he got to know the candidate and his family and took the view that if he won, the White House would have its most moral occupant since George Washington.

The audience gave a standing ovation.

"Experiences like that, where you see people get to know your dad and really learn to respect him and look at him as a potentially great leader," recalls Josh Romney, "those are great experiences."

Even as the pressure mounted, the Romneys weren't going to skip their annual family gathering. Nothing, not even a presidential campaign, would get in the way of that. Romney's eldest son, Tagg, knew that well. His father had instructed him during a previous summer that everyone would be at the New Hampshire lake home, even if Tagg had to beg forgiveness midseason from his then-bosses with the Los Angeles Dodgers.

It's a Romney rite of passage to spend a week at Lake Winnipesaukee, where they hire a professional photographer to snap the family portrait and enjoy a relaxing getaway. And, in true Romney fashion, they also compete in their own Olympics.

Events include a mini-triathlon of biking, swimming and running, but Romney also has added a few new, creative contests to give himself a good shot against his more athletic progeny: who can hang onto a pole the longest, who can throw a football the farthest, who can hammer the most nails into a board in two minutes.

That night in 2012, the family turned serious, engaging in frank discussions about the sons' careers and parenting worries. Romney also had another issue weighing on him: Whom should he pick as a running mate?

Romney had been on the other side of the equation in 2008, when his name surfaced as being on the short list of GOP nominee John McCain. Sarah Palin beat him out for that slot, but now it was Romney's big decision. Should he go with a tested politician such as former Minnesota Gov. Tim Pawlenty or Ohio Sen. Rob Portman, or should he look to Louisiana Gov. Bobby Jindal, an Indian-American who would add minority pizzazz to the ticket?

One name not in the mix: Jon Huntsman. He already had ruled it out — not that Romney would have thought about it anyway — since two Mormons on the same ticket would be a nonstarter. And they weren't exactly buddies at this point.

"There'd be too many jokes about that," Huntsman said. "No, I can't imagine it at all."

By late July, speculation was full throttle. Would Romney pick New Hampshire Sen. Kelly Ayotte or New Mexico Gov. Susana Martinez to add a Latina to the ticket? Would Florida Sen. Marco Rubio be the better Latino pick? How about New Jersey Gov. Chris Christie or Wisconsin Rep. Paul Ryan to shake up the race?

As the conjecture stirred, the news media picked their own favorites: Pawlenty, Portman and Jindal. Portman had his strengths as a respected senator, a budget wonk — he formerly headed the White House's Office of Management and Budget — and a man with foreign-policy credentials. Pawlenty would appeal to conservatives and was a well-liked surrogate for Romney on the trail. Jindal might be able to dig into Obama's lead with minorities.

But the choice would have to wait. Romney decided to showcase his own foreign knowledge and skills on a trip through London, Israel and Poland. It didn't go well, starting with an interview Romney gave just before England opened the Summer Olympics. Given his experience with Salt Lake City's 2002 Winter Games, he was asked the obvious question: Was London ready?

"It's hard to know just how well it will turn out," Romney ad-libbed. "There are a few things that were disconcerting. The stories about the private security firm not having enough people, the supposed strike of the immigration and customs officials — that obviously is not something which is encouraging."

The next day's Daily Telegraph blared the headline: "Mitt Romney questions whether Britain is ready for Olympic Games." Brits don't vote in American elections, but insulting the United States' strongest ally didn't play well there or at home.

Romney easily could have weathered that gaffe but quickly followed it up with others. At a breakfast fundraiser, he noted the gross domestic product of Israel was much higher than in areas managed by the Palestinian Authority, a comment guaranteed to outrage Palestinians. He also said it was good to be in Jerusalem, the capital of Israel, a status the United States doesn't officially recognize. Obama had once made that mistake, too.

In Poland, it was a press aide who caused a stir. A phalanx of reporters, whose news outlets had spent big money flying with the candidate, began shouting questions at Romney when he left the Tomb of the Unknown in Warsaw. Romney had answered only three questions the whole week, and the press was frustrated. So was spokesman Rick Gorka.

"Show some respect," he shouted back at the reporters who wanted to know why Romney was ignoring them. "Kiss my ass. This is a holy site for the Polish people. Show some respect."

Minutes later, Gorka told Politico's Jonathan Martin to "shove it."

Romney's team tried to put a happy spin on the trip. "I think it was a great success," adviser Stuart Stevens said unconvincingly.

Fortunately, the Romney campaign had a way to earn back some good press: the long-awaited vice-presidential announcement. After vetting candidates in secret — a small team pored over background information in a secure room at Romney's Boston headquarters — it came down to one name: Paul Ryan.

Picking the baby-faced, charismatic Wisconsin congressman would be heralded as one of the boldest moves of Romney's bid. Ryan, the architect of an aggressive budget-cutting plan, was beloved by conservatives and would energize the base voters who thought Romney was too moderate. Back from Europe, Romney sat down with aide Beth Myers, who had conducted the veep search and said it was a go.

Ryan, decked out in a baseball cap, sunglasses and jeans, flew to Hartford, Conn., and then drove to Myers' home in Brookline, Mass., to avoid pesky reporters. "By the time we met in person, I kind of knew it was gonna happen, and I was very humbled," Ryan later would say. "It was the biggest honor I've ever been given in my life."

The campaign had teased supporters that it would announce the pick on its smartphone app, though aides leaked it to a few outlets. The camp even dropped a large hint by announcing that Romney would welcome his new running mate in Norfolk, Va., on the USS Wisconsin. Hmm, who could it be?

The Romney-Ryan ticket bounded out for its introduction as "America's Comeback Team." The dynamic duo launched a national tour to highlight the change the two planned to bring to the White House. It was a highly coordinated, highly scripted affair, but nothing like the four-day national convention in Tampa.

For Romney's big moment, his team sought help from Broadway.

The gathering, essentially a long TV infomercial, offered a chance for the campaign to do something it had failed to accomplish so far: Paint a portrait of Romney as a leader, a family man, a caring neighbor and a man of faith, as opposed to the caricature pushed by Democrats that he was a robotic, uber-rich, out-of-touch political opportunist. To showcase their man, the team built one of the most intricate stages ever designed for a political convention. The $2.5 million Frank Lloyd Wright-inspired set — with its dark-wood finish and high-resolution screens craning into the rafters — was carefully selected to convey a sense of warmth, approachability and openness.

The background was designed to look like a photo display: 13 video screens, framed in dark wood. The podium staircases sloped into the audience to make the speakers, especially Romney, appear friendly and welcoming.

The convention carried four themes, one for each day: "We can do better," "We built it," "We can change it" and "We believe in America."

A bit of bad meteorological luck blew away the first night's plans. For the second GOP convention in a row, an approaching storm, this one Tropical Storm Isaac, forced organizers to cancel the first day's events. The second day featured the state delegates offering their enthusiastic votes for Romney as the nominee, culminating in Ann Romney's speech, designed to dazzle Americans with personal stories about her family and her husband.

She didn't want to talk politics; other speakers could cover that. She wanted to address the struggles that families face across the country, how it's sometimes hard to keep up with life, let alone get ahead. "And that is where this boy I met at a high-school dance comes in," she said. "His name is Mitt Romney, and you really should get to know him."

Ann, who strode onstage in a bright red dress, beaming to the welcome of hand-painted "Women Love Ann" signs, stayed poised as she talked about the couple's struggles during their first few years in a basement apartment with an ironing board for a dining-room table, of rearing five boys, of facing major health issues.

"I read somewhere that Mitt and I have a 'storybook marriage,' " she said. "Well, in the storybooks I read, there were never long, long, rainy winter afternoons in a house with five boys screaming at once. And those storybooks never seemed to have chapters called MS or breast cancer. A storybook marriage? No, not at all. What Mitt Romney and I have is a real marriage." Thunderous applause broke out. It was just what the campaign doctor ordered: a dose of real life.

"This is the man America needs," she said. "This is the man who will wake up every day with the determination to solve the problems that others say can't be solved, to fix what others say is beyond repair. This is the man who will work harder than anyone so that we can work a little less hard."

Mitt Romney couldn't have been prouder, nor their sons who watched from the VIP section. It was a good start to the convention rollout.

The next day would be Paul Ryan's turn. He had to wait several minutes for the crowd to settle down before he quickly accepted the nomination and declared the GOP team ready to give America's children the country of opportunity and promise their parents enjoyed.

"Our nominee is sure ready," Ryan said. "His whole life has prepared him for this moment — to meet serious challenges in a serious way, without excuses and idle words. After four years of getting the runaround, America needs a turnaround, and the man for the job is Gov. Mitt Romney."

Ryan's father, also named Paul, had told his son that life offers two choices: "You can be part of the problem, or you can be part of the solution."

"The present administration has made its choices," the vice presidential candidate said. "And Mitt Romney and I have made ours: Before the math and the momentum overwhelm us all, we are going to solve this nation's economic problems."

Ryan's parents struggled, too, he noted, continuing a convention theme meant to overcome the idea that the Romney-Ryan ticket didn't understand regular Americans' lives. He told the eager audience that his answer when Romney offered him a spot on the ticket was, "Let's get this done." He repeated the line as the culmination of that night's events.

The final night wouldn't go quite so well, although it started on a high note with a religious and patriotic display no other candidate could have pulled off.

A cadre of Olympians took the stage near the prime-time slot, heralding Romney for saving the Salt Lake City Games.

"I came here tonight because I believe that today our country is off-target," said Kim Rhode, a gold-medal-winning skeet shooter. "We need the leadership of Mitt Romney and Paul Ryan to turn our country around so the millions of Americans who have taken aim at their own dreams — whatever they may be — have the opportunity for those dreams to come true just like our Olympic dreams did."

Derek Parra, an Olympic speedskater mentioned often by Romney, noted that his greatest moment wasn't taking the gold but helping to carry the tattered and singed flag recovered from atop the World Trade Center after the Sept. 11, 2001, attacks into the 2002 Opening Ceremony.

"That moment came under the leadership of Mitt Romney, and it not only inspired me, but it inspired all of Team USA, and we went on to win a record number of medals," Parra said. "Today our country is struggling. But the right leaders can inspire us to push on, to overcome seemingly insurmountable challenges and to accomplish great things. Mitt Romney is that kind of leader."

Conventions are derided for being overly scripted, and Romney wanted to shake things up a bit. The GOP teased a "surprise" guest on the final night, and it delivered: Dirty Harry and a chair.

Clint Eastwood had given Romney a strong endorsement earlier in the summer, and the candidate was happy to flaunt a little Hollywood love that usually went to Democrats. "He just made my day," Romney told donors after getting the Oscar winner's support.

Romney's top campaign officials cleared the Eastwood appearance, handed him talking points and gave him a time limit. The actor/director promptly ignored these and asked a stagehand for a chair. The ad-libbed, sometimes off-color remarks went on for 12 minutes, with part of his shtick pretending that Obama was sitting in the chair beside him. The family-friendly, morals-and-values theme evaporated. In its place were moments like this:

"What do you want me to tell Romney?" Eastwood said to the imaginary Obama. "I can't tell him to do that. I can't tell him to do that to himself."

Romney aides quickly distanced themselves from the sideshow. "Not me," one adviser said when asked who was responsible. Others called it "strange" and "weird." Another dubbed it "theater of the absurd." One Romney aide said he actually vomited during Eastwood's routine.

The movie icon created such a spectacle that another longtime Romney adviser called the entire convention a disaster.

"They were literally winging it," he suggested.

That was an exaggeration, of course. Romney still had his moment in the spotlight, and he brought the delegates back to the convention's point.

Accepting the nomination to boisterous applause, he began reciting example after example of the difficulties Americans had faced during the previous four years.

"I wish President Obama had succeeded, because I want America to succeed," Romney said somberly. "But his promises gave way to disappointment and division. This isn't something we have to accept. Now is the moment when we can do something. With your help, we will do something."

As he stood there, basking in the attention, he evoked the one person he really wished could have been there to witness it.

"My dad had been born in Mexico and his family had to leave during the Mexican Revolution," he said. "I grew up with stories of his family being fed by the U.S. government as war refugees. My dad never made it through college and apprenticed as a lath and plaster carpenter. And he had big dreams. He convinced my mom, a beautiful young actress, to give up Hollywood to marry him. He moved to Detroit, led a great automobile company and became governor of the great state of Michigan."

Romney pivoted from his dad to his wife.

"I knew that her job as a mom was harder than mine," Romney said. "And I knew, without question, that her job as a mom was a lot more important than mine. And as America saw Tuesday night, Ann would have succeeded at anything she wanted to."

He addressed head-on concerns about leading Bain Capital, noting how he had helped turn Staples into an American success story, about how a great steel company grew out of an Indiana cornfield — and how Obama and his allies wanted to attack him for creating jobs.

He took some well-aimed shots at the president, who held a narrow lead, because he hadn't fulfilled the promise of his 2008 election. Hope and change were nice slogans, but four years later people still were waiting to see both.

"You know there's something wrong with the kind of job he's done as president when the best feeling you had was the day you voted for him," Romney said.

"The time has come to turn the page," he added. "Today the time has come for us to put the disappointments of the last four years behind us. To put aside the divisiveness and the recriminations. To forget about what might have been and to look ahead to what can be."

Balloons and confetti rained down, and the applause was deafening as Ann and their kids joined Mitt onstage. Paul Ryan and his family joined, too. They had made their case. Now the eyes of the political world would shift to Charlotte and the Democratic convention.

Obama's team lined up speaker after speaker to chip away at the Romney displayed at Tampa and reinforce the message delivered in hundreds of millions of dollars in negative ads: Romney isn't like you and doesn't understand your problems.

"Mitt Romney, quite simply, doesn't get it," declared San Antonio Mayor Julián Castro. "A few months ago he visited a university in Ohio and gave the students there a little entrepreneurial advice. 'Start a business,' he said. But how? 'Borrow money if you have to from your parents,' he told them. Gee, why didn't I think of that? Some people are lucky enough to borrow money from their parents, but that shouldn't determine whether you can pursue your dreams. I don't think Gov. Romney meant any harm. I think he's a good guy. He just has no idea how good he's had it."

A former steelworker lamented how Romney and his Bain cronies pocketed $12 million while the company fired 750 employees. Another plant worker noted Bain's purchase of her company cost 850 jobs.

Senate Majority Leader Harry Reid, one of Romney's sharpest critics despite their shared Mormon faith, chastised the Republican nominee and his party for believing in two sets of rules: one for millionaires and billionaires, and another for the middle class.

"And this year, they've nominated the strongest proponent — and clearest beneficiary — of this rigged game: Mitt Romney," the Nevada Democrat said. "Never in modern American history has a presidential candidate tried so hard to hide himself from the people he hopes to serve. When you look at the one tax return he has released, it's obvious why there's been only one."

Reid had been at the fore of that attack, taking to the Senate floor multiple times to call out Romney for not releasing more tax returns, noting his father, 1968 presidential hopeful George Romney, supplied 12 years' worth to the American people. Mitt Romney, Reid alleged, feared such disclosure because he hadn't paid taxes for a decade.

The feisty Senate majority leader wouldn't name his source, other than to say the person was an investor in Bain Capital. A later book about the campaign would identify the informant as Jon Huntsman Sr., whose business partner Bob Gay previously served as managing director of Bain Capital. Huntsman adamantly denied it.

"It's so ridiculous that people associate my name with Mitt Romney's tax returns, like I would have interest in it or know about it," Huntsman protested. "These fellows who wrote this book, they dwell on falsehoods and false rumors. They're nothing but supermarket tabloid trash. They ought to be ashamed of themselves."

Despite those unequivocal denials, Romney insiders still believe Huntsman was Reid's source.

Back at the Democratic convention, Michelle Obama played a similar role to Ann Romney in touting the kindhearted, family-oriented person her husband was. The first lady told of the couple's struggles early on, their first date in a car so rusty you could see through the door and using a coffee table they found in a dumpster. She highlighted the president's work to pay women more equitably, trim taxes for working families and pass health-care reform.

"So, in the end, for Barack, these issues aren't political, they're personal," Michelle Obama said. "Because Barack knows what it means when a family struggles. He knows what it means to want something more for your kids and grandkids. Barack knows the American Dream because he's lived it ... and he wants everyone in this country to have that same opportunity, no matter who we are, or where we're from, or what we look like, or who we love."

The star of the Democratic convention wasn't Michelle Obama or even her husband, it was a Southern blast from the past. President Bill Clinton gave a forceful and often ad-libbed defense of Obama's first term, everything from the publicly unpopular health-care law to his response to the financial crisis. So thorough and convincing was Clinton's speech that Obama's address the next day seemed a weak encore.

When Obama took the podium, he mentioned his opponent's name once and struck a more positive message, which also seemed to concede that he hadn't change Washington culture as much as he promised four years prior.

"America, I never said this journey would be easy, and I won't promise that now," the president said. "Yes, our path is harder — but it leads to a better place. Yes, our road is longer — but we travel it together. We don't turn back."

Obama hoped a bounce from the convention would propel him to victory. That bounce never came, but he did get an unexpected gift that made a big difference.

Earlier in the year, Romney had attended a $50,000-a-plate fundraiser in Boca Raton, Fla., at the home of Marc Leder, a controversial private-equity manager. Like most fundraisers, it was closed to the news media, so the candidate assumed he was safe in candidly answering a few questions.

"For the last three years, all everybody's been told is, 'Don't worry, we'll take care of you,' " an audience member quizzed Romney. "How are you going to do it, in two months before the elections, to convince everybody you've got to take care of yourself?"

Romney didn't hold back.

"There are 47 percent of the people who will vote for the president no matter what," Romney declared. "All right, there are 47 percent who are with him, who are dependent upon government, who believe that they are victims, who believe that government has a responsibility to care for them, who believe that they are entitled to health care, to food, to housing, to you name it — that that's an entitlement. And the government should give it to them.

"And they will vote for this president no matter what. And, I mean, the president starts off with 48, 49, 48 — he starts off with a huge number. These are people who pay no income tax. Forty-seven percent of Americans pay no income tax. So our message of low taxes doesn't connect. And he'll be out there talking about tax cuts for the rich. I mean, that's what they sell every four years. And so my job is not to worry about those people — I'll never convince them that they should take personal responsibility and care for their lives."

It was a stunningly frank response. Here was a presidential candidate saying he had written off 47 percent of Americans and that 47 percent of Americans essentially were moochers.

Scott Prouty, a bartender who was serving drinks at the fundraiser, had surreptitiously put his phone on the bar and hit record. After hearing the "47 percent" comment and others that surprised him, he weighed over and over again whether to release the video. He didn't want to lose his job. In late summer, he anonymously reached out to Mother Jones' David Corn. The story, and the video, went viral when the liberal muckraking magazine posted it in mid-September. It was a game changer, a remark so discordant with the public that it threatened to become Romney's version of his dad's infamous "brainwashing" line.

Within hours, Romney spokeswoman Gail Gitcho issued a statement that tried to speak to the recorded remarks without really addressing them. "Mitt Romney wants to help all Americans struggling in the Obama economy," the statement read in part. It wasn't nearly enough to stanch the bleeding. Aides hastily organized a news conference with Romney's traveling press corps in Costa Mesa, Calif. The desperation of the moment was best captured by the fact that the candidate appeared before the cameras with tousled hair.

"I understand there's been a video that's been on the Internet for a few weeks that has attracted some attention," Romney said in the understatement of the day. The point he had been trying to make, he said, was that Obama starts out with a good share of voters, 47 percent or 49 percent, who would vote for him no matter what. Romney said he, too, had a certain number of voters certain to swing his way. To win, he needed to draw some Obama folks to the Romney column. The explanation confused Reuters' Steve Holland.

"Are you not stepping away from anything, and do you worry you've offended this 47 percent you mentioned?"

"Well, um, it's not elegantly stated, let me put it that way," Romney responded. The "47 percent" comment would haunt him throughout the campaign.

As devastating as this secretly taped fundraiser turned out to be, it didn't end Romney's chances. Obama helped keep Romney in the contest when he made the next unforced error: a lackluster debate performance.

Romney twisted his fork into takeout spaghetti in his Denver hotel suite. "So any advice?" he asked Ann.

"Yes," she replied. "Conviction from your heart as to why you're running. Conviction that this country's on the wrong course and you're able to put it on the right one."

The debate that night would be huge. It was the first chance for Romney to be onstage with the incumbent. Obama was leading in national polls, and the "47 percent" remark was starting to erode Romney's brand among independent voters.

Do you think you'll be intimidated? son Matt asked.

"Sure," Romney said. "Are you kidding?"

"You should not be intimidated by him," Ann insisted. "I'm not joking, Mitt."

Obama is a good debater, Romney said, more effective than his GOP rivals. But he felt good about his preparations and wasn't willing to go easy on Obama just because he was the president.

"I represent the party that represents half the people in this country. I got selected by that party. I'm their nominee. I'm going to stand up to this guy because he's taking us in the wrong direction. I've got no problem doing that."

On their walk through the long hotel hallway, Ann joked that they should play a dirge while "Mitt walks to his execution." It would be anything but.

From the start of the University of Denver debate, hosted by PBS' Jim Lehrer, it was clear that the challenger came to tangle and the incumbent seemed to be wondering why he had interrupted his busy schedule to be there.

The first comments were jovial. It was the Obamas' anniversary and the president promised Michelle they wouldn't be doing the same thing next year. Romney quipped that he was sure the most romantic place Obama could commemorate his wedding was with him. Then the jabs started flying. The Republican was up for it, throwing out numbers and anecdotes to pummel his opponent with the steady message that he had failed Americans.

"The president has a view very similar to the view he had when he ran four years ago, that a bigger government, spending more, taxing more, regulating more — if you will, trickle-down government — would work," Romney charged out of the gate. "That's not the right answer for America. I'll restore the vitality that gets America working again."

In response, Obama rambled: from education to the tax code to oil and gas production to Romney's economic plan. Romney dove in again, reciting numbers, running through bullet points, ticking off a laundry list of Obama's failures. The pain was visible in the president's face; he knew he was offering a sleepy performance.

And it only got worse — so bad that former Vice President Al Gore later would blame the mile-high altitude of Denver for causing Obama to choke. Altitude or attitude, it was good for Romney, who exited the forum to cheers from supporters and family members.

Josh Romney had watched the debate, hoping it would end quickly before any gaffes by his dad. "I didn't want the president to somehow turn it around," Josh later said. "Unfortunately [for him], he never did. It was just a sound beating from beginning to end. You know, I think the president was overconfident and assumed he'd been president for four years and how dare anybody challenge him."

Back in his hotel suite, Romney jettisoned his tie and sat with his family discussing the debate. Presidents have a hard time in their first toe-to-toe encounter, he agreed, because they're stunned at this "whippersnapper" challenging them. He flipped through his notes and handed them to Matt. On the upper right corner, the word "DAD" was written in all caps.

"I wrote down 'DAD,' " Romney told his encircling family. "I always think about Dad, and about [how] I'm standing on his shoulders. There's no way I'd be able to run for president if Dad hadn't done what Dad did. He's the real deal."

Next to "DAD," Romney drew a sun — a reminder, the candidate said, to the biblical command to Christians to "let your light so shine."

This was Romney's moment, but it wouldn't last. Obama stepped up his game for the next debate. He wasn't going to take another pounding.

"Gov. Romney is a good man," Obama said. He "loves his family, cares about his faith. But I also believe that when he said behind closed doors that 47 percent of the country considered themselves victims who refuse personal responsibility, think about who he was talking about."

Obama hadn't referenced the 47 percent the first go-round and wasn't going to make that mistake again. He chided Romney for investing in companies, sending them to bankruptcy, laying off employees and stripping their pensions. Romney saw the chance to make a point. "Mr. President, have you looked at your pension?"

"I don't look at my pension," Obama snapped back. "It's not as big as yours, so it doesn't take as long."

Obama even got an assist from the moderator, CNN's Candy Crowley, when Romney tried to point out that it took the president 12 days to label as a terrorist attack the Sept. 11, 2012, ambush on the U.S. consulate in Benghazi, Libya, that killed four Americans.

Obama looked annoyed. A day after the deaths, he'd stood in the Rose Garden and said, "No acts of terror will ever shake the resolve of this great nation." To him, that was enough.

"Get the transcript," he challenged Romney, who tried to continue until Crowley interrupted him.

"He did, in fact, sir," she said.

"Can you say that a little louder, Candy?" Obama asked.

"He did call it an act of terror," Crowley said, though she gave Romney a point, too, for noting that the White House erroneously credited a web video offensive to Muslims for precipitating the attack.

The media labeled Obama the winner of the second debate, though Romney's people thought their man held his own. "Minus when Candy Crowley decided to join the debate against him," Josh Romney later would say.

The third, and final, sparring match came in Boca Raton, where Romney had made his now-infamous "47 percent" comment. Instead of economic issues, this one focused largely on foreign policy, and Romney didn't seem as combative as he had in the first two showdowns. Both candidates came armed with zingers. After Romney derided the idea of cutting the military budget, Obama pounced.

"I think Gov. Romney maybe hasn't spent enough time looking at how our military works," the president said. "You mention the Navy, for example, and that we have fewer ships than we had in 1916. Well, Governor, we also have fewer horses and bayonets. Because the nature of the military has changed."

"Attacking me is not an agenda," Romney later charged.

As the election neared, Romney and Ryan, and their families, jetted around the country to increasingly larger rallies. They felt momentum even as national polls showed Obama with a persistent lead in the swing states that would decide the election. Obama was leading in seven of the nine key states, including Ohio. Florida and Virginia leaned slightly Romney's way. Obama had big advantages with women and Latinos, not to mention energized black voters. Romney held sway with white men and older voters.

The outcome would be determined by which of those groups turned out.

As the country entered the final weeks of a bruising and historically expensive campaign, a harrowing hurricane hit New Jersey and New York. Hurricane Sandy devastated coastal towns and put a damper on the highly partisan campaign rhetoric. But the Romney people couldn't help but criticize New Jersey Gov. Chris Christie, supposedly an ally, for bringing Obama on a tour of the affected regions and heaping praise on the Democrat, calling his response "outstanding." Christie even gave his visitor a hug, allowing Obama to look presidential and bipartisan.

Romney folks, including some top donors, were furious. The GOP nominee tried to stay out of the dust-up, instead barnstorming the critical swing states. As did the president.

In Madison, Wis., Obama told supporters that Romney was a "talented salesman," trying to wrap old, bad ideas into a new package he called change.

"We've made progress these last four years," Obama said. "But the reason we're all gathered here … is because we know we've got more work to do. We've got more work to do. As long as there's a single American who wants a job but can't find one, our work is not yet done."

In Manchester, N.H., lines of Romney supporters snaked around the Verizon Wireless Arena for his final rally. The Republican hopeful said he was the real agent of change — the one who would fulfill the promises Obama hadn't — and that "Tomorrow we begin a new tomorrow."

"You hope that President Obama will live up to his promise to pull people together," Romney said. "He hasn't. I will."

On Election Day, Mitt and Ann voted in their hometown of Belmont, Mass., with cameras snapping. Obama went to the polls in Chicago. Landing in Pittsburgh, Romney was welcomed by hundreds of fans cheering from a parking garage.

"Intellectually I've felt that we're going to win this, and I've felt that for some time," Romney told reporters. "But, emotionally, just getting off the plane and seeing those people standing there — we didn't tell them we were coming. We didn't notify them when we'd arrive. Just seeing people there, cheering as they were, connected emotionally with me."

Back in the air, Romney napped, his arms crossed, his head nestled into a red seat cover embossed with his name.

"I always slept well before an election because I knew I'd given everything," he would say. "So, why worry? I did everything I could. After that, it's out of my hands."

It certainly was.

At the Boston Convention and Exhibition Center, the grand ballroom was set for Romney to celebrate a historic victory. Stars were projected on the entrance, and Romney's logo was plastered everywhere. Supporters milled before a flag-laden stage that sported the now-familiar "Believe in America" slogan. The Romneys huddled in an adjacent hotel, laughing and joking as they awaited results. That ended when CNN reported Romney was up 500 votes in Florida. The candidate knew he was in trouble.

"If it's a squeaker in Florida ... Ohio, no way," he said.

Romney started picking up trash left around the suite. Son Ben checked a laptop. Josh watched his phone. The predictable states were called as soon as polls closed. Others dripped in.

New Hampshire went for Obama. Wisconsin, too. Iowa fell next. Romney needed Ohio if he had any chance. He wouldn't get it. He wouldn't get any of the critical swing states.

NBC was the first network to call the race, at 11:12 p.m. Eastern Time. Fox News held out as Karl Rove argued the prediction was wrong. He couldn't believe the election results.

He wasn't the only one.

"I just can't believe you're going to lose," Josh told his dad, then tieless and lounging on the hotel sofa.

"It makes your life a lot better, doesn't it?" Romney countered.

"Yeah," Josh replied. "Still, I just don't believe it's possible."

Campaign manager Matt Rhoades came in to chat with the candidate, noting it didn't look good and he didn't want Romney to look like then-Sen. John Kerry did in 2004, waiting too long to acknowledge the loss.

Romney hadn't written a concession speech. He whipped out his iPad with the 1,118-word victory speech that would never be read.

"My time on the stage is over, guys," he told his family members who were ruminating about how he should be gracious in his concession but still make a point. "I'm grateful for the time I had, but my time is over."

Romney was depressed, not just for himself but for the country. Obama isn't an aberration, he said, and America is headed the wrong way. He wouldn't say so in his speech, though.

Just after 1 a.m., Romney entered the half-empty ballroom that had once teemed with excitement. He had called the president to congratulate him, Romney said, and he would pray for his success.

"I believe in America. I believe in the people of America," Romney told the hangers-on. "And I ran for office because I'm concerned about America. This election is over, but our principles endure. I believe that the principles upon which this nation was founded are the only sure guide to a resurgent economy and to a new greatness."

Six years or so of running for the highest office in the land, and Romney had lost. More than 51 percent of Americans had voted for Obama. Some 47 percent — a painfully ironic level of support — had picked Romney.

chapter fifteen

Dynasties

Every failed presidential nominee in the modern era eventually will be compared to Al Gore.

The former vice president lost a historically close race in 2000, so tight that it took the Supreme Court to step in and make George W. Bush the winner. So how did Gore respond? He got chubby and grew a beard, a physical transformation that fit public expectations. After going through a nail-biter that painful, Gore was supposed to feel defeated and depressed and ... he sure looked the part.

After his loss, Mitt Romney went into seclusion in his posh La Jolla, Calif., home, where he made thank-you calls, played around on an iPad and stared out the window at his neighbor's reconstruction project. He didn't gain weight and was never caught with any serious scruff. But when he did emerge, he was photographed with messy hair, which may be the Romney equivalent of letting yourself go.

His contest wasn't nearly as close as Gore's, but Romney was still "shell-shocked," as one adviser put it. Ann Romney cried on and off for weeks.

"There's nothing worse than when you think you're going to win and you don't," said another adviser. The Romney team incorrectly believed the polls were underplaying Republican enthusiasm.

In the middle of the campaign, Romney half joked about what a loss would mean, how he would be seen and remembered.

"I have looked at what happens to anybody in this country who loses as the nominee of their party," he said at a fundraiser. "They become a loser for life."

He formed an "L" shape with his fingers and put it on his forehead, then made a quip about Michael Dukakis having a hard time getting a job mowing lawns.

Romney saw how his dad had struggled after his 1968 campaign. George Romney spent a brief time in the Nixon White House, but then found it difficult to gain attention as he traveled the country to promote volunteerism.

"I remember my dad becoming quite frustrated," Mitt Romney said. "He used to say that Washington is the fastest place to go from 'Who's Who' to 'Who's That?' "

Making it even more painful, Romney is the first presidential also-ran to face the full force of social media. Two weeks after Obama's re-election, Mitt and Ann were spotted at a movie theater where they watched the latest "Twilight" flick, a vampire story written by fellow Mormon Stephenie Meyer. Afterward, they enjoyed some pizza. Why do we know details of this Romney date night? Someone on the street snapped pictures and sent them to TMZ. Two days later, multiple people caught Romney pumping gas in La Jolla, wearing a wrinkled blue dress shirt with his sleeves rolled and his hair mussed. The blurry images appeared on Twitter and Reddit. The next day, dozens of people pulled out their smartphones to document the Romney family's trip to Disneyland.

The photos didn't stop. There's the picture of him buying a McFlurry in Washington, the same day he met with President Barack Obama at the White House for lunch, a meal that included white turkey chili and Southwestern grilled chicken salad but apparently no dessert. There's one showing Romney pushing a cart out of Costco, a black ballcap riding high on his head. He bought two cases of water, paper towels, a down coat and a whole lot of V8.

The GOP's vanquished champion was seen frequently, but he wasn't heard from much. The first time he did speak, he got himself into trouble.

A week after conceding to Obama, Romney held a 20-minute conference call for his top donors during which he vacillated between abject disappointment and political pragmatism.

"I'm very sorry that we didn't win," he said. "I know that you expected to win. We expected to win. We were disappointed with the results; we hadn't anticipated it.

"And so now we're looking and saying, 'OK, what can we do going forward?' But, frankly, we're still so troubled by the past."

He pinned his loss on the "gifts" Obama gave to various voting blocs.

"With regards to the young people, for instance, a forgiveness of college-loan interests was a big gift," Romney said. "Free contraceptives were very big with young, college-aged women. And then, finally, Obamacare also made a difference for them."

He also said the president's controversial health-care plan lured black and Latino voters to turn out in higher-than-expected numbers.

Romney — still known for his "47 percent" comment — picked the wrong time to make this argument, and many ardent supporters criticized him for it.

New Hampshire Sen. Kelly Ayotte, a regular on the Romney campaign circuit, said she didn't know the context of the comments, but "I don't agree with them."

"The campaign is over," she said on cable news, "and what the voters are looking for us to do is to accept their votes and go forward."

It wasn't hard for the Republican Party to break up with Romney, because many in the GOP never fell in love with him — as evidenced by all of the primary-season flings with second- and third-tier candidates.

"I just don't think Romney ever established an emotional connection with much of anybody in the party," said Larry Sabato, a political scientist at the University of Virginia. "He was essentially a cyborg designed to win the presidency, and when he failed, he was placed in the disposal bin."

Weekly Standard editor Bill Kristol argued Romney may have been the first Republican candidate in recent memory to lose when people in the party expected him to win.

"So there's perhaps a particularly strong desire among Republicans," Kristol said, "to let his campaign disappear down the memory hole."

But Romney's people noted he was the first GOP candidate to raise $1 billion. He also captured 59 million votes, a few hundred thousand shy in key states of winning the Oval Office.

"Even those who have been critical of the campaign on our side realize, in the end, that Gov. Romney was resonating with millions of Americans and was running the kind of campaign we could all be proud of," said senior adviser Stuart Stevens. "I think the governor can have the political road of his choosing. I have no idea what that would be."

Mitt Romney took the road back to the world of venture capital and corporate boardrooms, where he was revered, respected and in command.

Less than a month after his defeat, he rejoined the board of Marriott International, the hotel behemoth created by his namesake, J. Willard Marriott. This was his third stint on the board after leaving to run for governor and then president.

A few months later, he took on a new role with Solamere Capital, named after the Deer Valley, Utah, community where Romney had owned a ski mansion. Tagg Romney and Spencer Zwick launched Solamere weeks after Mitt Romney dropped out of the 2008 race. They used the former governor's connections to help raise $244 million in venture capital. Mitt and Ann Romney also chipped in $10 million in seed money.

Now that the campaign was behind him, Mitt Romney wanted a bigger piece of the action. He agreed to serve as chairman of the executive committee, a one-week-per-month gig. He already had an office in Solamere's Boston headquarters that he mostly used for personal matters.

Just as he began to re-emerge in the business world, Romney inched his way back into the political debate. He gave his first post-campaign interview to Chris Wallace on "Fox News Sunday," where he said it "kills me" to not be in the White House, yet he sounded like a man coming to terms with the loss.

"We were on a roller coaster, exciting and thrilling, ups and downs. But the ride ends," Romney said. "And then you get off. And it's not like, 'Oh, can't we be on a roller coaster the rest of our life?' It's like, 'No, the ride's over.'"

Ann admitted having a harder time adjusting, equating the experience to a change in LDS Church callings.

"In our church, we're used to serving and, you know, you can be in a very high position, but you recognize you're serving. And now all of a sudden, you're released and you're nobody," she said. "We're used to that. It's like we came and stepped forward to serve. And, you know, the other part of it was an amazing thing, and it was really quite a lot of energy and a lot of passion and a lot of people around us and all of a sudden, it was nothing. But the good news is, fortunately, we like each other."

The Romneys made it clear, at least initially, that they weren't interested in a third bite at the apple.

"I did better this time than I did the time before," Mitt said. "And I won't get a third chance."

His political and business re-emergence was displayed simultaneously later that summer when Romney organized a public-policy conference at a lavish resort in Park City, Utah. Solamere held side events to recruit investors and sponsored the three-day summit, attended by potential presidential candidates such as New Jersey Gov. Chris Christie and Kentucky Sen. Rand Paul.

The conference, now an annual event, showed Romney's lasting political clout and the strength of his fundraising apparatus, both of which were irresistible to other politicians. It also reinforced his image as an agent of the rich and powerful.

In some ways he embraced it, sharing a new mansion in Deer Valley with another family and building a fourth house in Holladay, a Salt Lake City suburb where his son Josh lives. This one, which Mitt and Ann now call home, has a hidden room off the study and an outdoor spa attached to the master bathroom. The Romneys sold their town house in Belmont, Mass., and declared residency in Utah, a place where they are widely adored.

In his post-campaign life, Romney didn't devote himself to a single mission, as Gore did with climate change. Instead, he positioned himself as a leading critic of Obama and a counterpoint to the far right.

He and his allies went on an "I told you so" tour when Russian President Vladimir Putin annexed part of Ukraine. It was payback for the grief he had received from Obama after saying Russia was the "No. 1 geopolitical foe" of the United States. Since then, Romney hasn't missed opportunities to criticize the president — from the flawed rollout of Obamacare to the slow economic comeback to the flare-up of violence in Iraq.

Romney saved some of his fire for elements of his own party, namely tea-party groups. He criticized them for supporting a government shutdown as a way to fight the health-care law. He also argued against states moving away from primary elections and toward caucuses, a strategy that favors more ideologically rigid candidates.

"We should have the majority of the party's voters decide who they want as their nominee," he argued.

In May 2014, Romney bucked most Republicans to support a minimum-wage increase, arguing doing so would help reach out to black and Latino voters.

He used his fame and his deep donor lists to support like-minded Republicans, becoming a popular campaign surrogate during the 2014 midterms, which were a sweeping success for the GOP.

He supported former Sen. Scott Brown in New Hampshire (who lost) and Senate Minority Leader Mitch McConnell in Kentucky (who won and is now the majority leader), along with a dozen other high-profile Republicans. He raised money for the National Republican Senatorial Committee. He checked in regularly with Christie in New Jersey, Rep. Paul Ryan, R-Wis., his former running mate, and many of his top financial supporters.

He enjoyed a mini-renaissance, and it likely would not have happened if he hadn't let a guy with a camera tail his family for years.

Mitt and Ann Romney strolled down the red carpet in Salt Lake City when

Greg Whiteley's documentary "Mitt" premiered at the Sundance Film Festival in January 2014. The movie wasn't one of those inside-the-political-war-room tell-alls. It focused exclusively on intimate moments with Romney and his family during the 2008 and 2012 campaigns.

For many who saw it, the Mitt Romney on screen didn't resemble the one who ran for the highest office in the land. There was no sign of the political cyborg who had been ridiculed and reviled. In its place was a regular guy who picked up trash when his family made a mess, went sledding with his grandchildren and brushed off platitudes from his staff after the second debate, knowing he had badly botched the Benghazi line of attack.

The Romney in the documentary became frustrated during moments when any normal person would have done the same — at one point grumbling, "How many more debates do I have to go to?" He comforted his wife when she needed it. He seemed grounded, not aloof. He seemed competent, not calculating.

Where had this guy been during the campaign?

That's the reaction Whiteley had when he showed friends some of his raw footage. Romney and his team didn't let reporters get close to the candidate until the tail end of the campaign, months after his image had hardened for much of the public.

The documentary's more personal portrayal hit Netflix around the same time Christie tripped over a bridge connecting New Jersey to New York. A legislative investigation uncovered internal communications linking the governor's staffers to the temporary closure of two lanes of the George Washington Bridge. It appeared to be a punishment aimed at a Democratic mayor who wasn't playing ball. Christie previously had mocked reporters who asked about it, but now that there was proof, he fired people and said he had nothing to do with it. The investigations intensified. The embarrassing episode weakened Christie, a 2016 contender seen as one of the establishment GOP's best hopes.

Other early contenders included a trio of right-wing senators: Rand Paul of Kentucky, Ted Cruz of Texas and Marco Rubio of Florida. The political elites began turning to Jeb Bush, the former Florida governor and younger brother of President George W. Bush.

Jeb Bush has been out of office since 2007, but he still has the name to attract top conservative donors. He's a self-proclaimed introvert and far from a fire-breathing conservative. For instance, he supports giving undocumented immigrants a chance to be citizens. Bush also has been a critic of the Republican nomination process that gave voice to some fringe candidates.

More than one commentator thought of Jon Huntsman when they considered Bush, by which they meant a potentially strong general-election candidate who may struggle mightily in a GOP primary.

Party elders also worried voters may suffer from Bush fatigue after two of them already had occupied the White House. It didn't help that Hillary Clinton appears to be the odds-on favorite to be the Democratic nominee. A Clinton-Bush rehash? The first one didn't end well for papa George H.W. Bush.

With no clear front-runner, many pundits speculated anew about a third Romney run. Shortly after Christie's bridge scandal, CNN's Wolf Blitzer asked Mitt if he would consider it.

"No. I've answered that question a number of times, as you know, and the answer is no," Romney said. "I'm not running for president in 2016. It's time for someone else to take that responsibility. And I'll be supporting our nominee."

Blitzer wasn't done. He noted a poll of Republicans in New Hampshire found that Romney was the leading 2016 contender. "You see some of the folks out there in the Republican Party are saying, 'Well, Mitt Romney, maybe you should reconsider.'"

Romney said he appreciated the compliment, but tried, once again, to bury the issue. "I've had my turn. I gave it two good shots, didn't win. And now it's time for someone else to do it. So I'm not running for president, Wolf."

Blitzer was skeptical.

"All right, Mitt Romney telling us he's not going to run once again. But as I said, this is America. People can change their minds. You remember Barack Obama said he wasn't going to run and he decided to run. We'll see what happens."

Like many reporters, Blitzer had been conditioned to doubt politicians who say they are not going to run, because they often do.

In the months to come, Romney's hard "no" would soften considerably as those around him warmed up to the idea.

That May, former Utah Gov. Mike Leavitt, who likely would have been Romney's chief of staff, was jokingly asked about a third Romney campaign. He turned serious.

"If Mitt Romney concluded that he was interested in taking another run, I would be there with him, as I know thousands and thousands of others would."

Romney's friend and frequent campaign surrogate, Rep. Jason Chaffetz, R-Utah, told Chris Matthews on MSNBC that he fully expected Romney to make a third bid, though the congressman later said it was just a "gut feeling."

Ann Romney cryptically said: "Mitt and I, at this point, are not making plans."

Josh Romney even said he'd like to see his dad re-enter the arena.

"I'd love for there to be a third. I'd love to see him run again, but I don't get to make that decision," Josh said. "And he's not going to run again."

Asked the same question a few months later, Josh tweaked his answer: "I would like my dad to be president. I'm not entirely sure I would be up for another campaign."

As Mitt Romney barnstormed for Republican congressional candidates in August 2014, Zogby Analytics came out with a new poll showing him handily leading other GOP presidential prospects. He even held a commanding advantage among born-again Christians, a group normally seen as critical of Mormons.

Zogby summed it up this way: "Should Mitt Romney decide to run, he would be the man to beat."

Paul Ryan, considered a potential candidate in his own right, even chimed in: "I'd drive his bus if he asked me to."

When pressed by radio commentator Hugh Hewitt, Romney said there was a "one-in-a-million" chance that he would make a third run.

"You know circumstances can change, but I'm just not going to let my head go there," he said, suggesting he would consider it late in the campaign season only if Republicans were desperate for a candidate. "That's the one-in-a-million we are thinking about."

Romney even brought up the movie "Dumb and Dumber." Jim Carrey's character, Lloyd Christmas, tries to pick up the leading lady. She rejects him and, when pressed, says there's only a one-in-a-million shot she would change her mind.

"So you're telling me there's a chance," Christmas says. "Yeah!"

Romney was no longer so firm against another chance at the Oval Office. His financial network noticed it, reporters noticed it and so did other potential candidates.

For the most part, reporters treated the debate about whether Romney would run again seriously — if a bit far-fetched. That wasn't the case when Jon Huntsman said he would consider a future bid.

TV legend Larry King popped the question, and Huntsman initially ducked.

"I never thought I would run for governor. I never thought I would be in China as the United States ambassador," he said. "Things happen."

King pressed: "So, you're open?"

"I'm open," Huntsman said, "but here is the deal. You have to be able to create a pathway from point A to point B. I can tell you how I'd get to the finish line from Super Tuesday, but I can't tell you how I get through those early primary states, having been there and done that once before."

Washington Post political commentator Chris Cillizza pounced, saying there was no logic to justify another Huntsman run anytime soon.

"Here's some straight talk (with apologies to John McCain): Huntsman has as much chance as I do of being elected president in 2016. Part of that is due to who he is and part of that is because of what the current incarnation of the Republican Party looks like," Cillizza wrote in May 2014.

He was hardly alone. Many pundits threw cold water on the notion that a national candidate could rise by staking out the middle ground, especially in an era of inflated partisanship.

For all his arguments that a Huntsman return was fantasy, Cillizza allowed that Utah's former governor was only in his mid-50s and noted the shelf life of a presidential candidate runs into the early 70s.

So maybe not 2016, but perhaps 2020 or 2024.

That was the point Huntsman said he was trying to make. He may have explored a potential candidacy briefly, including a possible run as an independent, but he had taken none of the steps necessary to pursue the nation's highest office.

"I'm not organizing. I'm not fundraising for it, but politics is such serendipity," said Huntsman, who has moved his family to a posh Virginia suburb. "I don't think it'll be 2016, but will it be beyond? I just don't know."

Huntsman Sr. said he wouldn't contribute to any presidential race until he knows his son's intentions. In a radio interview, he coyly added: "Well, you know, I think that 2020 could be an interesting year for the Republicans."

He also hasn't ruled out a Senate campaign in Utah, though most of his attention has been focused on international relations and national politics.

The Huntsmans were dismissive of the early talk that Romney would run again, with Huntsman Jr. saying: "I don't think that's in the cards." But he heaped praise on another White House aspirant: Hillary Rodham Clinton.

"At the risk of totally destroying my future in politics, I have to say she is a very impressive public servant," said Huntsman, who worked for Clinton, then secretary of state, during his time as ambassador to China. "I have to say I haven't been around too many people as professional, as well briefed, as good with people at all levels of life, whether a head of state or the person holding open the door. I think that's the measure of a leader."

While he noted their different political allegiances, Huntsman called Clinton "a very, very capable person." The comment was reminiscent of Huntsman's note labeling Obama "a remarkable leader."

Conversely, one of the people who have consistently treated Huntsman as a serious presidential contender is Jim Messina, the man who ran Obama's 2012 re-election effort and who backed Clinton in 2016.

"The guy we were always the most afraid of was Jon Huntsman, the governor of Utah, who I think would be a smashingly great general-election candidate," Messina said on MSNBC.

The mutual admiration leads to a natural question: What about a potential Clinton-Huntsman unity ticket?

"That's highly unlikely and not even worth speculating on," Huntsman said in a classic nondenial denial.

There remains a more plausible role for Huntsman in the next administration, whether led by a Clinton, a Bush or someone else: secretary of state. Huntsman has built a résumé befitting the nation's top diplomat. He's a two-time ambassador, former deputy trade representative and governor, not to mention chairman of the Atlantic Council.

Most people outside D.C. haven't heard of this foreign-policy group, but it has been a stopping point for many future Cabinet members. Huntsman took over in January 2014, taking the reins previously held by retired Nebraska Sen. Chuck Hagel, a moderate Republican whom Obama tapped to be secretary of defense. Before Hagel, it was Gen. James L. Jones, who became Obama's national security adviser.

The Atlantic Council was established as a nonpartisan think tank focused on the relationship between the United States and Europe. As the globe has become more interconnected, the group has expanded its interests, which explains why a China expert is now its chairman.

At his first event as the council's new public face, Huntsman was asked if he would run for president.

"2016 you don't have to worry about," Huntsman assured as he sat next to Frederick Kempe, the council's president. "I'll be here with Fred, if Fred still wants me around."

One man in the crowd shouted, "Nominate the governor," while another asked him what it would take for a Republican to win the presidency. Huntsman launched into a history lesson focused on some of the most beloved GOP leaders. Abraham Lincoln ended slavery. Teddy Roosevelt protected national treasures. Dwight D. Eisenhower built interstate highways.

"If you look back over the past 150 years of Republican governance, you can find all kinds of examples that suggest that, in order to win, you've got to replay a couple of our greatest hits," he said, while at the same time acknowledging how hard it would be to replicate them.

Getting Republicans to spend heavily on public projects like the highway system or to set aside large swaths of wilderness seems unimaginable nowadays. Still, Huntsman envisions a political "sweet spot."

The GOP could succeed, he said, by being "a little more open and progressive on social issues, conservative on financial and budget issues and realistic on foreign policy."

Shortly after dropping out of the 2012 contest, Huntsman took a spot as chairman of the Huntsman Cancer Foundation. He also landed on some well-paying corporate boards such as Ford and Caterpillar. But the two organizations that command his attention are the Atlantic Council and No Labels, a political group that seeks to bypass partisanship to solve the nation's problems.

The group had a flashy beginning but has no real track record of accomplishments. No Labels and Huntsman plan to unveil a platform hoping to influence the 2016 contest. In the meantime, the group gave Huntsman a platform — a weekly satellite-radio show — to talk about election reform and other issues he raised during his time as governor and as a presidential candidate.

"It's money in politics; that is the cancer," he said. "It is driving people to do crazy things and make wrongful decisions and it is changing the priorities."

He has lamented closed primaries that reduce voter turnout and gerrymandered political districts that create more and more safe Republican or Democratic seats.

"We've diagnosed the problem, which nobody wants to talk about because if you do, you are not going to get too much in the way of fundraising support, you are not going to get too much in the way of the establishment political support," Huntsman said. "We are missing some low-hanging fruit that otherwise ought to be ours, and the political divide is making that almost impossible."

Huntsman may be the ultimate insider, the son of a prominent Republican donor, a man who has held vaunted party roles himself, but he always has seen himself as an outsider, a maverick in the John McCain mold, willing to tell the hard truths even if it complicates his political future.

While Mitt Romney's political future remained muddled, Ann Romney moved forward with purpose. At the suggestion of her son Josh, she wrote a cookbook full of family recipes and family pictures, with the proceeds going to the newly launched Ann Romney Center for Neurologic Diseases at the Brigham and Women's Hospital in Boston.

The center focuses not only on multiple sclerosis, which she continues to battle, but also on brain tumors and Alzheimer's, Lou Gehrig's and Parkinson's disease. With the help of her husband, Ann vowed to raise $50 million for the effort. As part of that fundraising push, the Romneys held a kickoff gala for the center in October 2014, and, as at all of their public appearances, they were asked about Mitt's political future.

Ann would have none of it.

"Done," she said. "Completely. Not only Mitt and I are done, but the kids are done. … Done. Done. Done."

And yet, among those in attendance that night were former campaign advisers and business associates who saw the event as a hint that the old team may get back together. Mitt Romney had just come off of a fundraising trip to Iowa to help Joni Ernst win a Senate seat. After revving up the crowd, some activists started chanting "Run, Mitt, run!"

Romney confidants described a scenario in which the establishment candidates like Bush and Christie stumble, allowing a far more conservative candidate such as Sen. Ted Cruz of Texas to gain an advantage. Then the party would implore Romney to save the day. So really Mitt could just enjoy the attention without having to make any serious moves until mid- to late 2015.

It was a fairy tale to begin with, and it came to an end during the winter holidays.

Jeb Bush started making a play for Romney's wealthy donors. Publicly, Romney had said nice things about Bush and his potential political future, but privately there were raw feelings. Team Romney remained upset that Bush had endorsed Mitt in 2012 only after he had mathematically wrapped up the nomination. And aides were irritated that Bush was now criticizing the way Romney had run his campaign, promising to be less publicly awkward and more aggressive in defending his own record.

Romney took his first serious counterswipe in early December, when he met with Wall Street donors whom Bush had been buttering up and urged them not to commit to a candidate who is not their "first choice and that they aren't excited about."

An insider told Politico that Romney let it be known that "he does not think much of the current field and does not think it is gelling. He still views himself as the leader of the establishment wing of the Republican Party."

If that didn't get the point across, Romney told the donors directly that he wouldn't defer to Bush. "He does not feel he owes the Bushes anything," the insider said.

Romney privately questioned Bush's political skill and warned that the former Florida governor was susceptible to many of the same Democratic attacks he had faced related to his work at Bain Capital. Bush had ties to financial giants Lehman Brothers and Barclays. He also had dabbled in other private-equity ventures.

In an interview with a Miami television station, Bush retorted that he wouldn't respond as passively to such critiques as Romney had. He said comparing their business careers would be like "comparing an apple to a peanut." Romney loyalists felt slighted again.

A few weeks later, Bush's advisers told reporters their man would likely release at least a decade of his personal tax returns, showing how he would be different than Romney, who had released only two years' worth. Bush may be rich, but he's not Romney rich.

Bush and his team decided in mid-December that it was time to make a play for the establishment GOP crown. He used a Facebook post to announce his exploratory committee and created a political-action committee so he could start accepting donations. He resigned from corporate boards and began untangling himself from complicated private-equity funds. And he kept calling those big donors, most of whom had been, or still were, loyal to Romney.

A Romney associate described Bush's actions this way: "It was like poking a bear."

During the holidays, Romney family members gathered at their Deer Valley ski chalet, and just as he had done with his past two presidential campaigns, Mitt Romney put the question before his wife, sons and daughters-in-law.

Should he give it one last go?

Ann Romney had once grabbed his husband's face and shook it side to side while saying, "No," when a TV interviewer asked that same question, and yet, over the months, she had warmed to the idea. She told the family she was ready for a third campaign. Tagg Romney, Mitt's eldest, had been saying the same thing for months. Some of his other sons were not as excited, but all of them said they would support his decision.

Spencer Zwick, Romney's key fundraiser, then invited 30 of Romney's biggest donors to gather at New York Jets owner Woody Johnson's Manhattan offices. Those who couldn't make it were patched in to the conference room by phone.

Romney thanked them for supporting Republicans in the 2014 election and then got to the point. He was contemplating a third White House run and wanted them to stay neutral until he made up his mind.

The contributors were encouraging, yet hesitant. They wanted to hear his rationale for a third campaign. He responded that he was driven to reduce poverty, improve the nation's long-term economic stability and stake out a stronger foreign policy.

Some urged him to drop his former campaign team, and Romney acknowledged he had received some bad advice.

They told him he needed to be more comfortable in public, be the Mitt from the movie "Mitt," not the Mitt voters saw in 2012. He agreed.

"I want to be president," he said, and then he left with a parting note: "Tell your friends."

The Wall Street Journal had the story within hours, documenting Romney's stunning reversal after spending two years denying any future presidential ambition. His advisers were energized and ready to go, arguing that none of the nearly two dozen Republican hopefuls had Romney's gravitas. They repeated to anyone who would listen that it took Ronald Reagan three tries to win the presidency.

That was a comparison that Reagan's campaign strategist, Stuart Spencer, didn't like at all. He said Romney, unlike Reagan, had failed to "win over hearts and minds" in his earlier campaigns.

"He was just the opponent of a guy [Republicans] didn't like, named Obama," Spencer said. "He can't just switch and say, 'I'm the new Romney,' and get away with it."

Bush's team also didn't enjoy the news or the stream of articles about the impending GOP clash of two titans.

"We're seeing the first shots of the war between clan Romney and clan Bush," said Alex Castellanos, a GOP strategist and TV commentator, who had worked for both men. "How ugly could it get? You're only competing to lead the free world."

Knowing that the Huntsmans and Romneys were far from friendly, reporters sought out Jon Huntsman's reaction. Asked what he thought of Mitt 3.0, Huntsman joked: "We'll see. The technology has not yet been developed."

While he tried to stay out of the fray, it wasn't hard to see where his allegiances would lie if it ever did come down to Bush vs. Romney. Huntsman had served under George H.W. Bush and then George W. Bush. Jeb Bush's son had endorsed him in 2012.

"The Bush connection is a centrifugal force," Huntsman said. "And it's drawing back a whole generation of public servants and politicos."

Still, Huntsman said it was too early to say anything definitive about the candidates. His daughter Abby was far less circumspect in her comments, using her platform on MSNBC to dismantle the idea of a third Romney run.

"Just because you can run for president doesn't mean you should. Even if you believe you are the chosen one, that you are destined to run this country, which he clearly believes, it doesn't mean it's the best thing for the country," she said. "This is why he lost the last two times. It wasn't the gaffes, although they certainly weren't helpful, or because he wasn't 'conservative enough' or even because he was too rich. He lost because he came across as computer-animated, like there was nothing real to him.

"Perception is everything in politics. If you can't connect with voters, and convince them that even in a small way you understand them and have compassion for them, you will never win. And if you can't do that after two tries, will the third time be the charm? I doubt it."

For good measure, she closed with a jab at Romney's wealth.

"He has had his chances, and now, as Barack Obama has said, America craves that new-car smell this time around. And no matter how many cars the Romneys have, 2016 in politics should be a new model."

Whether her father agreed with her analysis or not, he never would be so blunt publicly. Instead, Jon Huntsman tried to offer a more dispassionate view of Romney's sudden, unexpected move.

"So Mitt, because he was the last nominee, really does control most of the big funders in the Republican Party, and I think he has probably seen some of them slip away in the last little while with the rise of Jeb Bush," Huntsman said. "He was probably put in a position where he had to basically comment on his own aspirations, act quickly and decisively or threaten the loss of some of the funders he has built up over many, many years, and listen, that, in politics, is equity. You know what is your leverage as a politician or as a player in party politics? It's what kind of money you bring to the table. I hate to say that that's important, but it is."

There was a reason Romney announced his renewed interest to wealthy donors in New York. He had just entered the invisible primary in which candidates fight for financial backers and campaign operatives in advance of the public showdown. Romney called big-name backers to say that the news was real and that he "almost certainly" would run, tacking to the right of Bush.

Paul Ryan, the GOP's vice presidential nominee in 2012, and Tom Rath, a key Romney aide in New Hampshire, had no hesitation.

"If he's in," Rath said, "I'll make the coffee or drive the car, whatever he needs."

Mitt also phoned previous supporters such as former Minnesota Gov. Tim Pawlenty, former Massachusetts Sen. Scott Brown and Utah Rep. Jason Chaffetz. He even called Newt Gingrich.

Bush backers downplayed Romney's moves as a retread of a failed campaign, arguing it was time for someone new. The Romney people fired back.

"Regardless of what Mitt Romney does, I don't know how excited anybody could be with Jeb Bush's candidacy," Chaffetz said. "I'll support the nominee, and Bush, if he gets the nomination, I'll support him. But I want to win the White House, and I don't like the idea of another Bush-Clinton race. Been there, done that.

"Mitt Romney also has the ability to raise the billion dollars you are going to need to go up against the Clinton machine. There are no doubts about his integrity. He has been vetted," Chaffetz continued. "Are they going to bring up the dog atop his car? Is that it? Is that all they got?"

No, that's not all Romney's opponents had. They had the "47 percent" comment and the bevy of other slip-ups that made Romney look five steps removed from the lives of ordinary voters. Plenty of Republicans worried that Romney was damaged goods.

"He got defined early," said Sen. John Thune, R-S.D. "And those issues are still there. That doesn't change, and that narrative is still out there."

Matt Moore, chairman of the South Carolina Republican Party, said: "We've got a lot of talented candidates. ... We'll give Gov. Romney a chance. But no one's going to hand it to him on a silver platter."

Romney started spelling out his vision for a third run aboard the USS Midway aircraft carrier, which hosted the Republican National Committee's winter meeting in 2014. He began by trying to warm up the crowd.

"The most frequently asked question I get is, 'What does Ann think about all this?' " Romney said. "She believes people get better with experience. And heaven knows I have experience running for president."

He also turned to his wife when talking about his desire to focus on poverty and wage stagnation, while at the same time speaking in vague terms about his Mormon faith, something he was reluctant to do in the past.

"For over 10 years, as you know, I served as a pastor for a congregation and for groups of congregations," Romney said. "And so she's seen me work for people who are very poor, to get them help and some assistance. ... She knows where my heart is."

Romney insiders promised this wasn't an aberration. One of the most famous Mormons alive was ready to talk about his religion, the way his father had in the 1960s. The hope was that doing so would make him appear more authentic and sympathetic while giving him a new platform to talk about poverty, people and the economy.

One of the reasons Romney didn't open up in 2008 and 2012 was that he didn't want to be "a caricature of the Mormon candidate," said Kirk Jowers, a campaign-finance lawyer who once headed Mitt Romney's leadership PAC. But now that he had overcome the Mormon hurdle in 2012, Romney felt liberated. And the success of the "Mitt" documentary, which included scenes of him praying with his family, reinforced this view. Team Romney, though, didn't want it to seem as if Romney felt God had wanted him to run for president.

"He has been reluctant to speak too openly on the campaign trail about his faith out of a concern that people would believe his motivation for running was based on an attempt to convert others," Tagg Romney said. "If he were to run again, I believe he would be much more willing to open up and share who he is, not by asking others to learn the doctrines of his faith, but by speaking of the values of love and service that it has taught him."

Other prominent LDS politicians used religion to explain why Romney would even be willing to consider another exhausting campaign. Relating it to Mormon missionary work, Sen. Mike Lee, R-Utah, described it as the ability "to encounter rejection without suffering defeat."

Opinion polls consistently showed Romney leading the crowded conservative pack, and his team members had bushels of private data that were just as encouraging. Their plan was to lay it all on Jeb Bush when the two men had lunch, a private gathering that had the political world buzzing.

Planned well in advance of Romney's presidential revival, the original idea was for Bush to travel to Utah to kiss the ring of the former nominee. Now the get-together was far more uncomfortable.

Reporters met Bush at Salt Lake City International Airport, where he tried to argue that it was going to be two chums enjoying a nice meal. Asked what they would talk about, he said, "The future."

Aides described their conversation as wonky, focused largely on issues facing the nation. Romney handed off polling data for 20 states, explaining why he would consider running again.

It's unclear if that meeting changed either man's thinking or lightened the growing tension between them. And while more polls would emerge showing Romney in the lead, Bush clearly had surged ahead in that invisible primary, where donors reign supreme.

Chicago investor Craig Duchossois was among the former Romney supporters to back the for ner Florida governor.

"I've got great respect for Gov. Romney, and I busted my buns for him," he said. "But I have turned the page."

Far more damaging was the defection of David Kochel, a talented Republican strategist in Iowa, who was moving to Florida to lead Bush's presidential race. Days earlier, Kochel had been on Romney strategy conference calls.

Romney's aides held a four-hour meeting in Boston, where they dispensed with the cheerleading and sought to make a clear-eyed assessment of their chances. While they knew there would be naysayers, the Republican establishment did not rally around a Romney candidacy as they had hoped. Even some supporters seemed to lack enthusiasm. Money would be harder to raise, though he still had his Mormon network and plenty of billionaires in Republican circles.

They saw Bush as beatable, with one aide describing him as "basically a lighter version" of Romney. They thought he could fend off a challenge from the right. Essentially, they saw a path to the nomination, though it was one that would likely be even more painful than the 2012 contest.

"Yeah, he could win the nomination," Tagg Romney said, "but all of the guns were going to be trained on him."

The aides were ready for the bruising battle to come, and many thought it was all but a formality that Romney would run. But while they were meeting in Boston, Mitt Romney had come to a different conclusion in Utah.

It wasn't to be. Romney knew he would get so bloodied during a primary fight that he wouldn't have the political strength necessary to defeat Clinton. He told Tagg of his decision while the two were skiing, and they continued to talk about it between runs down the slope.

"There's a lot of sadness mixed with a lot of relief," Tagg said later. "We feel pretty deeply that he'd be the best president, so there's sadness there. But there's relief that we're not going to have to go through that process."

Romney decided to wait a few days in case he changed his mind. He didn't. He organized a series of calls Jan. 30, first to his closest advisers, then to a wider group of supporters.

"After putting considerable thought into making another run for president," he said, "I've decided it is best to give other leaders in the party the opportunity to become our next nominee."

Romney, now 67, told those on the broader conference call that he was confident he could win the GOP nod and believed in his message but that one of the newer candidates may be better positioned to win in 2016.

"It is critical that America elect a conservative leader to become our next president. You know that I have wanted to be that president. But I do not want to make it more difficult for someone else to emerge who may have a better chance of becoming that president," he said. "You can't imagine how hard it is for Ann and me to step aside."

His announcement set off a feeding frenzy as other hopefuls, namely Bush and Christie, rushed to recruit Romney's campaign bundlers.

Not everyone was willing to say that this was the definitive end to Romney's political career. Mike Leavitt, the former governor of Utah and one of Romney's close friends, said: "I always hoped that Mitt Romney would be president, so I'm disappointed that, at least for now, it is not the avenue he is pursuing."

For now?

Asked to clarify, Leavitt said: "Who knows what could happen? I don't."

Romney knows he'll likely face the same question now that he did after 2012 — the skepticism over whether he's finally done. He addressed that in his conference call to supporters.

"I've been asked and will certainly be asked again if there are any circumstances whatsoever that might develop that could change my mind," he said. "That seems unlikely."

Romney went from a sure no in late 2012 to a maybe and then to an unlikely. In the immortal words of Lloyd Christmas from "Dumb and Dumber," "So you're telling me there's a chance."

Mitt Romney always saw his political career as an extension of his father's.

"Like a baton has passed, like a relay team where the baton passed from generation to generation," he said during his first presidential campaign. "I am a shadow of the real deal."

Republicans in Massachusetts, Michigan and Utah were ready for Romney to pass the baton to other members of the family shortly after his 2012 defeat.

When Obama named Sen. John Kerry secretary of state, Massachusetts had a Senate seat to fill. The state's Republicans tried to recruit former GOP Sen. Scott Brown. When he declined, party leaders turned to the Romneys. GOP leaders wanted to know if Ann was interested or maybe Tagg. Ann Romney never seriously considered it, but Tagg did, feeling the need to send out a statement when he decided to stay on the sidelines.

"I have been humbled by the outreach I received this weekend encouraging me to become a candidate for the U.S. Senate. I love my home state and admit it would be an honor to represent the citizens of our great Commonwealth," he wrote in February 2013. "However, I am currently committed to my business and to spending as much time as I can with my wife and children. The timing is not right for me, but I am hopeful that the people of Massachusetts will select someone of great integrity, vision and compassion as our next U.S. senator."

The state eventually elected Democratic Rep. Edward Markey, not exactly whom the Republicans had in mind.

In Michigan, the party encouraged G. Scott Romney, Mitt's older brother, to take a stab at replacing retiring Sen. Carl Levin. The 71-year-old lawyer thought it over, but, like Ann and Tagg, opted out.

"I'm happy with my life," he said.

Michigan Republicans picked Ronna Romney McDaniel, Mitt's niece, to lead the state party in early 2015.

The closest any of Romney's immediate family came to running for public office was the third son, Josh, who considered a bid in 2009 for lieutenant governor in Utah on a ticket led by Kirk Jowers, who had headed Mitt Romney's leadership PAC. The Jowers-Romney duo created a buzz in Beehive State political circles but never organized a formal run.

"In a lot of ways," Josh explained, "it wouldn't have been the right fit for me."

Ann Romney hasn't been shy about sharing her maternal wisdom on the topic of her family's political future.

"My advice to my sons has always been, don't get involved in politics," she said on Boston Herald Radio. "I think all of my boys right now are in a place where they have young children at home and they need to be at home and they need to be supporting their wives. There's a time and a place for everything. So that's always been my advice, 'Not now, guys.' Someday in the future, that would be fine."

Mitt Romney wants his family's next generation to approach potential political careers the way he and his father did.

"If one of our boys or our daughters-in-law finds themselves in a position where they could make a real contribution," he said, "and they are needed — school board, mayor, Congress, whatever — I'd expect them to stand up and volunteer."

The Romney sons obviously have talked about running for office, and they did so publicly, chatting in front of a New York Times reporter. In that conversation, the sons agreed that Tagg and Josh were the two most likely to go into politics. Their mother came to a similar conclusion, at least for her eldest son.

"I can see only one son obviously ever being involved, and that would be Tagg," Ann Romney said. "He's a great kid, very smart, very sensitive, very tender. He's a wonderful, wonderful husband and father to his six young kids."

Her focus on Tagg may be explained by the fact that she was talking to a Massachusetts audience in his home state, but there could be more to it.

Tagg is the mini-Mitt. When he went to Brigham Young University, he rented the same basement apartment his parents did 20 years earlier. He served a mission in France, went to Harvard business school and made a career in venture capital. It's not a big leap to say that he'll enter politics at some point — just like his dad.

Tagg managed his father's lieutenant-governor pick in 2002, and he left a job as marketing director for the Los Angeles Dodgers to be a full-time aide when Romney ran for president the first time. He was the only son on hand to see Mitt Romney announce his second presidential bid. Tagg and Ann were the only Romneys gung-ho about a 2012 run from the beginning, and they were the duo who pushed him to the brink of running again in 2016.

Whether he wants to make the jump into politics is one thing; whether he has a place to land is another. Massachusetts hasn't gotten any less liberal since his dad became governor there in 2003, and the Romney name has lost some of its sheen.

"He is in a tough position," said Josh Romney. "I think being a conservative in Massachusetts is not an easy thing to do."

Tagg Romney bought some land in Park City, though he has yet to build on it. If he decided to relocate his wife, Jennifer, and their six children to Utah, he would land in a conservative bastion where he instantly would be a top-tier prospect for any elected office.

His younger brother brushed off that suggestion quite abruptly. "He's not a Utah resident," said Josh Romney, in what easily could be seen as protecting his own home turf.

The only other Romney offspring in Utah is Ben, a medical doctor and the least political of the clan.

Ann Romney stood before 600 business and political leaders in downtown Salt Lake City to pitch her new cookbook in late 2013, giving her a chance to talk about her sons' political futures. She certainly did not give Josh the stamp of approval she had Tagg in Massachusetts.

The well-dressed attendees, packed into the grand ballroom at the Marriott Hotel, dined on Mitt Romney's favorite dish: meatloaf. Some loved it; the rest were polite enough not to say anything.

The featured speaker touched on her family life, her health and politics, and then said: "I forbid my children to run for political office."

The crowd laughed. But some in the audience thought they detected more than a joke, particularly when she recounted her family's trials during the presidential run.

"She said it with a lot of fervor," said one attendee. "Her tone of voice was pretty serious."

Josh Romney, who sat a few feet away, didn't react.

He had relished his time on the campaign trail, where he talked up his dad in rallies across the nation. But he hated being separated from his wife and now six children. He also laments a campaign system that seems fixated on insignificant details and gaffes instead of big issues. It's an argument he uses to contrast Barack Obama, the more engaging politician, with his father.

"The thing about politics, in my opinion, is that a lot of times the people we elect are usually the best politicians, but the best politicians don't make the best governors or legislators or whatever they are," Josh said. "I think we look at the wrong things as important. You know, reading a teleprompter speech is not necessarily as important as having the experience of having run something in an executive position."

Josh Romney got a taste of the attention political celebrities regularly receive on the night of Thanksgiving 2013. He was the first person on the scene of a dramatic car accident in a Salt Lake City suburb, where an SUV carrying a family of four plowed into a home, finally coming to a stop in the kitchen.

"I opened the car door and spoke with the four passengers inside the car. Miraculously, they appeared to have no major injuries," Romney said. "I was able to help each of them get out of the car and lift them to the ground.

"What I did to help the people involved in the accident is what anyone else would do who witnessed such a potentially dangerous situation."

But what he did next was something that would cause social-media followers to cringe. He tweeted out a picture of himself smiling next to the wrecked car. The reaction was predictable: He was scolded for turning a tragedy into self-promotion. TheWrap.com, a site that reports on Hollywood, did an "analysis" of Josh Romney's tweet, giving him high marks for saying that no one was hurt, but essentially calling the rest of it a "humblebrag."

"All in all, great job on the car rescue, so-so job on the tweeting."

Like Tagg, Josh runs his own business. Romney Ventures is a real-estate development firm focusing on properties in Utah. He also has kept a toe in state politics, endorsing Republican candidates and getting involved in a group seeking to move the homeless shelter in Salt Lake City.

The most telegenic of the Romney boys, Josh remains careful and consistent when he talks about politics. He said he would consider a run for office if the right opportunity appeared.

"I'm not ruling anything in or out," he said. "But, obviously, having spent the last couple of years on the political trail, it's hard to give all that up."

He wouldn't hint if he's leaning toward an executive role such as governor or mayor or maybe a House or Senate seat. And while not closing the door to anything, he made it sound like he won't be a candidate anytime soon.

"The thought of running for office doesn't sound very fun and even governing would be very hard, but the impact you could have as a good leader, the impact you could have for generations, that's what drives me," he said. "That's what makes me think I would be open to doing something, because I could have a positive impact on people's lives."

Jon Huntsman Jr. isn't the only member of his family who has expressed interest in a future run at public office.

"I don't think I'd be totally opposed to it, but it'd have to be the right time, the right place," said Abby Huntsman, the second-eldest daughter of Jon and Mary Kaye. "I've learned so much from this past campaign, I would hopefully know how to do things differently."

She said if she ever did run, it would be in Utah, though she now lives in New York. Her family, from Huntsman Sr. on down, has stressed public service, and she's listened.

"There's the saying, 'Where much is given, much is expected,' " she said.

"I think about that all the time. I have been given a lot. And if I can in turn serve and give back in some way because I've been given so much, I feel that's what I hope to do."

Her father would be supportive if she tried her hand at politics, saying: "Abby would, I think, be a very, very good candidate at some point."

Mary Anne, the oldest, is an accomplished pianist who performed at Carnegie Hall; Liddy, the youngest of the Jon2012Girls, wants a career in the fashion industry. Liddy also dabbles in politics on Twitter and co-hosted a radio show with then-Utah Democratic Party Chairman Jim Dabakis.

Liddy married Eduardo Hernandez in August 2014 and three weeks later gave birth to Harrison Huntsman Hernandez. The little guy is Jon Huntsman's first grandchild. He said he was excited, even if the new title gave him pause.

"It's great once you mentally get over the idea that you're a grandfather," Huntsman said, "which, you know, as a rock 'n' roller, took me a moment to kind of let that sink in."

Becoming a grandfather has changed his outlook. He started seeing life in "longer-term increments."

"What's around the bend? What the country will be like for that child? What educational opportunities, job opportunities, dating opportunities will be around? What risks will be there? You think about it all."

What is new for Huntsman has become old hat for Romney, who welcomed his 23rd grandchild in early 2015. But one thing Romney hasn't experienced is children joining the military.

Jon Huntsman III graduated from the Naval Academy and trained to be a pilot. His younger brother, Will, also attended Annapolis, where he played football and hopes to become a Navy SEAL. Huntsman Sr. talks with pride about these young men becoming the latest generation of Huntsmans to join the Navy.

At this point, though, Huntsman Jr. finds it hard to believe his sons would pick the national stage.

"The boys are about as nonpolitical as any two people I have ever met, but that kind of stuff comes out later," he said. "They're beginning careers in the military, and they are going to learn a whole lot about national defense and the intersection between politics and security."

It's the kind of experience that could set the course of someone's life, not unlike their father's religious mission to Taiwan. But his sons could find themselves in places far more hostile than a roach-infested Taipei apartment.

The chance that the two could see action overseas already worries their parents. They have tracked deaths in Afghanistan and other hot spots closely, nervously. But Jon Huntsman said he supports their military careers.

"I know it sounds old and tired but it is a great nation, and to keep it great, you got to reinvest," he said, "not just as a taxpayer but through service and sacrifice. That's a part of it, and I'm glad they are doing it."

Unless Jon III or Will shifts course, Abby Huntsman seems like the best bet for a future in politics, which could be years, if not decades, away. She hasn't yet hit 30.

For now, she's following her first love, TV news, a career that supplies her with a daily dose of politics.

After his primary defeat in 2008, Romney became a loyal surrogate for McCain. Huntsman didn't do that in 2012 for Romney, and neither did his suddenly famous daughters.

Abby Huntsman landed a job hosting HuffPost Live, a daily video segment on the left-leaning Huffington Post, in part because of her past TV experience and her Jon2012Girls media attention. It seemed a natural, given her charisma and smarts.

Abby had long wanted a TV career, having worked as a booker for "Good Morning America." Now she had a chance. At the same time, she acted as a personal assistant to her father.

Those two responsibilities collided on live TV in 2012, when she appeared on the now-defunct Current TV's "The War Room," a program hosted by former Michigan Gov. Jan Granholm. On this liberal network, with this liberal host, just three months from Election Day, Huntsman let slip that her father had been disinvited to a GOP event.

"I haven't told a lot of people this, I might get in trouble for saying this," she said, "but [Jon Huntsman] was supposed to speak at a fundraiser in Florida and the RNC contacted him and said, 'Because you are speaking out about the need for a third voice, you're no longer invited to represent us at the fundraiser.' In fact, he's actually been disinvited to a lot of events."

She said the Republican Party was one of "noninclusion" that has left people like her and her dad sidelined. Granholm invited Abby to join the Democrats.

Abby responded: "I will join you there. I will join you."

The conservative press pounced, and Abby Huntsman responded to The Daily Caller by email, saying it was just playful banter and that she wasn't leaving the Republican Party. She then threw in a dig at the current state of the GOP, with Mitt Romney at the forefront.

"I've always been a Republican, but like many Americans right now, I feel without a home this election cycle."

Abby Huntsman received a promotion when S.E. Cupp bounced from MSNBC to CNN for a reboot of "Crossfire" in the summer of 2013. The liberal network designated Huntsman as a Republican voice on its show, "The Cycle," geared to millennials. She's one of four young hosts who debate politics without the standard bluster and vitriol of most political talk shows.

She has used the platform to push a Huntsman brand of Republican politics, complete with occasional on-air visits with her pop. It has allowed her to explore her own political viewpoints, with self-described "rants" under the title "Abby's Road."

In one such bit, where she talks directly to the audience instead of her cohosts, Huntsman argued Republicans should court young entrepreneurs who have embraced disruptive business models that have taken off through social media, everything from ride-hailing companies such as Uber to the hotel alternative Airbnb.

These "Uber-tarians" dislike government intervention that stifles innovation, she said, and tend to support gay marriage and legalizing marijuana.

"Here is the real deal on Uber-tarians or, as I like to call them, the Reagan Democrats of the 21st century: They might not swing elections in four or even eight years from now, but the tidal wave continues to build," she said. "We Republicans would be smart to bring them into our tent."

In many ways, the Huntsman and Romney offspring grew up in parallel circumstances, coming of age in prominent political families with a shared faith. They lament that voters never saw their fathers the way they did.

"What is very similar is that we love our dads so much, and we just want the best for them and we also see the best in them," said Abby Huntsman. "I definitely saw that in the Romneys during the campaign, and I sort of connected over that."

Another unifying factor is that the Huntsmans and the Romneys have little patience for the GOP's far right. In one of Abby's rants on "The Cycle," she argued that throwing the tea party overboard would be a good way to start reviving the GOP. She directed her ire at Sen. Mike Lee, R-Utah, her dad's former general counsel in the governor's office and the architect behind the strategy that shut down the government in 2013. Her grandfather has called Lee "an embarrassment," while her father has spoken fondly of the conservative firebrand.

"I hear Mitt Romney's son Josh Romney has been looking for an opening to run for office in Utah," she said. "Challenging the not-so-popular Lee actually sounds like a pretty good opportunity."

Josh Romney saw the bit and — while he had nothing to say about Lee — he thanked Huntsman for the shoutout.

"It was very nice of her," he said. "Very kind."

These two barely know each other and have little of the shared history of their fathers. Still, that history matters. They may not be part of a dynasty on the level of the Kennedys and the Bushes, but, for Utah and Mormonism, the Romneys and the Huntsmans are the royal families. They have a shared lineage and an intertwining history that has spanned generations. Yet they are separate and distant. The icy feud between them has lasted almost a decade, but a thaw is always possible.

"I feel that if Mitt and I were to get together and sit in this room, we'd have a great conversation," Jon Huntsman said from his Atlantic Council office. Huntsman Sr. said he would consider donating to Romney if he ever did go through with a third presidential run. A close Romney confidant added: "It's not that they don't like each other, it's that they don't know each other that well."

It seems like a stretch to say that a lack of quality time is what led to this rivalry, which in some ways seemed inevitable.

"We have very ambitious people, very successful people and generally, when you get into the political arena, there is only one microphone and someone is going to vie for that microphone," said Fred Lampropoulos, a former Utah gubernatorial candidate who counts Huntsman Sr. and Romney as friends. "They didn't get there by accident. They got there because they were smart, and they were competitive."

That competition hit an apex in the 2012 Republican primaries, but if past is prologue, it may not end there. The Romneys and the Huntsmans are not done with politics.

Even if Mitt Romney continues to say no to a third presidential pursuit, two of his sons — Tagg and Josh — are heirs to the Romney brand, positioned and destined to be mentioned in just about every campaign cycle until they make the leap.

And Jon Huntsman has sought to keep all options available, whether that means joining a Democratic administration, running as an independent or taking a second shot at becoming the Republican standard-bearer. The only thing off the table is leaving the political stage.

It's far less clear that the next generation of Huntsmans will vie for public office, but don't say that to Jon Huntsman Sr. He fully expects some of his grandchildren to launch political campaigns and some to work for the family charities, continuing a legacy he began.

"I would hope our children and grandchildren and great-grandchildren would feel equally comfortable in public office or philanthropy," he said in an interview from his office overlooking Salt Lake City, his chair just feet away from a table crammed with photos of each of those Huntsmans. Prominent among them is one of Abby.

It's intriguing to think about a future when Abby Huntsman and Josh Romney square off in the latest iteration of this rivalry, particularly since both have so thoroughly absorbed their fathers' respective political sensibilities.

Josh, who is about 10 years older than Abby, doesn't envision that race and won't talk about hypotheticals. But Abby's game.

"That," she quipped, "is when things are going to get really ugly."

About the authors

Matt Canham and Thomas Burr are political reporters for The Salt Lake Tribune and close friends. They staffed the Washington, D.C., bureau together for seven years before Canham returned to Utah in 2014. They also collaborated (with Tribune reporter Robert Gehrke) on "Mia Love: The Rise, Stumble and Resurgence of the Next GOP Star," a book The Tribune published in November 2014.

Canham is an investigative reporter, who specializes in campaign coverage, money in politics and data analysis. He covered Jon Huntsman's first years as Utah's governor and assisted in the newspaper's coverage of the 2012 presidential race. He's a recipient of the National Press Club's Regional Reporting Award. A proud University of Utah alumnus, Canham joined The Tribune staff in 2002. He's lucky to have the love and support of his committed partner, Leah Bryner, and his family. He'd particularly like to thank his parents, Steve and Lisa Canham.

Burr is the Washington correspondent for The Tribune and covered Mitt Romney's two White House runs as well as Jon Huntsman's short-lived presidential campaign. A native Utahn, and Washingtonian since 2005, Burr is vice president of the National Press Club and a member of the Gridiron Club and Foundation and the White House Correspondents' Association. He is a three-time winner of the Press Club's Regional Reporting Award. He thanks his parents, Jim and Ann Burr, for their loving support.

Acknowledgments

Editor and Publisher Terry Orme and former Managing Editor Lisa Carricaburu supported this project from its inception. Politics Editor Dan Harrie, who has covered the Romneys and the Huntsmans during his stellar career, guided the writing and editing masterfully. Without him, this book never would have happened. Managing Editor Dave Noyce and copy editor Cathy Reese Newton thoroughly fact-checked and polished our work. Designer Amy Lewis created the cover and its photo illustration. Their contributions were invaluable.

Notes and sources

This book is based on dozens of interviews, on and off the record, as well as numerous books, newspaper articles, magazine pieces, TV news stories and a documentary. In particular, we would like to note the work of *The Boston Globe*, the go-to source on Mitt Romney's background. The sources below are listed in chronological order.

1. Introduction

"Doctor Bill Frist, king of the wild frontier": Tom Curry, "Sen. Frist gets a ribbing in his home state," NBC News, March 11, 2006

"This sucking up to": John Dickerson, "60 seconds over Memphis," Slate, March 13, 2006

"Every child in America": Curry, "Sen. Frist gets a ribbing in his home state," NBC News, March 11, 2006

"I say, if you're going": Ibid.

"Mitt, well done in Memphis!": Jon Huntsman Jr., handwritten note, Utah State Archives

"Your grandfather would be": Interview with Jon Huntsman Jr., 2014

"There were some angry calls": Jason Horowitz, "Presidential hopefuls Huntsman, Romney share Mormonism and belief in themselves," The Washington Post, March 4, 2011

"...a perfectly lubricated weather vane": Thomas Burr, "Democrats remind: Huntsman hasn't been fond of Romney," The Salt Lake Tribune, Jan. 16, 2014

"It's almost like they are": Interview with source, 2014

"There is a thing called": Nicholas Confessore, "At a Romney Retreat, Republicans Seek a Way Forward," The New York Times, June 14, 2014

Pratt was among the pioneers: Matthew J. Grow, "The Extraordinary Life of Parley P. Pratt," Ensign Magazine, April 2007

Eleanor, wife No. 12: Steven Pratt, "Eleanor McLean and the murder of Parley P. Pratt," BYU Studies, Winter 1975

"I am dying a martyr": Ibid.

As many as 50,000 descendants: Jared Pratt Family Association and GENi

2. The rise of the Romneys

Five framed portraits: Michael Kranish and Scott Helman, The Real Romney (The Boston Globe, HarperCollins Publishers, 2012), page 32

He packed up his belongings: Mitt Romney, Turnaround (Washington, D.C., Regnery Publishing, 2004), page 8

The elder Miles, then 71, fell to his death: Kranish and Helman, The Real Romney, page 41

"… against the arid terrain": Romney, Turnaround, page 8

"They were trying to build": Interview with Mitt Romney, "60 Minutes," CBS-TV, May 13, 2007

"… a mass of putrid pus": Carol Sletten and Eric Kramer, Story of the American West (Pinetop, Ariz.: Wolf Water Press, 2010)

"I now publicly declare": LDS President Wilford Woodruff, Official Declaration 1, Oct. 6, 1890

The fighting began when George was just 4 years old: Clark R. Mollenhoff, George Romney: Mormon in

Politics (New York, Meredith Press, 1968), page 24

"We fed potatoes": Ibid., page 31

"It was the worst period": Ibid.

Gaskell almost regained his fiscal: Ibid., page 32

"From that time on": Ibid., page 35

While he was away, President Calvin Coolidge: Ibid., page 39

She soon caught the eye of a talent scout: Kranish and Helman, The Real Romney, page 13

"...the best selling job": The Associated Press, Lansing bureau, Jan. 1, 1963

"I had no intention of staying in Hollywood": Ibid.

… smoothing out her husband's "rough edges": Mollenhoff, George Romney: Mormon in Politics, page 52

He called it "a compact 18": The Associated Press Biographical Service, Jan. 1, 1963

"He set his eyes": Lawrence McCracken, American Motors public-relations material, Oct. 27, 1954

"We consider it a blessing": Kranish and Helman, The Real Romney, page 14

"Cars 19 feet long": Mollenhoff, George Romney: Mormon in Politics, page 117

American Motors was making $60 million: "Fortune 500: A database of 50 years of FORTUNE's list of America's largest corporations," Fortune.com

Romney's annual salary rose to $250,000: The Associated Press Biographical Service, Jan. 1, 1969

"Should I run as a Republican": New England Cable News, Oct. 31, 2002

"My final step in making": "Romney Final Step: To Seek Guidance," New York Times Service, Feb. 8, 1962

"As a gubernatorial candidate": Mollenhoff, George Romney: Mormon in Politics, page 173

It was also Mitt's first turn: Ibid., page 174

"It's really fun to be here": Neil Swidey, "Lessons of the Father," The Boston Globe Magazine, Aug. 13, 2006

"That wasn't a great line": Ibid.

"I would introduce myself": Romney, Turnaround, page 12

"This business of trying to put": Mollenhoff, George Romney: Mormon in Politics, page 174

At one event, he told an overwhelmingly black audience: Ibid., page 186

"I'm a citizen who is a Republican": The Associated Press Biographical Service, Jan. 1, 1963

"Associates complain that the governor": Charles A. Ferry, "George Romney Gone Bust," The New Republic, Jan. 25, 1964

"… elimination of injustice": Mollenhoff, George Romney: Mormon in Politics, page 203

"If his views deviate": Ibid., page 214

"I would remind you that extremism": Barry Goldwater, remarks at the Republican National Convention, 1964

"You further state": Mollenhoff, George Romney: Mormon in Politics, page 227

"I cannot accept the blame": George Romney, published letter, The New York Times, Nov. 29, 1966

"I don't think you can bring the North Vietnamese": Mollenhoff, George Romney: Mormon in Politics, page 245

"I have fought for 25 years": Ibid., page 260-261

"While you were there, you probably swiped": Ibid., page 260-261

"I am sure the American people": Lyndon B. Johnson, televised remarks after authorizing use of force in Detroit, July 24, 1967

"I think the president": Mollenhoff, George Romney: Mormon in Politics, page 284

"The Negro people are": Douglas L. Parker, "Romney Opens S.L. Visit, Sees Racial Issue Critical," The Salt Lake Tribune, Aug. 23, 1967

Hot Seat transcript: Swidey, "Lessons of the Father," The Boston Globe Magazine, Aug. 13, 2006

"Governor Romney's statements this week": Mollenhoff, George Romney: Mormon in Politics, page 295

"It is clear to me": The Associated Press Biographical Service, June 1, 1969

"It was a mini-campaign": Ron Scott, "Romney Comes 'Home'... to 'Friends,' " The Salt Lake Tribune, Feb. 18, 1969

"George won't run, he'll let": Brady Dennis, "For Mitt Romney, Mom's failed run offers cautionary tale," The Washington Post, Feb. 24, 2012

"Never before has the voice": Ibid.

"If I had sufficient reason to believe": Clark Lobb, "George Romney Keeps Candidacy Door Ajar," The Salt Lake Tribune, July 3, 1973

"I have searched diligently and prayerfully": Frank Hewlett, "George Romney Out of Race — Fans Other Senate Aspirations," The Salt Lake Tribune, Sept. 28, 1973

3. Building the Huntsman empire

"In my own family": Jon Huntsman Jr., remarks at inauguration, Jan. 3, 2005

The Huntsman past includes a proud farmer: Elaine Justesen, Huntsman Heritage (self-published, 1991), page 46

In Independence, James Huntsman was arrested: Ibid., page 48

"... exterminated or driven from the state": Military order, Missouri Gov. Lilburn W. Boggs, Oct. 27, 1838

... a fort out of large stones: Jeff Lindgren, trail guide, "Old Fillmore Fort"

"What I really came to ask you is": Stella Day, Huntsman family biographer, information provided by the Territorial Statehouse in Fillmore

... a filthy-mouthed rebel: Justesen, Huntsman Heritage, page 101

Hannah and Doc, who: Interview with Knox Huntsman, 2013

"It was the greatest saloon": "Huntsman's Fillmore roots run deep," The Salt Lake Tribune, Jan. 17, 2005

The family demolished the saloon: Interview with Knox Huntsman, 2013

"I've been in and out of hot water since": "Huntsman Brothers Work as One," The Salt Lake Tribune, March 10, 1974

"I wouldn't tolerate": Interview with Knox Huntsman, 2013

"My dad never let her drive": Kevin King, "The heart of Huntsman," Beaumont Business Journal, February 2014

"It would have been child abuse today": Interview with Jon Huntsman Sr., 2014

"I loved working out in the potato field": Todd Kunz, "Jon Huntsman Sr. Speaks About Idaho Roots and Funding Fight Against Cancer," KIDK Local News 8, May 22, 2012

"Most of my life growing up": Interview with Jon Huntsman Sr., "Latter-Day Profiles," BYUTV, March, 4, 2010

"With my parents and two brothers": Jon M. Huntsman Sr., Winners Never Cheat (New Jersey, Prentice Hall 2005), page 161

"I had never done that": Interview with Jon Huntsman Sr., 2014

"I was 15 before": Jon M. Huntsman Sr., Barefoot to Billionaire (New York City, N.Y., Overlook Press, 2014), page 50

"I had been in the right place": Huntsman Sr., Winners Never Cheat, page 177-178

"Jon came from zip": Nina Easton, "The Huntsmans: Inside an American dynasty," Fortune Magazine, June 18, 2010

"... great respect and admiration": Interview with Jon Huntsman Sr., 2014

He took the little money he had: Ibid.

He called it Continental Dynamics: "Huntsman Brothers Work as One," The Salt Lake Tribune, March 10, 1974

"I was in over my head": Ibid.

"To leave a company you're with": Interview with Jon Huntsman Sr., Rick Shenkman, KUTV, March 1988

"You will be interested to know": Greg Burton, "Watergate-Era Utah Leaders Share Reflections," The Salt Lake Tribune, June 16, 2002

"Are you a full tithe payer": Interview with Jon Huntsman Sr., Timothy Naftali, The Richard Nixon Presidential Library and Museum, March 10, 2008

"… by far, the most difficult job": Interview with Jon Huntsman Sr., Martha Kumar, White House Interview Program, Feb. 25, 2000

"He was one of the men in my life": Interview with Jon Huntsman Sr., 2011

"How did we ever get that guy": Interview with Jon Huntsman Sr., Naftali, The Richard Nixon Presidential Library and Museum, March 10, 2008

"He sort of set himself up as the Mormons' man": Thomas O'Toole, "Former Special Aide to Nixon LDS 'Man in White House,' " The Washington Post, Aug. 19, 1973

"His handwriting, honestly, was terrible": Interview with Jon Huntsman Sr., Kumar, White House Interview Program, Feb. 25, 2000

"The door flew open": Ibid.

"… a terrorizing time in my life": Ibid.

"If there had been employment": Huntsman Sr., Winners Never Cheat, page 19-20

"His passing saved me": Huntsman Sr., Barefoot to Billionaire, page 118

"There was obviously a dark side": Interview with Jon Huntsman Sr., Kumar, White House Interview Program, Feb. 25, 2000

"I didn't take anything but fear out": Ibid.

By 1973, Huntsman's assets topped: O'Toole, The Washington Post, "Former Special Aide to Nixon LDS 'Man in White House,'" Aug. 19, 1973

He wrote a letter to the state's GOP: "GOP Businessman Declines Bid for 1980 Gubernatorial Race," The Salt Lake Tribune, June 1, 1979

"… the riverboat gambler": Christopher Levenick, "The Fearless Philanthropist," Philanthropy magazine, Summer 2012

… by 1990 his net worth exploded: "Three Utahns Make Forbes 400 List," The Salt Lake Tribune, Oct. 11, 1989

Huntsman's son James was about to: Mike Carter, "Police Foil Ransom of Millionaire's Kidnapped Son," The Salt Lake Tribune, Dec. 10, 1987

Clegg was also attending: Interview with Cal Clegg, 2014

"I have never been as nervous": Huntsman Sr., Barefoot to Billionaire, page 254-255

"I'm OK, Dad": Huntsman Sr., Barefoot to Billionaire, page 256

"I thought he had hit me": Interview with Grant Alan Jacobsen, 2013

"This is Al Jacobsen of the FBI": Ibid.

"James was just beside himself": Interview with Cal Clegg, 2014

"Our family is deeply grateful to the FBI": Carter, "Police Foil Ransom of Millionaire's Kidnapped Son," The Salt Lake Tribune, Dec. 10, 1987

Years later, upon reflection, he says that event: Interview with Jon Huntsman Jr., 2014

"It changes your lifestyle": Interview with Jon Huntsman Sr., 2014

"I'm willing to deal with the consequences": Chris Jorgensen, "S.L. Teen-Ager Gets 5 Years For Huntsman Kidnapping," The Salt Lake Tribune, July 11, 1990

The Utah Board of Pardons and Parole released Byrd: Interview with spokesman from Utah Board of Pardons and Parole, 2014

"I know that James wasn't involved in this": Interview with Cal Clegg, 2014

Early polls had Bangerter a whopping: J. Roy Bardsley, "Huntsman Widens His Lead Over Bangerter," The Salt Lake Tribune, April 10, 1988

"I guess running for governor": Paul Rolly, "Tycoon Plans to Give Bangerter Run for His Money," The Salt Lake Tribune, March 17, 1988

"For a riverboat gambler, it seemed": Interview with Jon Huntsman Jr., 2014

"I'm here as a gentleman": Interview with Jon Huntsman Sr., Shenkman, KUTV, April 1988

"I have made this decision after": Rolly, "Tycoon Plans to Give Bangerter Run for His Money," The Salt Lake Tribune, March 17, 1988

"It's a free country": Ibid.

The governor argued Huntsman's entry: Ibid.

The Utah Poll: Bardsley, "Huntsman Widens His Lead Over Bangerter," The Salt Lake Tribune, April 10, 1988

A poll by Dan Jones: Bob Bernick Jr., "Bangerter Upstaged by Huntsman, Who's Upstaged by Wilson," Deseret News, March 20, 1988

Jon Jr. and John Romney: "Huntsman Team Boast Big-Name Players," The Salt Lake Tribune, April 7, 1988

Joe Cannon, the head of Geneva Steel: Douglas L. Parker, "Huntsman Picking Up More Support," The Salt Lake Tribune, March 23, 1988

"Jon Huntsman has an almost": Bernick, "Bangerter Upstaged by Huntsman, Who's Upstaged by Wilson," Deseret News, March 20, 1988

"Who the hell is Huntsman?": Interview with Rick Shenkman, 2014

"We both read it. It wasn't kind": Interview with Jon Huntsman Jr., 2014

"I love my sister Ruby": Interview with Dean Olson, Rick Shenkman, KUTV, March 1988

"It was a matter of integrity": Ibid.

"I don't think anybody should": Ibid.

"He hasn't followed the line": Ibid.

"I have never been involved in a church court": Interview with Jon Huntsman Sr., 2014

"… conflict-resolution committee": Huntsman Sr., Barefoot to Billionaire, page 143

"I think his greatest weakness": Interview with Dean Olson, Shenkman, KUTV, March 1988

George Hatch, a well-known Democrat, owned KUTV: Interview with Rick Shenkman, 2014

"This is the type of questions and trickery": Interview with Jon Huntsman Sr., Shenkman, KUTV, March 1988

"Mr. Olson is in his 80s": Ibid.

"What Mr. Olson wants to say": Ibid.

"I have made mistakes": Ibid.

"No, Lillian, I'm very": Ibid.

"This is out there": Rick Shenkman during interview with Jon Huntsman Sr.

"If there is any church apostle": Interview with Jon Huntsman Sr., Shenkman, KUTV, March 1988

"I'll be around this community": Ibid.

On the day after the third story aired: Interview with Rick Shenkman, 2014

"My personal reaction was": Ibid.

"He called every day for almost a week": Interview with Pat Shea, 2014

"… discovered that, as a private citizen": Douglas L. Parker, "Huntsman Abandons Race, Heals Rift With Bangerter," The Salt Lake Tribune, April 14, 1988

"I didn't think so": Interview with Lillian Garrett, 2014

"There were some pretty outlandish": McKay Coppins, "Huntsman's Big Daddy," The Daily Beast, June 28, 2011

"They weren't pleasant": Interview with Jon Huntsman Jr., 2014

"I'd been in the Nixon White House": Interview with Jon Huntsman Sr., 2014

"I never met anyone who is as mean-spirited": Ibid.

"I said, 'Thank you, Dean …' ": Ibid.

"From this day forward, I will work": Parker, "Huntsman Abandons Race, Heals Rift With Bangerter," The Salt Lake Tribune, April 14, 1988

Jon Huntsman Jr. told reporters at the time: Michael White, The Associated Press, Aug. 17, 1988

"We have gone through many interesting things": Paul Rolly, "Huntsman Vows to Deal with Prostate Cancer," The Salt Lake Tribune, Nov. 30, 1991

"Our prayers are with Mr. Huntsman": Mike Gorrell, "Huntsman Donates Millions to Needy on Eve of Surgery," The Salt Lake Tribune, Jan. 7, 1992

"Dad thought it would be nice": Dawn House, "Cancer Surgery Goes Well for Huntsman," The Salt Lake Tribune, Jan. 8, 1992

The surgery succeeded, though: Huntsman Sr., Barefoot to Billionaire, page 298

"I was terrified the whole time.": Levenick, "The Fearless Philanthropist," Philanthropy magazine, Summer 2012

"We both have had prostate cancer": Peter Scarlet, "A Memorable Meeting: Huntsman Visits Pope," The Salt Lake Tribune, May 22, 1993

"… greatest honors of my life": Interview with Jon Huntsman Sr., 2014

"I had to explain to Mr. Huntsman": Interview with Randy Dryer, 2010

"I am an emotional": Huntsman Sr., Barefoot to Billionaire, page 15

"I'm not supposed to say anything": Kirsten Stewart, "Huntsman Cancer Institute begins work on $105 million research wing," The Salt Lake Tribune, June 6, 2014

"My suggestion was to give 80 percent": Paul Sullivan, "Jon Huntsman Sr.'s Early Calling to Philanthropy," The New York Times, Nov. 1, 2013

"I am certain the genesis": Huntsman Sr., Barefoot to Billionaire, page 12

4. The rebel and the honor student

"He was your typical, gawky, tall": Marisa Schultz, "How Metro Detroit helped shape Mitt Romney," The Detroit News, Feb. 2, 2012

"That's not a car": Jason Horowitz, "Mitt Romney's prep school classmates recall pranks, but also troubling incidents," The Washington Post, May 10, 2012

"… no George Romney": Jonathan Cohn, "Parent Trap," The New Republic, July 2, 2007

"I had the impression that Mitt": Ibid.

"I just remember being like a deer": Horowitz, "Mitt Romney's prep school classmates recall pranks, but also troubling incidents," The Washington Post, May 10, 2012

"It wasn't a very funny joke": Schultz, "How Metro Detroit helped shape Mitt Romney," The Detroit News, Feb. 2, 2012

"He was just easy pickin's": Horowitz, "Mitt Romney's prep school classmates recall pranks, but also troubling incidents," The Washington Post, May 10, 2012

"If you should ever by chance": Ibid.

"He got an ovation like I never heard": Cohn, "Parent Trap," The New Republic, July 2, 2007

When young Romney had his appendix out: "Romney's Son OK Following Surgery," The Detroit News, May 18, 1965

Reporters wrote about the $2,000 he raised: Associated Press, appeared in The Detroit News, Oct. 29, 1964

"Romney Son Helps Fight School Fire": "Romney Son Helps Fight School Fire," The Detroit News, Feb. 23, 1965

"Things were so innocent": Horowitz, "Mitt Romney's prep school classmates recall pranks, but also troubling incidents," The Washington Post, May 10, 2012

"He dated a lot of my friends": Schultz, "How Metro Detroit helped shape Mitt Romney," The Detroit News, Feb. 2, 2012

"Chaperone rules were tightened": Ann Romney, The Romney Family Table (Salt Lake City, Shadow Mountain, 2013), page 39

"Friends will also shape your future": "Romney's Advice Caps Day for Son," The Detroit News, June 13, 1965

For the most part, he followed: Schultz, "How Metro Detroit helped shape Mitt Romney," The Detroit News, Feb. 2, 2012

"He didn't want his parents to know": Jack Thomas, "Ann Romney's Sweetheart Deal," The Boston Globe, Oct. 20, 1994

George Romney implored some of his son's: Kranish and Helmen, The Real Romney, page 58

He held a sign that said "Speak out, Don't sit in": Jason M. Breslow, "Artifact Two: Mitt Romney Protesting the Protesters," "Frontline," PBS, Sept. 17, 2012

Romney had no real fear of going to Vietnam: Kranish and Helmen, The Real Romney, page 61

Within weeks, she had decided she: Ibid., page 71

"Why even last Sat. night": Jason M. Breslow, "Artifact 12: Letters From Romney's Mission to France," "Frontline," PBS, Oct. 3, 2012

"As you can imagine, it's quite": Lawrence Wright, "Lives of the Saints," The New Yorker, Jan. 21, 2002

"This makes two converts here": Breslow, "Artifact 12: Letters From Romney's Mission to France," "Frontline," PBS Oct. 3, 2012

"Your gal looked lovely as always": Ibid.

"The rest of our system I know pretty well": Ibid.

"Your mother and I are not personally distressed": Thomas Burr, ' Romney's road to nomination began with father's aspiration," The Salt Lake Tribune, Aug. 24, 2012

"It happened so quickly that": Kranish and Helmen, The Real Romney, page 80

When the police arrived at the bloody scene: Romney, Turnaround, page 39

"He probably came within a hair": Kranish and Helmen, The Real Romney, page 82

While Romney's injuries were serious: "Governor's Son Hurt in Fatal Crash," UPI appearing in The Detroit News, June 17, 1968

"It was a very difficult and heart-wrenching experience": Kranish and Helmen, The Real Romney, page 83

"He became really, really distraught": Ibid., page 87

"He had served well, but like": R.B. Scott, Mitt Romney: An Inside Look at the Man and His Politics (Guilford, Conn., Globe Pequot Press, 2011), page 21

"I said yes without a second thought": "5 Things You Don't Know About Ann Romney," ABC News, Oct. 1, 2013

Miss Cleo said the couple "will be very happy": Eleanor Breitmeyer, The Detroit News, March 19, 1969

"… the picture of a very happy": Eleanor Breitmeyer, "Mitt Romney marries his boyhood sweetheart," The Detroit News, March 22, 1969

"We met exactly four years ago tonight": Ibid.

… one-bedroom basement apartment that cost them $62.50: "5 Things You Don't Know About Ann Romney," ABC News, Oct. 1, 2013

… a light blue Rambler sports car: Breitmeyer, "Mitt Romney marries his boyhood sweetheart," The Detroit News, March 22, 1969

At the same time, they used a fold-down: "5 Things You Don't Know About Ann Romney," ABC News, Oct. 1, 2013

"Even though they came from pretty": Interview with Alan Layton, 2014

"He was the smartest guy I knew": Ibid.

"I pray that this graduating class": Ben Bradlee Jr., "Romney seeks new chapter in success," The Boston Globe, Aug. 7, 1994

Three years later, Bain & Co. recruited him: Philip Rucker, "1984 Bain Capital money photo captured Romney on eve of major success," The Washington Post, June 19, 2012

"I always wondered about Mitt": Kranish and Helmen, The Real Romney, page 137

In a speech at BYU, Romney put it in terms of faith: Peggy Fletcher Stack, "Mormons Have Reared Titans in Business," The Salt Lake Tribune, July 13, 1996

"Mitt was often away": Romney, The Romney Family Table, page 10

"You can gripe and gripe": Bradlee, "Romney seeks new chapter in success," The Boston Globe, Aug. 7, 1994

"I kept asking myself": Romney, Turnaround, page 14

"I aspired, and though I achieved not": Burr, "Romney's road to nomination began with father's aspiration," The Salt Lake Tribune, Aug. 24, 2012

"Mitt's more like my mother": Swidey, "Lessons of the Father," The Boston Globe Magazine, Aug. 13, 2006

"I really believe the reason": Schultz, "How Metro Detroit helped shape Mitt Romney," The Detroit News, Feb. 2, 2012

"I thought he ought to get": Ibid.

"We recognized that there was no way": Romney, Turnaround, page 14

Romney preferred the term "socially innovative": "Kennedy Has Tough Opponent," P-I News Services, 1994

… "the living symbol of the family flaws": "Sobering Times," Newsweek, Dec. 8, 1991

"I recognize my own shortcomings": Curtis Wilkie, "Kennedy Admits Personal 'Faults' in Speech, Vows to 'Continue to Fight the Good Fight' for Liberal Causes," The Boston Globe, Oct. 26, 1991

"I will not embarrass you": Bradlee, "Romney seeks new chapter in success," The Boston Globe, Aug. 7, 1994

"He's better than a chip": Hugh McDiarmid, "Ex-Governor Basks in Son's Strong Bid," Detroit Free Press, Oct. 7, 1994

"Everything could always be tweaked": Kranish and Helmen, The Real Romney, page 5

Another aide said he had difficulty: Ibid., page 110

"Mitt is naturally a diplomat": Swidey, "Lessons of the Father," The Boston Globe Magazine, Aug. 13, 2006

"Look, I was an independent during": Louis Jacobson, "Mitt Romney once distanced himself from Ronald Reagan, but no longer," PolitiFact, May 17, 2012

"I was getting ready for this guy": Kranish and Helmen, The Real Romney, page 169

"He's not pro-choice, he's not anti-choice": Jonathan Cohn, "Parent Trap," The New Republic, July 2, 2007

"Where is Mr. Romney on those issues": Scot Lehigh, "Kennedy Believes Mormon-Racial Questions Proper," The Boston Globe, Sept. 27, 1994

He pulled over and wept with joy: Interview with Mitt Romney, "Meet the Press," NBC News, Dec. 16, 2007

"I do not speak for my church": Scot Lehigh and Frank Phillips, "Romney Hits Kennedy on Faith Issue," The Boston Globe, Sept. 28, 1994

"It is absolutely wrong": Ibid.

"All my life I've been guided": Ben Bradlee Jr. and Daniel Golden, "Strategies Shaped an Epic Race," The Boston Globe, Nov. 10, 1994

"We have a long tradition in our": Bradlee, "Romney seeks new chapter in success," The Boston Globe, Aug. 7, 1994

"He said that was part of the church": Ibid.

"The truth is, he's an incredibly": Ibid.

"I certainly can't say it could not": Scot Lehigh and Frank Phillips, "Romney admits advice against abortion," The Boston Globe, Oct. 20, 1994

"The loss felt worse than we": Romney, Turnaround, page 15

Lenore knew something was wrong: Kranish and Helmen, The Real Romney, page 197

"We hugged each other": Ibid., page 202

"It just didn't make sense to me": "Mitt," directed by Greg Whiteley (2014, Los Gatos, Ca., Netflix)

"I frankly would have rather died": Paula Parrish, "Mitt Romney Embraces Challenges, and This Might Be His Biggest," Scripps Howard News Service, Feb. 4, 2002

"Riding exhilarated me": Annie Eldridge, "Dressage Makes Ann Romney's Soul Sing," Chronicle of the Horse, Jan. 3, 2008

"She called me at the office": Romney, Turnaround, page 5

"You could walk around freely": Interview with Jon Huntsman Jr., 2011

More than anything, Huntsman remembers: Interview with Jon Huntsman Jr., 2014

"I thought George Romney was": Ibid.

"We were always kicked in the fanny": Ibid.

He relished those visits, going so far: Ibid.

"One thing that came to mind": Ibid.

"It was a shift. In Los Angeles": Ibid.

"I'm not going to say in isolation": Ibid.

"Everybody knew who the Huntsmans were": Scott Horsley, "Before Politics, Huntsman Aspired to Rock Star Fame," NPR, Oct. 12, 2011

"If you didn't know Jon was Jon": Ibid.

"In my late teens, you wouldn't": Jon Huntsman Jr., commencement address, University of South Carolina, May 7, 2011

"We might as well be moving to China": Interview with Mary Kaye Huntsman, 2014

"I'd never been to Utah": Tom Haraldsen, "Mary Kaye Huntsman: Instilling the power within," The Davis Clipper, April 30, 2005

"I was dating somebody else": Interview with Jon Huntsman Jr., 2014

"She had reminded me of": Ibid.

"We were best friends with a spark": Interview with Mary Kaye Huntsman, 2014

On their first outing, Huntsman picked Cooper: Ibid.

"Jon's easygoing personality": Yearbook, Highland High School, Salt Lake City, Utah, 1976-1977

After emerging from the outhouse: Interview with Jon Huntsman Jr., 2014

His chief rival, Kenneth Hadlock, didn't: Interview with Kenneth Hadlock, 2014

"... probably the most prestigious": Interview with Jon Huntsman Jr., 2014

"He was sort of depressed": Ben Smith and Kasie Hunt, "Huntsman, the rock 'n' roll years," Politico, April 4, 2011

"It's kind of like": Interview with Jon Huntsman Jr., 2014

"When Jon came on board": Smith and Hunt, "Huntsman, the rock 'n' roll years," Politico, April 4, 2011

"I always thought he was going": Interview with Howard Sharp, 2011

"In many young people": Interview with Jon Huntsman Sr., 2011

"It was the nicest equipment": Interview with Eric Malmquist, 2011

"I think he liked to fly underneath": Thomas Burr, "Huntsman's journey: From high school dropout to presidential hopeful," The Salt Lake Tribune, June 27, 2011

"Very few straddled in between": Smith and Hunt, "Huntsman, the rock 'n' roll years," Politico, April 4, 2011

"I think Jon probably — like most teenagers": Burr, "Huntsman's journey: From high school dropout to presidential hopeful," The Salt Lake Tribune, June 27, 2011

"We rolled in the ugliest green": Huntsman Jr., commencement address, University of South Carolina, May 7, 2011

"We'd play Eric Clapton's 'Cocaine' ": Horsley, "Before Politics, Huntsman Aspired to Rock Star Fame," NPR, Oct. 12, 2011

"Oh, he thought he was going": Melinda Henneberger, "Jon Huntsman: Why Democrats Fear Potential GOP Candidate," Time magazine, May 12, 2011

"He learned his first lesson": Burr, "Huntsman's journey: From high school dropout to presidential hopeful," The Salt Lake Tribune, June 27, 2011

"That's why I went into medicine": Dan Harrie, "The Ambassador," The Salt Lake Tribune, Oct. 24, 2004

"... never regret following": Huntsman Jr., commencement address, University of Southern California, May 7, 2011

"It was a momentary teenage desire": Burr, "Huntsman's journey: From high school dropout to presidential hopeful," The Salt Lake Tribune, June 27, 2011

"It's clear he really wanted": Horsley, "Before Politics, Huntsman Aspired to Rock Star Fame," NPR, Oct. 12, 2011

"I grew up right toward the end": Ben Leubsdorf, "For Huntsman, travel opened doors," Concord Monitor, Aug. 20, 2011

"We talked about if the band": Sheryl Gay Stolberg, "Huntsman Runs on His Name, and His Father's," The New York Times, Aug. 7, 2011

"That, for me, was an eye-opening": Interview with Jon Huntsman Jr., 2014

"… cockroach-infested dives": Jacob Weisberg, "Jon Huntsman: The Outsider," Vogue, Aug. 18, 2011

"There were no organized classes": Interview with Jon Huntsman Jr., Foreign Affairs Oral History Project, The Association for Diplomatic Studies and Training, Feb. 25, 1994

"I got to Taiwan and wondered": Weisberg, "Jon Huntsman: The Outsider," Vogue, Aug. 18, 2011

"… knocking on a lot of inhospitable doors": Interview with Jon Huntsman Jr., 2014

"It was so colorful. It was so complex": Ibid.

"We were there on God's errand": Leubsdorf, "For Huntsman, travel opened doors," Concord Monitor, Aug. 20, 2011

"He was very sharp back then": Ibid.

"… an opportunity to discover your strengths": Ibid.

"You get to see your own country": Weisberg, "Jon Huntsman: The Outsider," Vogue, Aug. 18, 2011

"I said, 'I hope you told him to come back' ": Interview with Mary Kaye Huntsman, 2014

"It was a pretty quick conversation": Interview with Jon Huntsman Jr., 2014

"It's a way of life": Interview with Mary Kaye Huntsman, 2014

"I didn't feel I needed to": Ibid.

"He asked if I was willing": Thomas Burr, "Huntsman and son: namesake and role model," The Salt Lake Tribune, July 5, 2011

"There's nothing more exciting": "White House Advance Man Follows Dad's Footsteps," The Salt Lake Tribune, Sept. 19, 1983

"Thanks for being such a good friend": Interview with Jon and Mary Kaye Huntsman, BrideAccess.com, Jan. 19, 2009

"I was so baffled": Interview with Mary Kaye Huntsman, 2014

"I said, 'You didn't ask me' ": Interview of Jon and Mary Kaye Huntsman, BrideAccess.com, Jan. 19, 2009

"… the awkward romantic encounter": Interview with Jon Huntsman Jr., 2014

"I didn't know what to get you": Interview with Mary Kaye Huntsman, 2014

"I hope you're ready for": Interview with Jon Huntsman Jr., 2011

"The way it happened so abruptly": Interview with a Sigma Chi member, 2014

"He's probably a Sigma Chi": Interview with a Sigma Chi member, 2014

"I just didn't want to hang around": Interview with Jon Huntsman Jr., 2014

"… there were things going on": Ibid.

"I don't recall that I had": Interview with Jon Huntsman Sr., 2014

"This was a real chance to build": Interview with Jon Huntsman Jr., Foreign Affairs Oral History Project, The Association for Diplomatic Studies and Training, Feb. 25, 1994

"I remember sitting in Art Hummel's": Ibid.

"… excellent grades": Interview with Jon Huntsman Sr., 2011

… his "political guru": Harrie, "The Ambassador," The Salt Lake Tribune, Oct. 24, 2004

"You know I'm very proud": Ibid.

"I thought that was maybe a career": Interview with Jon Huntsman Jr., 2014

A relative called Huntsman's secretary: Ibid.

"He doesn't take no for an answer": Stolberg, "Huntsman Runs on His Name, and His Father's," The New York Times, Aug. 7, 2011

"Competent, capable and hardworking": Ibid.

"I was of the opinion that": Interview with Jon Huntsman Jr., Foreign Affairs Oral History Project, The Association for Diplomatic Studies and Training, Feb. 25, 1994

"I'm keeping all the options open": "Huntsman Jr. Could Trade Commerce Job for Politics," The Associated Press printed in The Salt Lake Tribune, July 10, 1991

"I thought that this was silly": Interview with Jon Huntsman Jr., Foreign Affairs Oral History Project, The Association for Diplomatic Studies and Training, Feb. 25, 1994

"I don't think there's much question": Stolberg, "Huntsman Runs on His Name, and His Father's," The New York Times, Aug. 7, 2011

"Our families have been very close": Ibid.

"He called me into his office": Interview with Jon Huntsman Jr., Foreign Affairs Oral History Project, The Association for Diplomatic Studies and Training, Feb. 25, 1994

"'Please don't hold age against me'": Ibid.

"I was fearful that they were": Ibid.

"He is very street smart": Interview with Pat Shea, 2014

"He is young, but he's had": Lee Davidson, "Huntsman Jr. Wins Over Demo Senate Questioner," Deseret News, July 23, 1992

"I have some concerns about": Ibid.

"That's not a large amount really": Ibid.

"Even though I do not": Ibid.

"I was staggered": Harrie, "The Ambassador," The Salt Lake Tribune, Oct. 24, 2004

"Jake personally called me": Davidson, "Huntsman Jr. Wins Over Demo Senate Questioner," Deseret News, July 23, 1992

"My dad was just so happy": Interview with Abby Huntsman, 2014

"When I reflect back on that": Ibid.

"I've always kind of used his life": Harrie, "The Ambassador," The Salt Lake Tribune, Oct. 24, 2004

5. The Games begin

… Toilet of the West!: Kirk Johnson, "Tarnished Gold: a special report; From an Innocent Bid to Olympic Scandal," The New York Times, March 11, 1999

"It shows you how unsophisticated": Ibid.

"We'd have been horrified if we won": John Keahey, "Utah's Long Road to Olympics Started With a Craving for Tourist Dollars," The Salt Lake Tribune, June 4, 1995

"What are you going to do": Ibid.

"'When we arrived there, the Greeks'": Johnson, "Tarnished Gold: a special report; From an Innocent Bid to Olympic Scandal," The New York Times, March 11, 1999

"Everyone was giving wonderful gifts": Ibid.

The night before the vote, Jean-Jacques Ganga: Ibid.

"Some may say that this is a blessing": John Keahey and Jack Fenton, "IOC Foils Utah Olympic Bid," The Salt Lake Tribune, June 16, 1991

"He could tell us their favorite toothpaste": Dan Egan, "Once Best and Brightest, Is Johnson a Falling Star?," The Salt Lake Tribune, Jan. 9, 1999

Ganga received medical treatment for hepatitis: Mike Gorrell, "Olympic Bid Run Amok: It Was Long in the Making," The Salt Lake Tribune, Jan. 10, 1999

The largesse to these two men: Mike Gorrell, "IOC Official: Games Are for Sale," The Salt Lake Tribune, Dec. 13, 1998

"Where's my check?": Johnson, "Tarnished Gold: a special report; From an Innocent Bid to Olympic Scandal," The New York Times, March 11, 1999

"You didn't have to be a brain surgeon": Ibid.

"If you are part of this family": Linda Fantin and Rebecca Walsh, "Scandal Began in Birmingham," The Salt Lake Tribune, Jan. 31, 1999

Beyond cash payments, Welch and Johnson: Greg Burton, "SLOC Gifts May Make Some Blush," The Salt Lake Tribune, Sept. 30, 2000

"What I am saying is not popular": Paul Rolly, "Huntsman: Olympics May Do More Harm Than Good," The Salt Lake Tribune, Sept. 8, 1994

"To say we no longer need the Olympics": John Keahey, "Bid Official: Olympics Won't Save Economy," The Salt Lake Tribune, Nov. 30, 1994

"This process put a great deal": Gordon Monson, "Road to 2002 Gold Was Long and Personally Wrenching," The Salt Lake Tribune, June 25, 1995

"We are comfortable with the fact": John Keahey, "Heat's On, But Utahns Play It Cool While Warming Up to the IOC," The Salt Lake Tribune, June 14, 1995

"There's nothing like coming home": Katherine Kapos, "Olympic Team Brings Home the Gold," The Salt Lake Tribune, June 18, 1995

Alma told Officer David Rowley: Mike Gorrell, "Olympics Chief Investigated Over Domestic Incident," The Salt Lake Tribune, July 18, 1997

"I have concluded that the costs": Mike Gorrell, "Welch's 2002 Olympic Reign Ends," The Salt Lake Tribune, July 30, 1997

Alma said he "made the right decision": Ibid.

"I have been encouraged to look": Mike Gorrell, "Is Search for Olympic Boss Over?," The Salt Lake Tribune, Aug. 24, 1997

... to see Joklik's "little heart burst": Linda Fantin and Rebecca Walsh, "Welch's Secretary Supplied Memo That Started Bid Scandal," The Salt Lake Tribune, Dec. 11, 2001

"This is the letter Olympic folks": Alicia C. Shepard, "An Olympian Scandal," American Journalism Review, April 1999

"Under the current budget structure": Mike Gorrell, "Panel Paid Tuition for IOC Voter's Relative," The Salt Lake Tribune, Nov. 26, 1998

"Sonia never would have had": Ibid.

"... looks like, walks like and quacks like a bribe": Mike Gorrell, "Bribery Accusations Are Unfair, S.L. Olympic Officials Say," The Salt Lake Tribune, Dec. 6, 1998

"You know how important the Cameroon": Ibid.

"Certainly, it's a bribe": Mike Gorrell, "IOC to Investigate Olympic Payments," The Salt Lake Tribune, Dec. 11, 1998

Reporters identified men marketing: Gorrell, "IOC Official: Games Are for Sale," The Salt Lake Tribune, Dec. 13, 1998

"Everything was done by Tom Welch": Ibid.

"Salt Lake City was the victim": Mike Gorrell, "Olympic Scandal Details Unfold," The Salt Lake Tribune, Dec. 15, 1998

"I would say it is a sad day": Bob Mims, "S.L. Bid Process was 'Out of Control,' Huntsman Says," The Salt Lake Tribune, Dec. 18, 1998

"... absolutely clear that the actions": Mike Gorrell, "Joklik hopes his sacrifice will push Games forward," The Salt Lake Tribune, Jan. 9, 1999

"... a systematic cover-up": Mike Gorrell, "Olympic Bid Run Amok: It Was Long in the Making," The Salt Lake Tribune, Jan. 10, 1999

"Our mission statement was": Egan, "Once Best and Brightest, Is Johnson a Falling Star?," The Salt Lake Tribune, Jan. 9, 1999

"I'd been in her home": Mike Gorrell, "Welch Says Board Had Access to All Dealings," The Salt Lake Tribune, Jan. 11, 1999

"You support your friends": Ibid.

"You can come in and be the hero": Linda Fantin, "SLOC Official to Unveil Plan to Find New Leader," The Salt Lake Tribune, Jan. 22, 1999

"… someone with an understanding of Utah": Ibid.

"Oh, honey, it's not": Interview with Alan Layton, 2014

"Everything about Tom seemed made": Romney, Turnaround, page 4

"There seemed to be an implied association": Ibid., page 4

"He grilled me for about two hours": Interview with Mitt Romney, 2014

"We just didn't see Jon Jr.": Interview with a SLOC board member, 2014

"They just were not sure": Interview with a SLOC board member, 2014

"I had to call and explain that": Romney, Turnaround, page 19

"He would be a tremendous choice": Mike Gorrell, "Romney Is Considered as New SLOC Boss," The Salt Lake Tribune, Feb. 3, 1999

"When I first heard his name": Linda Fantin, "Leavitt Discusses SLOC Top Job With BYU-Graduate Mitt Romney," The Salt Lake Tribune, Feb. 5, 1999

"I can pull Utah": Huntsman Sr., Barefoot to Billionaire, page 330

"I nearly choked on": Ibid.

"… who could stand on the international stage": Terry Gildea, "Utah's Olympic Legacy: The Impact of the 2002 Winter Games. Part Four: The Making of Mitt Romney," KUER, Feb. 15, 2012

"The first thing I needed": Romney, Turnaround, page 27

"When Alan came in to see me": Ibid., page 33

"It was an emotional day for me": Interview with Alan Layton, 2014

"We cannot change history": Kirk Johnson and Jo Thomas, "Olympics; Salt Lake Panel Enacts Changes as It Tries to Chart a 'New Beginning,' " The New York Times, Feb. 12, 1999

"Where were you when I needed you?": Romney, Turnaround, page 34

"… the highest levels of ethical conduct": Johnson and Thomas, "Olympics; Salt Lake Panel Enacts Changes as It Tries to Chart a 'New Beginning,' " The New York Times, Feb. 12, 1999

"The Olympics is about sport": Linda Fantin, "New SLOC Boss Motivated By Olympic Tradition of Toil," The Salt Lake Tribune, Feb. 12, 1999

"I would expect any of you": Philip Hersh, "Utah Olympic Panel Clings To Traditional Social Order," Chicago Tribune, Feb. 12, 1999

The only real criticism came: Paul Rolly and JoAnn Jacobsen-Wells, "Huntsman Sr. Sees Another Olympic Sham," The Salt Lake Tribune, Feb. 12, 1999

"We were pretty much faxed": Interview with Jon Huntsman Jr., 2014

"He was pretty bent out of shape": Stolberg, "Huntsman Runs on His Name, and His Father's," The New York Times, Aug. 7, 2011

"I told him to screw off": Interview with Jon Huntsman Jr., 2014

"I wasn't that good of a": Ibid.

"I had no plans to parlay": Romney, Turnaround, page 19

Rick Reed, who had advised Romney: Kranish and Helmen, The Real Romney, page 206

"It was serendipitous": Ibid.

"It's hard to say what is going": Glen Warchol, "This Is the Place, But Politics May Lead Romneys Elsewhere," The Salt Lake Tribune, Feb. 14, 1999

"You can't look out over the valley": Brandon Loomis, "New Envision Utah Boss, Jon Huntsman Jr., Sees Growth as State's Most Pressing Issue," The Salt Lake Tribune, April 10, 1999

"This is one of the greatest exercises": Ibid.

"It was heartbreaking": Doug Robinson, "Greatest gift: Adoption like a fairytale for the Huntsmans," Deseret News, Dec. 26, 2004

Huntsman weighed the offer: Paul Rolly and JoAnn Jacobsen-Wells, "Huntsman Urged to Run Against Cook," The Salt Lake Tribune, March 15, 2000

"It was a quick and unhappy encounter": Interview with Jon Huntsman Jr., 2014

"I was in my worst state": Interview with Ann Romney, Shauna Lake, "Person 2 Person," KUTV, Dec. 1, 2013

"There have been studies shown": "Mitt," directed by Greg Whiteley

"MS has been my best teacher": Interview with Ann Romney, Lake, "Person 2 Person," KUTV, Dec. 1, 2013

"He loves emergencies and catastrophes": John Powers, "Hub's Romney takes on Salt Lake City Games," The Boston Globe, Feb. 12, 1999

"We were in a psychological zombie-land": Jo-Ann Barnas, "Romney Gives His All to Games," Detroit Free Press, Feb. 14, 2011

"The tsunami of financial, banking, legal": Romney, Turnaround, page 52

"It was a mess in a public-relations": Amy Shipley, "10 years after Salt Lake City Olympics, questions about Romney's contributions," The Washington Post, Feb. 12, 2012

"If this doesn't work": Kranish and Helmen, The Real Romney, page 207

"I think he took it because": John Powers, "Golden Opportunity," The Boston Globe Magazine, Feb. 3, 2002

... if he was "completely nuts": Romney, Turnaround, page 192-193

"His first day in Utah, he called": Kranish and Helmen, The Real Romney, page 218

"SLOC would have credibility": Romney, Turnaround, page 176

"... caught in a combination of cronyism": Linda Fantin, "Huntsman Blasts Oly Fund Raising," The Salt Lake Tribune, July 11, 1999

"The governor has to make his position": Ibid.

"He's politically driven. He's probably": Ibid.

"The world needs public-spirited citizens": Ibid.

"Who could possibly measure up": Ibid.

"Clearly, when you have a state": Ibid.

"I pressed my view that our": Romney, Turnaround, page 273

"Many citizens are not excited": Mike Gorrell, "Huntsman Changes Course, Supports Games," The Salt Lake Tribune, July 17, 1999

"And I made a mistake in judgment": Ibid.

"I am touched by his sentiments": Ibid.

"We didn't want to do it.": Linda Fantin and Rebecca Walsh, "Gateway Plaza Poised to Become Salt Lake City's Olympic Keepsake," The Salt Lake Tribune, Jan. 21, 2002

"As nice and philanthropic as": Mike Gorrell, "Park Would Honor Oly Donors, Volunteers," The Salt Lake Tribune, Jan. 5, 2000

"... would send the wrong message": Matt LaPlante, "The Myth of Mitt," Salt Lake Magazine, April 19, 2012

"Mitt called and said he thought": Kranish and Helmen, The Real Romney, page 215

"It strains credulity to believe": Linda Fantin, "So Why Is This Guy Smiling?," The Salt Lake Tribune, Aug. 13, 2000

"Several times during the history": Linda Fantin, "Olympic bribery case dismissed," The Salt Lake Tribune, Dec. 5, 2003

"How I regret that you": Ibid.

"The legal process is not for": Ibid.

"Of course, not being convicted of a crime": Romney, Turnaround, page 23

"Mitt Romney, as far as I know": Kranish and Helmen, The Real Romney, page 216

"It didn't smell like burning jet fuel": Romney, Turnaround, page 302

"Mitt wondered inwardly": Powers, "Golden Opportunity," The Boston Globe Magazine, Feb. 3, 2002

"As a testament to the courage": Romney, Turnaround, page 304

"In the annals of Olympism": Ibid., page 305

"What the Olympic Games, supposedly": Sen. John McCain, remarks on Senate floor, Sept. 19, 2000

"He told me that he believed it": Romney, Turnaround, page 309

"It's been much more somber": Powers, "Golden Opportunity," The Boston Globe Magazine, Feb. 3, 2002

"That was so much fun": Joe Baird, "It's Here," The Salt Lake Tribune, Feb. 8, 2002

"It was an amazing thing": Shira Schoenberg, "Trail No Obstacle for Ann Romney," The Boston Globe, Sept. 22, 2011

"It was a more emotional moment": Romney, Turnaround, page 346

"I expressed my frustration": Ibid., page 365

"Who the f--- are you and": Michael Vigh, "Officer Reports Romney Apologized for Outburst," The Salt Lake Tribune, March 6, 2002

"I have not used that word since": Kranish and Helmen, The Real Romney, page 219

"There were a lot of people": Ibid., page 219

"I have no doubt whatsoever": Ibid., page 213

"I'm not saying other people": Shipley, "10 years after Salt Lake City Olympics, questions about Romney's contributions," The Washington Post, Feb. 12, 2012

"I never thought there was a time": LaPlante, "The Myth of Mitt," Salt Lake Magazine, April 19, 2012

"Any well-trained chimpanzee could": Peter Henderson, "Special report: Mitt Romney's thrill of victory at the Olympics," Reuters, Nov. 22, 2011

"What's offensive to me is he": Shipley, "10 years after Salt Lake City Olympics, questions about Romney's contributions," The Washington Post, Feb. 12, 2012

"Mitt's objective was to look": Kranish and Helmen, The Real Romney, page 216

"It's tough to prove a negative": Henderson, "Special report: Mitt Romney's thrill of victory at the Olympics," Reuters, Nov. 22, 2011

6. Capitol gains

"I have to be honest": Linda Fantin, "SLOC Boss May Seek Utah Office," The Salt Lake Tribune, July 4, 2001

Fined $1,250 for using: Brian Mooney, "Taking office, remaining an outsider," The Boston Globe, June 29, 2007

"I know you're really busy now": Ibid.

"… getting a lot of pressure": Mike Gorrell, "All Eyes on Romney," The Salt Lake Tribune, Feb. 4, 2002

His advisers rented out a big hotel ballroom: Kranish and Helmen, The Real Romney, page 225

"It's obvious to anyone what the": Pam Belluck, "In Massachusetts, Governor Steps Aside for a Juggernaut," The New York Times, March 20, 2002

"Lest there be any doubt, I'm in": Mooney, "Taking office, remaining an outsider," The Boston Globe, June 29, 2007

"I learned in my race against Sen. Kennedy": New England Cable News, Oct. 31, 2002

"I have to tell you, I'm really": Dan Harrie, "Ambiguity May Tarnish Romney's Rising Star," The Salt Lake Tribune, March 31, 2002

… gushing that his "too-perfect Ken doll": "50 Most Beautiful People, Mitt Romney: Politician," People magazine, May 13, 2002

"Nothing embarrasses Mitt more": Ibid.

"His looks": Harrie, "Ambiguity May Tarnish Romney's Rising Star," The Salt Lake Tribune, March 31, 2002

"The Olympic-size challenge that we face": Ibid.

"I respect what he's done": Ibid.

"Mitt has always been consistent": Dan Harrie, "Romney on Abortion: New State, New Stand?," The Salt Lake Tribune, July 11, 2001

"That upset him to be characterized": Ibid.

"I make an unequivocal answer: yes": Interview with Mitt Romney, WBZ-TV, Boston, 2002

"The truth is, no candidate": Mitt Romney, questionnaire, National Abortion Rights Action League, April 8, 2002

"At a very young age, my parents": Mitt Romney, questionnaire, Bay Windows, 2002

"Any effort to try to remove": Frank Phillips and Rick Klein, "Democrats File to Halt Romney Bid," The Boston Globe, June 8, 2002

"He never asked for it": Jim Woolf, "When Is a House a Home? Taxing Dilemma for Mitt," The Salt Lake Tribune, June 6, 2002

The Deseret News fought the request: Elizabeth Neff, "Deseret News Reporter Signs Affidavit on Residency Issue," The Salt Lake Tribune, June 18, 2002

"I don't know": Ibid.

"It would not surprise me that": Ibid.

"I've lived, voted, raised a family": Pam Belluck, "Massachusetts man, Mitt insists to board," New York Times News Service, June 18, 2002

"… a lot of sound and fury signifying nothing": Ibid.

"… credible in all respects": Filing, Massachusetts State Ballot Law Commission, June 25, 2002

"I wasn't a particularly good": Mitt Romney, No Apology (New York City, St. Martin's Press, 2010), page 267

"Massachusetts doesn't need a": Frank Phillips, "It's O'Brien for Democrats," The Boston Globe, Sept. 18, 2002

"… as disgraceful as it is inaccurate": Mooney, "Taking office, remaining an outsider," The Boston Globe, June 29, 2007

"It was the Ted Kennedy punch": Ibid.

"We need to do a better job": Christopher Smith, "The Utah Factor," The Salt Lake Tribune, Nov. 4, 2002

"The most familiar usage of that term": Pam Belluck, "Tight and Heated Race Rages in Massachusetts," The New York Times, Nov. 2, 2002

Romney's 10-point disadvantage: Frank Phillips, "Poll Finds Romney and O'Brien in Dead Heat," The Boston Globe, Nov. 1, 2002

"We took on an entrenched machine": Frank Phillips, "Romney Sails to Victory," The Boston Globe, Nov. 6, 2002

"We are facing a financial emergency": Mitt Romney, remarks at inauguration, Jan. 2, 2003

"The spirit of Massachusetts is": Ibid.

"My usual approach": Kranish and Helmen, The Real Romney, page 236

"Here is a person who": Ibid.

"The Legislature had really killed": transcript, State House News Service, July 17, 2003

"It was very irritating to lawmakers": Michael Barbaro, "Legislators Recall Governor Who Didn't Mingle," The New York Times, March 9, 2012

"Mitt Romney is not a schmoozer": Ibid.

"His theory of government was": Kranish and Helmen, The Real Romney, page 242

"He forced all of us to bring": David Weber, "Democrats Take Sole Control of Statehouse as Romney Leaves Office," The Associated Press, Jan. 4, 2007

"I wanted to change the environment": Mooney, "Taking office, remaining an outsider," The Boston Globe, June 29, 2007

"They were trying to change": Jerry Markon and Alice Crites, "As governor, Mitt Romney backtracked on promised reforms in appointing judges," The Washington Post, May 30, 2012

"… San Francisco east": Peter Wallsten, "Activists Remember a Different Romney," Los Angeles Times, March 25, 2007

"There was, a long time ago": Christopher Smith, "GOP gay-wed bill gets Hatch's support," The Salt Lake Tribune, June 23, 2004

"My daughters sat me down": Leubsdorf, "For Huntsman, travel opened doors," Concord Monitor, Aug. 20, 2011

"My first and foremost priority is": Christopher Smith, "Huntsman Resigns as Trade Rep," The Salt Lake Tribune, March 29, 2003

"…a fresh look at things": Dan Harrie, "Huntsman Jr. joins race," The Salt Lake Tribune, Sept. 11, 2003

"I can't look my kids": Ibid.

"Nothing ventured, nothing gained": Ibid.

"He had 94 percent name ID": Stolberg, "Huntsman Runs on His Name, and His Father's," The New York Times, Aug. 7, 2011

"If we can't raise money": Harrie, "Huntsman Jr. joins race," The Salt Lake Tribune, Sept. 11, 2003

"We certainly had a lot more": Dan Harrie, "Silver spooner or dishwasher?," The Salt Lake Tribune, April 29, 2004

"We weren't born into a family": Harrie, "The Ambassador," The Salt Lake Tribune, Oct. 24, 2004

"I bounce ideas and thoughts": Ibid.

"There is a place for a tailored": Harrie, "Huntsman Jr. joins race," The Salt Lake Tribune, Sept. 11, 2003

"It is hard to fight against Grandma": Interview with former Huntsman aide, 2014

"… shackles of incumbency": Dan Harrie, "Walker's in, the race is on," The Salt Lake Tribune, March 7, 2004

"I'd like Mr. Huntsman to tell us": Interview with Fred Lampropoulos, 2013

"Jon was upset at that": Ibid.

" 'You know, Fred, we have great' ": Ibid.

Then, on an April day loaded: Paul Rolly and JoAnn Jacobsen-Wells, "Candidate a man about town(s)," The Salt Lake Tribune, April 21, 2004

"This represents a significant": Dan Harrie, "Herbert's rural ties bolster Huntsman ticket," The Salt Lake Tribune, April 21, 2004

Lampropoulos' campaign responded: Paul Rolly and JoAnn Jacobsen-Wells, "Workers hope 'bonus' sends a message to the Legislature," The Salt Lake Tribune, April 23, 2004

"The big risk for me was": Dan Harrie, "Karras takes chance with Greene party ticket," The Salt Lake Tribune, April 25, 2004

"She is very well respected": Ibid.

"I don't have the advantages": Dan Harrie, "Karras puts emphasis on his financial know-how," The Salt Lake Tribune, April 30, 2004

"It's my money and this is America": Dan Harrie, "GOP spend like drunken sailors in race for governor," The Salt Lake Tribune, May 4, 2004

"We knew we were surging": Dan Harrie, "Walker KO'd," The Salt Lake Tribune, May 9, 2004

"Congratulations, I knew I picked": Dan Harrie, "Huntsman, Karras begin to spar, probe for soft spots," The Salt Lake Tribune, May 14, 2004

"There are a lot of extremely": Rebecca Walsh, "Walker: Controversy over vetoes, and her moderate stands, played a part in her ouster from the race," The Salt Lake Tribune, May 9, 2004

"They got rid of a woman": Rebecca Walsh, "GOP outcome is no tilt to the right," The Salt Lake Tribune, May 11, 2004

"It produced two candidates": Ibid.

"I don't think there's any": Harrie, "Huntsman, Karras begin to spar, probe for soft spots," The Salt Lake Tribune, May 14, 2004

"Just tell Jon Sr. to be": Dan Harrie, "Mud flies in GOP primary contest," The Salt Lake Tribune, May 21, 2004

Foxley, who denies any connection: Interview with Doug Foxley, 2014

"The threat against my family": Harrie, "Mud flies in GOP primary contest," The Salt Lake Tribune, May 21, 2004

"I could have wrung Spencer's neck": Interview with Nolan Karras, 2013

"He renounces the statement": Harrie, "Mud flies in GOP primary contest," The Salt Lake Tribune, May 21, 2004

"I'm embarrassed by this": Ibid.

"It served a very useful": Dan Harrie, "Huntsman, Karras lay out visions," The Salt Lake Tribune, May 31, 2004

"I've been at the highest levels": Interview with Nolan Karras, 2013

"Voters are going to look": Dan Harrie, "Matheson says it's a horse race," The Salt Lake Tribune, June 24, 2004

"Well, what makes me tick?": Dan Harrie, "The Academic: Matheson is thoughtful, deliberate, detail-driven," The Salt Lake Tribune, Oct. 24, 2004

"... people with mutual economic interests": Rebecca Walsh, "Huntsman proposes new partner rights," The Salt Lake Tribune, Aug. 25, 2004

"Taking shots, that was just": Interview with Mike Zuhl, 2013

"He taught me the importance": Peggy Fletcher Stack, "Eldest Elder Loves Life — Pure & Simple Elder Embraces Life with a Tender Touch," The Salt Lake Tribune, Sept. 30, 1995

"Philanthropist. Chemical plant owner": Judy Fahys, Rebecca Walsh and Dan Harrie, "Huntsman paradox: Cancer claims vs. cancer research," The Salt Lake Tribune, Aug. 8, 2013

"I really don't kind of blame": Ibid.

"... humbled by your support": Dan Harrie, "Utah's top office stays Republican," The Salt Lake Tribune, Nov. 3, 2004

"He put his personal reputation": Raphael Lewis, "GOP Falls Short in State," The Boston Globe, Nov. 3, 2004

7. From friends to foes

"Being a Republican governor": Jason Bergreen, "Romney wows GOP in a return to SLC," The Salt Lake Tribune, Feb. 26, 2005

"America cannot continue": Ibid.

"He is principled. He is brilliant": Ibid.

"It is not uncommon for people": Huntsman Sr., Winners Never Cheat, page 73

"Over the years": Ibid.

"I've told [Romney] that I'd": Bob Bernick Jr. and Lisa Riley Roche, "Huntsman gets behind Romney bid," Deseret News, May 25, 2005

"I'll do whatever I can": Ibid.

"We had conversations": Interview with Jon Huntsman Jr., 2014

"I stand before you with": Jon Huntsman Jr, remarks at inauguration, Jan. 3, 2005

"My father, one of the great": Ibid.

"I turned them down": Interview with Jon Huntsman Jr., 2014

"My whole family tree": Tom Harvey, "Huntsman's Fillmore roots run deep," The Salt Lake Tribune, Jan. 17, 2005

A few weeks later, Chaffetz: "Governor's chief of staff on leave," The Salt Lake Tribune, July 8, 2005

The office announced Chaffetz: Rebecca Walsh and Matt Canham, "Right hand waves guv goodbye," The Salt Lake Tribune, Oct. 11, 2005

"We have always had": Ibid.

"Everyone expected Kennedy to": Kranish and Helmen, The Real Romney, page 271

"No more free riding": Scott S. Greenberger, "Romney Eyes Penalties for Those Lacking Insurance," The Boston Globe, June 22, 2005

"Romney knew his best": Kranish and Helmen, The Real Romney, page 272

"… the plane is circling": Ibid., page 273

"How often does the governor": Ibid.

"He did everything he could": Ibid.

"Today, Massachusetts has": Scott Helman, "Mass. Bill Requires Health Insurance," The Boston Globe, April 4, 2006

"This is a politician's dream": Mitt Romney, signing of Massachusetts health-care bill, C-SPAN video, 2006

"It's law!": Ibid.

"I have to admit that I'm": Kranish and Helmen, The Real Romney, page 277

"I don't know if what": Brian C. Mooney, Stephanie Ebbert and Scott Helman, "Ambitious goals; shifting stances," The Boston Globe, June 30, 2007

"As long as the symbol": Brian C. Mooney, " 'RomneyCare' — a revolution that basically worked," The Boston Globe, June 26, 2011

"It's almost as though he": Kranish and Helmen, The Real Romney, page 259

You don't need to decide: Interview with Bob Bennett, 2014

"I didn't know if I": Kranish and Helmen, The Real Romney, page 252

"For a great job of": Scott Helman, "A Breakfast Best Served Cold," The Boston Globe, March 20, 2006

"I thought he gave up": Danny Hakim, "As Massachusetts Governor, Romney Was Often Away," The New York Times, Oct. 13, 2012

"Democrats who are carping": Ibid.

"I think there's really": Molly Ball, "Was Mitt Romney a Good Governor?," The Atlantic, May 31, 2012

"The one mistake I think": Rebecca Walsh, "Huntsman hopes hardball works second time around," The Salt Lake Tribune, March 12, 2006

"I'm just a simple dweeb": Rebecca Walsh, "Tax cut faded as chaos hit session," The Salt Lake Tribune, March 5, 2006

Huntsman was one of three: Matthew D. LaPlante, "Guv greets Utahns on Iraq tour," The Salt Lake Tribune, March 26, 2006

"We must win in Iraq": Rebecca Walsh, "McCain's cross-country trip stops in Utah," The Salt Lake Tribune, May 14, 2006

"He knew it was going": Interview with a Huntsman aide, 2014

"He just assumed": Interview with Jon Huntsman Jr., 2014

"If Mitt had really involved": Interview with a Huntsman aide, 2014

"… share common viewpoints": Thomas Burr, "Utah governor throws support to McCain for president," The Salt Lake Tribune, July 19, 2006

"Not even a phone call": Interview with a Huntsman aide, 2014

8. Making the leap

"He was basically never here": Thomas Burr, "Romney unpopular as he leaves governor's post," The Salt Lake Tribune, Jan. 15, 2007

Before the first phone call: Suzanne Struglinski, "Romney overwhelmed by $6.5 million in trial fundraiser," Deseret Morning News, Jan. 9, 2007

"You guys today are my hope": Thomas Burr, "Romney raises millions to explore presidential bid," The Salt Lake Tribune, Jan. 8, 2007

"This is an exciting day": Ibid.

"It's not a hard sale": Thomas Burr, "Mitt rakes in dough, proves his political viability," The Salt Lake Tribune, Jan. 9, 2007

"We're excited about what he's doing:" Struglinski, "Romney overwhelmed by $6.5 million in trial fundraiser," Deseret Morning News, Jan. 9, 2007

"I don't like the influence of money": Isabel Lopez, "Romney in 1994: 'I'd abolish PACs… I don't like them," Rachel Maddow Show, MSNBC, Aug. 7, 2012

"… akin to a nightmare": Kranish and Helmen, The Real Romney, page 289

"It is time for innovation and transformation": Thomas Burr, "It's official: Romney is a candidate," The Salt Lake Tribune, Feb. 14, 2007

"My dad is my life hero": Steve LeBlanc, "Romney's life is his father's legacy," Associated Press in USA Today, Nov. 4, 2007

"If people really get to know": Michael Luo, "The Romney-Rockwell video," The New York Times, June 29, 2007

"I don't think you have a choice": Ibid.

"We felt like McCain's not that guy": Interview with former senior Romney aide, 2013

"At the beginning of the campaign": Dan Balz and Haynes Johnson, The Battle for America (New York City, Viking Adult, 2008), page 239

Democrats wanted in on the action, too: Thomas Burr, "Romney facing more fire than other GOP hopefuls," The Salt Lake Tribune, Jan. 28, 2007

Jon Huntsman Sr. was a big help: Linda Fantin, "Romney appears reconciled to cash politics," The Salt Lake Tribune, March 5, 2007

"It's time to take government": Kathryn Jean Lopez, "The Turnaround," National Review, March 2, 2007

Of the 1,705 votes: Tom Hamburger, "Conservative activists choose Romney in straw poll," Los Angeles Times, March 3, 2007

"Change begins in Iowa": Adam Nagourney and Jeff Zeleny, "Romney Wins Iowa Straw Poll by a Sizable Margin," The New York Times, Aug. 12, 2007

Ames did produce one surprise: Thomas Beaumont and Jennifer Jacobs, "Romney wins Iowa straw poll, Huckabee second," The Des Moines Register, Aug. 13, 2007

Mid-2007 saw a mass exodus: Jonathan Martin and Mike Allen, "McCain drain: Inside the implosion," Politico, July 10, 2007

"Sen. John Edwards": Jay Leno, "Laugh Lines: Jay Leno, David Letterman and Conan O'Brien," The New York Times, July 15, 2007

Weaver, an ever-present political pro: BuzzFeed staff, "Meet the man behind Jon Huntsman's failed presidential bid," BuzzFeed, Jan. 16, 2012

"We had a spending problem": Geoffrey Gray, "Off the bus," New York Magazine, July 13, 2007

"He's not dead yet": Interview with Beth Myers, Campaigning for President: The Managers Look at 2008," John F. Kennedy School of Government, (Boston, Harvard University, 2009), page 65

"Be the last man standing": Balz and Johnson, The Battle for America, page 261

"The key is, we don't": transcript, Republican debate, University of New Hampshire, Sept. 5, 2007

"I thought that was a pretty good line": Ibid.

Romney called Huckabee's: Scott Conroy, "Romney: Huckabee's Press Conference Was 'Confusing' To Iowans," CBS News, Dec. 31, 2007

"Now it's your turn to kick his butt": Balz and Johnson, The Battle for America, page 280

"Wow, you guys are crazy": Michael Levenson, "Romney returns, shifts focus to N.H.," The Boston Globe, Jan. 4, 2008

It was gold and said, "Winner": Ibid.

"Had I been a Baptist minister": Thomas Burr, "Romney attributes Iowa loss to faith," The Salt Lake Tribune, Jan. 5, 2008

"You know, Governor, don't": Transcript, ABC News/Facebook/WMUR debate, Jan. 5, 2008

His aides sent out talking points: Alex Gage, "The path to victory," memo, Romney for President, Jan. 9, 2008

"I don't know about the": Mitt Romney, remarks to the Detroit Economic Club, Jan. 14, 2008

"The people of Nevada": Nancy Cook, "Romney Wins GOP Caucuses in Nevada," NPR, Jan. 19, 2008

"With the nature of the challenges": Josh Hafenbrack, "Republicans blitz Florida," Florida Sun-Sentinel, Jan. 22, 2008

Huntsman played the good soldier: Thomas Burr, "Huntsman: My fellow guv Palin will 'raise a little hell,' " The Salt Lake Tribune, Sept. 5, 2008

9. A diplomat in China

A Salt Lake Tribune poll showed him with 78 percent: Robert Gehrke, "Huntsman's 2nd term goals: Health care reform, ending food sales tax," The Salt Lake Tribune, March 12, 2008

At his monthly news conference in April: Gov. Jon Huntsman Jr. and Utah reporters, transcript, KUED, April 2008

"Anyone with a pulse": Gov. Jon Huntsman Jr. and Utah reporters, transcript, KUED, August 2008

"I'm in the best position already": Ibid.

Huntsman, Bader assured Obama: Thomas Burr, "Utah guv answers presidential call," The Salt Lake Tribune, May 16, 2009

"I apologize for wasting your time": Mark Halperin and John Heilemann, Double Down: Game Change 2012 (New York City, Penguin Press, 2013), page 147

"This is something that was very tough for him": Thomas Burr, "Utah guv answers presidential call," The Salt Lake Tribune, May 16, 2009

"Are you sitting down": Interview with Jon Huntsman Jr., 2014

"The lieutenant governor doesn't": Robert Gehrke, "Huntsman to accept ambassadorship to China," The Salt Lake Tribune, May 15, 2009

"I grew up understanding the most basic responsibility": Burr, "Utah guv answers presidential call," The Salt Lake Tribune, May 16, 2009

"I hope the good people of Utah": Ibid.

"I am grateful for the graciousness": Jonathan Strong, "Jon Huntsman's love letters," The Daily Caller, April 15, 2011

"Ambassador to Singapore": Interview with Utah Republican, 2013

"When you leave": Burr, "Utah guv answers presidential call," The Salt Lake Tribune, May 16, 2009

"It is not necessarily a fun place": Interview with former Huntsman aide, 2013

"[Mary Kaye] couldn't just": Ibid.

"We could still wander around": Interview with Abby Huntsman, 2014

"It was also a memorable": Ibid.

… an "effective" team player: Thomas Burr, "White House: Huntsman 'effective' ambassador until campaign rumors," The Salt Lake Tribune, July 31, 2011

"As one observer and": Press briefing by White House Press Secretary Robert Gibbs and Ambassador to China Jon Huntsman, transcript, Nov. 17, 2009

"I've got to say some of the reporting": Christopher Bodeen, "U.S. envoy criticizes coverage of Obama's China visit," The Associated Press, Nov. 20, 2009

The Chinese even had their own name: Cai Hong, "Obama names Utah governor as China envoy," China Daily, May 15, 2009

"I can tell you that": Interview with Jon Huntsman Jr., Erin Burnett, CNBC, May 27, 2010

"… worked really well as part of a team": Burr, "White House: Huntsman 'effective' ambassador until campaign rumors," The Salt Lake Tribune, July 31, 2011

"You know, I'm really focused": McKay Coppins, "The Manchurian Candidate," Newsweek, Jan. 1, 2011

"It swirled out of control": Interview with former senior Huntsman aide, 2013

"You guys don't know me": Thomas Burr, "Huntsman at China rally by accident," The Salt Lake Tribune, April 29, 2011

"There wasn't a split": Burr, "White House: Huntsman 'effective' ambassador until campaign rumors," The Salt Lake Tribune, July 31, 2011

A different type of coordination was going on: Interview with former senior Huntsman aides

"I couldn't be happier": Jeff Zeleny, "Envoy to China to resign, weighing '12 G.O.P. bid," The New York Times, Jan. 31, 2011

"I'm a little biased towards": Thomas Burr, "Obama on Huntsman: 'Love that guy,' " The Salt Lake Tribune, March 13, 2011

"My buddy": President Barack Obama, remarks at the White House Correspondents' Dinner, transcript, May 1, 2011

"There's a vicious rumor floating around": Ibid.

10. Late to the party

"He had really good answers": Interview with former senior Huntsman adviser, 2013

"I was maybe living in naive land": Interview with Jon Huntsman Jr., 2014

"Thank you all for an interest in our cause": Ibid.

"I can't do that": Ibid.

"I thought [Romney] had compromised himself": Ibid.

"I thought there had been that": Ibid.

"We thought we had a winning candidate": Interview with former senior Huntsman aide, 2013

Before Huntsman stepped off the plane: Utah Election Office records, accessed 2013

"This is a paperwork step": Jonathan Martin, "Jon Huntsman takes step toward 2012 bid," Politico, May 4, 2011

"Give back -- as much as you're able": Thomas Burr, "Huntsman to grads: 'Give back,'" The Salt Lake Tribune, June 21, 2011

"The way I saw it": Ibid.

"I've met him once in my life": Thomas Burr, "GOP presidential hopefuls: So who is this Huntsman guy?" The Salt Lake Tribune, June 6, 2011

"I've certainly heard": Ibid.

"I don't know him well": Ibid.

"We literally realized a couple days out": Interview with former senior Huntsman aide, 2013

"I worked for the president of the United States": Suzan Clarke, "Transcript: Exclusive interview with Jon Huntsman," ABC News, May 20, 2011

"That was probably the highest moment": Interview with former senior Huntsman aide, 2013

"I will say my dad, up until that point": Interview with Abby Huntsman, 2014

"I was very surprised. I didn't see it coming": Interview with former senior Huntsman adviser, 2013

"I had enough of a feel of the marketplace": Interview with Jon Huntsman Jr., 2014

"Dear Mr. President:" Jonathan Strong, "Jon Huntsman's love letters," The Daily Caller, April 15, 2011

"I must report that Sec.": Ibid.

There were more questions about Huntsman's record: Travis Waldron, "Report: Jon Huntsman's secret life as a progressive," Think Progress, May 19, 2011

"Until we put a value on carbon": Ibid.

He felt so burned by the former governor: Patrick M. Byrne, "Backed Huntsman once, but never again," Politico, Aug. 4, 2011

"Well, first of all, I don't change": Suzan Clarke, "Transcript: Exclusive interview with Jon Huntsman," ABC News, May 20, 2011

Romney's announcement: John DiStaso, "Romney makes it official, says Obama 'has failed America,' " The Union Leader, June 2, 2011

"At the time, we didn't know": Ibid.

"I had no choice": Interview with Jon Huntsman Jr., 2014

"Mr. Huntsman is trying something different": Neil King, "The making of Brand Huntsman," The Wall Street Journal, July 16, 2011

"Guys! We're about to start this live-shot": Alex Klein, "Riding the Huntsman bus to nowhere," The New Republic, June 22, 2011

"A father couldn't ask for a better birthday gift": Thomas Burr, "Jon Huntsman Jr. launches 2012 presidential bid," The Salt Lake Tribune, June 22, 2011

"Today, I'm a candidate": Ibid.

Not that many Americans saw it: Sean P. Means, "Huntsman's speech longer than cable TV's attention," The Salt Lake Tribune, June 21, 2011

"I was furious": Interview with Jon Huntsman Jr., 2014

"If the Titanic is sinking": Interview with former senior Huntsman adviser, 2014

"It was an annoyance": Interview with former senior Romney aide, 2013

11. The Mormon question

"I don't like coming on the air": Katie Glueck, "Mitt Romney Mormon video goes viral," Politico, Nov. 5, 2012

"Nobody was more surprised": Interview with Jan Mickelson, The American Review, Aug. 11, 2007

"We have to own this": Interview with Matt Rhoades, 2013

"I'm not changing my religion": Kranish and Helman, The Real Romney, page 281

The first Mormon to run for president: Richard D. Poll, "Joseph Smith and the Presidency, 1844," Dialogue: A Journal of Mormon Thoughts, 1969

"We have had Democratic": Ibid.

"Can't we get on to something else": Andrew J. Glass, "Romney Declares Mormon Doctrine on Priesthood 'Not Racist,' " The Washington Post, May 4, 1967

"But I have been raised": Ibid.

"People don't understand": "Racist position denial," UPI, May 4, 1967

Romney, on his initial trip: Jules Witcover, The making of an ink-stained wretch: Half a century pounding the political beat (Baltimore, Johns Hopkins University Press, 2005), pages 86-87

The Romneys were seated on the dais: McKay Coppins, "When George Romney Invited the Press to Church," BuzzFeed, July 3, 2012

… Romney denied he'd said such a thing: Hugh Hewitt, A Mormon in the White House (Washington, D.C., Regnery Publishing, 2007), page 24

The greatest crisis facing the nation: Steve Bouser, "Both Romney and McCarthy Fight Loser Image in State," Janesville Daily Gazette, Jan. 22, 1968

"One of them was not": Hewitt, A Mormon in the White House, page 43

Udall took stout liberal positions: Richard Severo, "Morris K. Udall, Fiercely Liberal Congressman, Dies at 76," The New York Times, Dec. 14, 1998

But Coleman Young: Mark Shields, "Missing and needing Mo Udall," Creator's Syndicate, Dec. 22, 1998

Even though Udall had broken: Lee Davidson, "LDS faith has been obstacle for string of presidential candidates," The Salt Lake Tribune, June 2, 2011

"I'm a one-eyed Mormon from conservative Arizona": Ibid.

"If I had a revelation": John Heilprin, "Did Hatch Allude to LDS Prophecy," The Salt Lake Tribune, Nov. 11, 1999

"They tolerate everything that's": Interview with Sen. Orrin Hatch, "The Doug Wright Show," KSL, Nov. 9, 1999

A Hatch spokeswoman later clarified: Heilprin, "Did Hatch Allude to LDS Prophecy?" The Salt Lake Tribune, Nov. 11, 1999

"Not in Iowa": John Heilprin, "In Iowa, Latecomer Hatch Hopes Straw Poll Will Jump-Start His Campaign," The

Salt Lake Tribune, Aug. 2, 1999

A December debate allowed Hatch: Transcript, Republican presidential debate in Phoenix, Ariz., Dec. 6, 1999

"Bigotry has raised its ugly head here": Jerry Spangler, "Religious bigotry plagues Hatch," Deseret News, Aug. 13, 1999

"They are just not political": Leslie Wayne, "The 2000 campaign: The Longshot; Senator Hatch Runs With Credentials Far Weightier Than His Ratings," The New York Times, Jan. 22, 2000

"We're planning on going": John Heilprin, "Hatch: Re-evaluating options," The Salt Lake Tribune, Jan. 25, 2000

"No, Orrin": Thomas Burr, "Utah's Hatch officially ends White House bid," The Salt Lake Tribune, Aug. 14, 2013

"There's a perception out there": Interview with Beth Myers, Campaign for President: The Managers Look at 2008, The Institute of Politics, page 13

Romney wondered aloud: Hewitt, A Mormon in the White House, page 43

... nearly a quarter of Americans said they wouldn't vote: Thomas Burr, "Republicans warming up to idea of Mormon president," The Salt Lake Tribune, July 11, 2012

DeMoss added the cherry: Adam Nagourney and Laurie Goodstein, "Mormon Candidate Braces for Religion as Issue," The New York Times, Feb. 8, 2007

"When they'd ask me the question": Interview with Kevin Madden, 2013

"Former Massachusetts Gov. Mitt Romney pops into Pennsylvania": Brett Lieberman, "Romney makes a cash call," The Patriot-News, Oct. 24, 2007

Andrew Sullivan of The Atlantic posted: Andrew Sullivan, "Mormon Sacred Underwear," The Atlantic online, Nov. 24, 2006

It wasn't just the media: Thomas Burr, "McCain's Iowa campaign chief stirs Mormons' ire by sniping at Romney's LDS faith," The Salt Lake Tribune, June 22, 1007

"The only thing Christianity": Thomas Burr, "Romney GOP presidential foe Brownback sorry for staffer's e-mail questioning LDS faith," The Salt Lake Tribune, June 19, 2007

"I found people who are faithful": Thomas Burr, "Romney: It's politics over pulpit," The Salt Lake Tribune, Feb. 4, 2007

"My goal is not to affiliate": Ibid.

"I believe that, in our state": Interview with Mitt Romney, 2007

"I could serve alcohol in the White House": Jonathan Darman and Lisa Miller, "A Mormon's Journey," Newsweek, Oct. 8, 2007

"The current situation is similar": Thomas Burr, "Romney bid an opportunity, challenge for Mormon church," The Salt Lake Tribune, June 11, 2012

"We can't even recognize": Ibid.

"According to [Romney friend Kem Gardner]": Scott Helman and Michael Levenson, "E-mails offer details of LDS, Romney campaign planning," The Boston Globe, Oct. 22, 2006

"We have no responsibility": Ibid.

"The single biggest obstacle to his election was his religion": Steve Shaw, "JFK and the So-Called Religious Issue," Huffington Post, March 7, 2012

"Contrary to common newspaper usage": John F. Kennedy, remarks to Greater Houston Ministerial Association, Sept. 12, 1960

At the meeting in Romney's pinkish: Kranish and Helmen, The Real Romney, page 286

"There really isn't a": Interview with a former Romney aide, 2007

"You see, I have been hearing": Mark DeMoss, remarks to the National Religious Broadcasters Convention, Feb. 18, 2007

Romney was more than just a Mormon: Peggy Fletcher Stack, "Mitt and his faith: Remembering when candidate Romney was Bishop Romney," The Salt Lake Tribune, Jan. 11, 2008

"By the way": Kathryn Jean Lopez, "Funny Line," The Corner, National Review, Oct. 19, 2007

John McCain and his 95-year-old: Thomas Burr, "McCain's mom slams Romney," The Salt Lake Tribune, Nov. 9,

2007

"Faith doesn't just influence": Michael Luo, "Huckabee Lays Out His Claim as 'Authentic Conservative,' " The New York Times, Nov. 27, 2007

Romney's advisers gave the candidate: Mike Allen and Jonathan Martin, "Romney speech is a huge gamble," Politico, Dec. 3, 2007

Former President George H.W. Bush previously had offered: Interview with former senior Romney adviser, 2013

"Freedom requires religion": Mitt Romney, remarks at the presidential library of George H.W. Bush, Dec. 6, 2007

"Mitt Romney, who sure": Kate O'Beirne, "The Speech," The Corner, National Review, Dec. 6, 2007

"For the first time in this campaign": Chris Matthews, MSNBC, Dec. 6, 2007

"It was a magnificent speech": Pat Buchanan, MSNBC, Dec. 6, 2007

"Gov. Romney's speech was a": Mark Silva, "Romney: No church above duty of office," Chicago Tribune, Dec. 7, 2007

"Each of us, whether": Statement from Sen. Ted Kennedy, 2007

"We pray that thou": "Mitt," directed by Greg Whiteley

"Ooh, that's not good": Ibid.

"Don't Mormons believe that Jesus": Laurie Goodstein, "Huckabee Is Not Alone in Ignorance on Mormonism," The New York Times, Dec. 14, 2007

"Mike had a terrific base": Thomas Burr, "An Iowa also-ran, Romney looks to New Hampshire to reverse his primary fortunes," The Salt Lake Tribune, Jan. 4, 2008

"This is a personal visit": Peggy Fletcher Stack, "Mitt Romney attends Hinckley funeral," The Salt Lake Tribune, Feb. 2, 2008

"When this is over": "Mitt," directed by Greg Whiteley

"I want to bring up something, " Barbara Walters, "The View," ABC, 2007

"My path to conservativism": Mitt Romney, remarks to the Conservative Political Action Conference, Feb. 10, 2012

"People of different faiths": Philip Rucker, "Romney delivers spiritual address at Liberty University, but doesn't mention Mormonism," The Washington Post, May 12, 2012

"It was just so hard": Interview with former senior Romney aide, 2013

"Rick Perry's a Christian": Alexander Burns, "Rick Perry backer Robert Jeffress: Mitt Romney not a Christian," Politico, Oct. 7, 2011

"The fact that, you know": Thomas Burr, "Huntsman calls pastor who criticized Mormonism a 'moron,' " The Salt Lake Tribune, Oct. 11, 2011

"When Mitt and I met": Ann Romney, remarks at the Republican National Convention, Tampa, Fla., Aug. 28, 2012

"I've seen him drop": Ibid.

"As we began working": Grant Bennett, remarks at the Republican National Convention, Tampa, Fla., Aug. 30, 2012

"How many men do": Pat Oparowski, remarks at the Republican National Convention, Tampa, Fla., Aug. 30, 2012

"There has never been as much": Emily Friedman, "JW Marriott Thanks Romney for Bringing Attention to Mormonism," ABC News, Sept. 2, 2012

"Give back — as much": Jon Huntsman Jr., commencement address, University of South Carolina, May 7, 2011

Instead, Huntsman headed to Seacoast: Thomas Burr, "Is Huntsman distancing himself from LDS faith?," The Salt Lake Tribune, June 27, 2011

"I look forward to continuing": Statement from Jon Huntsman Jr., Feb. 4, 2008

"I'm a very spiritual person": Melinda Henneberger, "Jon Huntsman: The potential Republican presidential candidate Democrats fear most," Time magazine, May 12, 2011

A poll showed that some 77 percent: Pew Research Religion and Public Life Project, Jan. 12, 2012

"That's always been who he is": Interview with Abby Huntsman, 2014

"Mormons believe that Mitt Romney": Interview with Utah State Sen. Todd Weiler, 2014

"They want him to wear it": Interview with Abby Huntsman, 2014

… someone "you want to sit next to": Thomas Burr, "Huntsman and son: namesake and role model," The Salt Lake Tribune, July 14, 2011

"I believe in God": Thomas Burr, "Huntsman signs up for first-in-the-South presidential contest," The Salt Lake Tribune, June 24, 2011

"In '12, with Huntsman in the race, it was a shared burden": Interview with former senior Romney aide, 2013

"And at that point I said": "Mormon in America," "Rock Center With Brian Williams," NBC News, Aug. 23, 2012

"The other half was horrible": Interview with Abby Huntsman, 2014

"But I still think": Ibid.

"We are the combination of a lot": Interview with Mary Kaye Huntsman, 2014

"My dad and Romney": Interview with Abby Huntsman, 2014

12. The showdown

Where Romney was leading in the polls: Rebecca Stewart, "Poll: Romney still ahead in New Hampshire," CNN, July 5, 2011

"Good to see you": John Heilemann, "Running for Grown Up," New York Magazine, July 30, 2011

"It's nothing against Huntsman": Thomas Burr, "Chaffetz endorses Romney for president over former boss Jon Huntsman," The Salt Lake Tribune, July 7, 2011

"Throughout his life, Mitt": Mark Halperin, "Utah for Romney," Time magazine, July 6, 2011

… nabbed 63 percent in a statewide poll: Tom Jensen, "Bad news for Huntsman, Hatch," Public Policy Polling, July 13, 2011

That wasn't all the bad news: Thomas Burr, "In Utah, Huntsman son hits Romney rally," The Salt Lake Tribune, June 30, 2011

"Will wanted to see another campaign event": Ibid.

"I don't think he has a speaking problem": Interview with former senior Huntsman aide, 2013

Lynn Forester de Rothschild, a Manhattan socialite: Jeff Zeleny, "Huntsman finishes opening day with big money haul," The New York Times, June 22, 2011

Aides were shocked, even more: Interview with former senior Huntsman aides, 2013

"This is not a Washington-based campaign": Aaron Deslatte, "Jon Huntsman picks Florida for presidential campaign headquarters," Orlando Sentinel, May 18, 2011

"I was being told to hire, hire, hire": Interview with former senior Huntsman aide, 2013

"I hate big money in politics": Interview with Jon Huntsman Jr., 2014

"A lot of the donors": Ibid.

"Then it became, 'OK' ": Ibid.

"Now the campaign is moving": Aaron Blake, "Huntsman campaign manager Susie Wiles resigns," The Washington Post, July 21, 2011

"If the election were next week": Andrew Romano, "Huntsman bets on Boehner," The Daily Beast, July 27, 2011

"He acted like a hall monitor": Erin McPike, "Longtime confidant of Huntsman is forced out of campaign," Real Clear Politics, July 31, 2011

"I look forward to a future": Jonathan Martin, "Jon Huntsman 2012 campaign: Inside the 'drama,' " Politico, Aug. 4, 2011

"Dave Fischer tried to threaten the campaign": Ibid.

"Some people have suggested": Transcript, Republican presidential debate, Ames, Iowa, Aug. 13, 2011

"Look, I'm not going": Ibid.

"But in case Mitt wins": Ibid.

"If you can only do certain": Zeke Miller, "Jon Huntsman trashes GOP, expresses campaign regrets," BuzzFeed, April 22, 2012

"You stand up on the stage": Robert Gehrke, "Inside a Huntsman fundraiser," The Salt Lake Tribune, Aug. 28, 2011

"You look at everything": Interview with Josh Romney, 2014

"I wish you would speak to": Rachel Streitfeld, "Romney faces rowdy town hall crowd," CNN, Aug. 24, 2011

Former Democratic presidential candidate: Jarrett Stepman, "Huntsman amassing long list of politically toxic backers," Human Events, Aug. 24, 2011

Soon, filmmaker Michael Moore: Maggie Haberman, "Michael Moore likes Jon Huntsman 2012: From the Dept. of Unhelpful Praise," Politico, Sept. 28, 2011

"Then you have Annie Leibovitz": Interview with Jon Huntsman Jr., 2014

"A few weeks into the race": Weisberg, "Jon Huntsman: The Outsider," Vogue, Aug. 18, 2011

Huntsman also had fired: Sarah Kunin, "Jon Huntsman fires New Hampshire campaign manager," ABC News, Sept. 1, 2011

Weaver "doesn't suffer fools": Interview with former senior Huntsman aide, 2013

"I prefer having a governor who is No. 1": Lisa Lerer, "Huntsman doubts Perry or Romney could win U.S. presidential race," Bloomberg, Sept. 17, 2011

"To be clear. I believe": Shira Schoenberg, "Jon Huntsman now less certain of science on climate change," The Boston Globe, Dec. 7, 2011

He was, essentially, the DNC's: Alexander Burns, "Democratic National Committee's new surrogate: Jon Huntsman," Politico, Aug. 21, 2011

"When you need to stand up": Amy Bingham, "Huntsman sharpens his Romney rhetoric," ABC News, Aug. 13, 2011

"I knew my only option then was": Interview with Jon Huntsman Jr., 2014

"I didn't call him back": Michael Falcone, "Donald Trump, Jon Huntsman Feud Continues: 'He went negative,'" ABC News, Sept. 30, 2011

"The 9-9-9 plan that": Transcript, Republican presidential debate, Hanover, N.H., Oct. 11, 2011

"Since some might see you": Ibid.

Huntsman's three eldest daughters: The Reliable Source, "Jon Huntsman daughters on the campaign trail and YouTube," The Washington Post, Oct. 31, 2011

In response to Romney's debate vow: Michael Brendan Dougherty, "Abby Huntsman on her father, the campaign and the 'Jon 2012 Girls,' " The Atlantic, Oct, 2011

"We are shamelessly promoting": Matt Negrin, "For Huntsman Daughters, a Ticket to Ride ... to TV?" ABC News, Jan. 16, 2012

"The video was produced without authorization": Rachel Weiner, "Jon Huntsman's strange viral video strategy," The Washington Post, Dec. 2, 2011

"Herman Cain accused": Jonathan Martin, Maggie Haberman, Anna Palmer and Kenneth P. Vogel, "Herman Cain accused by two women of inappropriate behavior," Politico, Oct. 31, 2011

"You can't be a perfectly lubricated": "Huntsman: Romney's a 'perfectly lubricated weather vane,' " CNN, Oct. 28, 2011

"Now, Gov. Huntsman, do": Transcript, CNN, Nov. 22, 2011

"Well, let me respond": Ibid.

"Listen, I think it's important": Ibid.

The next day, The Washington Post: Chris Cillizza, "CNN Republican debate: Winners and losers," The Washington Post, Nov. 22, 2011

The Jon Huntsman signs: Thomas Burr, "Romney leading in N.H., Huntsman down," The Salt Lake Tribune, Oct. 10, 2011

"This is truly the intrepid": Thomas Burr, "Through storms, bad polls and fundraising, Huntsman forges on," The Salt Lake Tribune, Nov. 6, 2011

"I just feel totally convinced": Ibid.

"At least he's one of the sane": Ibid.

He had one hope left: Thomas Burr, "Pro-Huntsman group to air ads in New Hampshire," The Salt Lake Tribune, Nov. 6, 2011

"Any efforts will help": Ibid.

Another web spot took: Zeke Miller, "Huntsman Attacks Romney With Back-Flipping Toy Monkey," Business Insider, Oct. 28, 2011

Two punches thrown: Kevin Spak, "Jon Huntsman's New Website: 'Scared Mittless,' " Newser, Nov. 8, 2011

"It was more about ideas": Interview with Jon Huntsman Jr., 2014

"And so you ratchet up": Ibid.

"You know what? You've raised": Transcript, Republican presidential debate, ABC News, Dec. 11, 2011

"I can see my daughter nodding": Thomas Burr, "Huntsman, Gingrich shun sound bites in N.H. debate," The Salt Lake Tribune, Dec. 12, 2011

"The only one that was worth": Interview with Jon Huntsman Jr., 2014

… so Huntsman took his turn at the swivel chair: Sean Means, "Jon Huntsman flatters New Hampshire on 'Saturday Night Live,' " The Salt Lake Tribune, Dec. 9, 2011

Romney, too, was up for a bit of comedy: Lucy Madison, "Romney does Letterman's Top 10 list, asks 'Newt Gingrich, really?' " CBS News, Dec. 20, 2011

"I thought I could make it big": "'Late Show with David Letterman': Jon Huntsman rocks out with Paul Shaffer and the band," The Huffington Post, Dec. 22, 2011

A Christmastime poll: Maeve Reston, "Poll: Mitt Romney in command in New Hampshire," The Los Angeles Times, Dec. 25, 2011

The Huntsman Sr.-funded Our Destiny: Steve Peoples and Holly Ramer, "Our Destiny group, pro-Jon Huntsman group, runs anti-Mitt Romney ad in New Hampshire," The Associated Press, Dec. 30, 2011

"We started with a blank piece": Philip Rucker, "For Romney, stealth campaign brings real hopes of winning Iowa," The Washington Post, Dec. 27, 2011

"I don't have any predictions": Ibid.

Romney was gracious, offering congrats: Tom Beaumont, "Iowa Caucus Results: Rick Santorum & Mitt Romney took opposite paths to victory," The Associated Press, Jan. 4, 2012

Romney and Santorum got more than 30,000 votes: Stephanie Condon, "Iowa caucus results: Mitt Romney beats Rick Santorum by 8 votes," CBS News, Jan. 4, 2012

"It's with some nostalgia": "John McCain endorses Romney," Fox News, Jan. 4, 2012

"It's another example of the establishment": Thomas Burr, "Romney rolls into New Hampshire as a big favorite," The Salt Lake Tribune, Jan. 5, 2012

Privately, Huntsman cared. Very much: Alex Pappas, "Huntsman felt betrayed by McCain's endorsement of Romney," The Daily Caller, April 4, 2012

"I didn't mean to offend": Mike Allen, Evan Thomas, "Inside the Circus," Politico, 2012

"The establishment is going to say": Maeve Reston, "Jon Huntsman to New Hampshire voters: 'Upend conventional wisdom,'" The Los Angeles Times, Jan. 3, 2012

Doubling down, Gingrich rolled out: Beth Fouhy, "Seeking New Hampshire buzz, Mitt Romney hits president as others swat at him," The Associated Press, Jan. 5, 2012

"American values? Or Chinese?": "Huntsman criticizes ad featuring adopted kids," The Associated Press, Jan. 6, 2012

"I congratulate Gov. Huntsman on the success": Thomas Burr, "Romney slams Huntsman for serving in Obama's administration," The Salt Lake Tribune, Jan. 8, 2012

"I'm sorry, Governor, you were": Ibid.

"Here's a guy who usually tries": Ibid.

"We take nothing for granted": Ibid.

"There was no sleep": Interview with Jon Huntsman Jr., 2014

This time, Huntsman was ready: Thomas Burr, "Huntsman hits Romney back over putting 'country first,' " The Salt Lake Tribune, Jan. 9, 2012

"We serve our country first": Ibid.

"Over the last two years": Ibid.

"It was a moment for": Ibid.

"I'm not sure he really": Ibid.

"I feel a little momentum": Thomas Burr, "With campaign at stake, Huntsman counting on surge," The Salt Lake Tribune, Jan. 9, 2012

"I like being able to fire people": Lucy Madison, "Romney: 'I like being able to fire people' for bad service," CBS News, Jan. 9, 2012

"He really said that?": Interview with senior Huntsman adviser, 2013

"That's what I hate about politics": Interview with Jon Huntsman Jr., 2014

"Gov. Romney enjoys firing people": Madison, "Romney: 'I like being able to fire people' for bad service," CBS News, Jan. 9, 2012

Izak, the second goat: Alexis Levinson, "Huntsman bitten by goat while campaigning in New Hampshire," The Daily Caller, Oct. 31, 2011

"You know, I'm feeling it": "Huntsman plans to ride momentum into primary day," WMUR, Jan. 9, 2012

"Can you feel a little momentum": Thomas Burr, "Romney looks for victory, Huntsman for a 'surprise' in New Hampshire," The Salt Lake Tribune, Jan. 9, 2012

..the tiny town of Dixville Notch: Martha T. Moore and Susan Page, "N.H. voters head to the polls as Romney fends off attacks," USA Today, Jan. 10, 2012

Huntsman called his cousin: Emily Goodin, "Huntsman insists he's staying in race despite third-place NH finish," The Hill, Jan. 11, 2012

"I say third place": David Jackson, "Huntsman claims 'ticket to ride' in N.H.," USA Today, Jan. 10, 2012

13. A tepid endorsement

"Romney comes in here 2-0": Jonathan Allen, "Mitt Romney's South Carolina primary strategy: Divide and conquer," Politico, Jan. 11, 2012

"I don't want to be overconfident": "Romney blitzing S. Carolina as front-runner," The Associated Press in The Christian Science Monitor, Jan. 12, 2012

"What happened after Massachusetts": Rachel Weiner, "Newt Gingrich hits Mitt Romney on abortion in South Carolina ad," The Washington Post, Jan. 10, 2012

"People of this state don't": John Hoeffel, "Huntsman's 'ticket to ride' lands him in South Carolina," Los Angeles Times, Jan. 11, 2012

Stephen Colbert, a South Carolina native: M.J. Lee, "Stephen Colbert ponders 2012 presidential campaign," Politico, Jan. 12, 2012

… the endorsement of The State newspaper: Felicia Sonmez, "Huntsman, Romney win South Carolina newspaper endorsements," The Washington Post, Jan. 15, 2012

"I knew in the back of my mind": Interview with Jon Huntsman Jr., 2014

"I wanted to just make sure": Ibid.

"We were sitting in the middle of dinner": Ibid.

The libation-fueled party: Interview with former senior Huntsman aide, 2013

The two discussed the "state of the race": Reid J. Epstein and Juana Summers, "Jon Huntsman's endorsement of Mitt Romney: A cold embrace," Politico. Jan. 16, 2012

"Jon Huntsman should win": Thomas Burr, "Jon Huntsman to pull out of presidential race, endorse Romney," The Salt Lake Tribune, Jan. 15, 2012

A Huntsman friend saw the end differently: McKay Coppins, "Beijing to Myrtle Beach: Jon Huntsman's long way down," BuzzFeed, Jan. 16, 2012

"Good morning, everybody": Jon Huntsman Jr., remarks upon withdrawing from the presidential race, C-SPAN video, Jan. 16, 2012

"Today I am suspending": Ibid.

"You still think he's completely": Ibid.

"If you looked at the endorsement": Interview with Romney confidant, 2014

"I mean for them, I think": Interview with Jon Huntsman, 2014

"I'm not going to look back": Interview with John Weaver, January 2012

Romney, for his part, called: David A. Farenthold and Debbie Wilgoren, "Santorum finished 34 votes ahead of Romney in new Iowa tally," The Washington Post, Jan. 19, 2012

"How could he ask me for a divorce": Alan Duke, "Newt Gingrich wanted 'open marriage,' ex-wife says," CNN, Jan. 20, 2012

"No, but I will": Transcript, Republican presidential debate, CNN, South Carolina, Jan. 20, 2012

"John, let's get on to": Ibid.

A poll later showed that: Samuel Best, "How Newt Gingrich won the South Carolina primary," CBS News, Jan. 22, 2012

"Tonight, I want to congratulate": Transcript, remarks in Columbia after the South Carolina primary, American Presidency Project, Jan. 21, 2012

Romney hammered home the point: Paul Blumenthal, "Mitt Romney Florida primary comeback fueled by deep pockets, big advertising spending," Huffington Post, Jan. 28, 2012

Romney needed a big win: Samuel Best, "How Mitt Romney won the Florida primary, CBS News, Jan. 31, 2012

"Don't worry, Mr. President": Ibid.

"Newt doesn't control the board anymore": Reed Epstein, "Mitt Romney claims return to inevitability in Florida primary win," Politico, Jan. 31, 2012

Romney also won a another cool prize: Emily Friedman and John Berman, "Exclusive: Mitt Romney to receive Secret Service protection," ABC News. Jan. 31, 2012

"… not a surrogate for anybody": Amy Bingham, "Jon Huntsman calls for the rise of a third party," ABC News, Feb. 23, 2012

"We're going to have problems": Ibid.

"I would hope he would do it": Tim Mak, "Christine Todd Whitman to Jon Huntsman: Run third party," Politico, Dec. 2, 2011

"You can't help but have your mind wander": Interview with Jon Huntsman Jr., 2014

"… not that I was seriously": Ibid.

"They had everything but": Ibid.

One example: He had been scheduled: Zeke Miller, "Jon Huntsman dropped from RNC event for 'third party' call," BuzzFeed, March 2, 2012

"In fact, he has actually been uninvited": Eric W. Dolan, "Abby Huntsman: GOP uninvited my father for talking about 'a third voice,' " RawStory, Aug. 7, 2012

"This is what they do in China": Zeke Miller, "Jon Huntsman Trashes GOP, Expresses Campaign Regrets," Buzz-Feed, April 22, 2012

"I felt like the lone voice in the wilderness": Interview with Jon Huntsman Jr., 2014

"No, I feel educated": Ibid.

"Obviously there were better advisers": Interview with Jon Huntsman Sr., 2014

"He has such respect around": Ibid.

"We made a decision over the weekend": Katherine W. Seelye and Jim Rutenberg, "Santorum quits race, clearing way for Romney," The New York Times, April 10, 2012

"This is not a choice between Mitt": Brian Montopoli, "Newt Gingrich suspends presidential campaign," CBS News, May 2, 2012

"I encourage a return to the party": Thomas Burr, "Huntsman scolds GOP for losing focus, will skip convention," The Salt Lake Tribune, July 11, 2012

14. Taking the silver

"Ever once have you thought": "Mitt," directed by Greg Whiteley

"If you're tempted": Ibid.

"We finally got there": Ginger Gibson, "Mitt Romney clinches GOP nomination, Politico, May 29, 2012

"Experiences like that": Interview with Josh Romney, 2014

Events include a mini-triathlon: Philip Rucker, "Mitt Romney's summer vacation full of competitive sports and family meetings," The Washington Post, June 30, 2012

"There'd be too many jokes": Steve Krakauer, "Would Jon Huntsman consider being Rep. Michele Bachmann's running mate," CNN, Aug. 22, 2011

By late July, the speculation was full throttle: Steve Holland, "Romney appears in final stages of running-mate decision," Reuters, July 16, 2012

"It's hard to know": Jim Acosta, "Romney's Olympics false start," CNN, July 26, 2012

"Show some respect": Jim Acosta, "Romney aide loses cool, curses at press in Poland," CNN, July 31, 2012

Romney's team tried to put a happy spin: Jim Acosta, "Was Romney's trip 'a great success' or gaffe-filled disaster?," CNN, July 31, 2012

"By the time we met in person": Alex Altman, "Inside the VP pick: How Romney decided on Ryan — and kept the secret," Time magazine, Aug. 12, 2012

The background was designed to look: Jeremy W. Peters, "G.O.P. packaging seeks to reveal a warm Romney," The New York Times, Aug. 20, 2012

"I read somewhere that Mitt": Ann Romney, remarks at the Republican National Convention, Tampa, Fla., Aug. 28, 2012

"Our nominee is sure ready": Paul Ryan, remarks at the Republican National Convention, Tampa, Fla., Aug. 29, 2012

"I came here tonight": Transcript, Republican National Convention, Tampa, Fla., Aug. 30, 2012

Romney's top campaign officials: Michael Barbaro and Michael D. Shear, "Before Eastwood's talk with a chair, clearance from the top," The New York Times, Aug. 31, 2012

"What do you want me": Ibid.

"I wish President Obama had": Mitt Romney, remarks at the Republican National Convention, Tampa, Fla., Aug. 30, 2012

"I knew that her job": Ibid.

"The time has come to turn": Ibid.

"Mitt Romney, quite simply": Julián Castro, remarks at the Democratic National Convention, Charlotte, N.C., Sept. 4, 2012

"And this year, they've nominated": Sen. Harry Reid, remarks at the Democratic National Convention, Charlotte, N.C., Sept. 4, 2012

"It's so ridiculous that people associate": Thomas Burr, "Huntsman denies he was source for tax claim against Mitt Romney," The Salt Lake Tribune, Nov. 1, 2013

"So, in the end": Michelle Obama, remarks at the Democratic National Convention, Charlotte, N.C., Sept. 4, 2012

"America, I never said this journey": Barack Obama, remarks at the Democratic National Convention, Charlotte, N.C., Sept. 6, 2012

"For the last three years": "Full transcript of the Mitt Romney secret video," Mother Jones, Sept. 19, 2012

"There are 47 percent": Ibid.

"Mitt Romney wants to help all Americans": Romney campaign news release, 2012

"I understand there's been": Transcript, Mitt Romney news conference, The New York Times, Sept. 17, 2012

"Well, um, it's not elegantly stated": Ibid.

"So any advice?": "Mitt," directed by Greg Whiteley

"The president has a view very": Transcript, first presidential debate, Oct. 3, 2012

And it only got worse: Cavan Sleczkowski, "Al Gore blames Denver's high altitude for Obama's dismal debate performance," The Huffington Post, Oct. 4, 2012

"I didn't want the president to somehow": Interview with Josh Romney, 2014

"I wrote down 'DAD' ": "Mitt," directed by Greg Whiteley

"Gov. Romney is a good man": Transcript, second presidential debate, Oct. 16, 2012

"No acts of terror": Transcript, remarks of the president, The White House, Sept. 12, 2012

"Minus when Candy Crowley decided": Interview with Josh Romney, 2014

"I think Gov. Romney maybe": Transcript, third presidential debate, Oct. 22, 2012

"… talented salesman": Anita Kumar, William Douglas and David Lightman, "Obama and Romney race across map in final weekend," Nov. 3, 2012

"You hope that President Obama would live": Thomas Burr, "Romney, Obama make final pitches," The Salt Lake Tribune, Nov. 6, 2012

"Intellectually I've felt that we're going": Philip Rucker, "Romney's belief in himself never wavered," The Washington Post, Nov. 7, 2012

"I always slept well before": "Mitt," directed by Greg Whiteley

The Romneys huddled in the adjacent hotel: Ibid.

"I just can't believe you're": Ibid.

"I believe in America": Transcript, Mitt Romney's concession speech, Nov. 7, 2012

15. Dynasties

After the loss, Mitt Romney went: Philip Rucker, "A detached Romney tends wounds in seclusion after failed White House bid," The Washington Post, Dec. 1, 2012

"There's nothing worse": Jan Crawford, "Adviser: Romney 'shellshocked' by loss," CBS News, Nov. 8, 2014

"I have looked at": "Mitt," directed by Greg Whiteley

"I remember my dad": Mark Leibovich, "Mitt Isn't Ready to Call It Quits," The New York Times, Sept. 30, 2014

Two weeks after Obama's re-election: J.K. Trotter, "Mitt Romney's Bizarre Post-Election Life: A Timeline in Photos," The Wire, March 1, 2013

"I'm very sorry that we": Ashley Parker, "Romney Blames Loss on Obama's 'Gifts' to Minorities and Young Voters," The New York Times, Nov. 14, 2012

"With regards to the young": Ibid.

"I don't agree with them": Ginger Gibson, "GOP returns Mitt Romney 'gifts,' " Politico, Nov. 15, 2012

"I just don't think Romney": James Hohmann, "Republicans run from Mitt Romney," Politico, Nov. 19, 2012

"So there's perhaps a particularly": Ibid.

"Even those who have been": Dan Eggen, "Romney sinks quickly in Republicans' esteem," The Washington Post, Nov. 16, 2012

"We were on a roller coaster": "Romney likens 2012 race to 'roller coaster' in exclusive 'Fox News Sunday' interview," Fox News, Feb. 28, 2013

"In our church, we're used": Ibid.

"I did better this time": Ibid.

"We should have": Matt Viser and Michael Kranish, "Mitt Romney carefully looks to raise public voice," The Boston Globe, Nov. 4, 2013

In May 2014, Romney bucked most: Paul Singer, "Romney: We should raise minimum wage," USA Today, May 9, 2014

That's the reaction Whiteley: Tierney Sneed, "The Man Behind 'Mitt' Talks Making the Romney Netflix Documentary," U.S. News & World Report, Jan. 23, 2014

"No. I've answered that": Interview with Mitt Romney, "The Situation Room," CNN, Feb. 5, 2014

"All right, Mitt Romney telling": Ibid.

"If Mitt Romney concluded": Matt Canham, "Giant In Our City: Romney calls Leavitt the quintessential volunteer," The Salt Lake Tribune, April 10, 2014

"... gut feeling": Matt Canham, "Jason Chaffetz has gut feeling Mitt Romney runs again," The Salt Lake Tribune, July 8, 2014

"Mitt and I, at this point": Lucy McCalmont, "Ann Romney: Dem rhetoric 'offensive,' " Politico, Sept. 23, 2014

"I'd love for there to be": McKoye Mecham, "Josh Romney discusses 'Mitt' documentary," Fox13 TV, Feb. 11, 2014

"I would like my dad to be": Interview with Josh Romney, 2014

"Should Mitt Romney decide": memo, Zogby Analytics, Aug. 19, 2014

"I'd drive his bus if he": Interview with Paul Ryan, Bloomberg Television, Aug. 20, 2014

"You know circumstances can": Interview with Mitt Romney, "Hugh Hewitt Show," Aug. 26, 2014

"I never thought I would": Matt Canham, "Former Utah Gov. Jon Huntsman open to another presidential run," The Salt Lake Tribune, May 6, 2014

"Here's some straight talk": Chris Cillizza, "Jon Huntsman for president? Come on, man," The Washington Post, May 7, 2014

... a possible run as an independent: Ruby Cramer and McKay Coppins, "Jon Huntsman, Independent for President?," BuzzFeed, Sept. 16, 2014

"I'm not organizing": Interview with Jon Huntsman Jr., 2014

Huntsman Sr. said he wouldn't contribute: Interview with Jon Huntsman Sr., 2014

"Well, you know, I think": Interview with Jon Huntsman Sr., "The Alan Colmes Show," Fox News Radio, Oct. 29, 2014

"I don't think that's in": Thomas Burr, "Huntsman: Romney third run 'isn't in the cards,' " The Salt Lake Tribune, Aug. 12, 2014

He also hasn't ruled out: Thomas Burr, "Huntsman 'not likely' running against Lee," The Salt Lake Tribune, Feb. 17, 2015

"At the risk of totally destroying": Canham, "Former Utah Gov. Jon Huntsman open to another presidential run," The Salt Lake Tribune, May 6, 2014

"The guy we were always": Interview with Jim Messina, "Ronan Farrow Daily," MSNBC Feb. 2, 2015

"That's highly unlikely": Interview with Jon Huntsman Jr., 2014

"2016 you don't have": Nikki Schwab, "Jon Huntsman Eyeing the Sidelines in 2016," U.S. News & World Report, March 12, 2014

"If you look back over": Ibid.

"It's money in politics": Interview with Jon Huntsman Jr., at opening of fourth phase of Huntsman Cancer Center, 2014

"We've diagnosed the problem": Ibid.

"Done," she said. "Completely": Maeve Reston, "Ann Romney launches new center to study neurological diseases," The Los Angeles Times, Oct. 13, 2014

After revving up the crowd: Philip Rucker and Robert Costa, "Can't quit Mitt: Friends say Romney feels nudge to consider a 2016 presidential run," The Washington Post, Oct. 13, 2014

"… first choice and that they": Ben White, "Morning Money," Politico, Dec. 5, 2014

"He does not feel": Ibid.

"…comparing an apple to": Philip Rucker and Robert Costa, "For Jeb Bush and Mitt Romney, a history of ambition fuels a possible 2016 collision," The Washington Post, Jan. 10, 2015

A few weeks later, Bush's advisers: Ben White, "Jeb to come clean," Politico, Jan. 7, 2015

"It was like poking a bear": Dan Balz and Philip Rucker, "Mitt Romney bows out of GOP presidential race over potential for political injury," The Washington Post, Jan. 30, 2015

During the holidays, Romney family members: Matt Viser, "Mitt Romney will not run for president in 2016," The Boston Globe, Jan. 30, 2015

The contributors were encouraging, yet: Matt Viser, "Mitt Romney crafting a rationale for 2016 run," The Boston Globe, Jan. 14, 2015

"I want to be president": Rucker and Costa, "For Jeb Bush and Mitt Romney, a history of ambition fuels a possible 2016 collision," The Washington Post, Jan. 10, 2015

"Tell your friends": Steve Holland, "Romney tells donors he's considering a 2016 White House run," Reuters, Jan. 9, 2015

That was a comparison that Reagan's: Seema Mehta and Mark Z. Barabak, "Mitt Romney's new focus on poverty has many allies baffled," The Los Angeles Times, Jan. 18, 2015

"We're seeing the first shots": Rucker and Costa, "For Jeb Bush and Mitt Romney, a history of ambition fuels a possible 2016 collision," The Washington Post, Jan. 10, 2015

"We'll see. The technology": Interview with Jon Huntsman Jr., "State of the Union," CNN, Jan. 25, 2015

"The Bush connection is a": Rucker and Costa, "For Jeb Bush and Mitt Romney, a history of ambition fuels a possible 2016 collision," The Washington Post, Jan. 10, 2015

"Just because you can run": Abby Huntsman, "If Mitt Romney is the answer, what is the question?," MSNBC, Jan. 16, 2015

"So Mitt, because he was": Interview with Jon Huntsman Jr., "Matt Lewis Show," podcast audio, Jan. 13, 2015

"…almost certainly" would run: Robert Costa, Philip Rucker and Karen Tumulty, "Romney moves to reassemble campaign team for 'almost certain' 2016 bid," The Washington Post, Jan. 12, 2015

"If he's in": Ibid.

"Regardless of what Mitt Romney does": Robert Costa, "Jason Chaffetz on Bush 2016: 'Been there, done that,' " The Washington Post, Jan. 13, 2015

"He got defined early": Jonathan Martin, "Third Chance for Romney? GOP Is Torn," The New York Times, Jan. 13, 2015

"We've got a lot of talented": Kasie Hunt, "Can Mitt Romney rally the support of his party in time for 2016?" MSNBC, Jan. 15, 2015

"The most frequently asked question": Matt Viser, "Mitt Romney makes case for possible third run," The Boston Globe, Jan. 16, 2015

"For over 10 years, as": Ibid.

"… a caricature of the Mormon candidate": Ashley Parker and Alex Thompson, "Romney's Consideration of Candidacy Is Closely Tied to His Faith, Alles Say," The New York Times, Jan. 25, 2015

"He has been reluctant to speak": Philip Rucker, "Romney, ahead of 2016 run, now calls Utah home, talks openly about Mormon influence," The Washington Post, Jan. 27, 2015

"… to encounter rejection without": Ashley Parker and Alex Thompson, "Romney's Consideration of Candidacy Is Closely Tied to His Faith, Alles Say," The New York Times, Jan. 25, 2015

"… the future": Matt Canham, "Mitt Romney and Jeb Bush to recognize 'awkward' situation in Utah meeting," The Salt Lake Tribune, Jan. 22, 2015

Aides described the conversation as wonky: Balz and Rucker, "Mitt Romney bows out of GOP presidential race over potential for political injury," The Washington Post, Jan. 30, 2015

"I've got great respect for": Thomas Beaumont and Steve Peoples, "As Mitt Romney weighs '16 bid, his past donors commit to Jeb Bush," The Associated Press, Jan. 29, 2015

Romney's aides held a four-hour: Jonathan Martin and Michael Barbaro, "Mitt Romney Won't Run in 2016 Presidential Election," The New York Times, Jan. 30, 2015

"... basically a lighter version": Viser, "Mitt Romney will not run for president in 2016," The Boston Globe, Jan. 30, 2015

"Yeah, he could win": Ibid.

"There's a lot of sadness": Ibid.

"After putting considerable thought": Transcript, Mitt Romney conference call, Jan. 30, 2015

"I always hoped that Mitt Romney": Thomas Burr and Matt Canham, "Romney's friends say he's far from retired despite not running in 2016," The Salt Lake Tribune, Jan. 30, 2015

"I've been asked and will": Transcript, Mitt Romney conference call, Jan. 30, 2015

"Like a baton has passed": David D. Kirkpatrick, "For Romney, a Course Set Long Ago," The New York Times, Dec. 18, 2007

"I have been humbled": Kristen A. Lee and Dan Hirschhorn, "Mitt Romney's son Tagg decides against a run for John Kerry's seat," New York Daily News, Feb. 4, 2013

"I'm happy with my life": Todd Spangler, "Mitt Romney's brother G. Scott Romney won't run for Levin's seat," Detroit Free Press, March 12, 2013

Michigan Republicans picked Ronna: "Romney's niece picked to head Michigan Republican Party," The Associated Press, Feb. 21, 2015

"In a lot of ways": Interview with Josh Romney, 2014

"My advice to my sons": Colneth Smiley Jr., "Ann Romney sees son Tagg 'obviously' involved in politics in future," Boston Herald, Dec. 5, 2013

"If one of our boys or": Jake Tapper, "Mrs. Romney on sons running for office: Don't do it," The Lead with Jake Tapper, CNN, June 6, 2013

In that conversation, the sons agreed: Ashley Parker, "Romney Times Four," The New York Times, Jan. 6, 2012

"I can see only one son": Smiley Jr., "Ann Romney sees son Tagg 'obviously' involved in politics in future," Boston Herald, Dec. 5, 2013

"He is in a tough position": Interview with Josh Romney, 2014

"He's not a Utah resident": Ibid.

"I forbid my children": Interviews with attendees of luncheon sponsored by Zions Bank, November 2013

"She said it with a": Interview with attendee of luncheon sponsored by Zions Bank, November 2013

"The thing about politics": Interview with Josh Romney, 2014

"I opened the car door": Erin Alberty and Matthew Piper, "Josh Romney helped Utah crash victims on Thanksgiving," The Salt Lake Tribune, Nov. 29, 2013

"All in all, great job": Ibid.

"I'm not ruling anything in": Lisa Riley Roche, "Josh Romney not ruling out run for office in Utah," Deseret News, June 5, 2013

"The thought of running for": Interview with Josh Romney, 2014

"I don't think I'd be totally": Interview with Abby Huntsman, 2014

"There's the saying, 'Where ...' ": Ibid.

"Abby would, I think": Interview with Jon Huntsman Jr., 2014

"It's great once you mentally": Interview with Jon Huntsman Jr., "Person 2 Person," KUTV, Dec. 1, 2014

"What's around the bend": Ibid.

"The boys are about as": Interview with Jon Huntsman Jr., 2014

"I know it sounds old": Ibid.

"I haven't told a lot of": Patrick Gavin, "Abby Huntsman teases party switch," Politico, Aug. 8, 2012

"I've always been a Republican": Alex Pappas, "Abby Huntsman: I was kidding about joining the Democratic Party," The Daily Caller, Aug. 8, 2012

"Here is the real deal": Abby Huntsman, "What Abby Huntsman sees as the GOP's future," MSNBC's The Cycle, Jan. 23, 2014"What is very similar": Interview with Abby Huntsman, 2014

"I hear Mitt Romney's son": Transcript, "The Cycle," MSNBC, Nov. 1, 2013

"It was very nice": Interview with Josh Romney, 2014

"I feel that if Mitt and I": Interview with Jon Huntsman Jr., 2014

"It's not that they don't": Interview with Mitt Romney advisor, 2014

"We have very ambitious people": Interview with Fred Lampropoulos, 2013

"I would hope our children": Interview with Jon Huntsman Sr., 2014

"That," she quipped: Interview with Abby Huntsman, 2014

Index

CPSIA information can be obtained at www.ICGtesting.com
Printed in the USA
BVOW05s2125160415

396399BV00001B/1/P

9 780986 224522